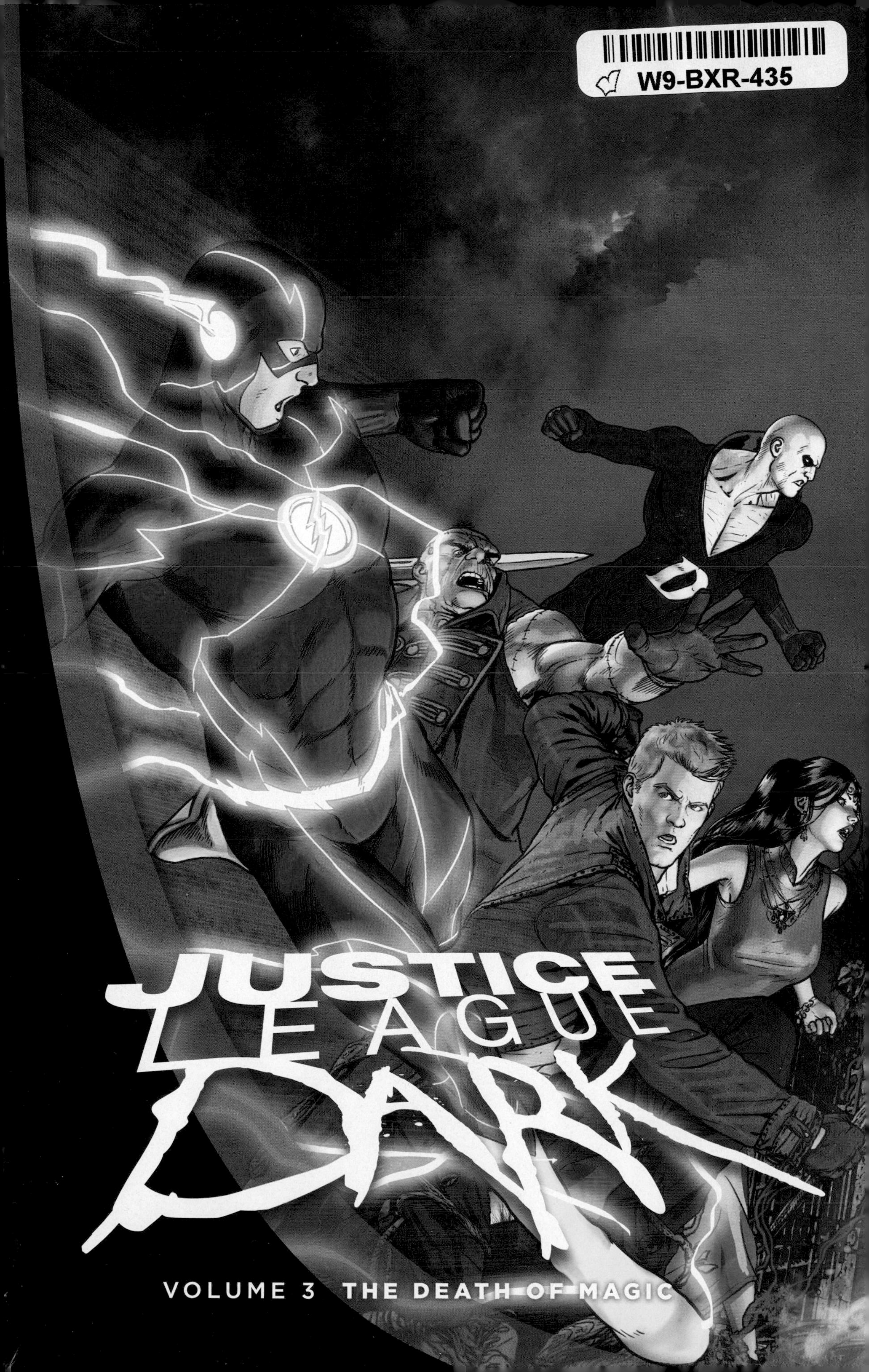
JUSTICE
LEAGUE
DARK
VOLUME 3 THE DEATH OF MAGIC

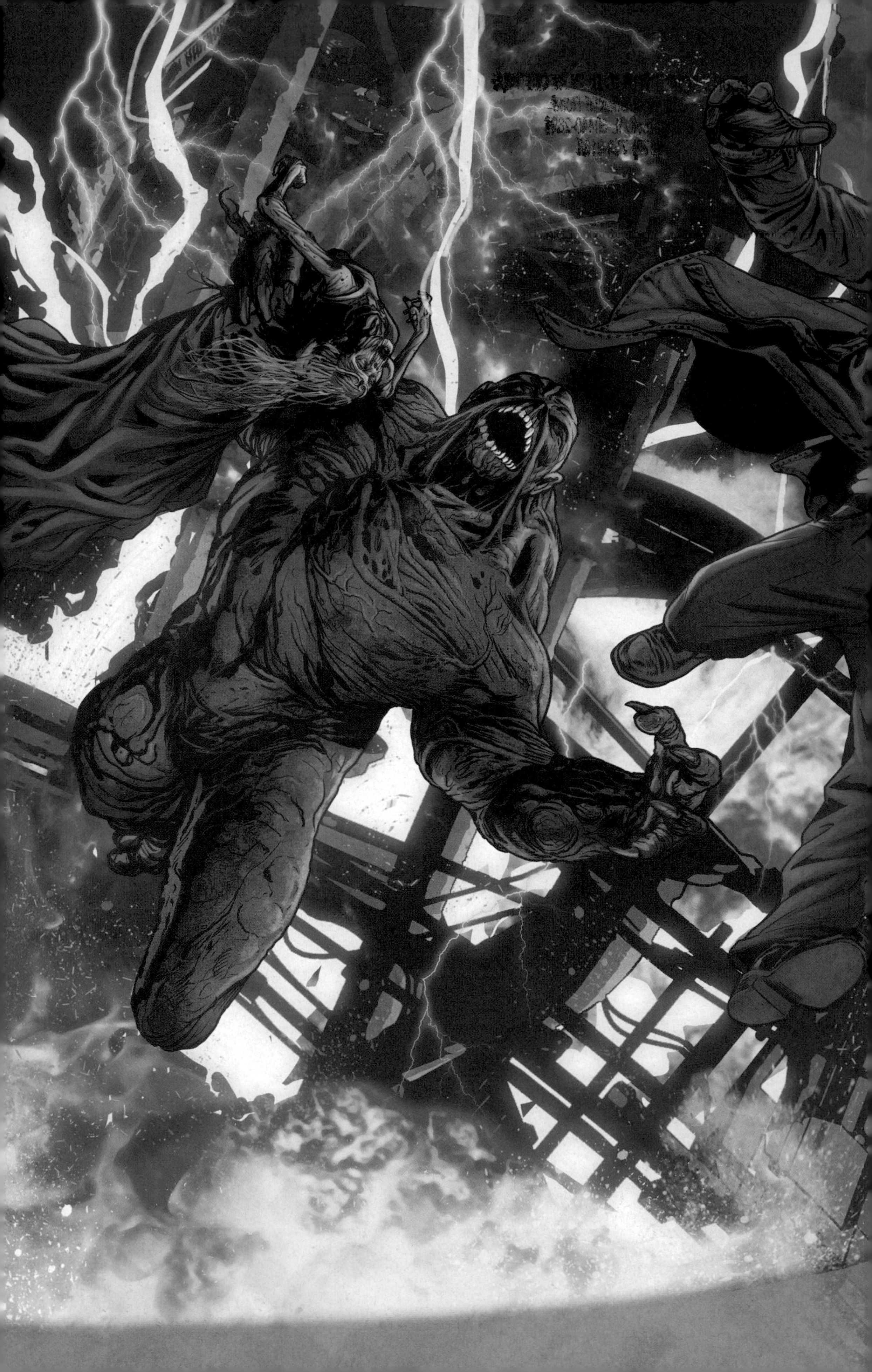

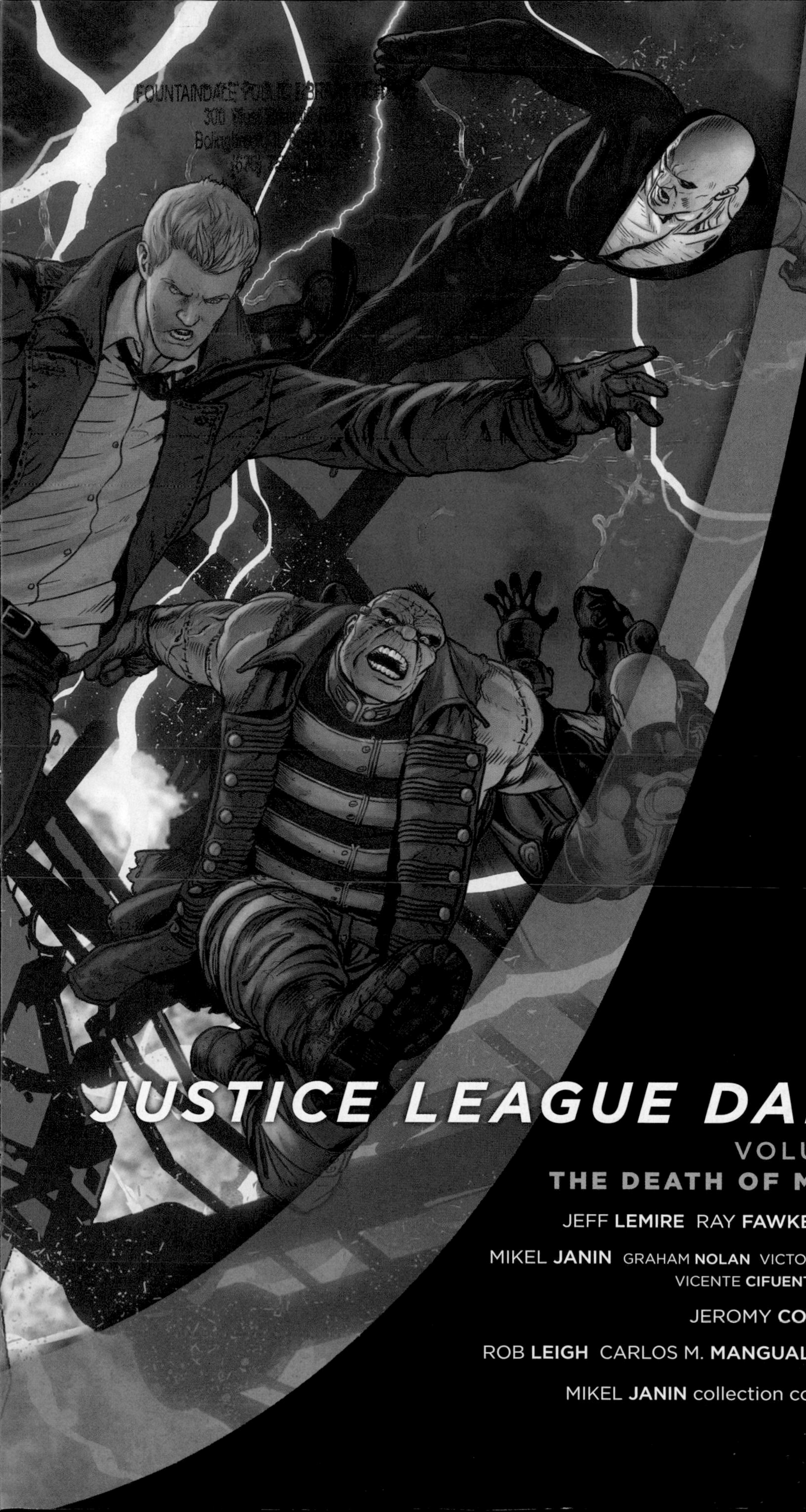

JUSTICE LEAGUE DARK

VOLUME 3
THE DEATH OF MAGIC

JEFF **LEMIRE** RAY **FAWKES** writers

MIKEL **JANIN** GRAHAM **NOLAN** VICTOR **DRUJINIU**
VICENTE **CIFUENTES** artists

JEROMY **COX** colorist

ROB **LEIGH** CARLOS M. **MANGUAL** letterers

MIKEL **JANIN** collection cover artist

BRIAN CUNNINGHAM Editor – Original Series KATIE KUBERT KATE STEWART Assistant Editors – Original Series
ROBIN WILDMAN Editor ROBBIN BROSTERMAN Design Director – Books ROBBIE BIEDERMAN Publication Design

BOB HARRAS Senior VP – Editor-in-Chief, DC Comics

DIANE NELSON President DAN DIDIO and JIM LEE Co-Publishers GEOFF JOHNS Chief Creative Officer
JOHN ROOD Executive VP – Sales, Marketing and Business Development AMY GENKINS Senior VP – Business and Legal Affairs
NAIRI GARDINER Senior VP – Finance JEFF BOISON VP – Publishing Planning
MARK CHIARELLO VP – Art Direction and Design JOHN CUNNINGHAM VP – Marketing
TERRI CUNNINGHAM VP – Editorial Administration ALISON GILL Senior VP – Manufacturing and Operations
HANK KANALZ Senior VP – Vertigo and Integrated Publishing JAY KOGAN VP – Business and Legal Affairs, Publishing
JACK MAHAN VP – Business Affairs, Talent NICK NAPOLITANO VP – Manufacturing Administration
SUE POHJA VP – Book Sales COURTNEY SIMMONS Senior VP – Publicity BOB WAYNE Senior VP – Sales

JUSTICE LEAGUE DARK VOLUME 3: THE DEATH OF MAGIC

DC Comics, 1700 Broadway, New York, NY 10019
A Warner Bros. Entertainment Company.
Printed by RR Donnelley, Salem, VA, USA. 01/29/14. First Printing.

ISBN: 978-1-4012-4245-9

Library of Congress Cataloging-in-Publication Data

Lemire, Jeff.
Justice League Dark. Volume 3, The death of magic / Jeff Lemire.
pages cm. – (The New 52!)
This volume collects issues #14-21 of Justice League Dark" – Provided by publisher.
ISBN 978-1-4012-4245-9 (pbk.)
1. Graphic novels. I. Title. II. Title: Death of magic.
PN6728.J87L47 2014
741.5'973-dc23
2013039605

SUSTAINABLE FORESTRY INITIATIVE
Certified Chain of Custody
At Least 20% Certified Forest Content
www.sfiprogram.org
SFI-01042
APPLIES TO TEXT STOCK ONLY

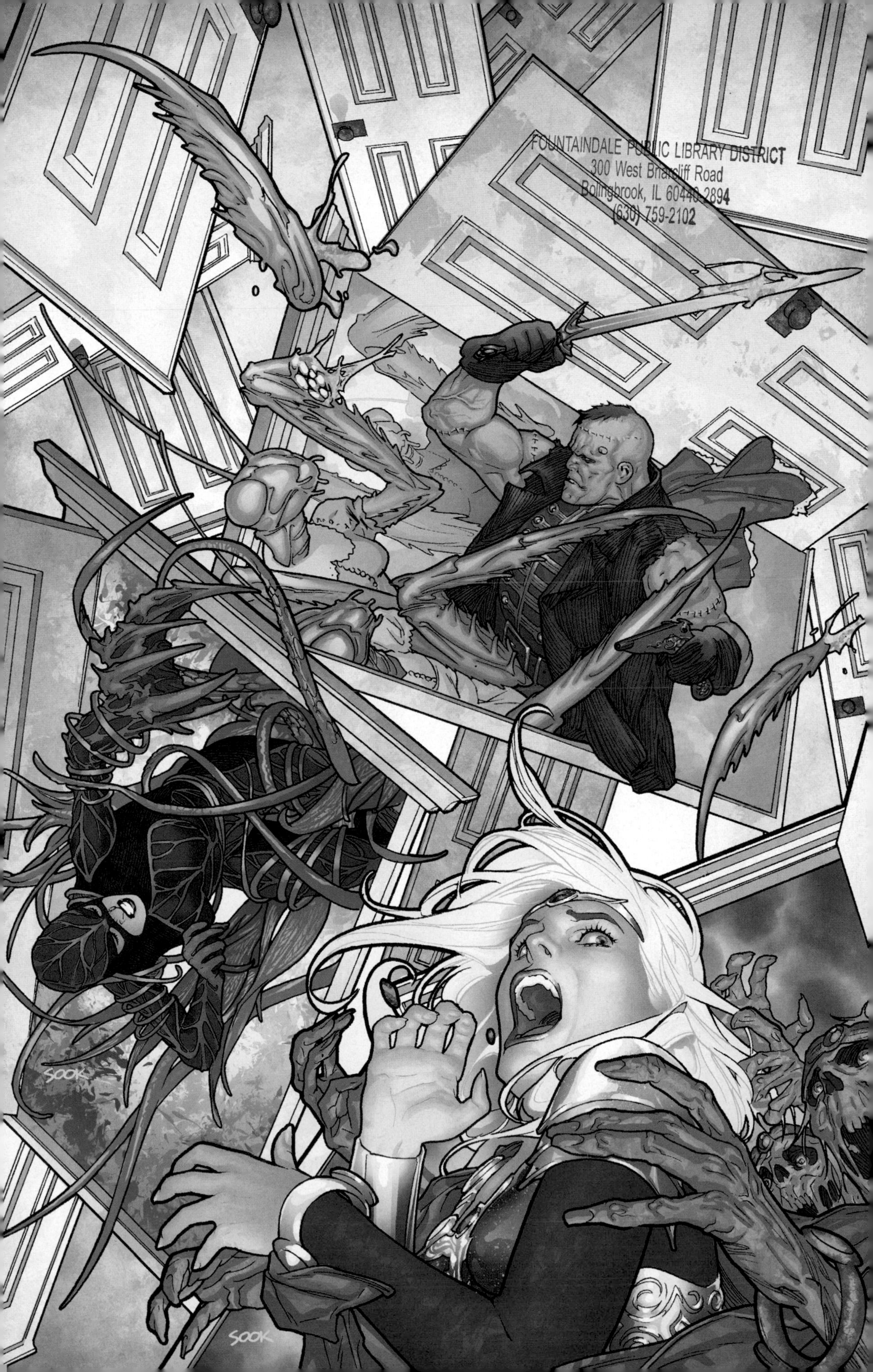
SOOK
SOOK

ENTER THE HOUSE OF MYSTERY

JEFF LEMIRE
writer

GRAHAM NOLAN
layouts

VICTOR DRUJINIU
finishes

RYAN SOOK
cover artist

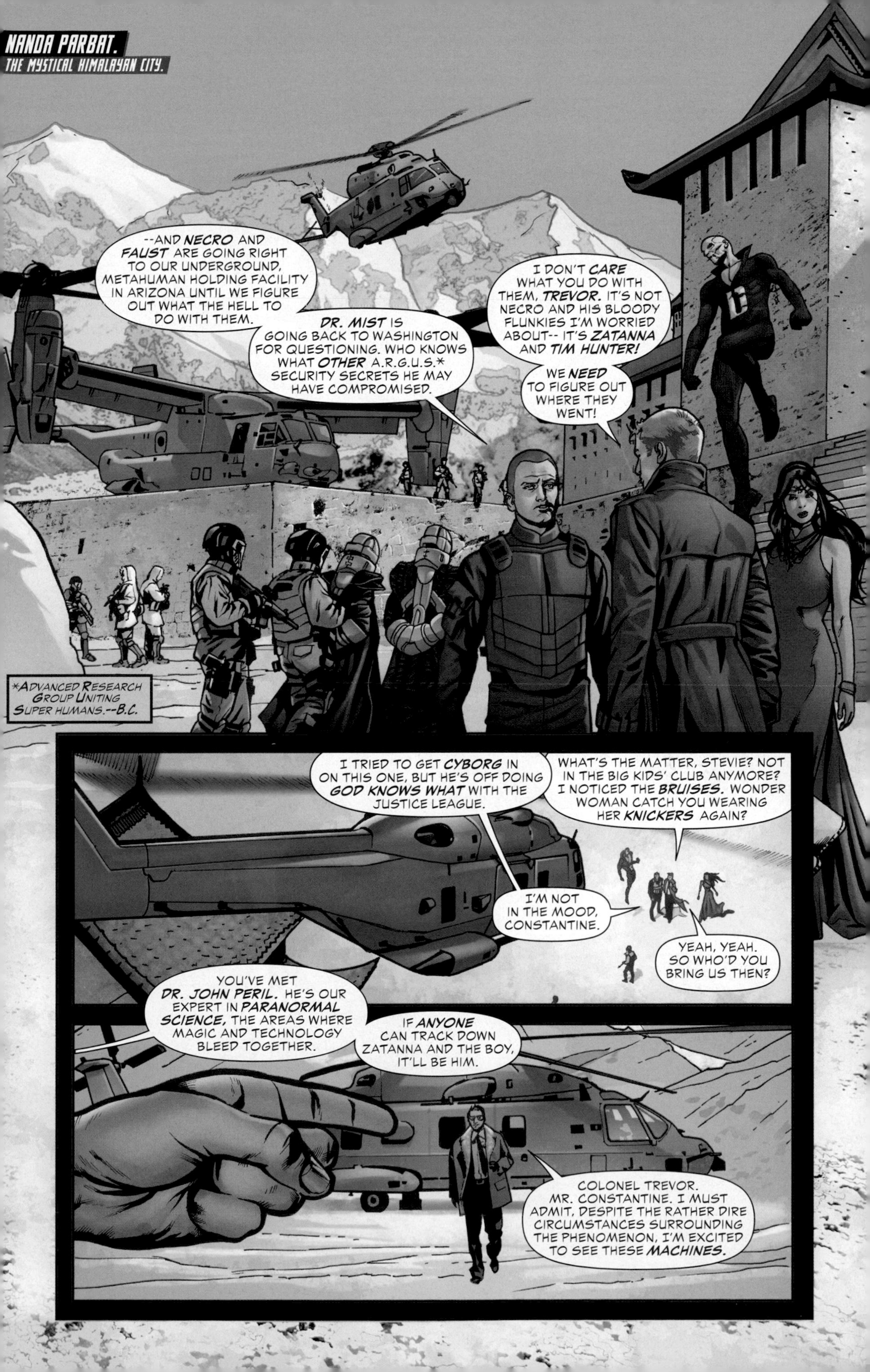
NANDA PARBAT.
THE MYSTICAL HIMALAYAN CITY.
--AND NECRO AND FAUST ARE GOING RIGHT TO OUR UNDERGROUND, METAHUMAN HOLDING FACILITY IN ARIZONA UNTIL WE FIGURE OUT WHAT THE HELL TO DO WITH THEM.
DR. MIST IS GOING BACK TO WASHINGTON FOR QUESTIONING. WHO KNOWS WHAT OTHER A.R.G.U.S.* SECURITY SECRETS HE MAY HAVE COMPROMISED.
I DON'T CARE WHAT YOU DO WITH THEM, TREVOR. IT'S NOT NECRO AND HIS BLOODY FLUNKIES I'M WORRIED ABOUT-- IT'S ZATANNA AND TIM HUNTER!
WE NEED TO FIGURE OUT WHERE THEY WENT!
*ADVANCED RESEARCH GROUP UNITING SUPER HUMANS.--B.C.
I TRIED TO GET CYBORG IN ON THIS ONE, BUT HE'S OFF DOING GOD KNOWS WHAT WITH THE JUSTICE LEAGUE.
WHAT'S THE MATTER, STEVIE? NOT IN THE BIG KIDS' CLUB ANYMORE? I NOTICED THE BRUISES. WONDER WOMAN CATCH YOU WEARING HER KNICKERS AGAIN?
I'M NOT IN THE MOOD, CONSTANTINE.
YEAH, YEAH. SO WHO'D YOU BRING US THEN?
YOU'VE MET DR. JOHN PERIL. HE'S OUR EXPERT IN PARANORMAL SCIENCE, THE AREAS WHERE MAGIC AND TECHNOLOGY BLEED TOGETHER.
IF ANYONE CAN TRACK DOWN ZATANNA AND THE BOY, IT'LL BE HIM.
COLONEL TREVOR. MR. CONSTANTINE. I MUST ADMIT, DESPITE THE RATHER DIRE CIRCUMSTANCES SURROUNDING THE PHENOMENON, I'M EXCITED TO SEE THESE MACHINES.

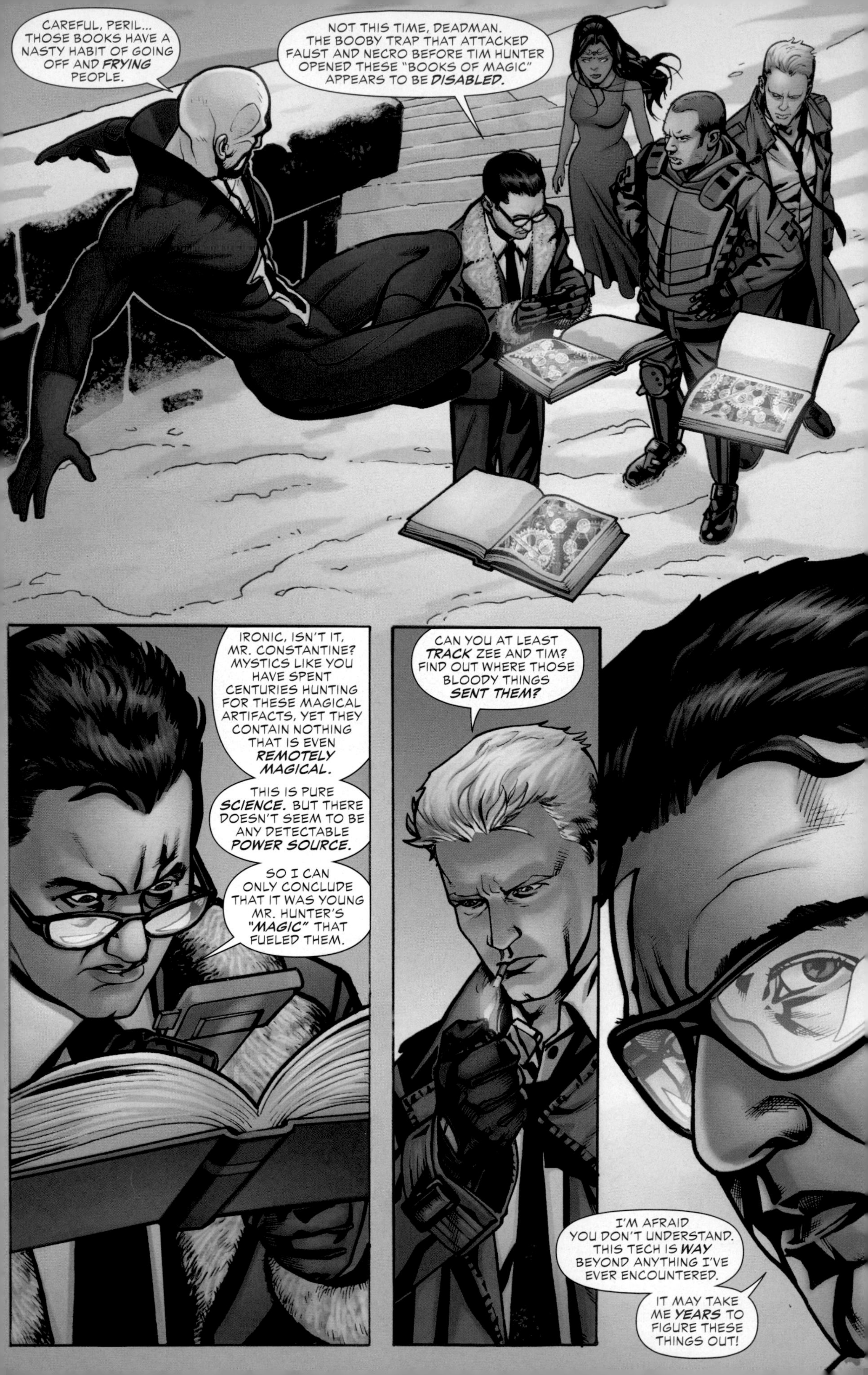
CAREFUL, PERIL... THOSE BOOKS HAVE A NASTY HABIT OF GOING OFF AND FRYING PEOPLE.
NOT THIS TIME, DEADMAN. THE BOOBY TRAP THAT ATTACKED FAUST AND NECRO BEFORE TIM HUNTER OPENED THESE "BOOKS OF MAGIC" APPEARS TO BE DISABLED.
IRONIC, ISN'T IT, MR. CONSTANTINE? MYSTICS LIKE YOU HAVE SPENT CENTURIES HUNTING FOR THESE MAGICAL ARTIFACTS, YET THEY CONTAIN NOTHING THAT IS EVEN REMOTELY MAGICAL.
THIS IS PURE SCIENCE. BUT THERE DOESN'T SEEM TO BE ANY DETECTABLE POWER SOURCE.
SO I CAN ONLY CONCLUDE THAT IT WAS YOUNG MR. HUNTER'S "MAGIC" THAT FUELED THEM.
CAN YOU AT LEAST TRACK ZEE AND TIM? FIND OUT WHERE THOSE BLOODY THINGS SENT THEM?
I'M AFRAID YOU DON'T UNDERSTAND. THIS TECH IS WAY BEYOND ANYTHING I'VE EVER ENCOUNTERED.
IT MAY TAKE ME YEARS TO FIGURE THESE THINGS OUT!

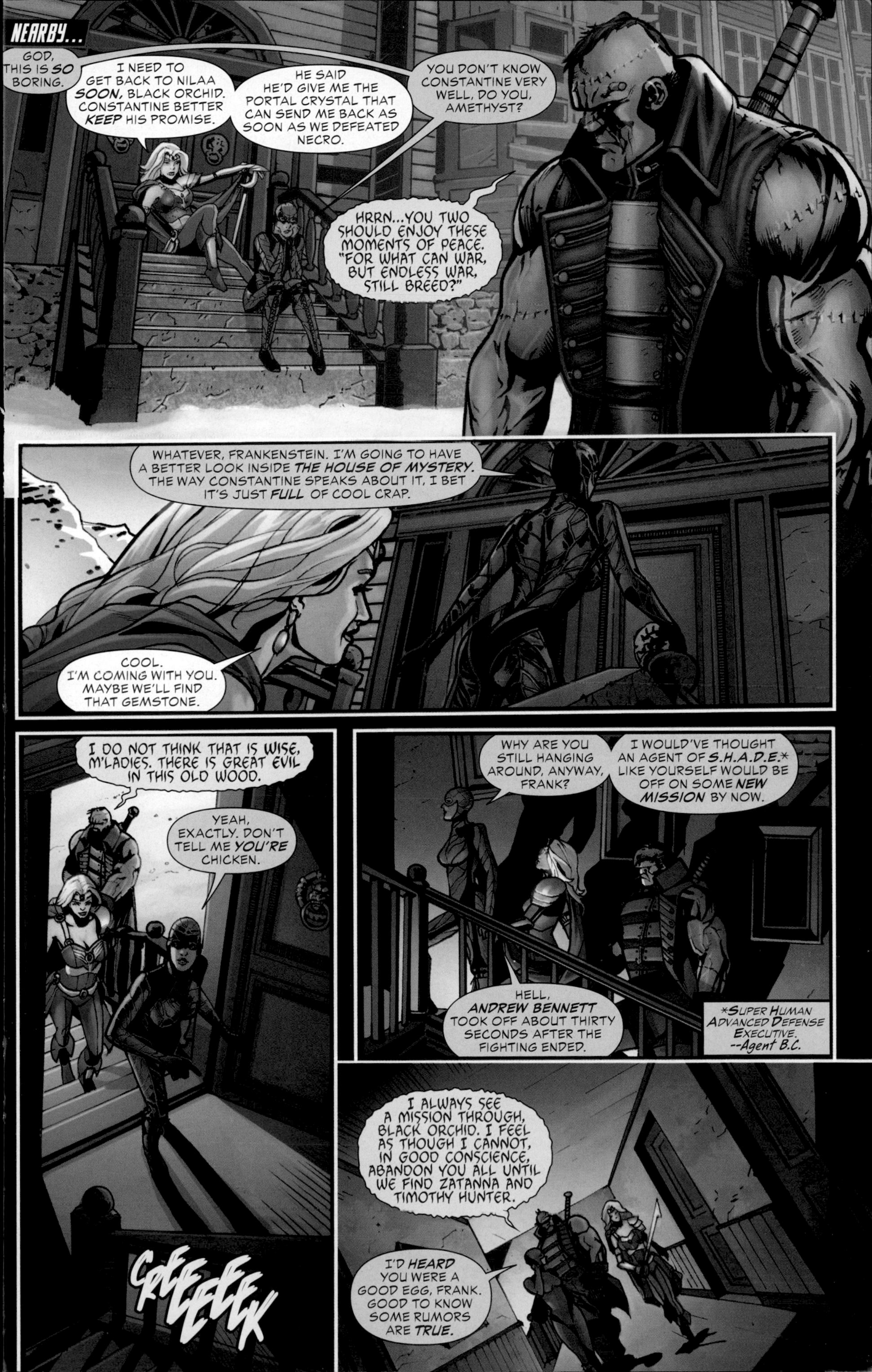
NEARBY...
GOD, THIS IS SO BORING.
I NEED TO GET BACK TO NILAA SOON, BLACK ORCHID. CONSTANTINE BETTER KEEP HIS PROMISE.
HE SAID HE'D GIVE ME THE PORTAL CRYSTAL THAT CAN SEND ME BACK AS SOON AS WE DEFEATED NECRO.
YOU DON'T KNOW CONSTANTINE VERY WELL, DO YOU, AMETHYST?
HRRN...YOU TWO SHOULD ENJOY THESE MOMENTS OF PEACE. "FOR WHAT CAN WAR, BUT ENDLESS WAR, STILL BREED?"
WHATEVER, FRANKENSTEIN. I'M GOING TO HAVE A BETTER LOOK INSIDE THE HOUSE OF MYSTERY. THE WAY CONSTANTINE SPEAKS ABOUT IT, I BET IT'S JUST FULL OF COOL CRAP.
COOL. I'M COMING WITH YOU. MAYBE WE'LL FIND THAT GEMSTONE.
I DO NOT THINK THAT IS WISE, M'LADIES. THERE IS GREAT EVIL IN THIS OLD WOOD.
YEAH, EXACTLY. DON'T TELL ME YOU'RE CHICKEN.
CREEEEK
WHY ARE YOU STILL HANGING AROUND, ANYWAY, FRANK?
I WOULD'VE THOUGHT AN AGENT OF S.H.A.D.E.* LIKE YOURSELF WOULD BE OFF ON SOME NEW MISSION BY NOW.
HELL, ANDREW BENNETT TOOK OFF ABOUT THIRTY SECONDS AFTER THE FIGHTING ENDED.
*SUPER HUMAN ADVANCED DEFENSE EXECUTIVE. --Agent B.C.
I ALWAYS SEE A MISSION THROUGH, BLACK ORCHID. I FEEL AS THOUGH I CANNOT, IN GOOD CONSCIENCE, ABANDON YOU ALL UNTIL WE FIND ZATANNA AND TIMOTHY HUNTER.
I'D HEARD YOU WERE A GOOD EGG, FRANK. GOOD TO KNOW SOME RUMORS ARE TRUE.

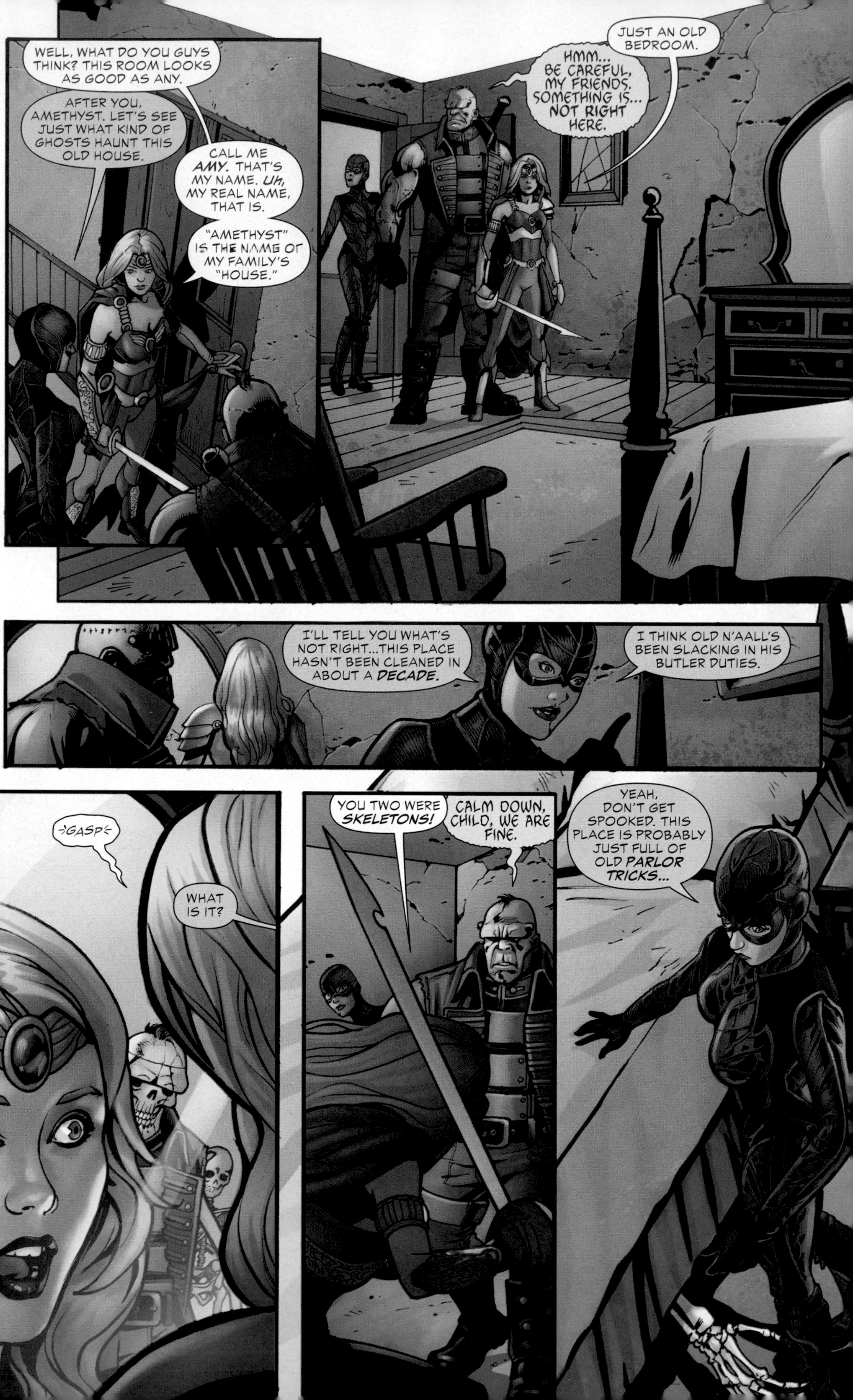
WELL, WHAT DO YOU GUYS THINK? THIS ROOM LOOKS AS GOOD AS ANY.
AFTER YOU, AMETHYST. LET'S SEE JUST WHAT KIND OF GHOSTS HAUNT THIS OLD HOUSE.
CALL ME AMY. THAT'S MY NAME. UH, MY REAL NAME, THAT IS.
"AMETHYST" IS THE NAME OF MY FAMILY'S "HOUSE."
JUST AN OLD BEDROOM.
HMM... BE CAREFUL, MY FRIENDS. SOMETHING IS... NOT RIGHT HERE.
I'LL TELL YOU WHAT'S NOT RIGHT...THIS PLACE HASN'T BEEN CLEANED IN ABOUT A DECADE.
I THINK OLD N'AALL'S BEEN SLACKING IN HIS BUTLER DUTIES.
GASP
WHAT IS IT?
YOU TWO WERE SKELETONS!
CALM DOWN, CHILD, WE ARE FINE.
YEAH, DON'T GET SPOOKED. THIS PLACE IS PROBABLY JUST FULL OF OLD PARLOR TRICKS...

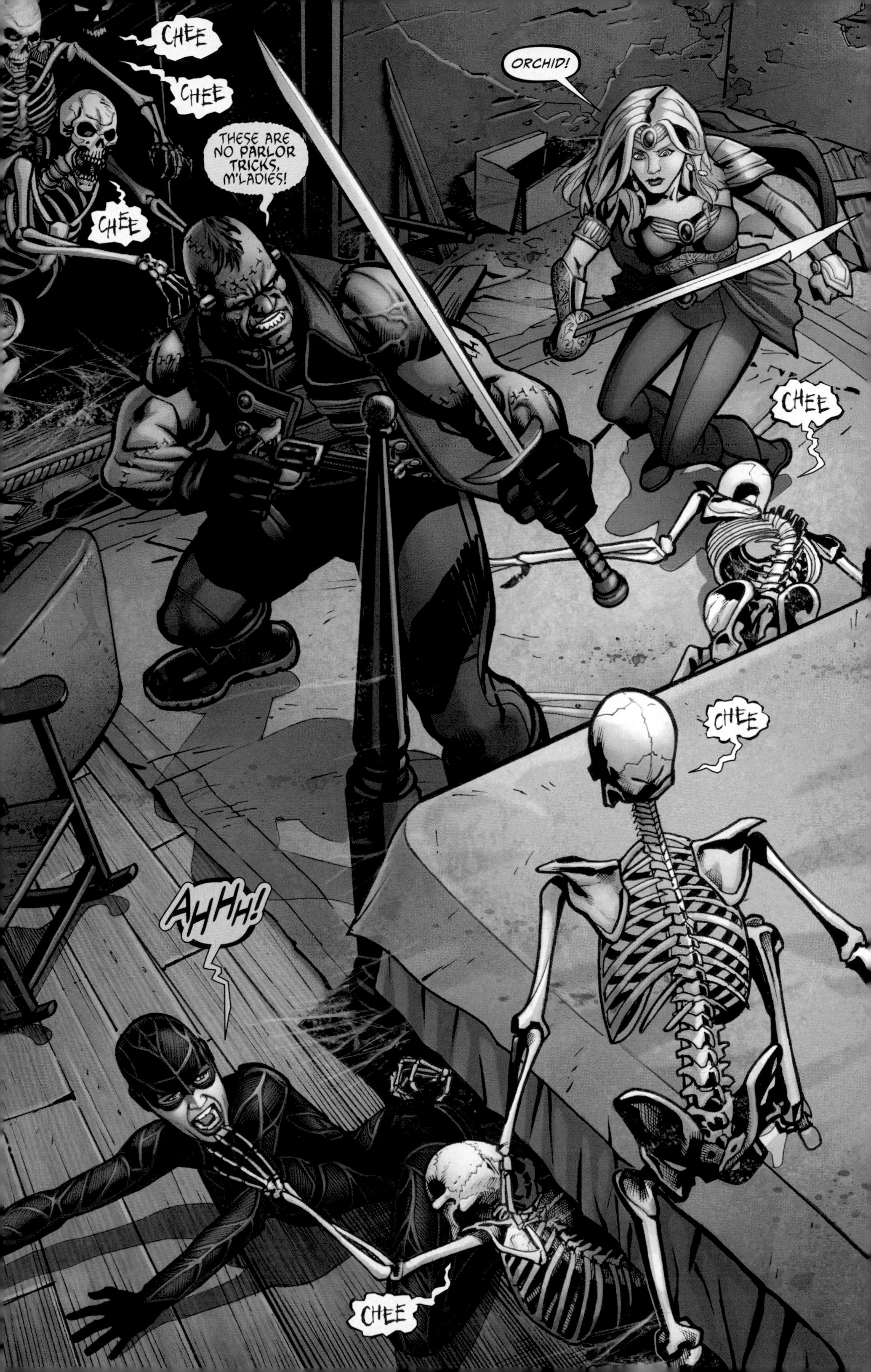
CHEE
CHEE
THESE ARE NO PARLOR TRICKS, M'LADIES!
CHEE
ORCHID!
CHEE
CHEE
AHHH!
CHEE

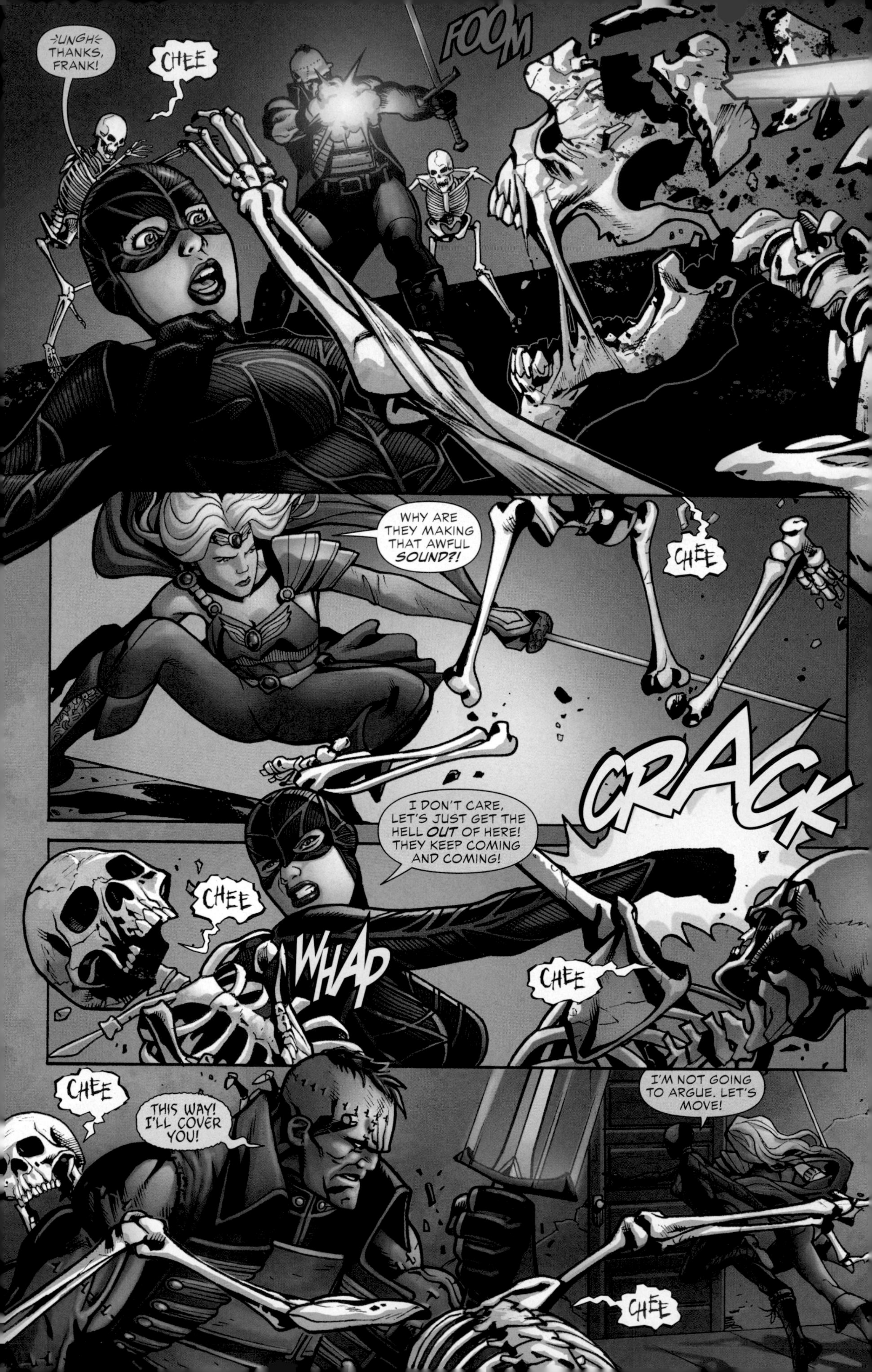
FOOM
-UNGH- THANKS, FRANK!
CHEE
WHY ARE THEY MAKING THAT AWFUL SOUND?!
CHEE
CRACK
I DON'T CARE, LET'S JUST GET THE HELL OUT OF HERE! THEY KEEP COMING AND COMING!
CHEE
WHAP
CHEE
CHEE
THIS WAY! I'LL COVER YOU!
I'M NOT GOING TO ARGUE. LET'S MOVE!
CHEE

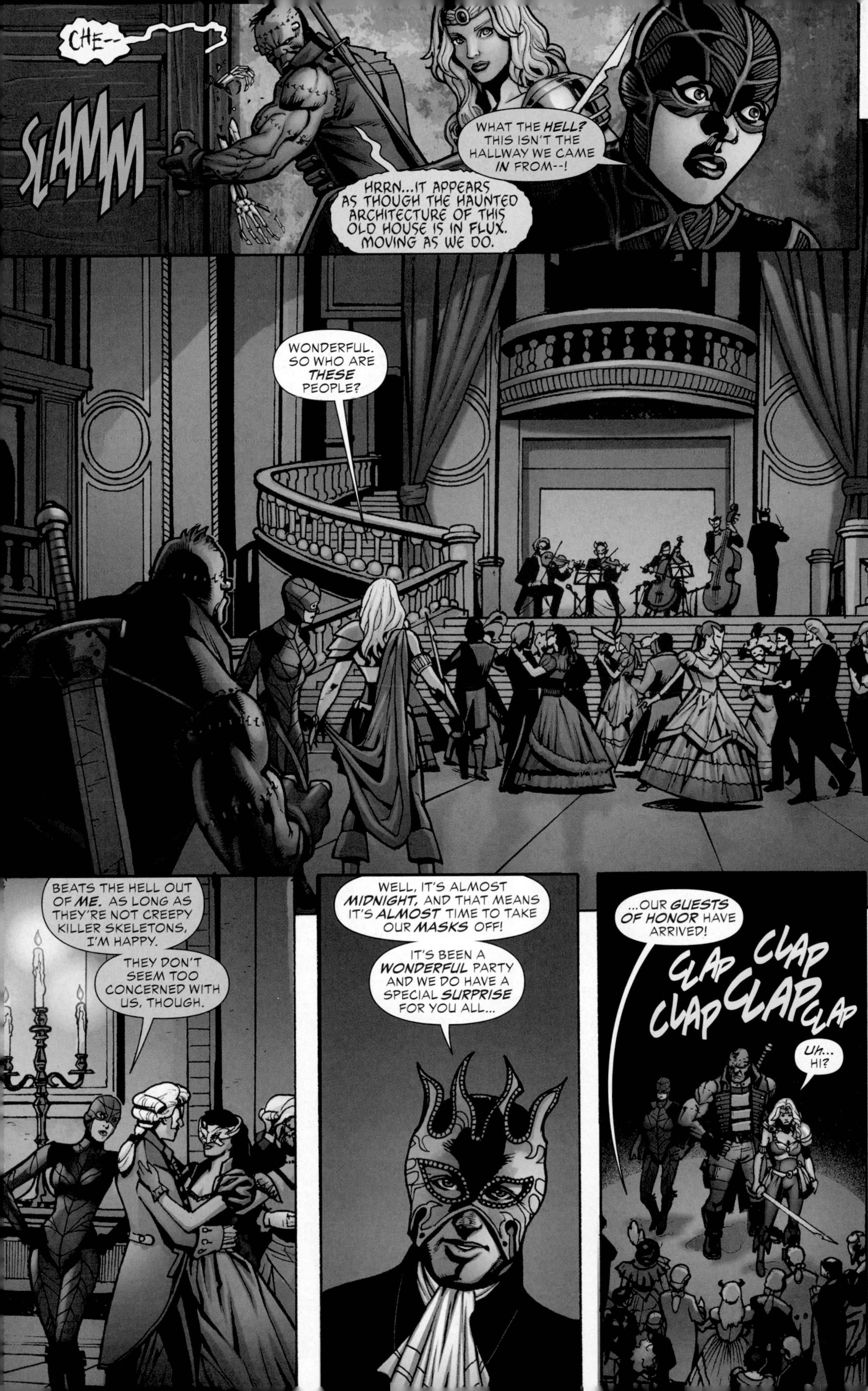
CHE--
SLAMM
WHAT THE HELL? THIS ISN'T THE HALLWAY WE CAME IN FROM--!
HRRN...IT APPEARS AS THOUGH THE HAUNTED ARCHITECTURE OF THIS OLD HOUSE IS IN FLUX. MOVING AS WE DO.
WONDERFUL. SO WHO ARE THESE PEOPLE?
BEATS THE HELL OUT OF ME. AS LONG AS THEY'RE NOT CREEPY KILLER SKELETONS, I'M HAPPY.
THEY DON'T SEEM TOO CONCERNED WITH US, THOUGH.
WELL, IT'S ALMOST MIDNIGHT, AND THAT MEANS IT'S ALMOST TIME TO TAKE OUR MASKS OFF!
IT'S BEEN A WONDERFUL PARTY AND WE DO HAVE A SPECIAL SURPRISE FOR YOU ALL...
...OUR GUESTS OF HONOR HAVE ARRIVED!
CLAP CLAP CLAP CLAP CLAP
Uh... HI?

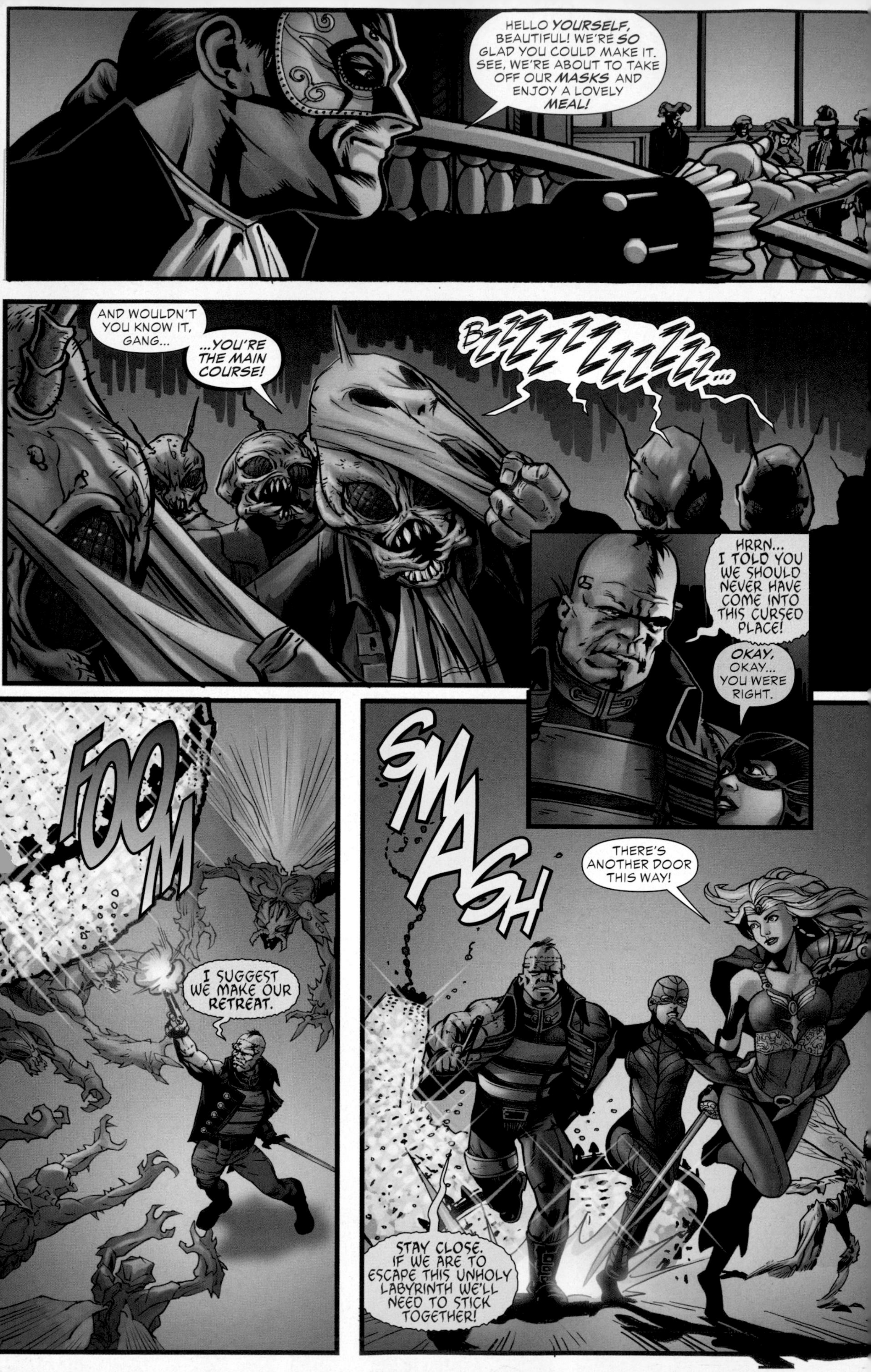
HELLO YOURSELF, BEAUTIFUL! WE'RE SO GLAD YOU COULD MAKE IT. SEE, WE'RE ABOUT TO TAKE OFF OUR MASKS AND ENJOY A LOVELY MEAL!
AND WOULDN'T YOU KNOW IT, GANG...
...YOU'RE THE MAIN COURSE!
BZZZZZZZZZZZZ...
HRRN... I TOLD YOU WE SHOULD NEVER HAVE COME INTO THIS CURSED PLACE!
OKAY, OKAY... YOU WERE RIGHT.
FOOM
I SUGGEST WE MAKE OUR RETREAT.
SMASH
THERE'S ANOTHER DOOR THIS WAY!
STAY CLOSE. IF WE ARE TO ESCAPE THIS UNHOLY LABYRINTH WE'LL NEED TO STICK TOGETHER!

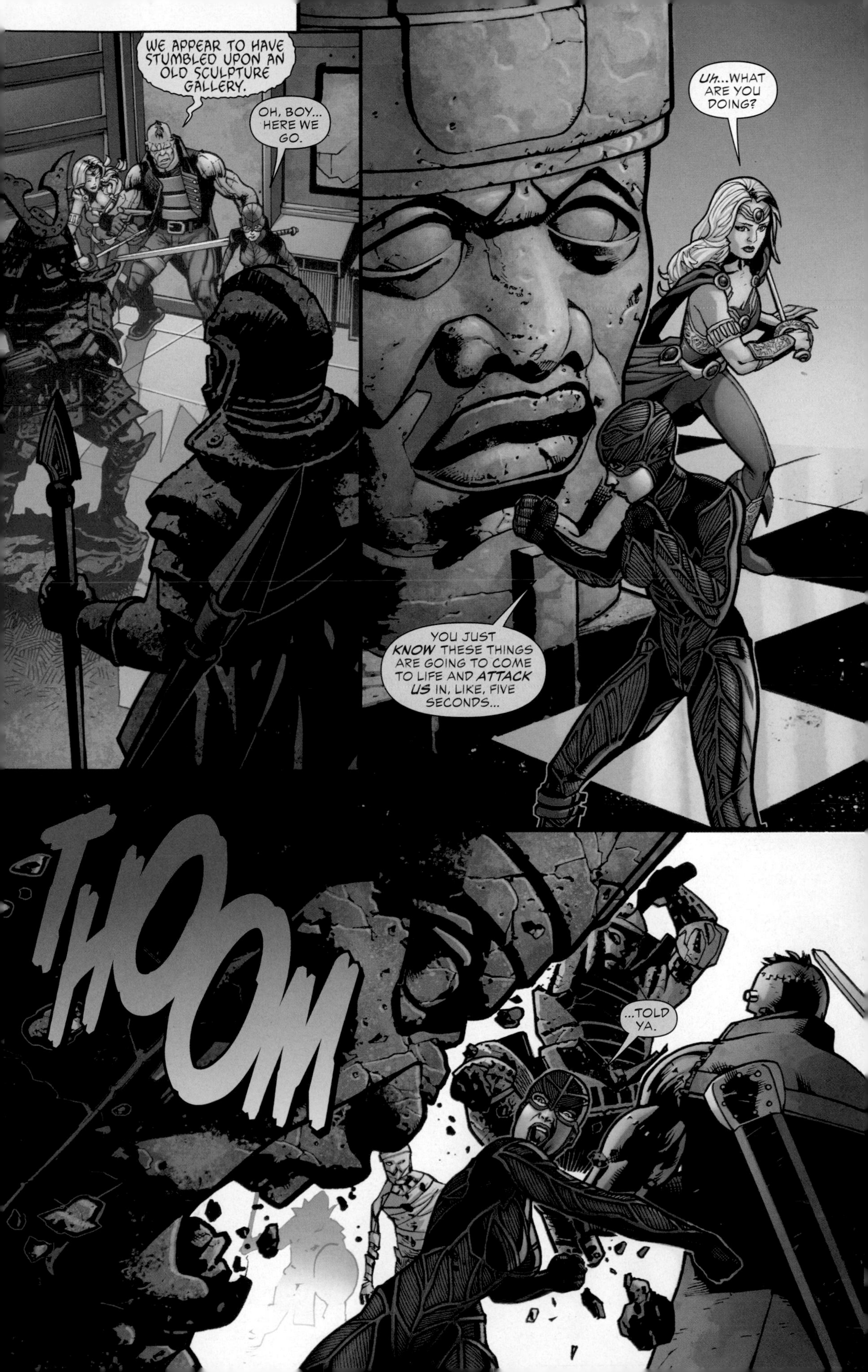
WE APPEAR TO HAVE STUMBLED UPON AN OLD SCULPTURE GALLERY.
OH, BOY... HERE WE GO.
Uh...WHAT ARE YOU DOING?
YOU JUST KNOW THESE THINGS ARE GOING TO COME TO LIFE AND ATTACK US IN, LIKE, FIVE SECONDS...
THOOM
...TOLD YA.

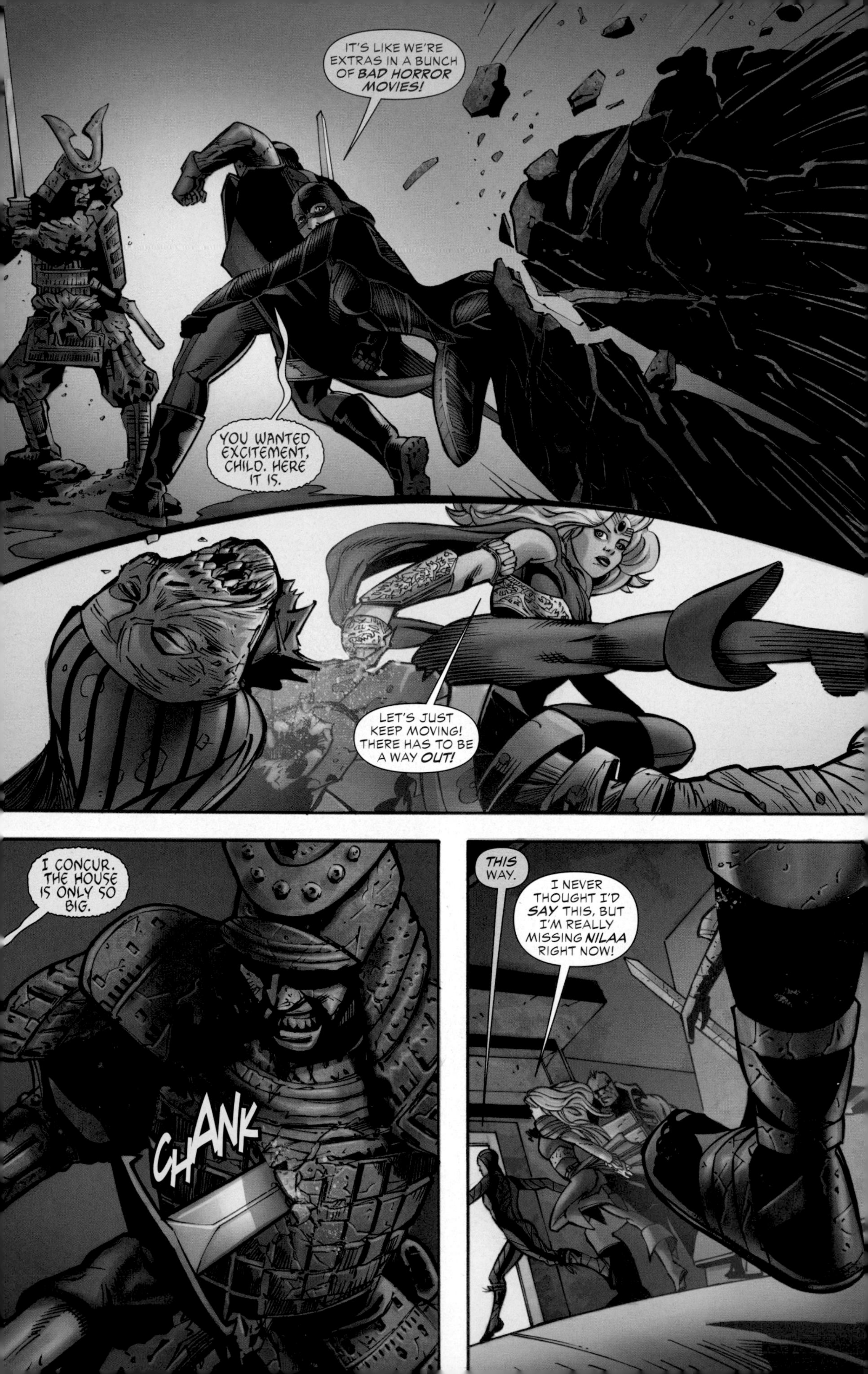
IT'S LIKE WE'RE EXTRAS IN A BUNCH OF BAD HORROR MOVIES!
YOU WANTED EXCITEMENT, CHILD. HERE IT IS.
LET'S JUST KEEP MOVING! THERE HAS TO BE A WAY OUT!
I CONCUR. THE HOUSE IS ONLY SO BIG.
CHANK
THIS WAY.
I NEVER THOUGHT I'D SAY THIS, BUT I'M REALLY MISSING NILAA RIGHT NOW!

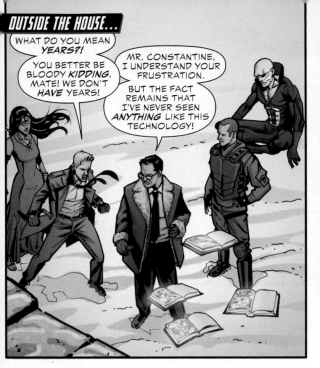

WHAT DO YOU MEAN *YEARS*?!

YOU BETTER BE BLOODY *KIDDING*, MATE! WE DON'T *HAVE* YEARS!

MR. CONSTANTINE, I UNDERSTAND YOUR FRUSTRATION. BUT THE FACT REMAINS THAT I'VE NEVER SEEN *ANYTHING* LIKE THIS TECHNOLOGY!

BOLLOCKS! YOU'RE SUPPOSED TO BE THE EXPERT! IF *YOU* CAN'T DO IT, THEN WE NEED TO CALL SOMEONE ELSE WHO *CAN*! WE MIGHT AS WELL HAVE *MADAME XANADU* HERE READ HER BLOODY *TAROT CARDS* AND TELL US WHAT'LL HAPPEN A BLOODY YEAR FROM NOW...

NO NEED TO BE *HASTY* HERE.

I CAN'T CRACK THE MACHINES THEMSELVES, BUT MAYBE I CAN RECREATE THE EFFECT THAT *TRIGGERED* THEM.

WHAT DO YOU MEAN?

YEAH, DOC, SPELL IT OUT FOR THE SLOW KIDS...

PERHAPS I COULD TRY THE ECTO-DISPLACEMENT METHOD TO CREATE A TEMPLATE OR MAP OF TIMOTHY HUNTER'S DISTINCT *MAGICAL SIGNATURE.*

IF WE HAD *THAT*, WE MIGHT BE ABLE TO CHANNEL THOSE ENERGIES INTO IT AND *TRICK* THE MACHINES INTO THINKING HE'S *ACTIVATING* THEM AGAIN.

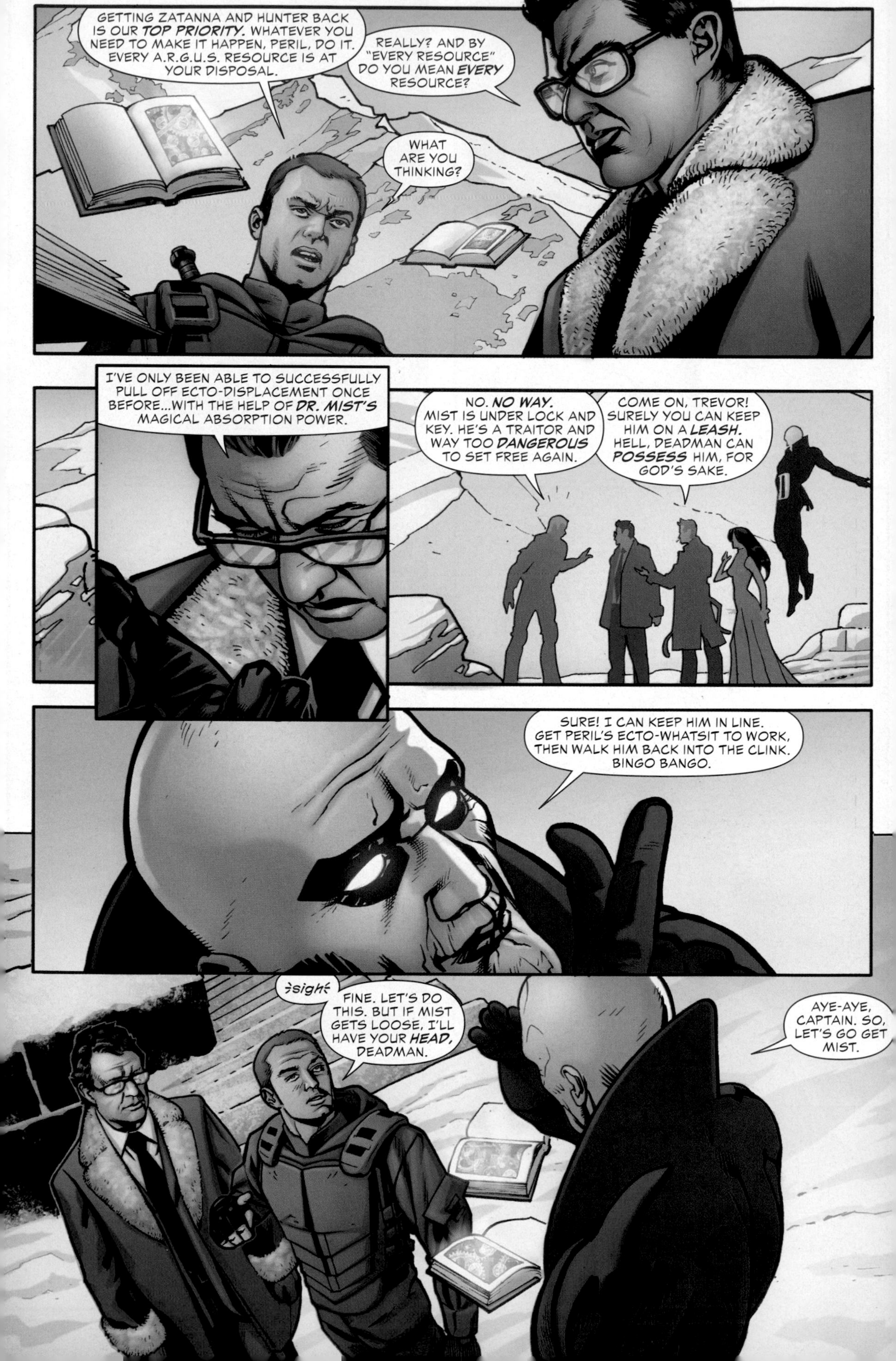
GETTING ZATANNA AND HUNTER BACK IS OUR TOP PRIORITY. WHATEVER YOU NEED TO MAKE IT HAPPEN, PERIL, DO IT. EVERY A.R.G.U.S. RESOURCE IS AT YOUR DISPOSAL.
REALLY? AND BY "EVERY RESOURCE" DO YOU MEAN EVERY RESOURCE?
WHAT ARE YOU THINKING?
I'VE ONLY BEEN ABLE TO SUCCESSFULLY PULL OFF ECTO-DISPLACEMENT ONCE BEFORE...WITH THE HELP OF DR. MIST'S MAGICAL ABSORPTION POWER.
NO. NO WAY. MIST IS UNDER LOCK AND KEY. HE'S A TRAITOR AND WAY TOO DANGEROUS TO SET FREE AGAIN.
COME ON, TREVOR! SURELY YOU CAN KEEP HIM ON A LEASH. HELL, DEADMAN CAN POSSESS HIM, FOR GOD'S SAKE.
SURE! I CAN KEEP HIM IN LINE. GET PERIL'S ECTO-WHATSIT TO WORK, THEN WALK HIM BACK INTO THE CLINK. BINGO BANGO.
sigh
FINE. LET'S DO THIS. BUT IF MIST GETS LOOSE, I'LL HAVE YOUR HEAD, DEADMAN.
AYE-AYE, CAPTAIN. SO, LET'S GO GET MIST.

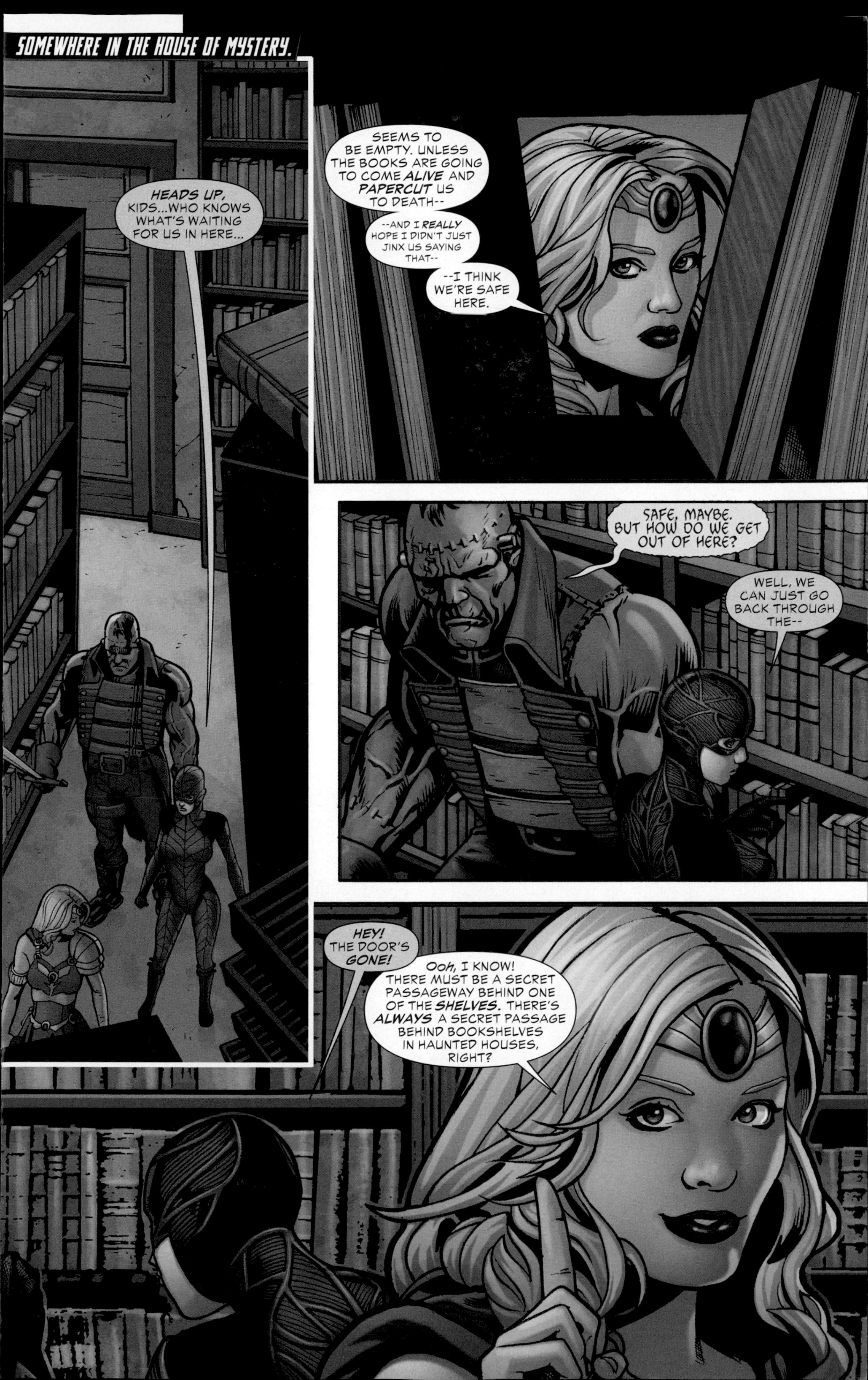
SOMEWHERE IN THE HOUSE OF MYSTERY.
HEADS UP, KIDS...WHO KNOWS WHAT'S WAITING FOR US IN HERE...
SEEMS TO BE EMPTY. UNLESS THE BOOKS ARE GOING TO COME ALIVE AND PAPERCUT US TO DEATH--
--AND I REALLY HOPE I DIDN'T JUST JINX US SAYING THAT--
--I THINK WE'RE SAFE HERE.
SAFE, MAYBE. BUT HOW DO WE GET OUT OF HERE?
WELL, WE CAN JUST GO BACK THROUGH THE--
HEY! THE DOOR'S GONE!
Ooh, I KNOW! THERE MUST BE A SECRET PASSAGEWAY BEHIND ONE OF THE SHELVES. THERE'S ALWAYS A SECRET PASSAGE BEHIND BOOKSHELVES IN HAUNTED HOUSES, RIGHT?

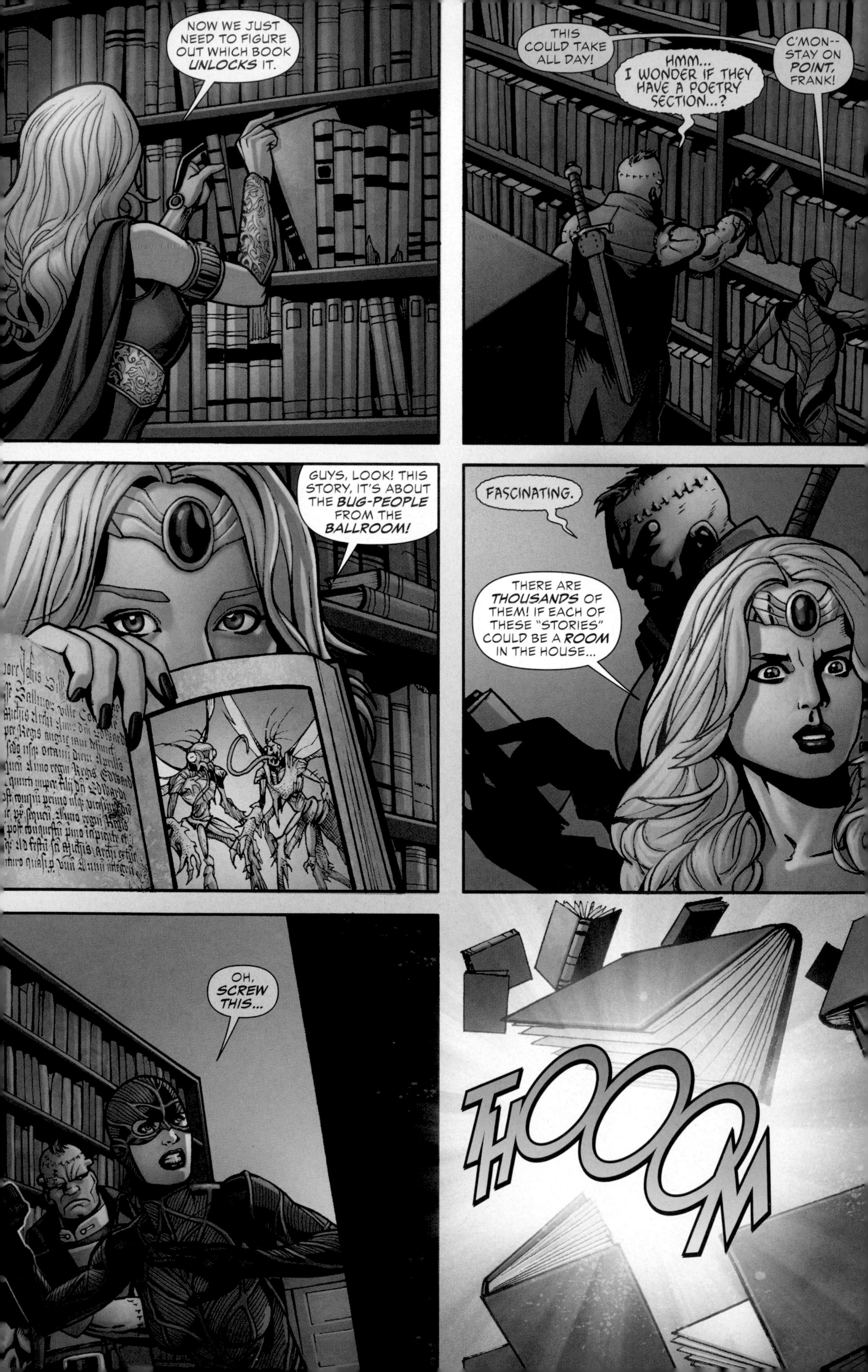

NOW WE JUST NEED TO FIGURE OUT WHICH BOOK UNLOCKS IT.
THIS COULD TAKE ALL DAY!
HMM... I WONDER IF THEY HAVE A POETRY SECTION...?
C'MON-- STAY ON POINT, FRANK!
GUYS, LOOK! THIS STORY, IT'S ABOUT THE BUG-PEOPLE FROM THE BALLROOM!
FASCINATING.
THERE ARE THOUSANDS OF THEM! IF EACH OF THESE "STORIES" COULD BE A ROOM IN THE HOUSE...
OH, SCREW THIS...
THOOOM

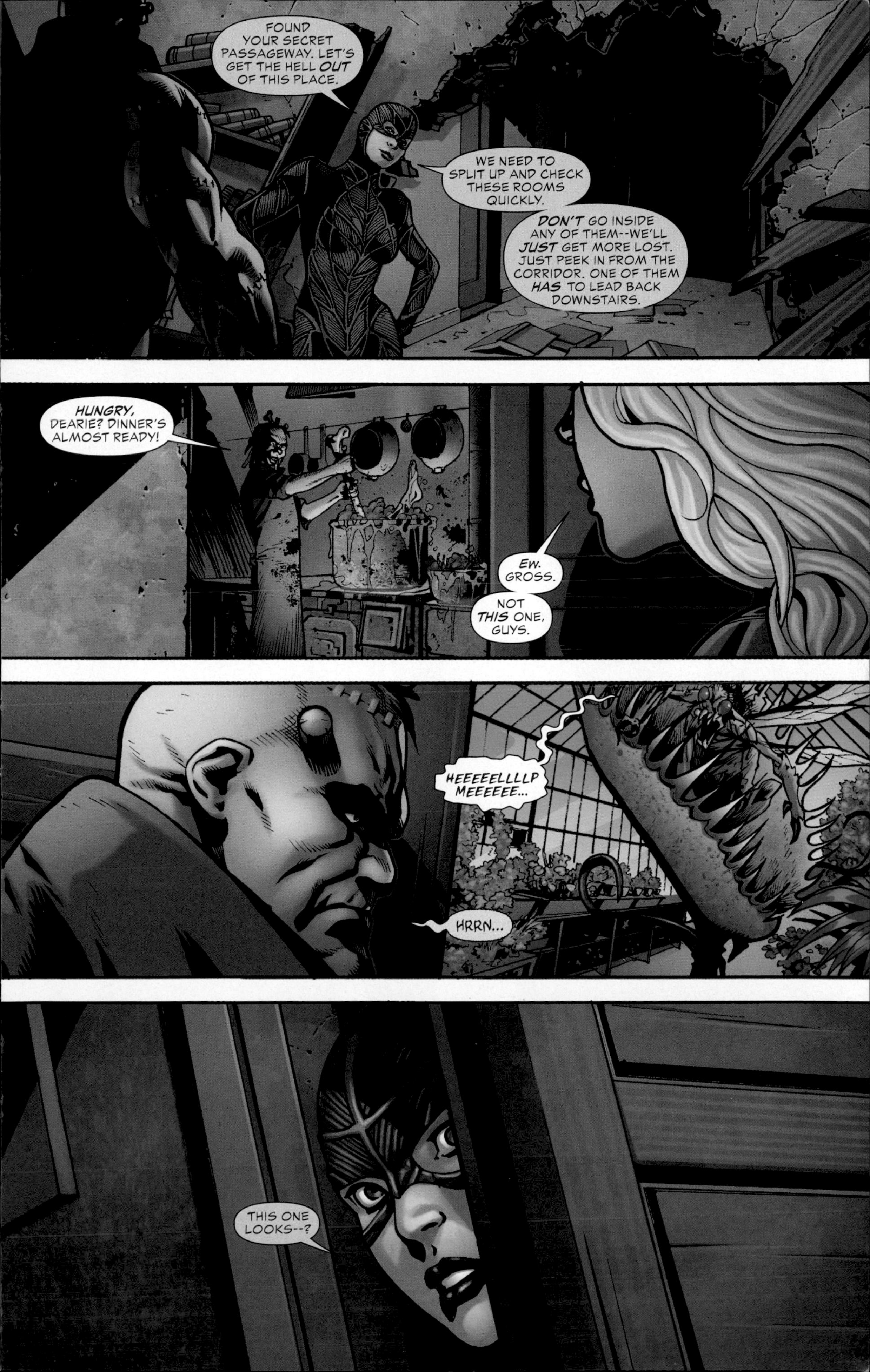
FOUND YOUR SECRET PASSAGEWAY. LET'S GET THE HELL OUT OF THIS PLACE.
WE NEED TO SPLIT UP AND CHECK THESE ROOMS QUICKLY.
DON'T GO INSIDE ANY OF THEM--WE'LL JUST GET MORE LOST. JUST PEEK IN FROM THE CORRIDOR. ONE OF THEM HAS TO LEAD BACK DOWNSTAIRS.
HUNGRY, DEARIE? DINNER'S ALMOST READY!
EW. GROSS.
NOT THIS ONE, GUYS.
HEEEEELLLLP MEEEEEE...
HRRN...
THIS ONE LOOKS--?

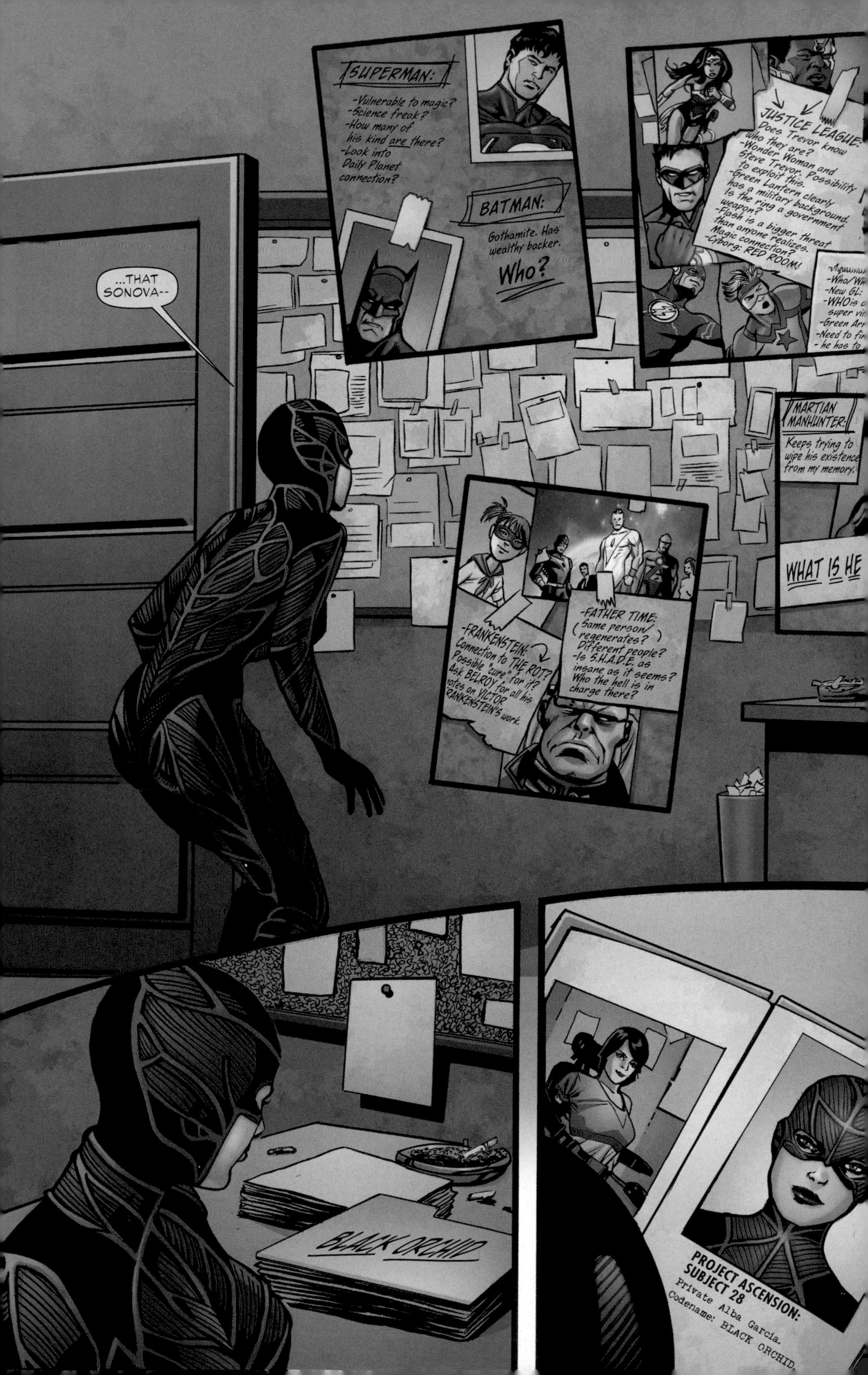

...THAT SONOVA--
SUPERMAN:
-Vulnerable to magic?
-Science freak?
-How many of his kind are there?
-Look into Daily Planet connection?
BATMAN:
Gothamite. Has wealthy backer.
Who?
JUSTICE LEAGUE:
Does Trevor know who they are?
-Wonder Woman and Steve Trevor. Possibility to exploit this.
-Green Lantern clearly has a military background. Is the ring a government weapon?
-Flash is a bigger threat than anyone realizes. Magic connection?
-Cyborg: RED ROOM!
MARTIAN MANHUNTER:
Keeps trying to wipe his existence from my memory.
-FRANKENSTEIN:
Connection to THE ROT? Possible "cure" for it? Ask BELROY for all his
-FATHER TIME:
(Same person/ regenerates?) Different people?
-Is S.H.A.D.E. as insane as it seems? Who the hell is in charge there?
BLACK ORCHID
PROJECT ASCENSION: SUBJECT 28
Private Alba Garcia.
Codename: BLACK ORCHID.

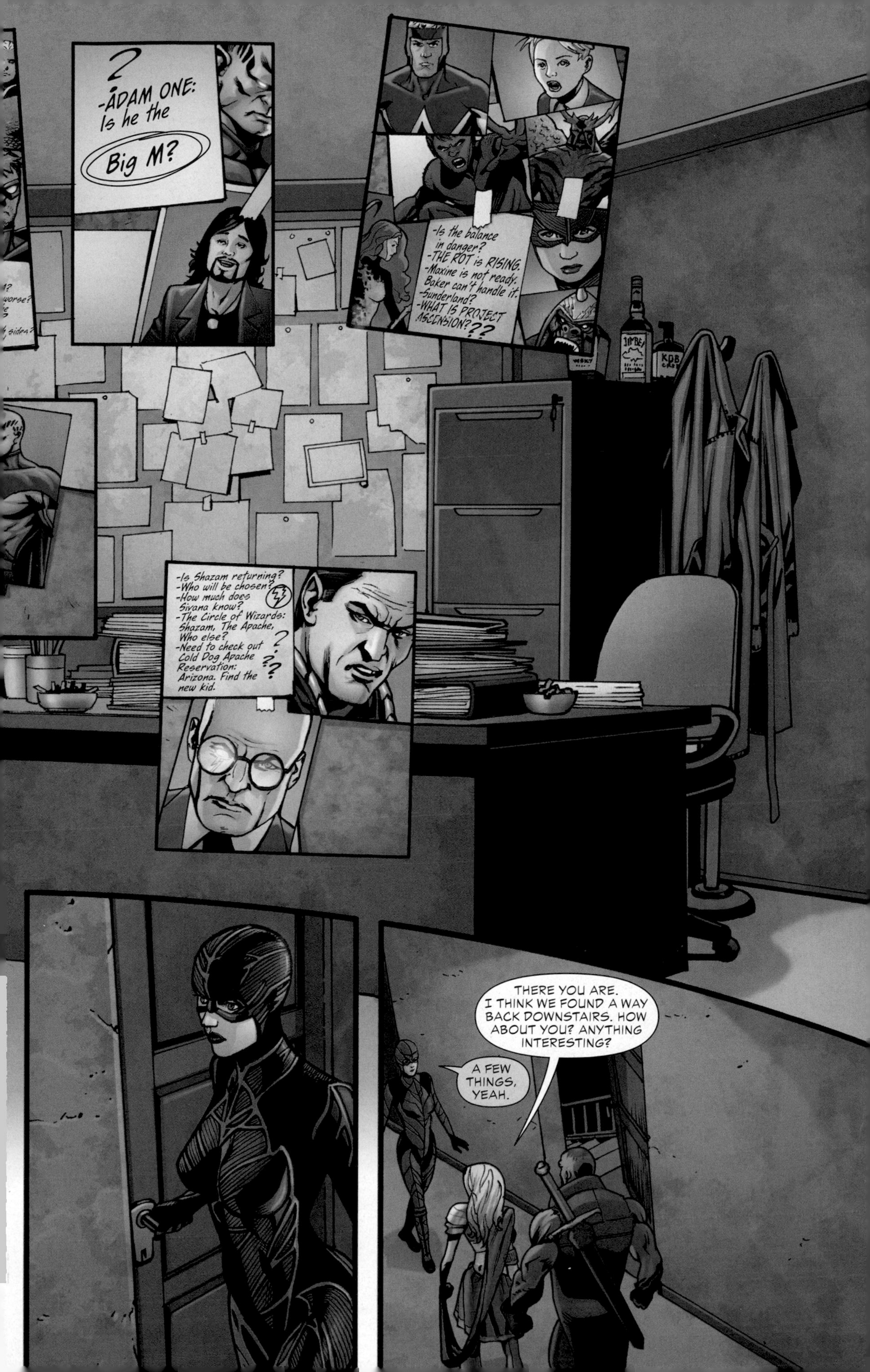
?
-ADAM ONE:
Is he the
Big M?
-Is the balance in danger?
-THE ROT is RISING.
-Maxine is not ready. Baker can't handle it.
-Sunderland?
-WHAT IS PROJECT ASCENSION???
-Is Shazam returning?
-Who will be chosen?
-How much does Sivana know?
-The Circle of Wizards: Shazam, The Apache, Who else?
-Need to check out Cold Dog Apache Reservation: Arizona. Find the new kid.
???
THERE YOU ARE. I THINK WE FOUND A WAY BACK DOWNSTAIRS. HOW ABOUT YOU? ANYTHING INTERESTING?
A FEW THINGS, YEAH.

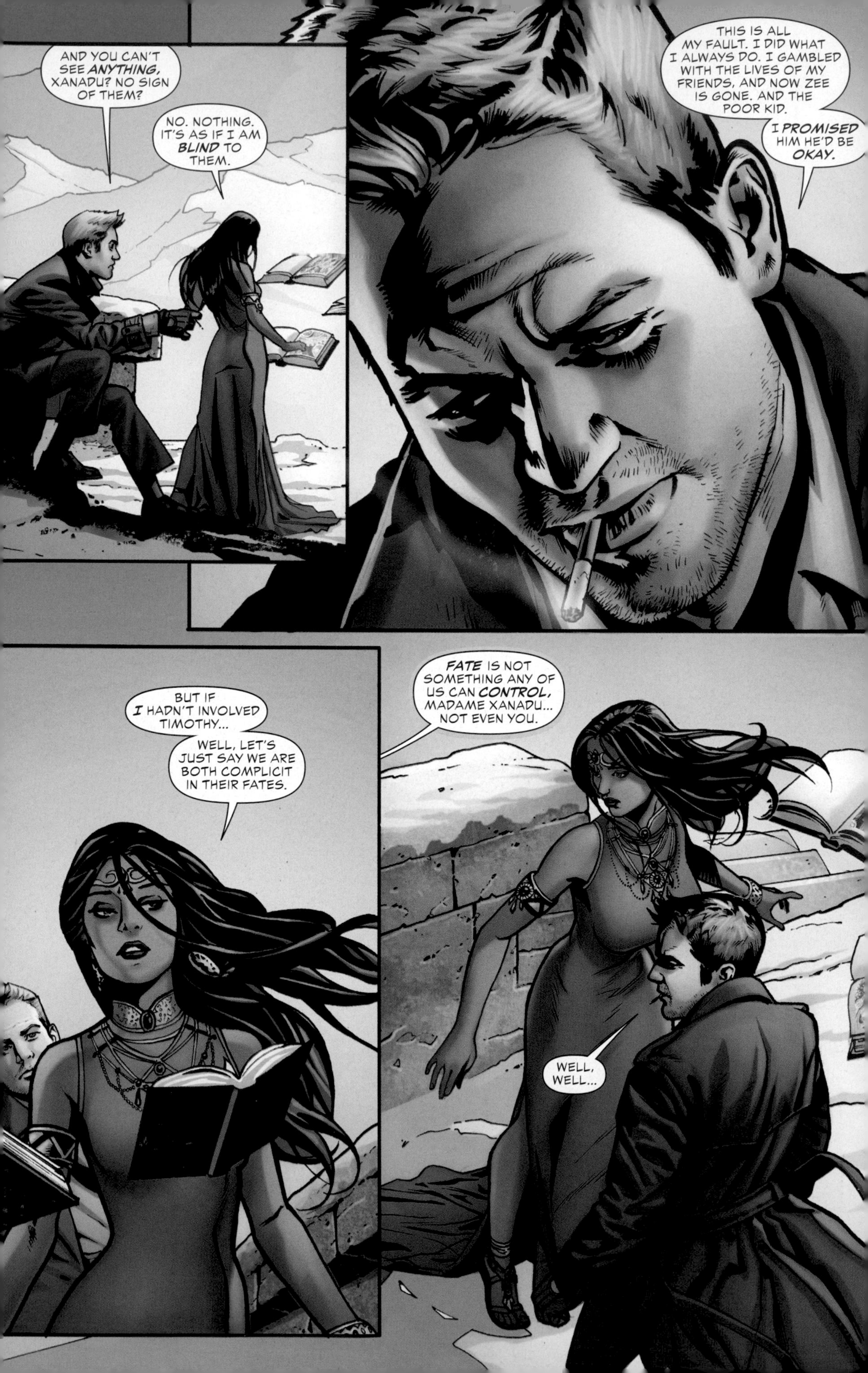
AND YOU CAN'T SEE ANYTHING, XANADU? NO SIGN OF THEM?
NO. NOTHING. IT'S AS IF I AM BLIND TO THEM.
THIS IS ALL MY FAULT. I DID WHAT I ALWAYS DO. I GAMBLED WITH THE LIVES OF MY FRIENDS, AND NOW ZEE IS GONE. AND THE POOR KID.
I PROMISED HIM HE'D BE OKAY.
BUT IF I HADN'T INVOLVED TIMOTHY...
WELL, LET'S JUST SAY WE ARE BOTH COMPLICIT IN THEIR FATES.
FATE IS NOT SOMETHING ANY OF US CAN CONTROL, MADAME XANADU... NOT EVEN YOU.
WELL, WELL...

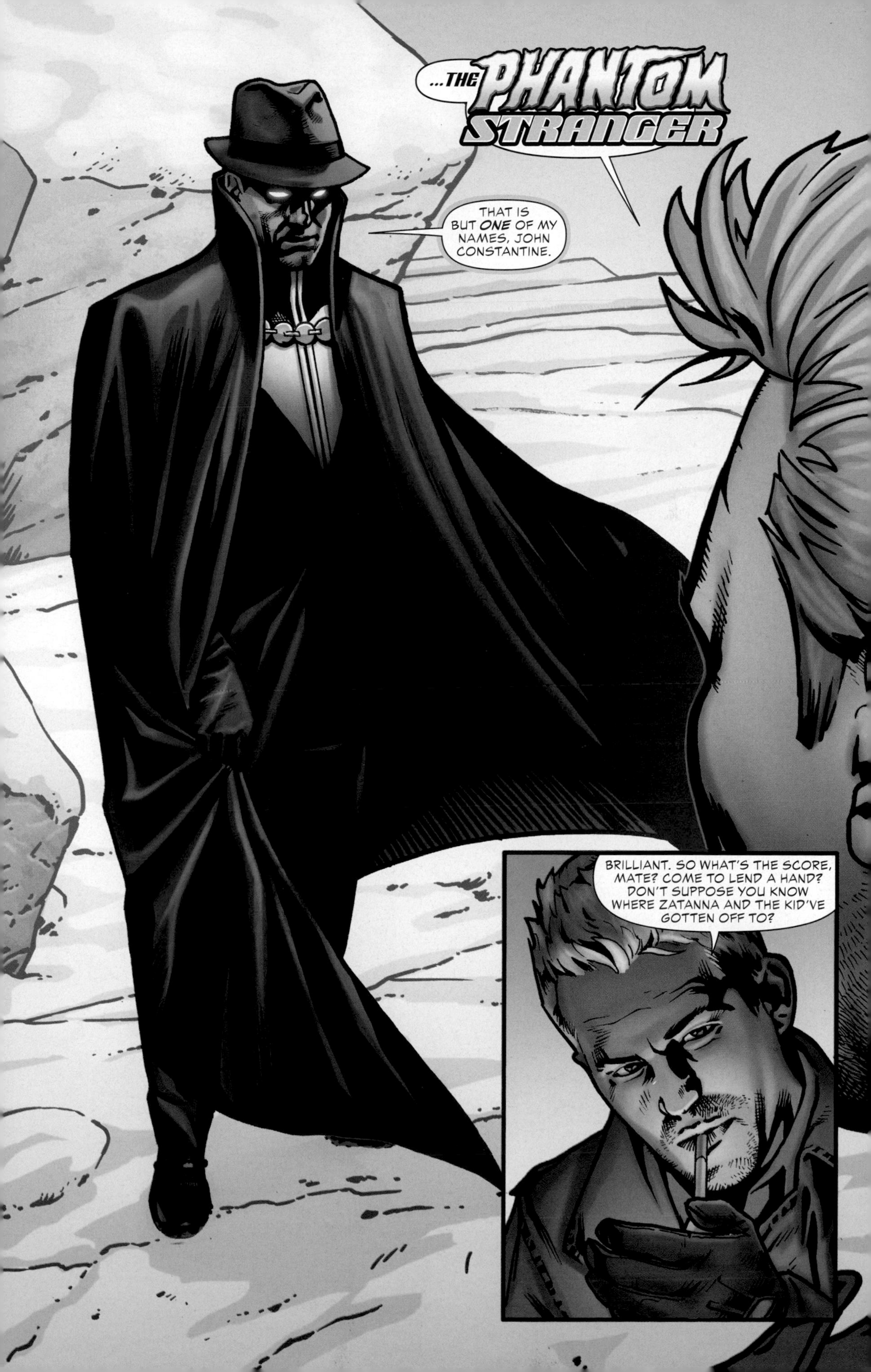
...THE PHANTOM STRANGER
THAT IS BUT ONE OF MY NAMES, JOHN CONSTANTINE.
BRILLIANT. SO WHAT'S THE SCORE, MATE? COME TO LEND A HAND? DON'T SUPPOSE YOU KNOW WHERE ZATANNA AND THE KID'VE GOTTEN OFF TO?

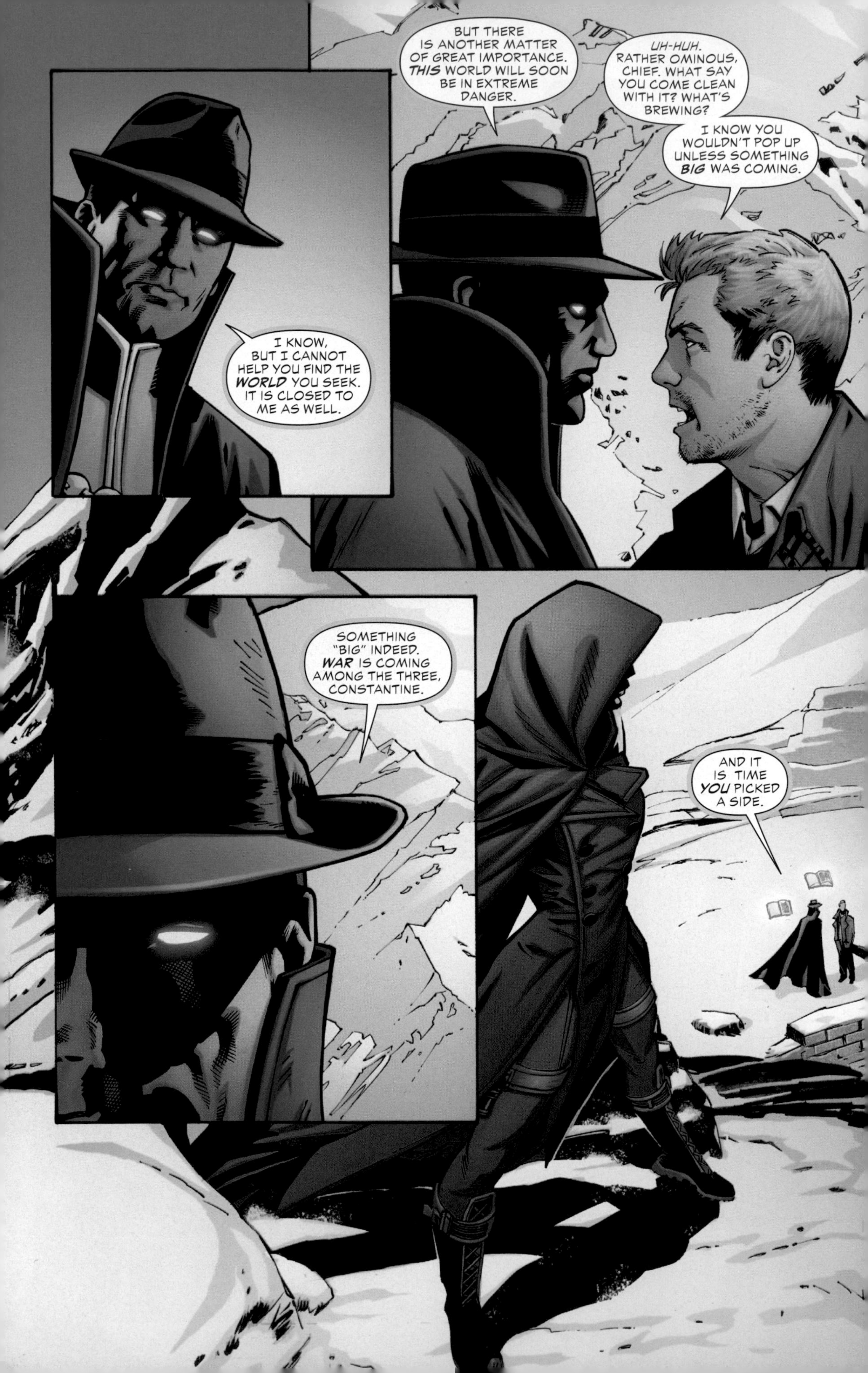
I KNOW, BUT I CANNOT HELP YOU FIND THE WORLD YOU SEEK. IT IS CLOSED TO ME AS WELL.
BUT THERE IS ANOTHER MATTER OF GREAT IMPORTANCE. THIS WORLD WILL SOON BE IN EXTREME DANGER.
UH-HUH. RATHER OMINOUS, CHIEF. WHAT SAY YOU COME CLEAN WITH IT? WHAT'S BREWING?
I KNOW YOU WOULDN'T POP UP UNLESS SOMETHING BIG WAS COMING.
SOMETHING "BIG" INDEED. WAR IS COMING AMONG THE THREE, CONSTANTINE.
AND IT IS TIME YOU PICKED A SIDE.

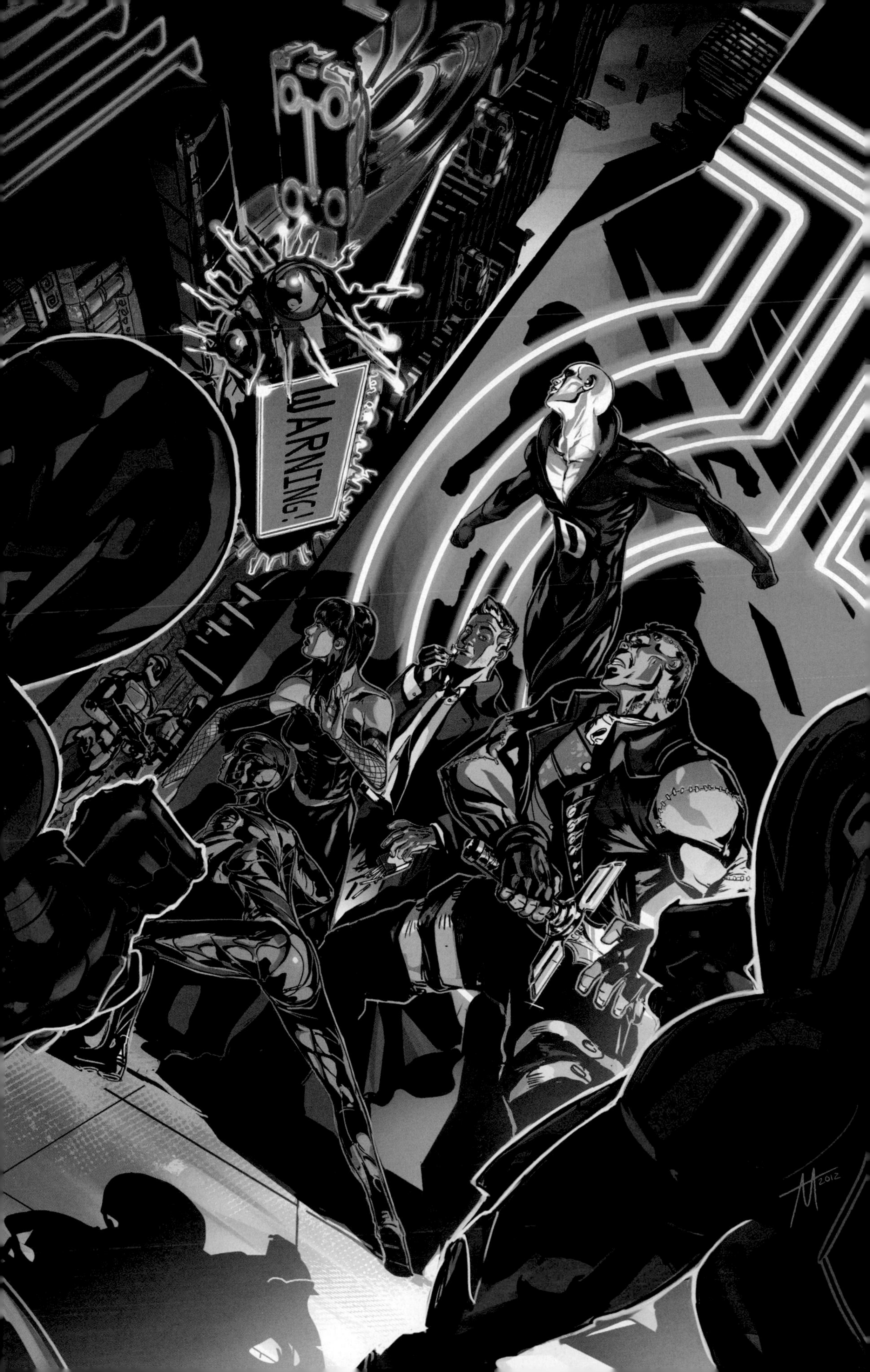
WARNING!

THE DEATH OF MAGIC part one
UP IS DOWN

JEFF LEMIRE
RAY FAWKES
writers

MIKEL JANIN
artist

TREVOR McCARTHY
cover artist

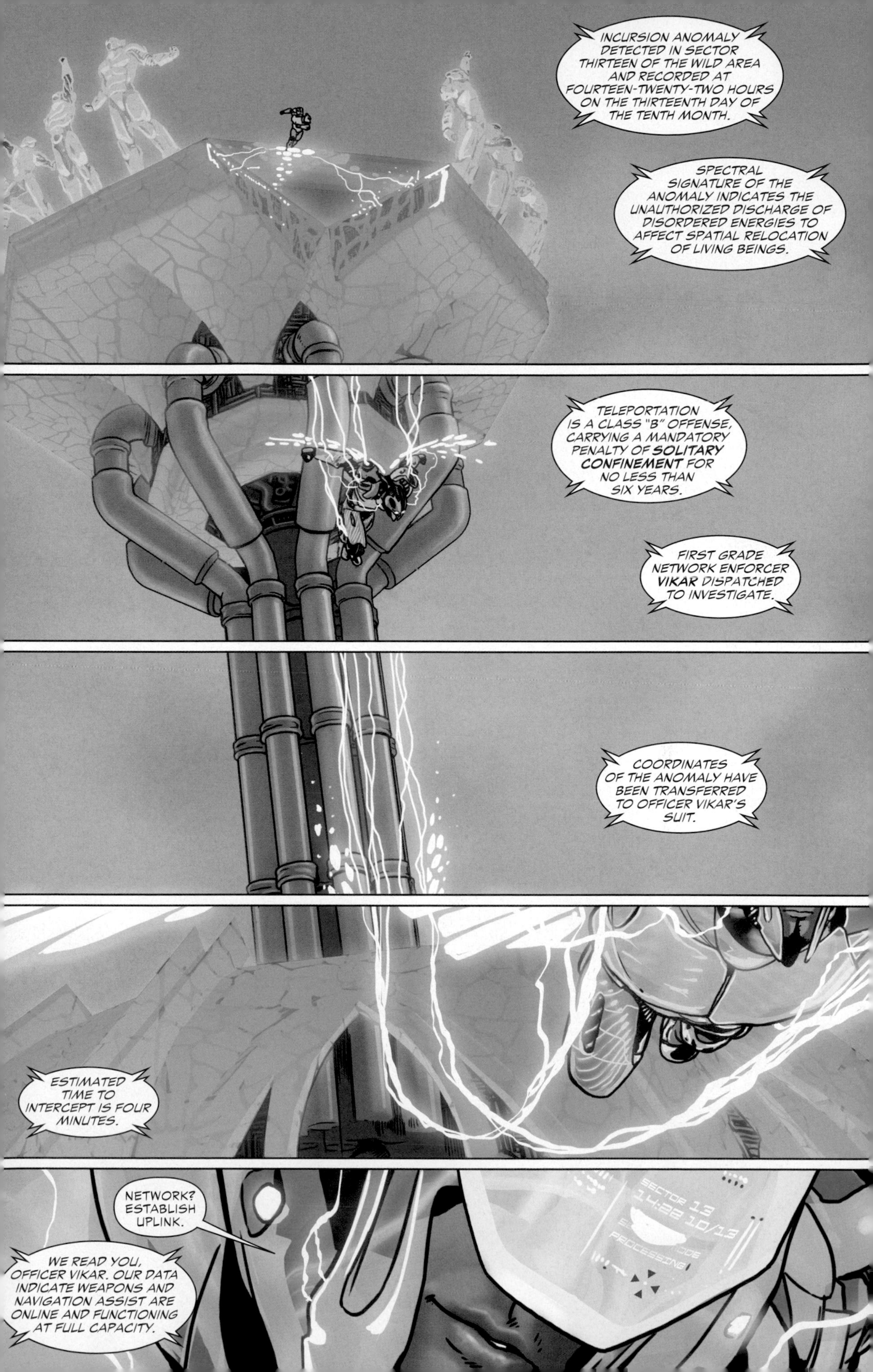
INCURSION ANOMALY DETECTED IN SECTOR THIRTEEN OF THE WILD AREA AND RECORDED AT FOURTEEN-TWENTY-TWO HOURS ON THE THIRTEENTH DAY OF THE TENTH MONTH.
SPECTRAL SIGNATURE OF THE ANOMALY INDICATES THE UNAUTHORIZED DISCHARGE OF DISORDERED ENERGIES TO AFFECT SPATIAL RELOCATION OF LIVING BEINGS.
TELEPORTATION IS A CLASS "B" OFFENSE, CARRYING A MANDATORY PENALTY OF **SOLITARY CONFINEMENT** FOR NO LESS THAN SIX YEARS.
FIRST GRADE NETWORK ENFORCER **VIKAR** DISPATCHED TO INVESTIGATE.
COORDINATES OF THE ANOMALY HAVE BEEN TRANSFERRED TO OFFICER VIKAR'S SUIT.
ESTIMATED TIME TO INTERCEPT IS FOUR MINUTES.
SECTOR 13
14:28 10/13
PROCESSING
NETWORK? ESTABLISH UPLINK.
WE READ YOU, OFFICER VIKAR. OUR DATA INDICATE WEAPONS AND NAVIGATION ASSIST ARE ONLINE AND FUNCTIONING AT FULL CAPACITY.

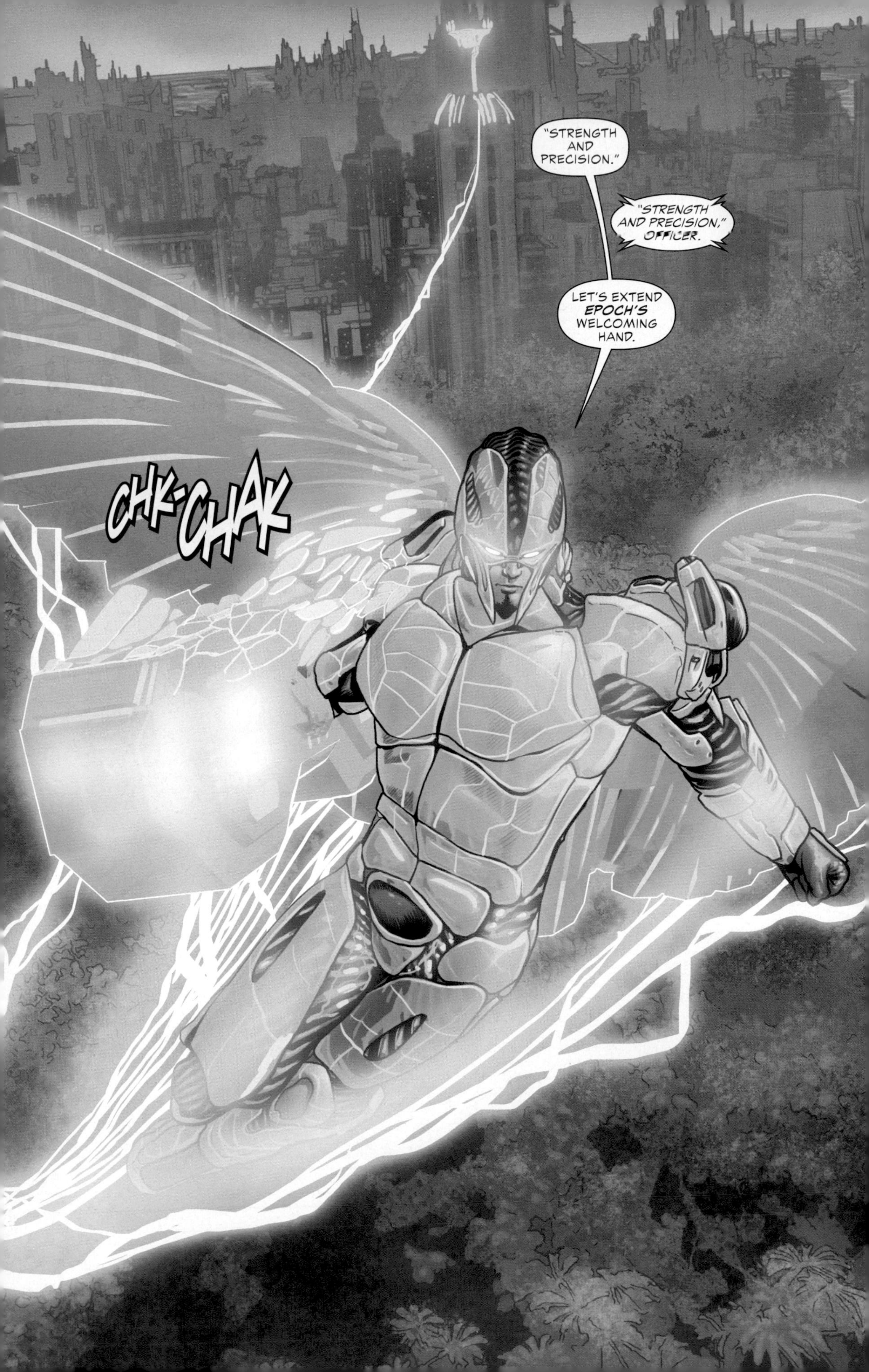
"STRENGTH AND PRECISION."
"STRENGTH AND PRECISION," OFFICER.
LET'S EXTEND **EPOCH'S** WELCOMING HAND.
CHK-CHAK

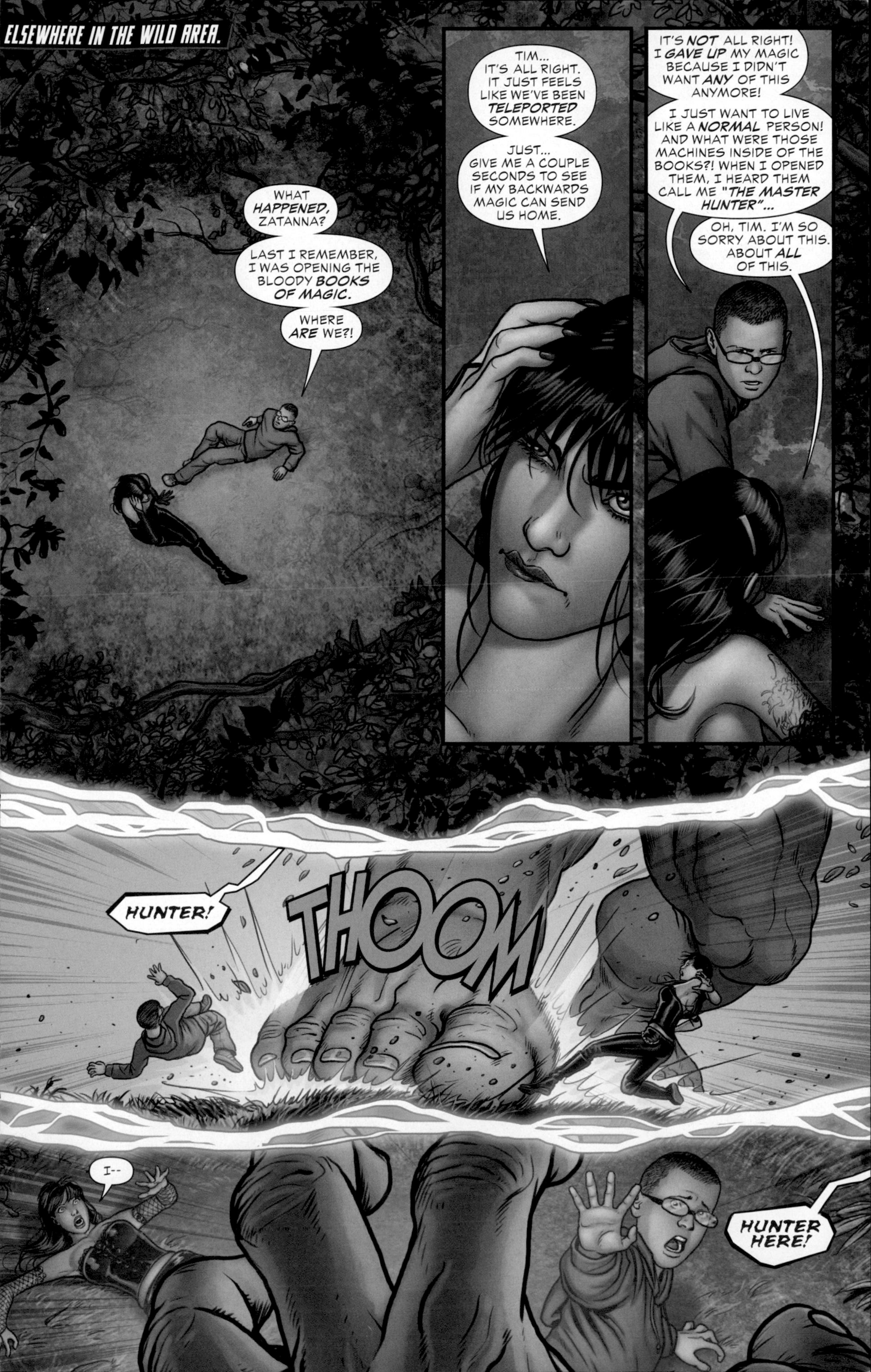
ELSEWHERE IN THE WILD AREA.
WHAT HAPPENED, ZATANNA?
LAST I REMEMBER, I WAS OPENING THE BLOODY BOOKS OF MAGIC.
WHERE ARE WE?!
TIM... IT'S ALL RIGHT. IT JUST FEELS LIKE WE'VE BEEN TELEPORTED SOMEWHERE.
JUST... GIVE ME A COUPLE SECONDS TO SEE IF MY BACKWARDS MAGIC CAN SEND US HOME.
IT'S NOT ALL RIGHT! I GAVE UP MY MAGIC BECAUSE I DIDN'T WANT ANY OF THIS ANYMORE!
I JUST WANT TO LIVE LIKE A NORMAL PERSON! AND WHAT WERE THOSE MACHINES INSIDE OF THE BOOKS?! WHEN I OPENED THEM, I HEARD THEM CALL ME "THE MASTER HUNTER"...
OH, TIM. I'M SO SORRY ABOUT THIS. ABOUT ALL OF THIS.
HUNTER!
THOOM
I--
HUNTER HERE!

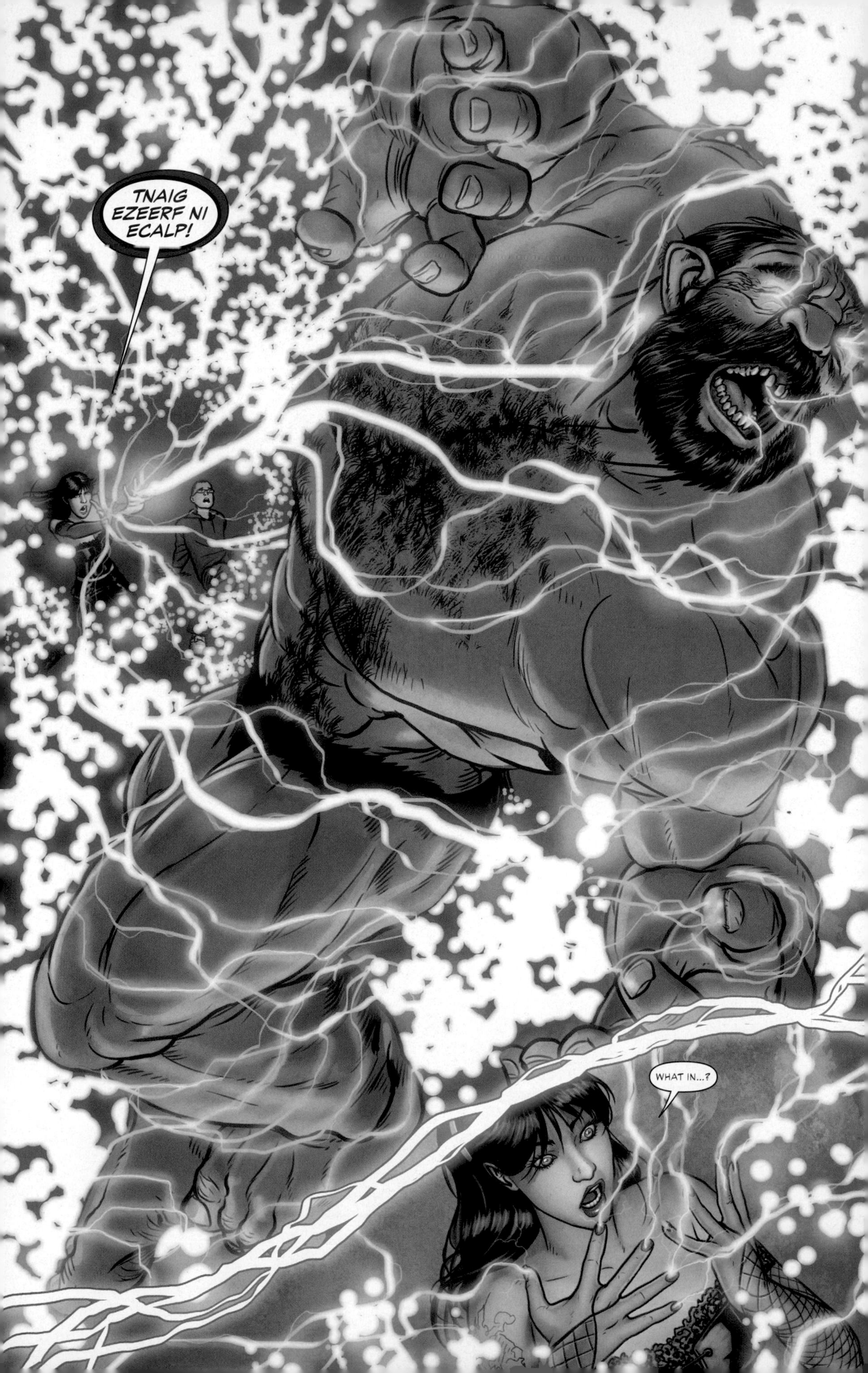
TNAIG EZEERF NI ECALP!
WHAT IN...?

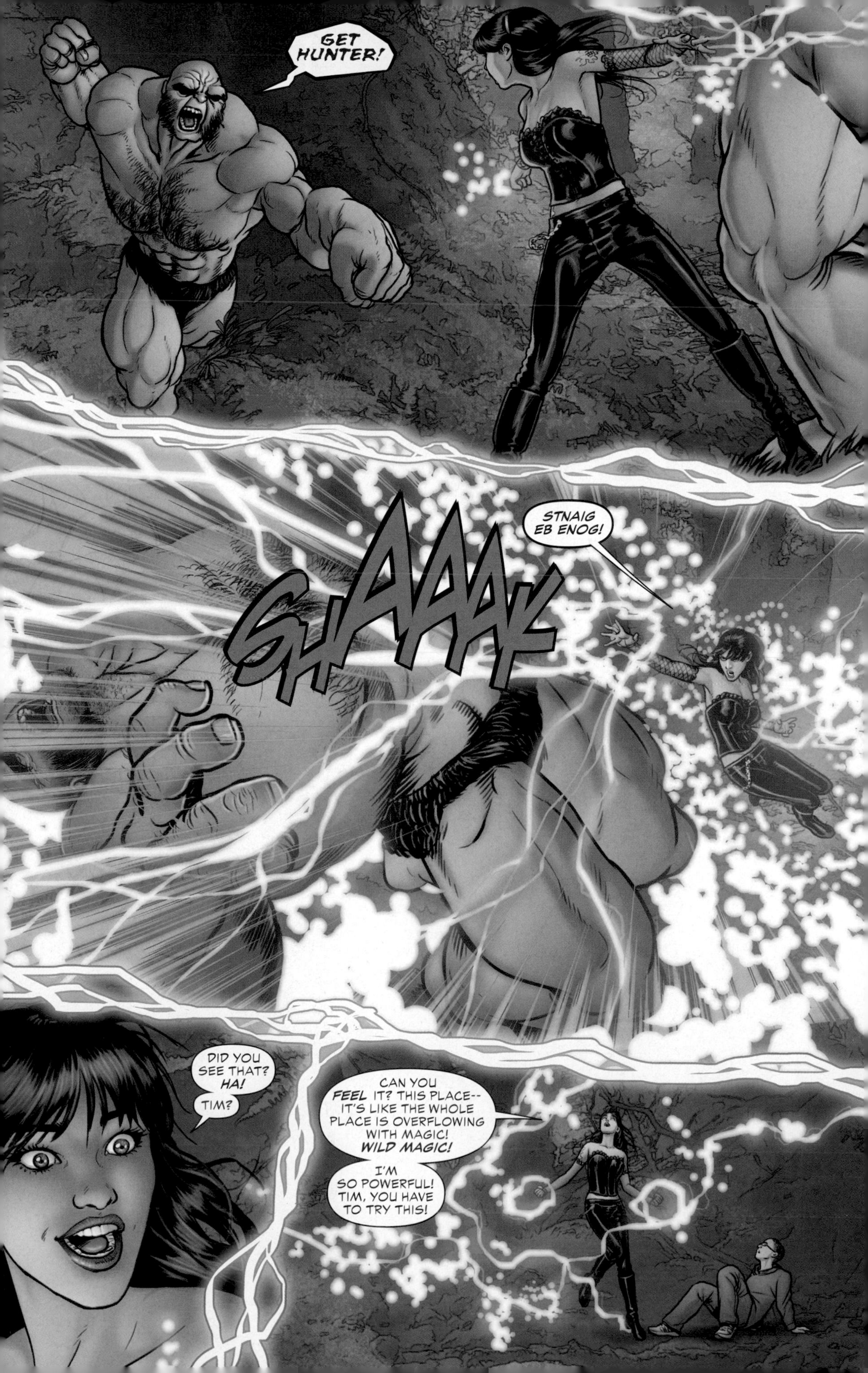
GET HUNTER!
STNAIG EB ENOG!
SHAAAK
DID YOU SEE THAT? HA!
TIM?
CAN YOU FEEL IT? THIS PLACE-- IT'S LIKE THE WHOLE PLACE IS OVERFLOWING WITH MAGIC! WILD MAGIC!
I'M SO POWERFUL! TIM, YOU HAVE TO TRY THIS!

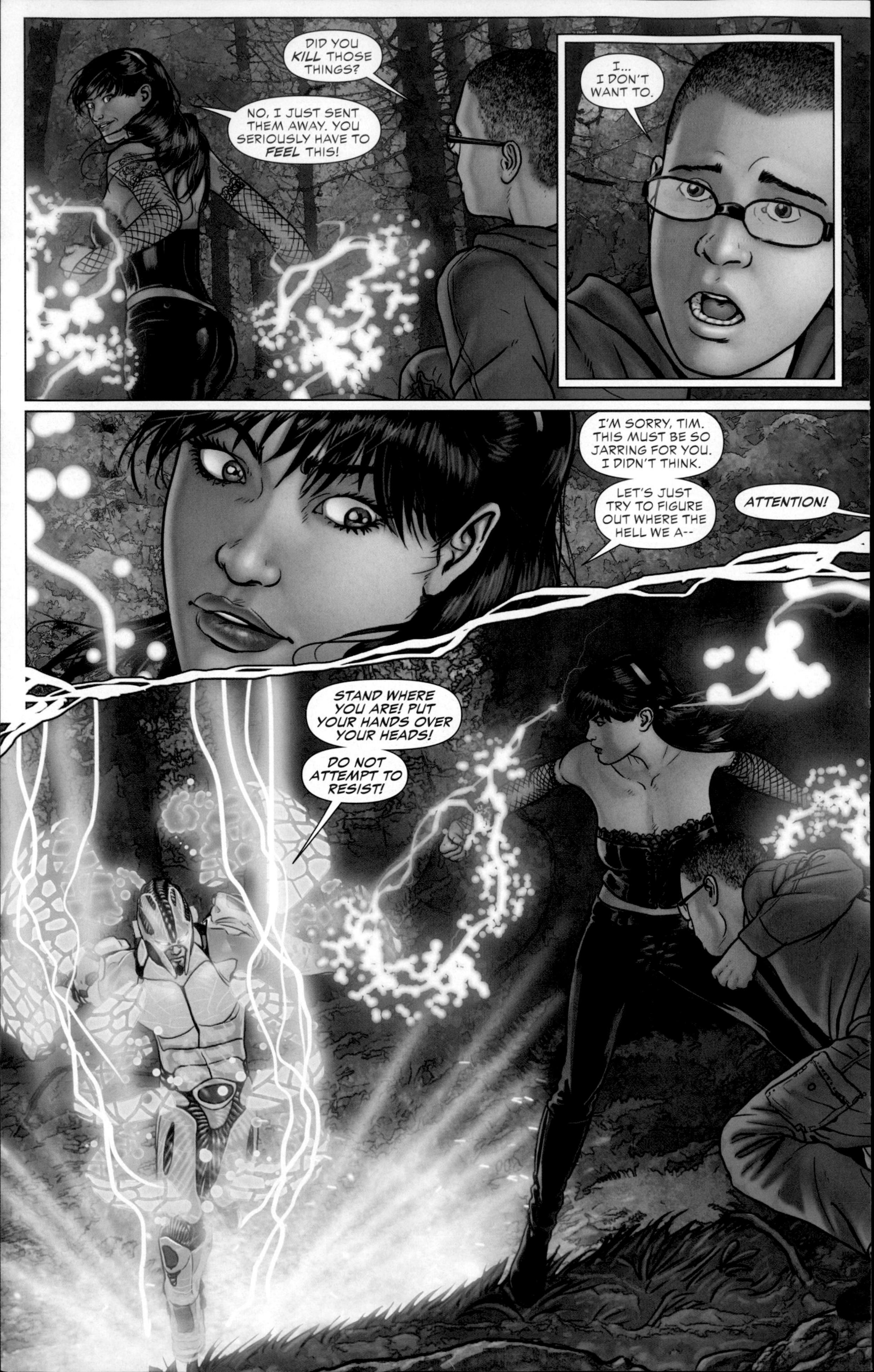
DID YOU *KILL* THOSE THINGS?
NO, I JUST SENT THEM AWAY. YOU SERIOUSLY HAVE TO *FEEL* THIS!
I... I DON'T WANT TO.
I'M SORRY, TIM. THIS MUST BE SO JARRING FOR YOU. I DIDN'T THINK.
LET'S JUST TRY TO FIGURE OUT WHERE THE HELL WE A--
ATTENTION!
STAND WHERE YOU ARE! PUT YOUR HANDS OVER YOUR HEADS!
DO NOT ATTEMPT TO RESIST!

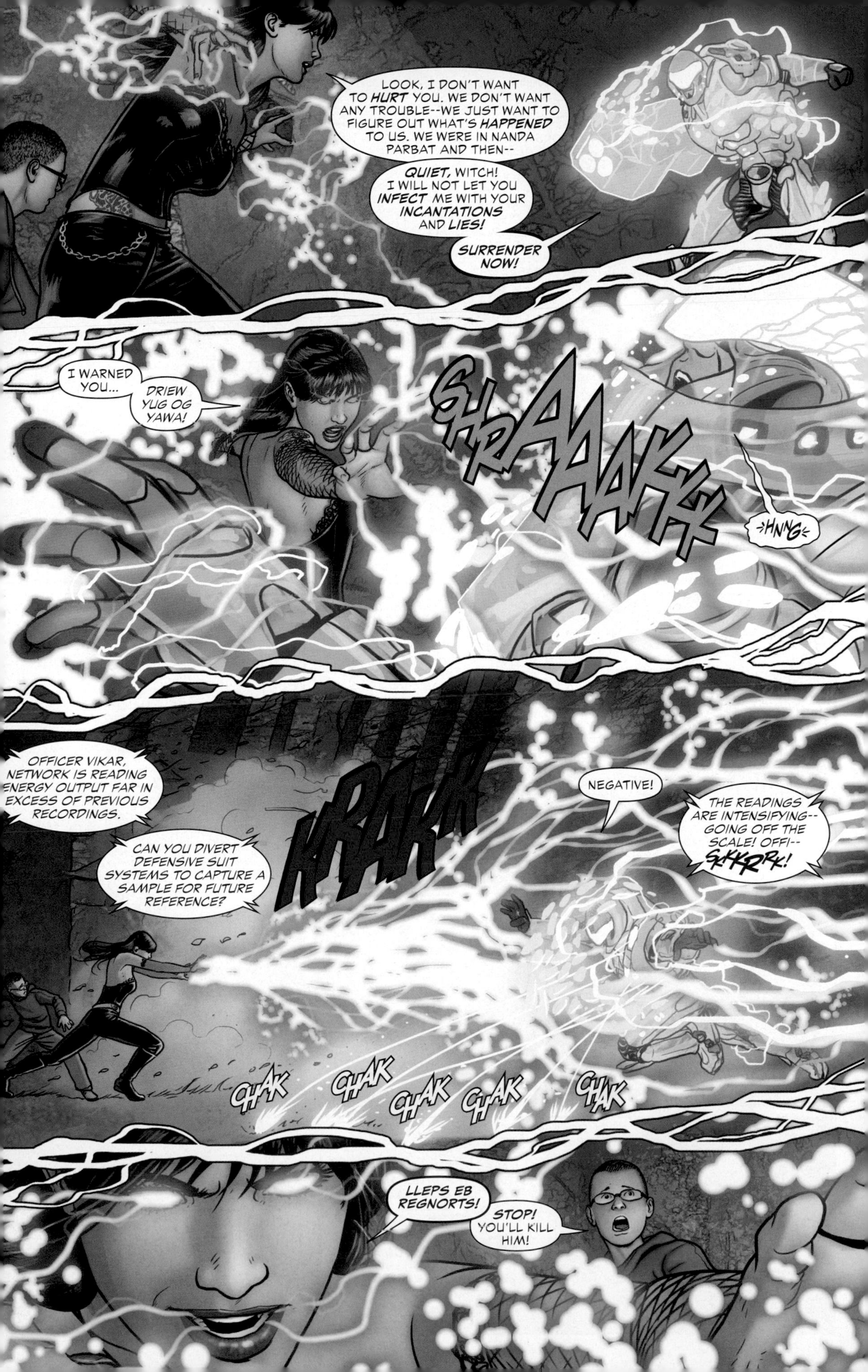
LOOK, I DON'T WANT TO HURT YOU. WE DON'T WANT ANY TROUBLE--WE JUST WANT TO FIGURE OUT WHAT'S HAPPENED TO US. WE WERE IN NANDA PARBAT AND THEN--
QUIET, WITCH! I WILL NOT LET YOU INFECT ME WITH YOUR INCANTATIONS AND LIES!
SURRENDER NOW!
I WARNED YOU...
DRIEW YUG OG YAWA!
SHRAAAKKK
HNNG
OFFICER VIKAR, NETWORK IS READING ENERGY OUTPUT FAR IN EXCESS OF PREVIOUS RECORDINGS.
CAN YOU DIVERT DEFENSIVE SUIT SYSTEMS TO CAPTURE A SAMPLE FOR FUTURE REFERENCE?
KRAKK
NEGATIVE!
THE READINGS ARE INTENSIFYING-- GOING OFF THE SCALE! OFFI-- SKKKRRK!
CHAK
CHAK
CHAK
CHAK
CHAK
LLEPS EB REGNORTS!
STOP! YOU'LL KILL HIM!

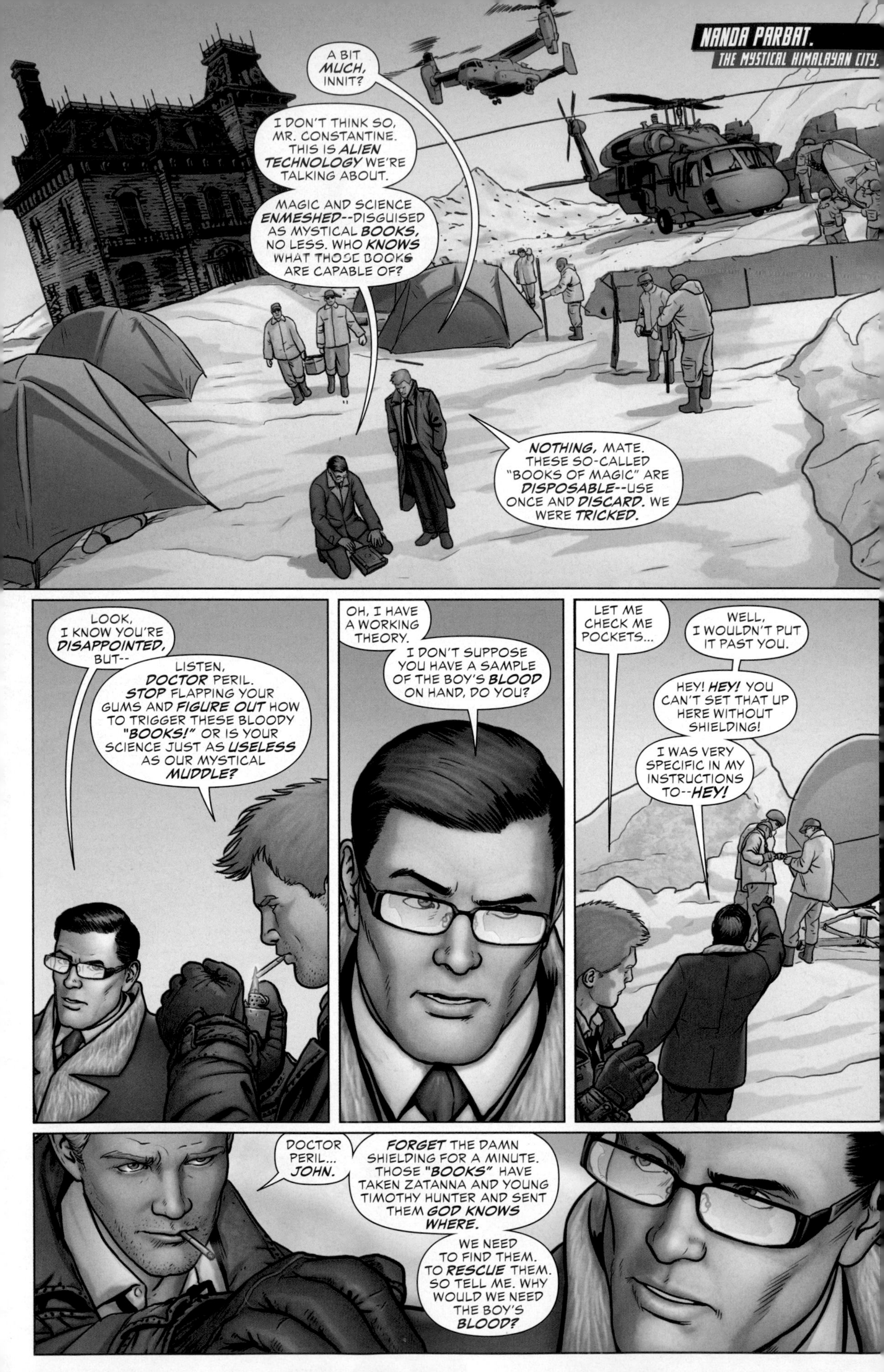
NANDA PARBAT.
THE MYSTICAL HIMALAYAN CITY.
A BIT MUCH, INNIT?
I DON'T THINK SO, MR. CONSTANTINE. THIS IS ALIEN TECHNOLOGY WE'RE TALKING ABOUT.
MAGIC AND SCIENCE ENMESHED--DISGUISED AS MYSTICAL BOOKS, NO LESS. WHO KNOWS WHAT THOSE BOOKS ARE CAPABLE OF?
NOTHING, MATE. THESE SO-CALLED "BOOKS OF MAGIC" ARE DISPOSABLE--USE ONCE AND DISCARD. WE WERE TRICKED.
LOOK, I KNOW YOU'RE DISAPPOINTED, BUT--
LISTEN, DOCTOR PERIL. STOP FLAPPING YOUR GUMS AND FIGURE OUT HOW TO TRIGGER THESE BLOODY "BOOKS!" OR IS YOUR SCIENCE JUST AS USELESS AS OUR MYSTICAL MUDDLE?
OH, I HAVE A WORKING THEORY.
I DON'T SUPPOSE YOU HAVE A SAMPLE OF THE BOY'S BLOOD ON HAND, DO YOU?
LET ME CHECK ME POCKETS...
WELL, I WOULDN'T PUT IT PAST YOU.
HEY! HEY! YOU CAN'T SET THAT UP HERE WITHOUT SHIELDING!
I WAS VERY SPECIFIC IN MY INSTRUCTIONS TO--HEY!
DOCTOR PERIL... JOHN.
FORGET THE DAMN SHIELDING FOR A MINUTE. THOSE "BOOKS" HAVE TAKEN ZATANNA AND YOUNG TIMOTHY HUNTER AND SENT THEM GOD KNOWS WHERE.
WE NEED TO FIND THEM. TO RESCUE THEM. SO TELL ME. WHY WOULD WE NEED THE BOY'S BLOOD?

OF COURSE. OF COURSE, I'M SORRY.

IN THE WORLD OF MAGIC, WHEN ONLY ONE PERSON CAN UNLOCK A DEVICE, WE CALL IT DESTINY OR PROPHECY. *FATE* HAS SELECTED THEM.

SCIENCE AND MAGIC ARE NOT ENEMIES, MR. CONSTANTINE. I DO BELIEVE IN *SERENDIPITY.*

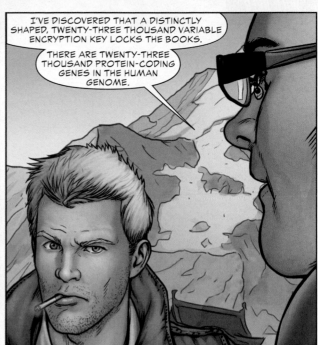

I'VE DISCOVERED THAT A DISTINCTLY SHAPED, TWENTY-THREE THOUSAND VARIABLE ENCRYPTION KEY LOCKS THE BOOKS.

THERE ARE TWENTY-THREE THOUSAND PROTEIN-CODING GENES IN THE HUMAN GENOME.

THE BOY'S MAGICAL SIGNATURE PROVIDES THE "SHAPE" WE SEEK. BUT I BELIEVE THE KEY IS HIS *DNA.*

...

WHAT ABOUT A CLOSE RELATIVE? WOULD THAT DO THE TRICK?

IT'S WORTH A SHOT.

THEN I'LL BE RIGHT BACK. SO GATHER EVERYBODY.

AND BE READY TO TRIGGER THOSE BLOODY BOOKS.

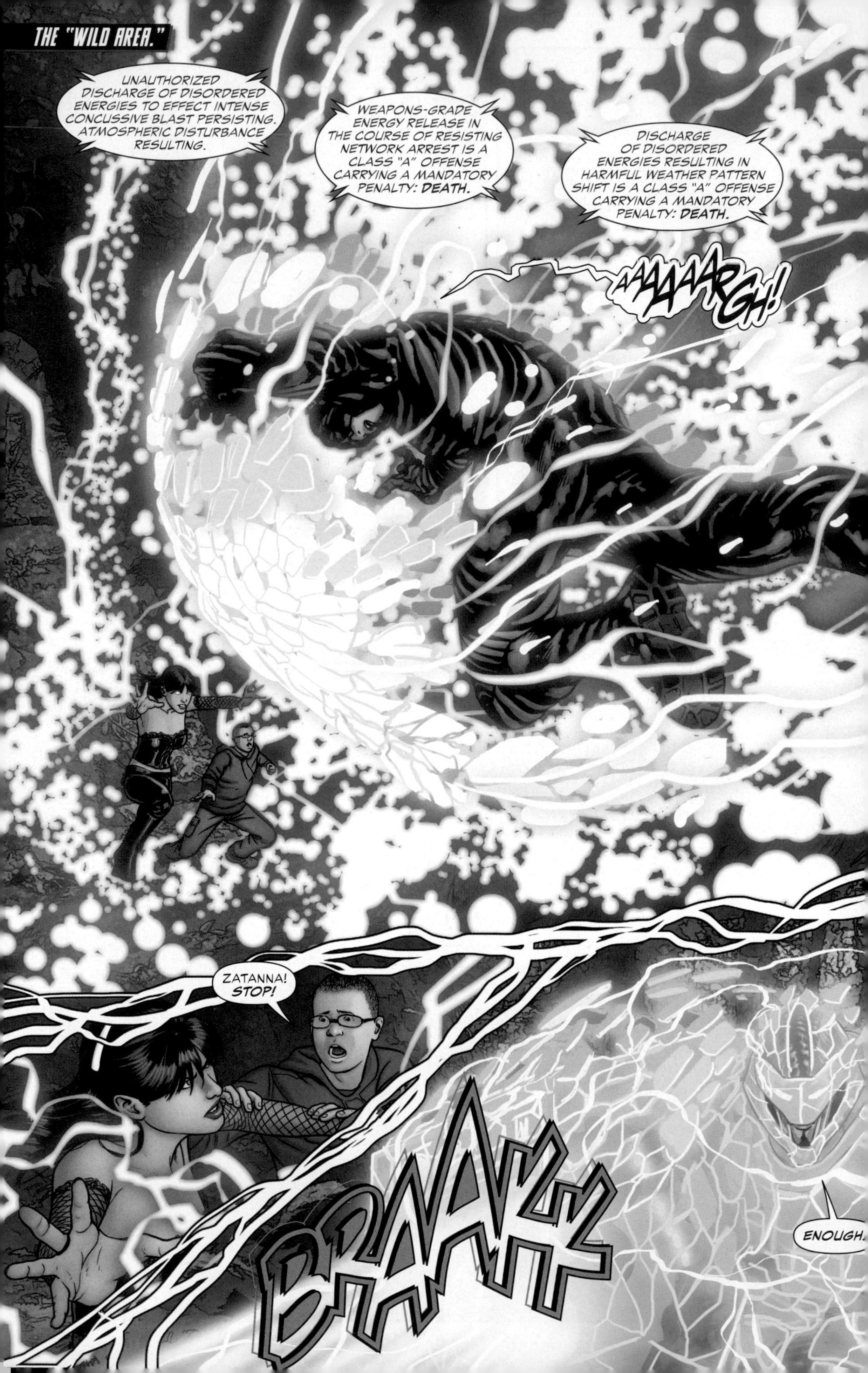
THE "WILD AREA."
UNAUTHORIZED DISCHARGE OF DISORDERED ENERGIES TO EFFECT INTENSE CONCUSSIVE BLAST PERSISTING. ATMOSPHERIC DISTURBANCE RESULTING.
WEAPONS-GRADE ENERGY RELEASE IN THE COURSE OF RESISTING NETWORK ARREST IS A CLASS "A" OFFENSE CARRYING A MANDATORY PENALTY: DEATH.
DISCHARGE OF DISORDERED ENERGIES RESULTING IN HARMFUL WEATHER PATTERN SHIFT IS A CLASS "A" OFFENSE CARRYING A MANDATORY PENALTY: DEATH.
AAAAAAARGH!
ZATANNA! STOP!
BRAKK
ENOUGH.

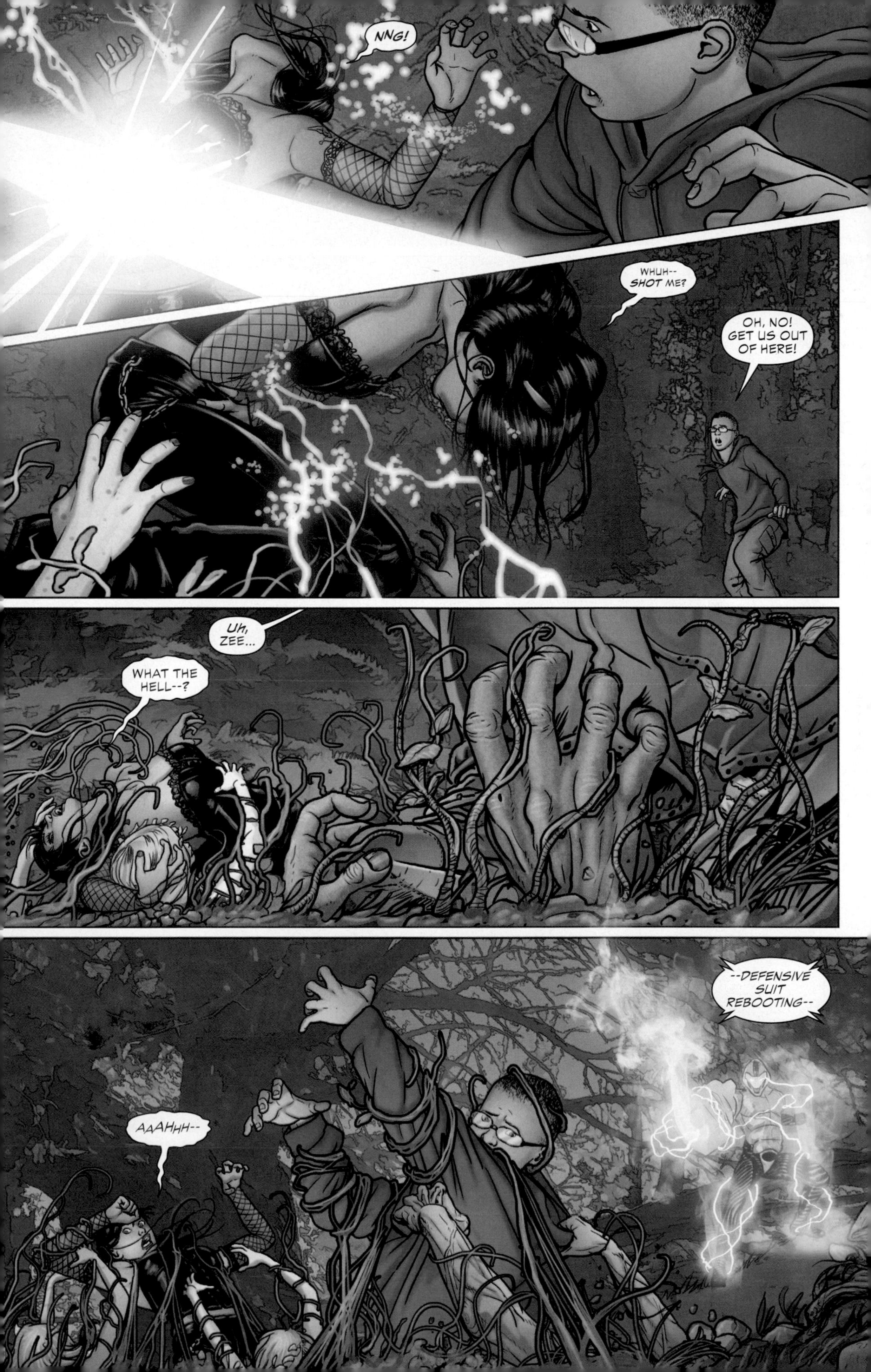
NNG!
WHUH--
SHOT ME?
OH, NO!
GET US OUT
OF HERE!
UH,
ZEE...
WHAT THE
HELL--?
--DEFENSIVE
SUIT
REBOOTING--
AAAHHH--

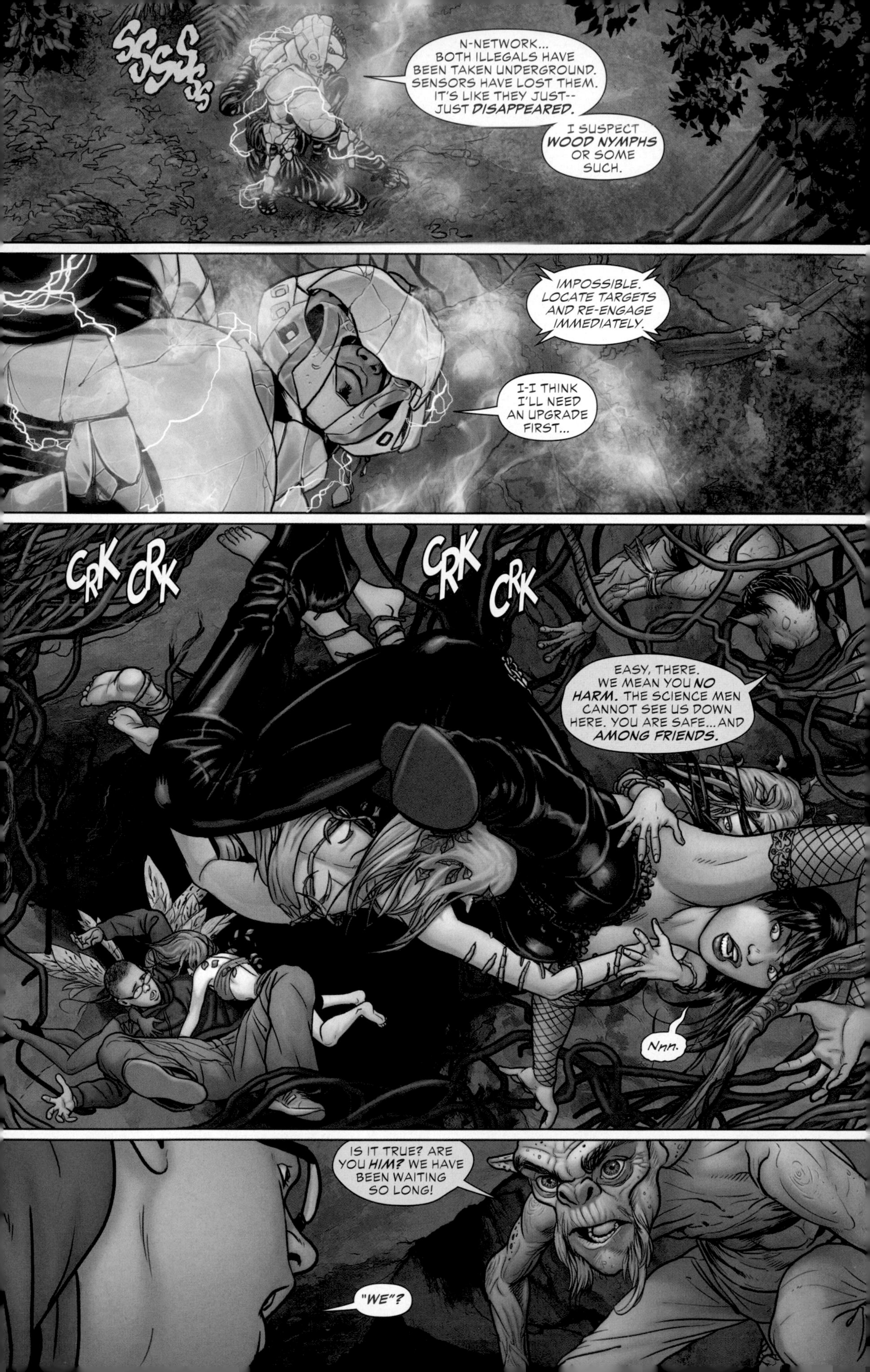
SSSSsss
N-NETWORK... BOTH ILLEGALS HAVE BEEN TAKEN UNDERGROUND. SENSORS HAVE LOST THEM. IT'S LIKE THEY JUST-- JUST DISAPPEARED.
I SUSPECT WOOD NYMPHS OR SOME SUCH.
IMPOSSIBLE. LOCATE TARGETS AND RE-ENGAGE IMMEDIATELY.
I-I THINK I'LL NEED AN UPGRADE FIRST...
CRK CRK
CRK CRK
EASY, THERE. WE MEAN YOU NO HARM. THE SCIENCE MEN CANNOT SEE US DOWN HERE. YOU ARE SAFE...AND AMONG FRIENDS.
Nnn.
IS IT TRUE? ARE YOU HIM? WE HAVE BEEN WAITING SO LONG!
"WE"?

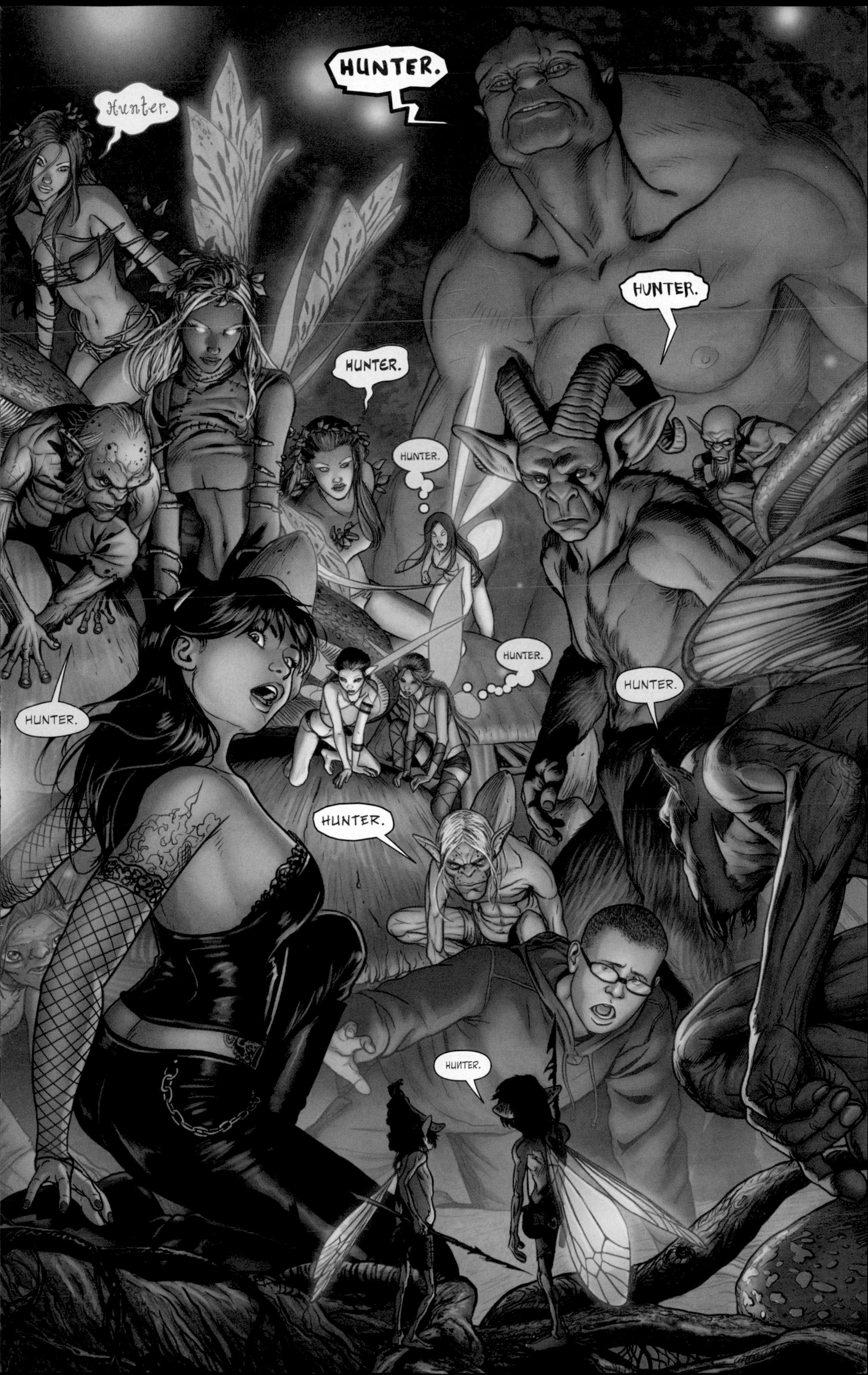

Hunter.
HUNTER.
HUNTER.
HUNTER.
HUNTER.
HUNTER.
HUNTER.
HUNTER.
HUNTER.
HUNTER.

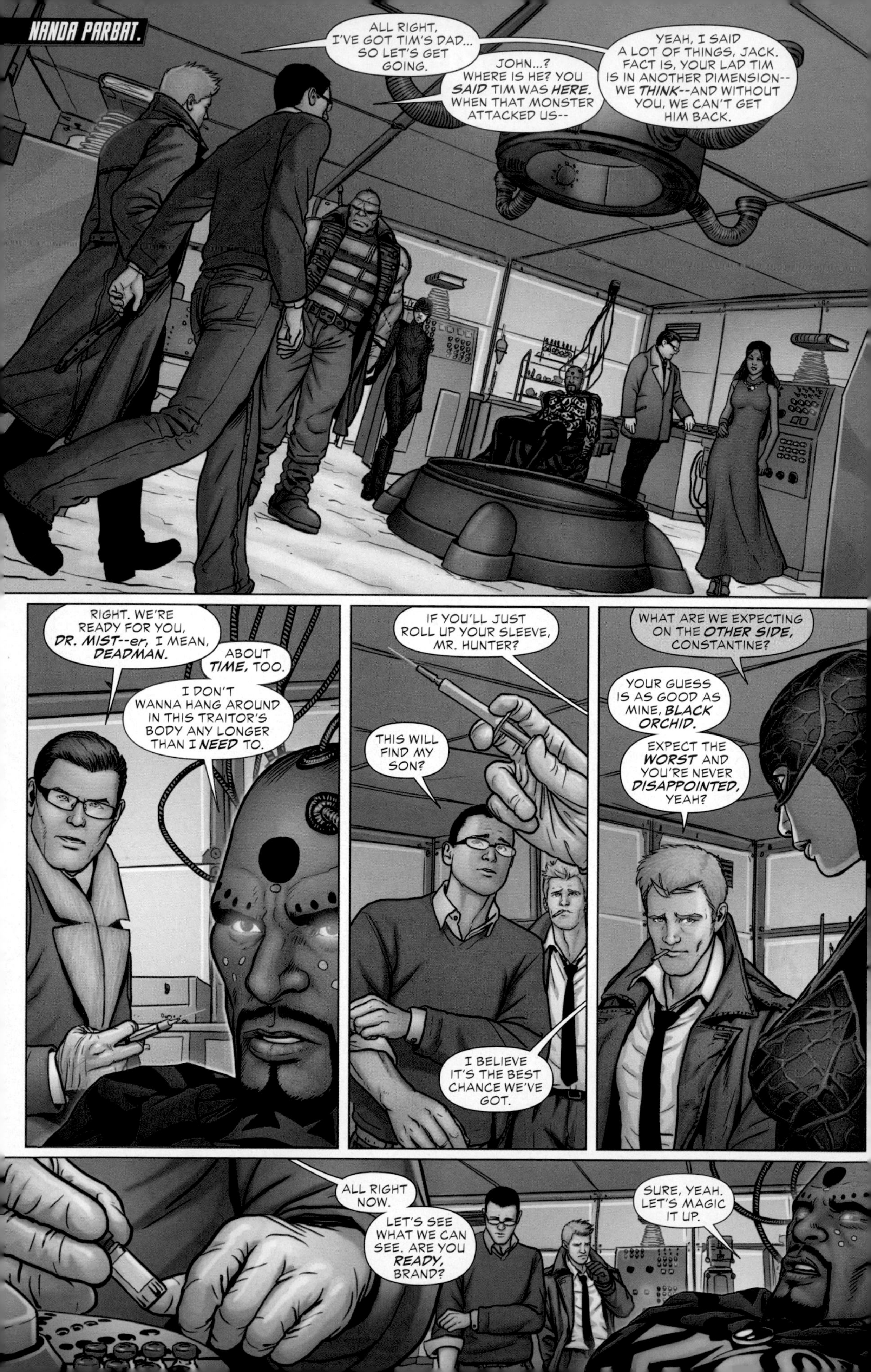
NANDA PARBAT.
ALL RIGHT, I'VE GOT TIM'S DAD... SO LET'S GET GOING.
JOHN...? WHERE IS HE? YOU SAID TIM WAS HERE. WHEN THAT MONSTER ATTACKED US--
YEAH, I SAID A LOT OF THINGS, JACK. FACT IS, YOUR LAD TIM IS IN ANOTHER DIMENSION--WE THINK--AND WITHOUT YOU, WE CAN'T GET HIM BACK.
RIGHT. WE'RE READY FOR YOU, DR. MIST--er, I MEAN, DEADMAN.
ABOUT TIME, TOO.
I DON'T WANNA HANG AROUND IN THIS TRAITOR'S BODY ANY LONGER THAN I NEED TO.
IF YOU'LL JUST ROLL UP YOUR SLEEVE, MR. HUNTER?
THIS WILL FIND MY SON?
I BELIEVE IT'S THE BEST CHANCE WE'VE GOT.
WHAT ARE WE EXPECTING ON THE OTHER SIDE, CONSTANTINE?
YOUR GUESS IS AS GOOD AS MINE, BLACK ORCHID.
EXPECT THE WORST AND YOU'RE NEVER DISAPPOINTED, YEAH?
ALL RIGHT NOW.
LET'S SEE WHAT WE CAN SEE. ARE YOU READY, BRAND?
SURE, YEAH. LET'S MAGIC IT UP.

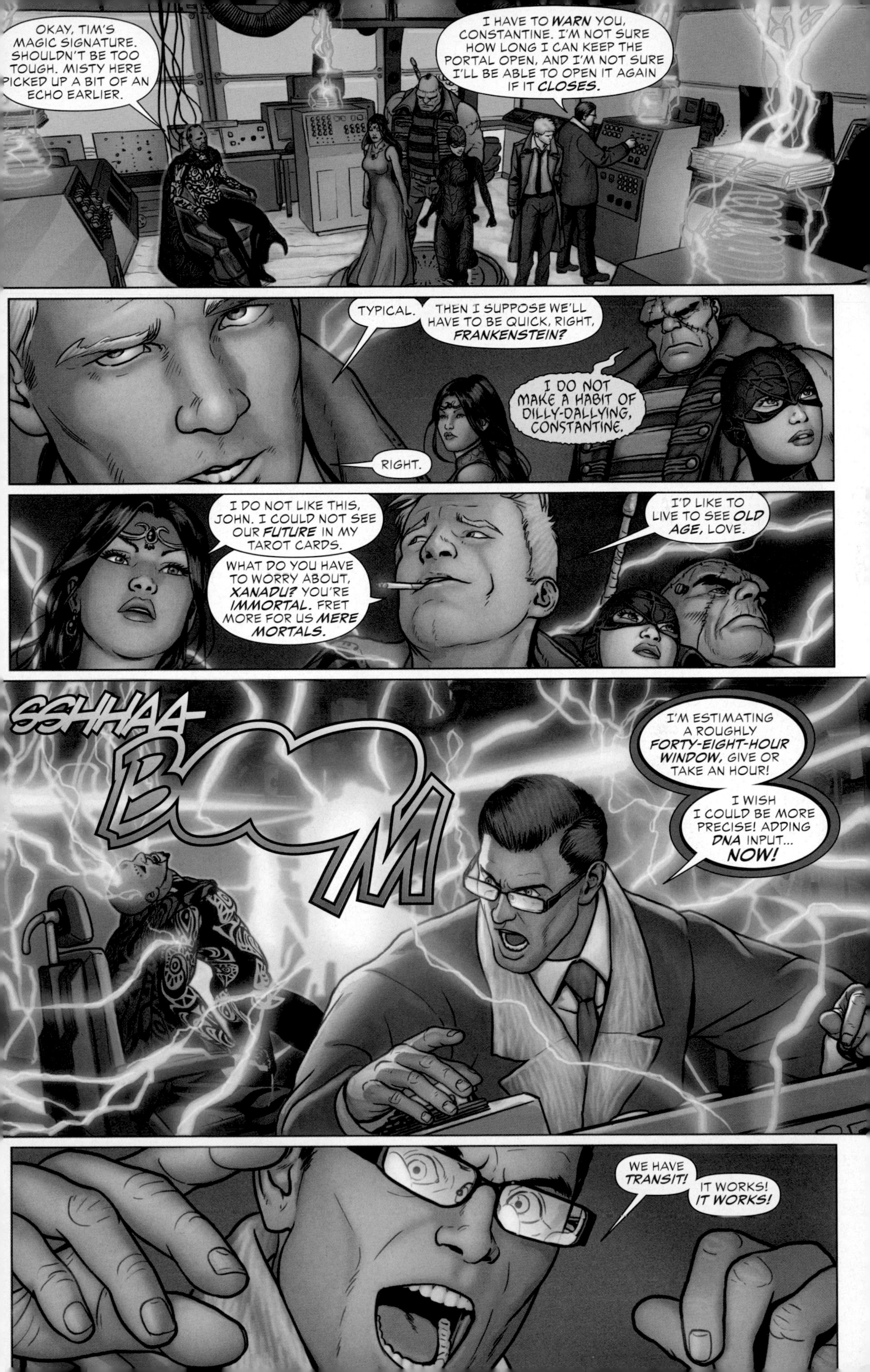
OKAY, TIM'S MAGIC SIGNATURE. SHOULDN'T BE TOO TOUGH. MISTY HERE PICKED UP A BIT OF AN ECHO EARLIER.
I HAVE TO WARN YOU, CONSTANTINE. I'M NOT SURE HOW LONG I CAN KEEP THE PORTAL OPEN, AND I'M NOT SURE I'LL BE ABLE TO OPEN IT AGAIN IF IT CLOSES.
TYPICAL.
THEN I SUPPOSE WE'LL HAVE TO BE QUICK, RIGHT, FRANKENSTEIN?
I DO NOT MAKE A HABIT OF DILLY-DALLYING, CONSTANTINE.
RIGHT.
I DO NOT LIKE THIS, JOHN. I COULD NOT SEE OUR FUTURE IN MY TAROT CARDS.
WHAT DO YOU HAVE TO WORRY ABOUT, XANADU? YOU'RE IMMORTAL. FRET MORE FOR US MERE MORTALS.
I'D LIKE TO LIVE TO SEE OLD AGE, LOVE.
SSHHAA BOOM
I'M ESTIMATING A ROUGHLY FORTY-EIGHT-HOUR WINDOW, GIVE OR TAKE AN HOUR!
I WISH I COULD BE MORE PRECISE! ADDING DNA INPUT... NOW!
WE HAVE TRANSIT!
IT WORKS! IT WORKS!

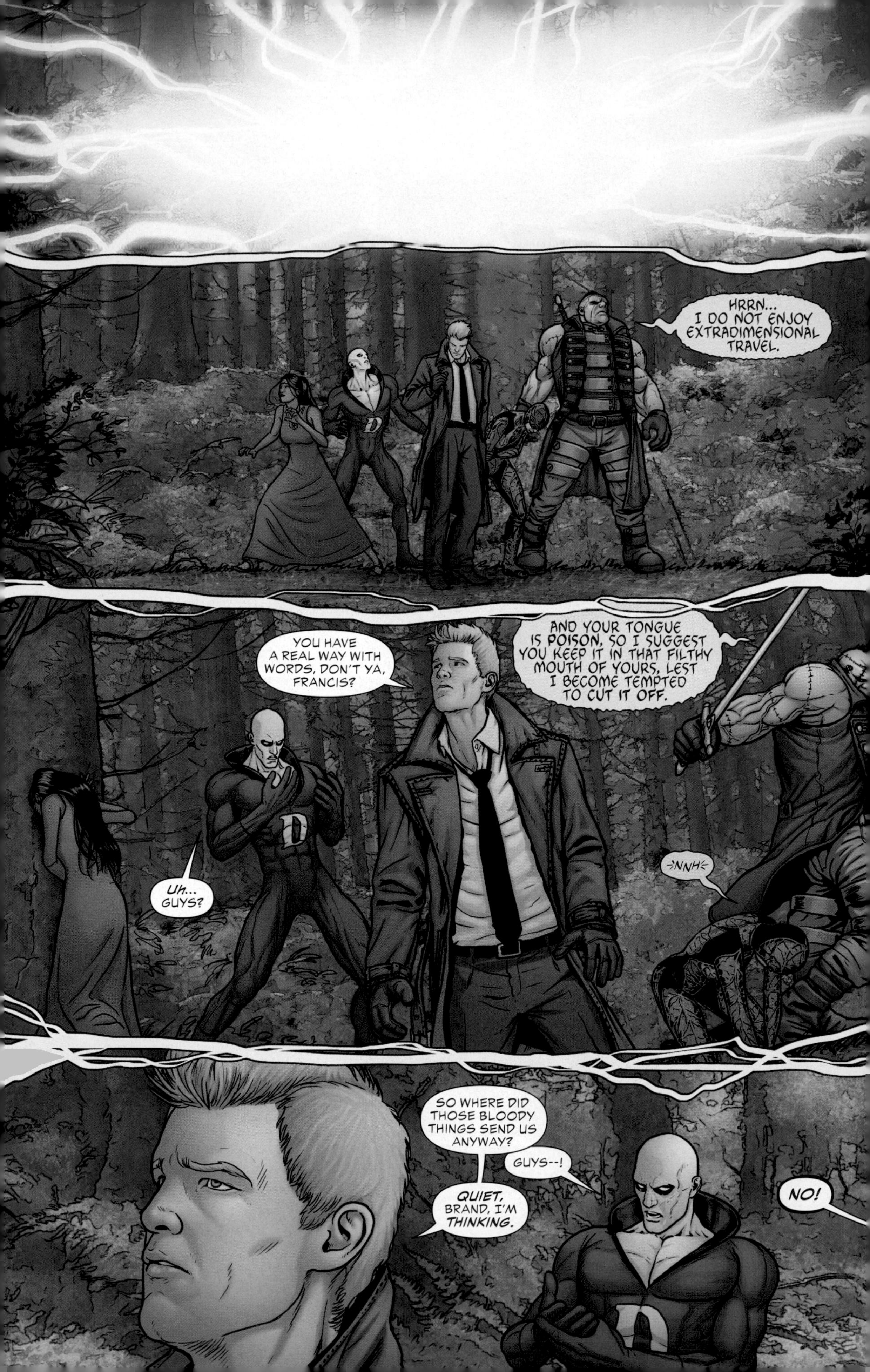

HRRN... I DO NOT ENJOY EXTRADIMENSIONAL TRAVEL.
YOU HAVE A REAL WAY WITH WORDS, DON'T YA, FRANCIS?
AND YOUR TONGUE IS POISON, SO I SUGGEST YOU KEEP IT IN THAT FILTHY MOUTH OF YOURS, LEST I BECOME TEMPTED TO CUT IT OFF.
UH... GUYS?
NNH
SO WHERE DID THOSE BLOODY THINGS SEND US ANYWAY?
GUYS--!
QUIET, BRAND, I'M THINKING.
NO!

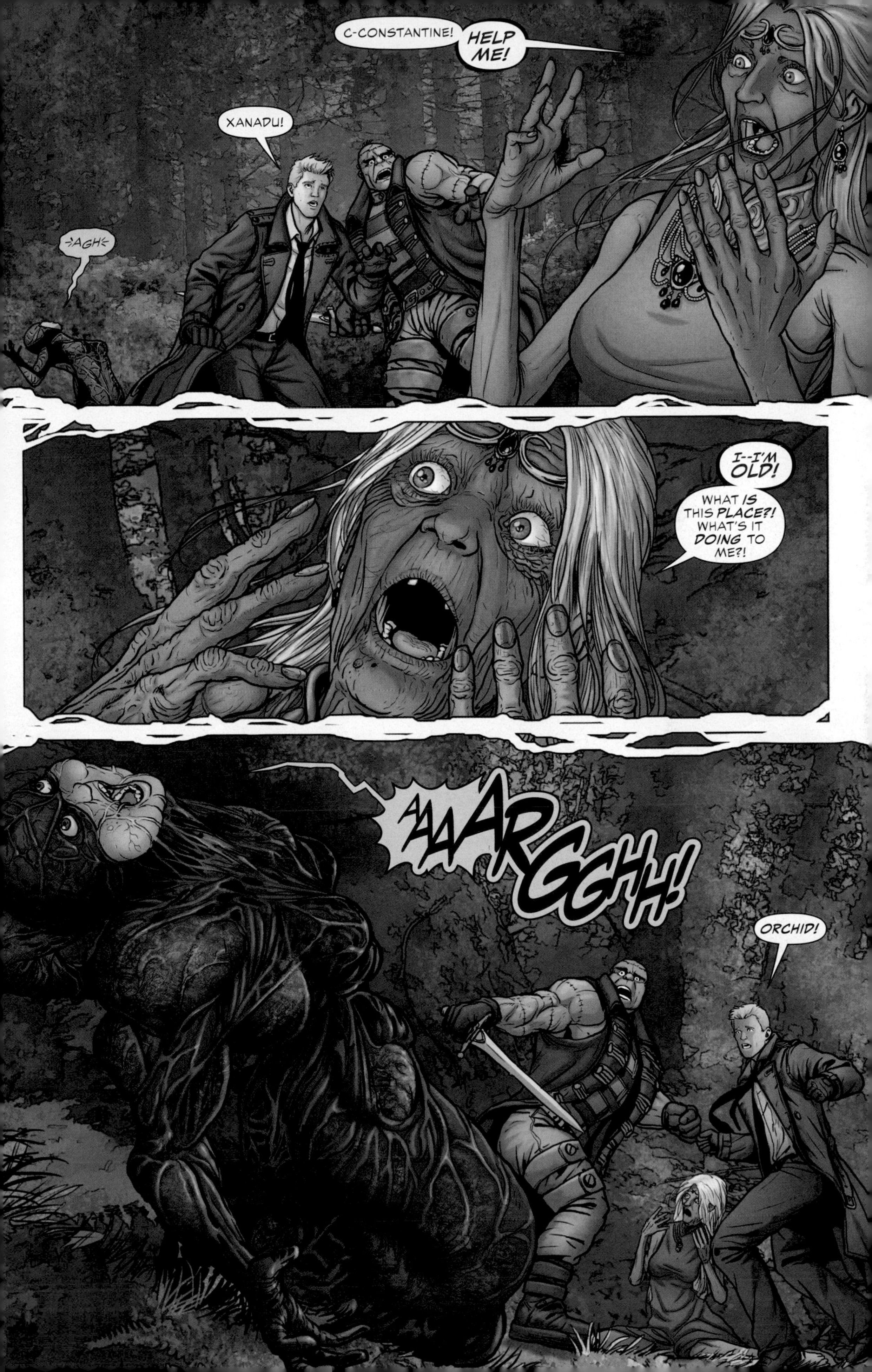
C-CONSTANTINE!
HELP ME!
XANADU!
AGH
I--I'M OLD!
WHAT IS THIS PLACE?! WHAT'S IT DOING TO ME?!
AAAARGGHH!
ORCHID!

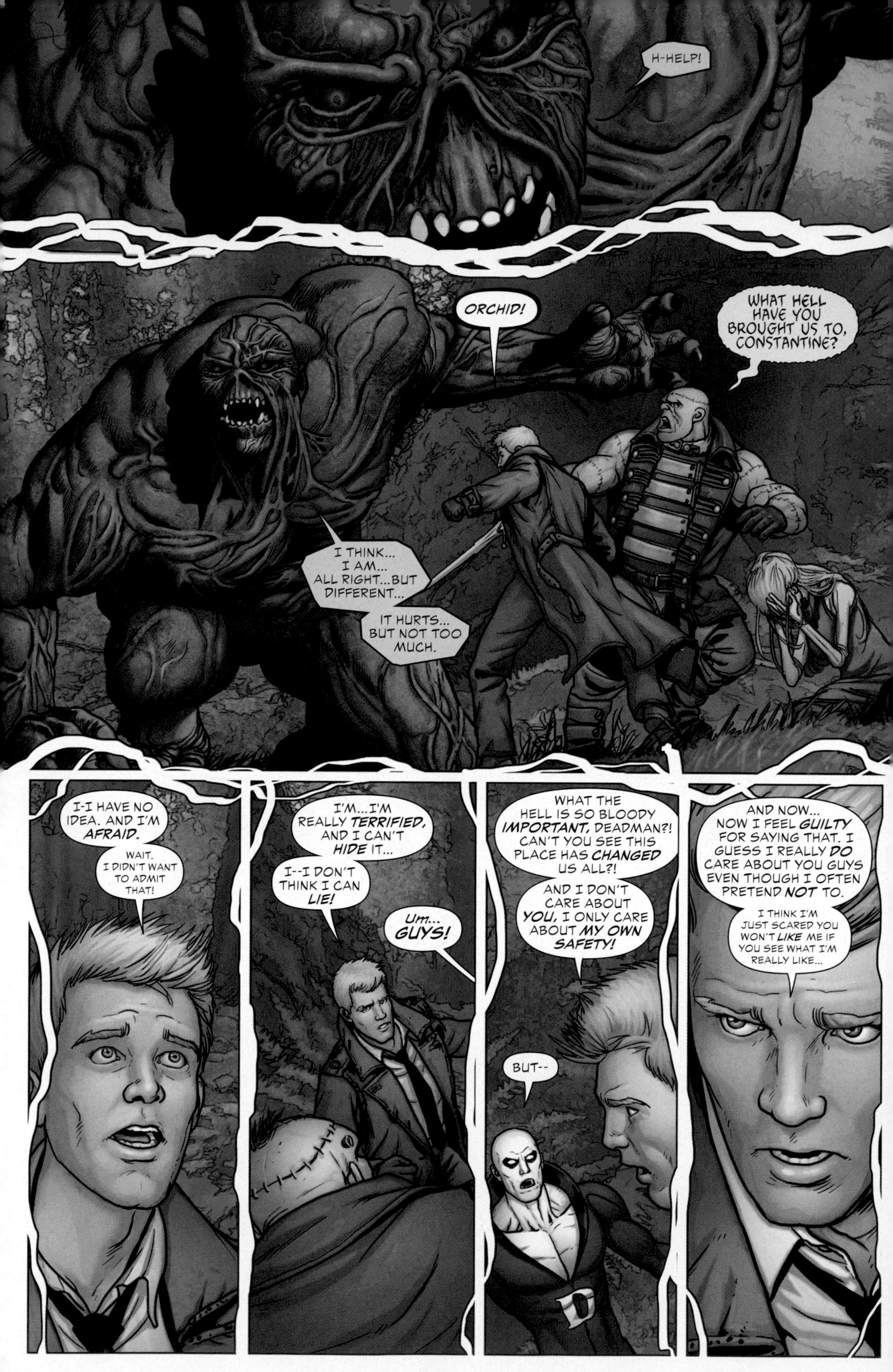
H-HELP!
ORCHID!
WHAT HELL HAVE YOU BROUGHT US TO, CONSTANTINE?
I THINK... I AM... ALL RIGHT...BUT DIFFERENT...
IT HURTS... BUT NOT TOO MUCH.
I-I HAVE NO IDEA. AND I'M AFRAID.
WAIT. I DIDN'T WANT TO ADMIT THAT!
I'M...I'M REALLY TERRIFIED, AND I CAN'T HIDE IT...
I--I DON'T THINK I CAN LIE!
Um... GUYS!
WHAT THE HELL IS SO BLOODY IMPORTANT, DEADMAN?! CAN'T YOU SEE THIS PLACE HAS CHANGED US ALL?!
AND I DON'T CARE ABOUT YOU, I ONLY CARE ABOUT MY OWN SAFETY!
BUT--
AND NOW... NOW I FEEL GUILTY FOR SAYING THAT. I GUESS I REALLY DO CARE ABOUT YOU GUYS EVEN THOUGH I OFTEN PRETEND NOT TO.
I THINK I'M JUST SCARED YOU WON'T LIKE ME IF YOU SEE WHAT I'M REALLY LIKE...

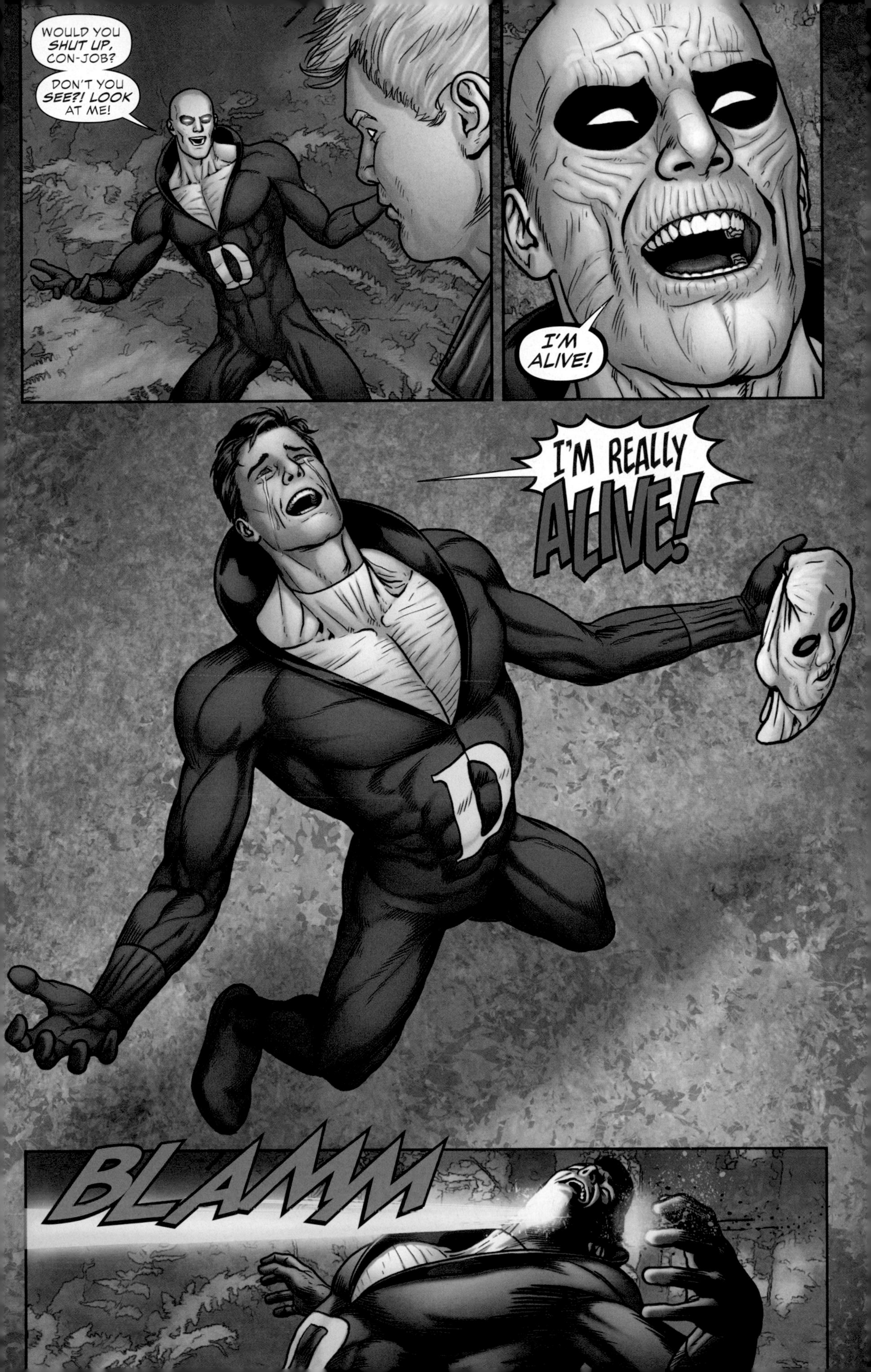
WOULD YOU SHUT UP, CON-JOB?
DON'T YOU SEE?! LOOK AT ME!
I'M ALIVE!
I'M REALLY ALIVE!
BLAMM

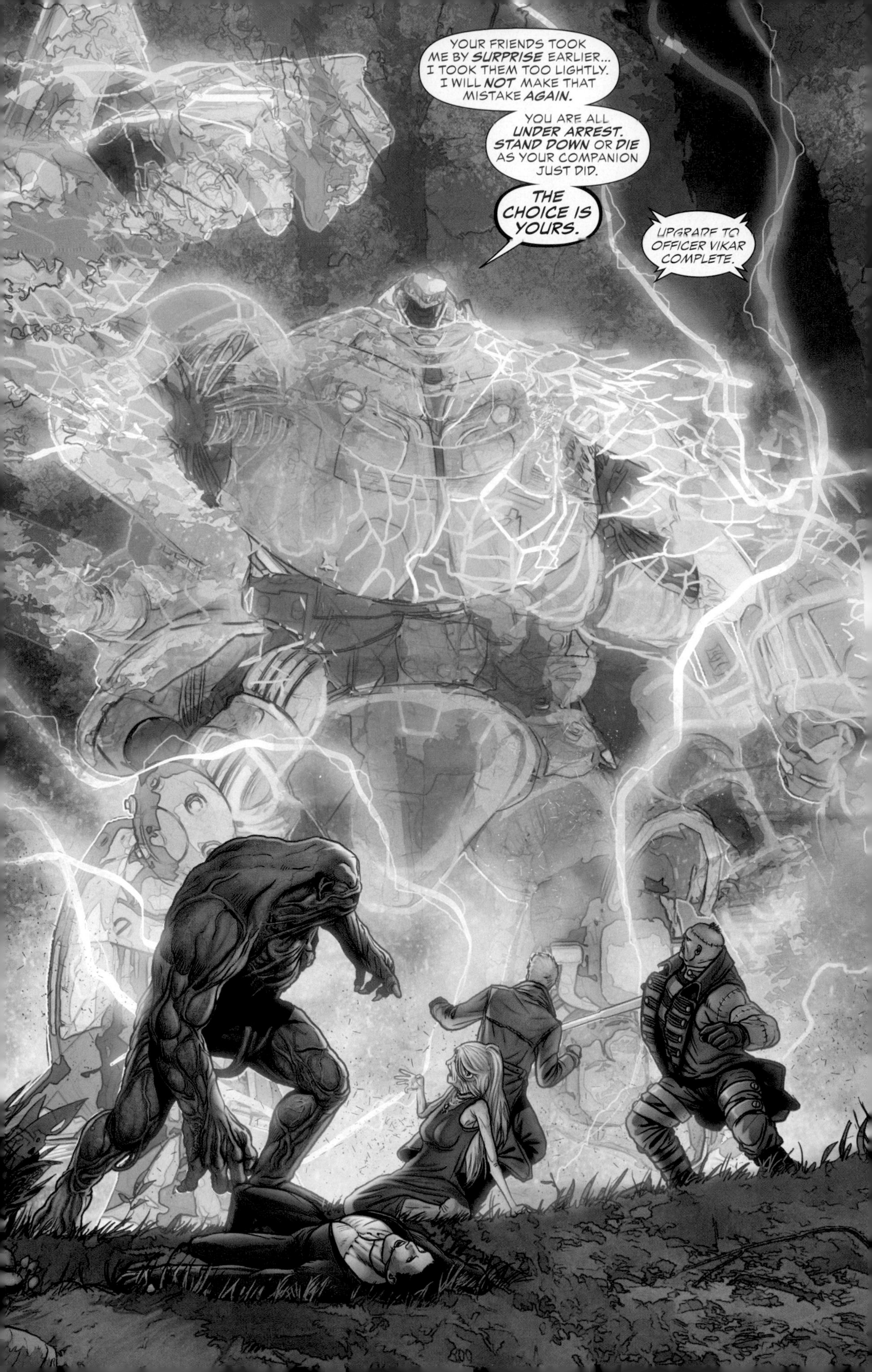
YOUR FRIENDS TOOK ME BY SURPRISE EARLIER... I TOOK THEM TOO LIGHTLY. I WILL NOT MAKE THAT MISTAKE AGAIN.
YOU ARE ALL UNDER ARREST. STAND DOWN OR DIE AS YOUR COMPANION JUST DID.
THE CHOICE IS YOURS.
UPGRADE TO OFFICER VIKAR COMPLETE.

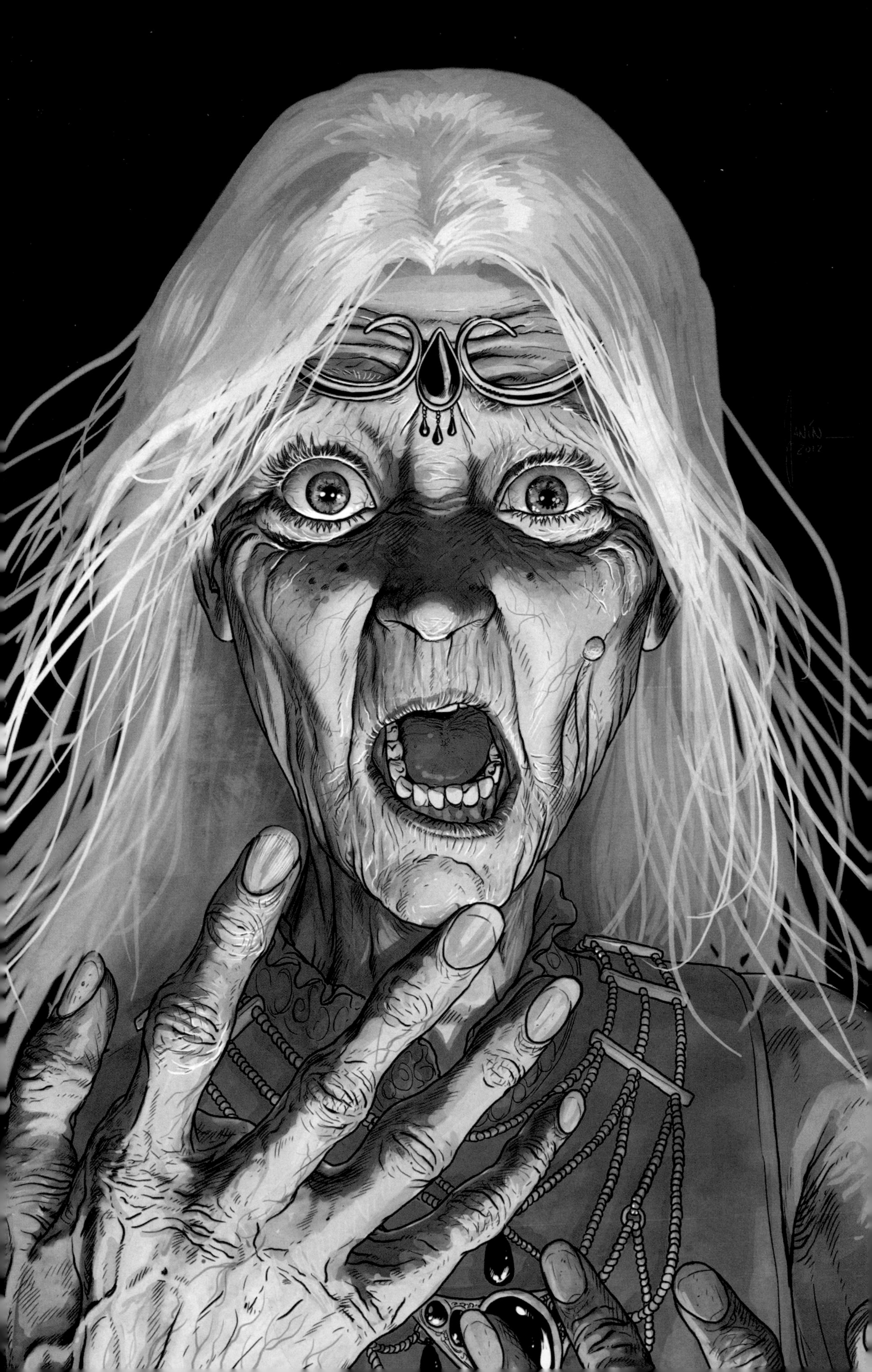

**THE DEATH OF MAGIC part two
NIGHT OF THE HUNTER**

JEFF LEMIRE
RAY FAWKES
writers

MIKEL JANIN
artist

MIKEL JANIN
cover artist

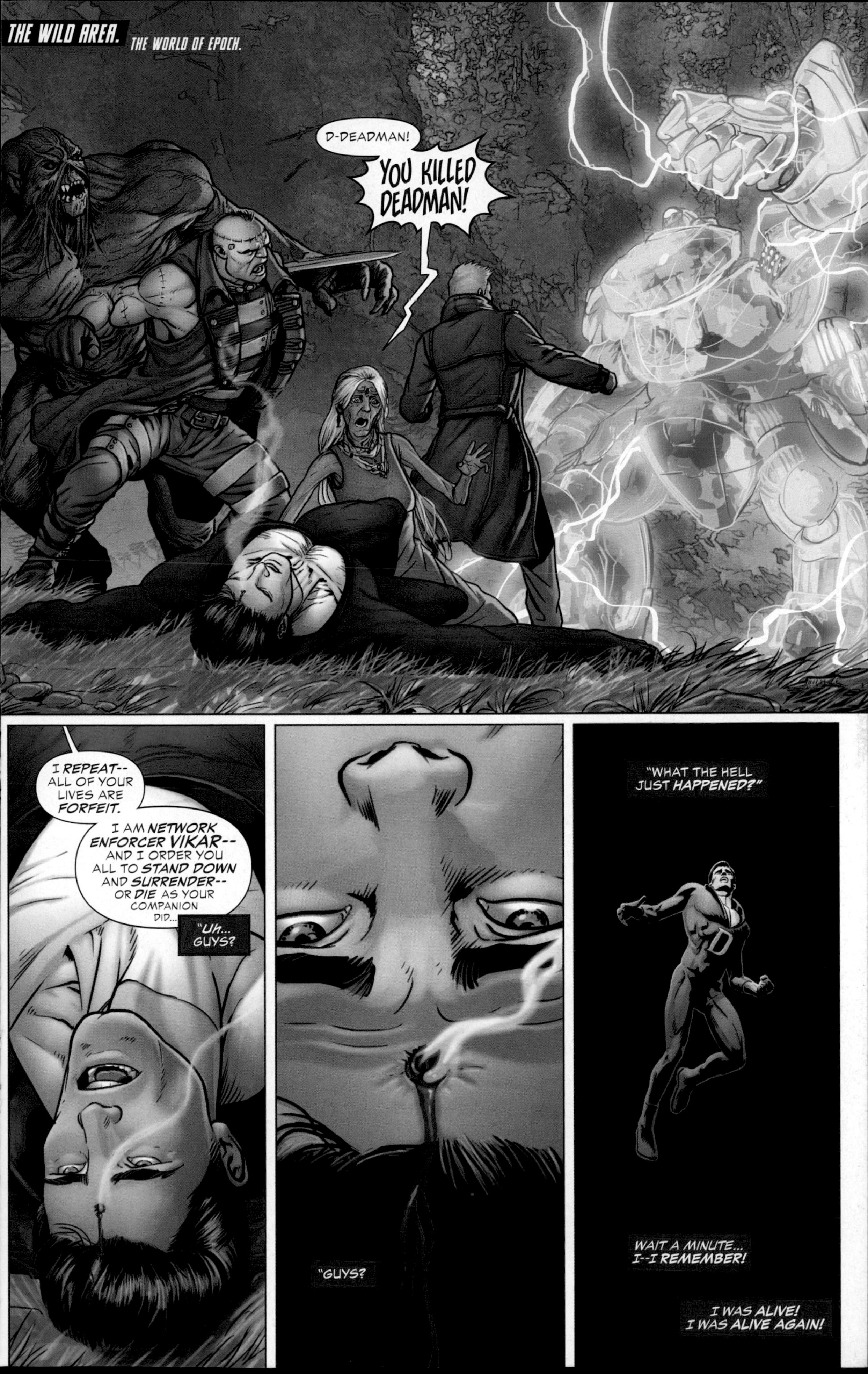
THE WILD AREA.
THE WORLD OF EPOCH.
D-DEADMAN!
YOU KILLED DEADMAN!
I REPEAT-- ALL OF YOUR LIVES ARE FORFEIT.
I AM NETWORK ENFORCER VIKAR-- AND I ORDER YOU ALL TO STAND DOWN AND SURRENDER-- OR DIE AS YOUR COMPANION DID...
"UH... GUYS?
"GUYS?
"WHAT THE HELL JUST HAPPENED?"
WAIT A MINUTE... I--I REMEMBER!
I WAS ALIVE! I WAS ALIVE AGAIN!

I REMEMBER COMING TO THIS WEIRD DIMENSION WITH THE OTHERS--TO FIND THE MISSING *ZATANNA* AND *TIM HUNTER.*

CROSSING OVER INTO THIS MESSED-UP WORLD... *RESURRECTED* ME.

I'D FORGOTTEN WHAT IT FELT LIKE TO REALLY *FEEL* AGAIN. TO BREATHE THE AIR...TO FEEL PAIN.

BUT AS SOON AS I REALIZED WHAT HAD HAPPENED TO ME, THAT BASTARD, *VIKAR,* TOOK IT ALL AWAY.

NOW I'M JUST *PISSED OFF.*

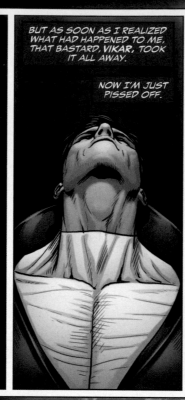

GONNA *KILL* THAT SONOVA...!

THE AFTERLIFE IS MESSED UP *HERE,* TOO. *DIFFERENT.* BUT IT DOESN'T TAKE AN EGGHEAD LIKE JOHN PERIL TO REALIZE *THAT'S* MY WAY BACK.

ALMOST THERE. I CAN FEEL THE LAND OF THE DEAD FALLING AWAY BEHIND ME.

WHERE DO YOU THINK *YOU'RE* GOING, LITTLE GHOST? YOU SEEK REFUGE FROM *DEATH?* YOU SEEK TO CROSS OVER WITHOUT PAYING *THE TOLL?*

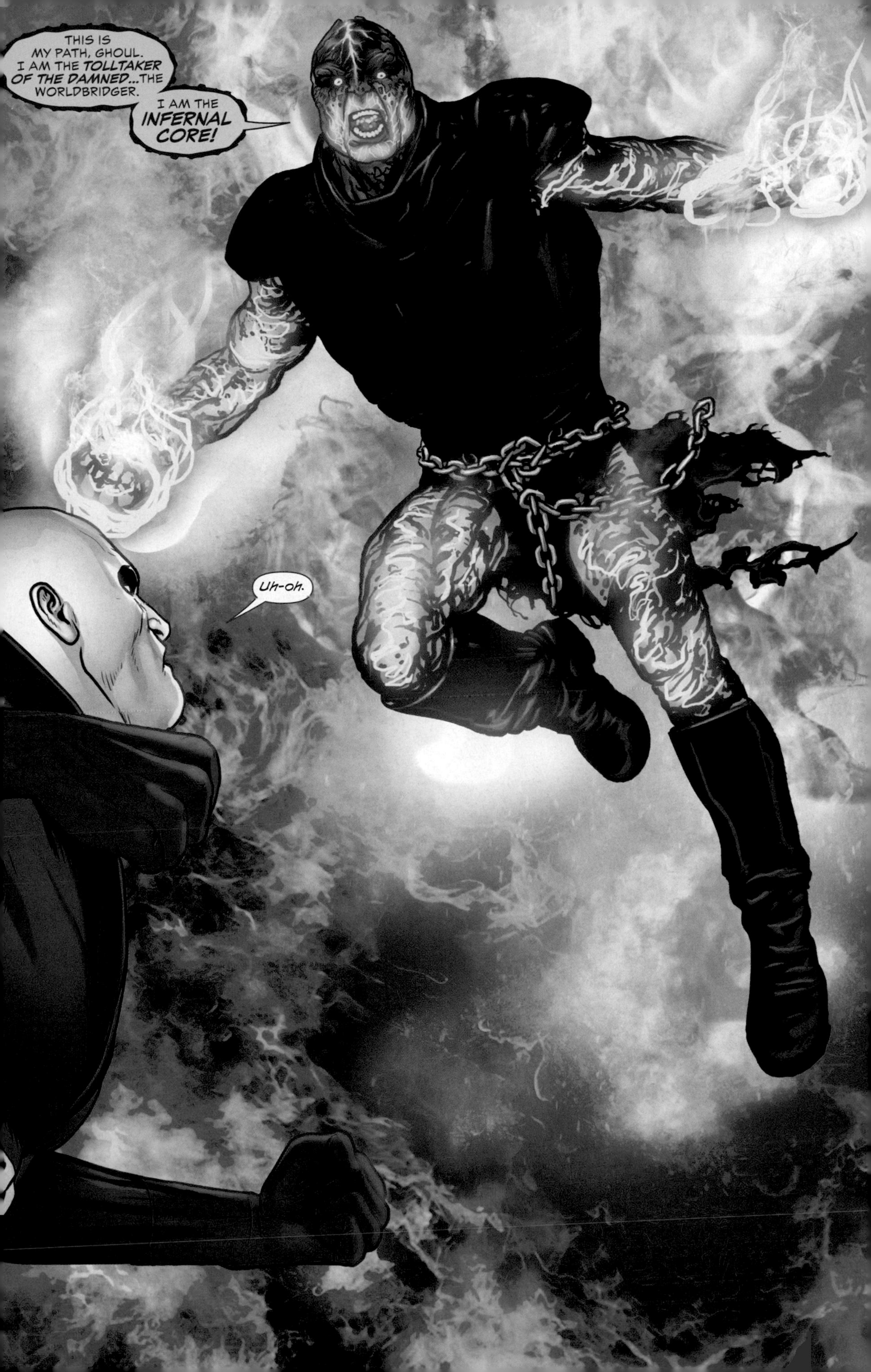
THIS IS MY PATH, GHOUL. I AM THE TOLLTAKER OF THE DAMNED...THE WORLDBRIDGER.
I AM THE INFERNAL CORE!
Uh-oh.

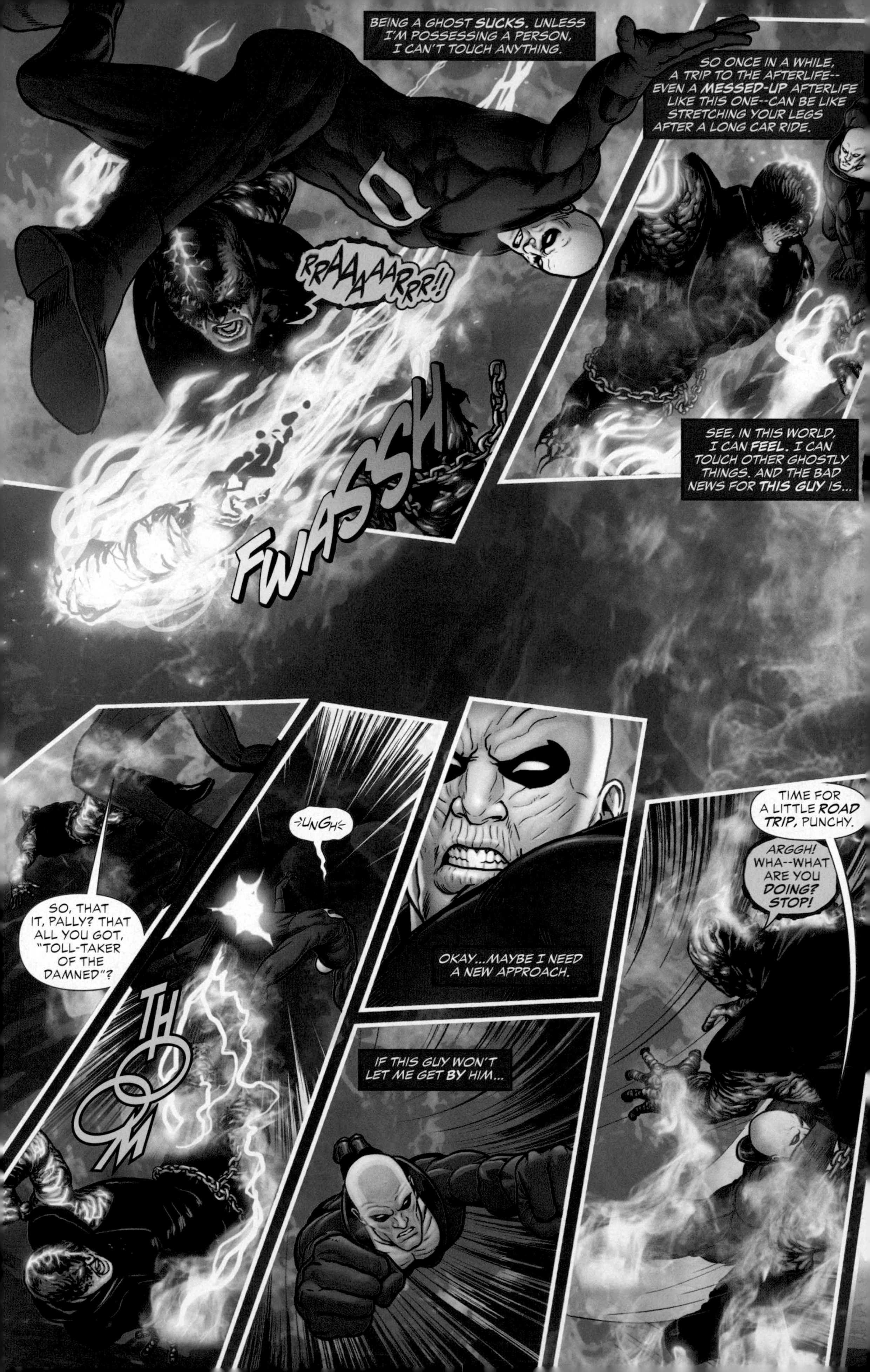
BEING A GHOST SUCKS. UNLESS I'M POSSESSING A PERSON, I CAN'T TOUCH ANYTHING.
SO ONCE IN A WHILE, A TRIP TO THE AFTERLIFE--EVEN A MESSED-UP AFTERLIFE LIKE THIS ONE--CAN BE LIKE STRETCHING YOUR LEGS AFTER A LONG CAR RIDE.
RRAAAAARRR!!
FWASSH
SEE, IN THIS WORLD, I CAN FEEL. I CAN TOUCH OTHER GHOSTLY THINGS. AND THE BAD NEWS FOR THIS GUY IS...
SO, THAT IT, PALLY? THAT ALL YOU GOT, "TOLL-TAKER OF THE DAMNED"?
THOOM
UNGH
OKAY...MAYBE I NEED A NEW APPROACH.
IF THIS GUY WON'T LET ME GET BY HIM...
TIME FOR A LITTLE ROAD TRIP, PUNCHY.
ARGGH! WHA--WHAT ARE YOU DOING? STOP!

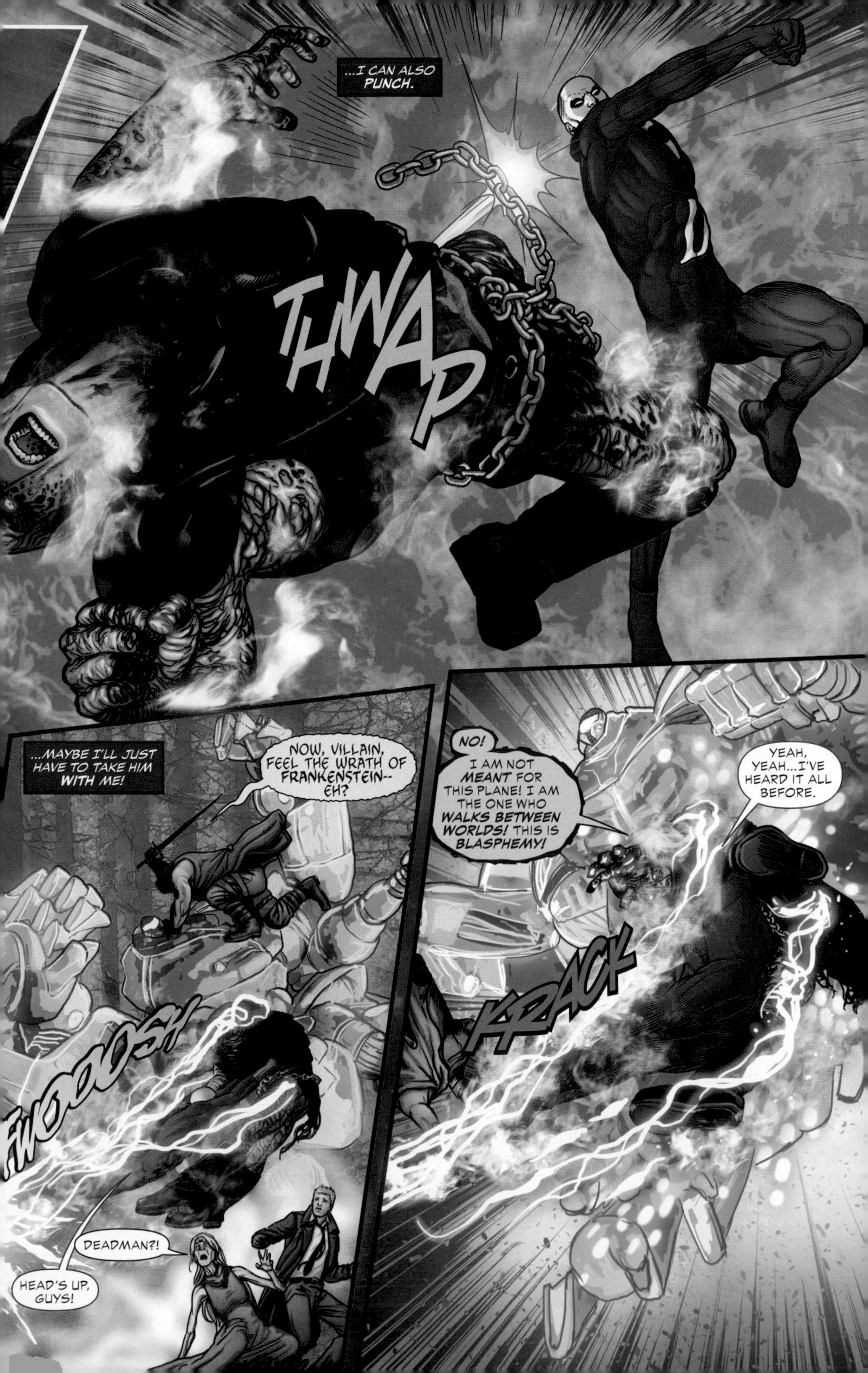
...I CAN ALSO PUNCH.
THWAP
...MAYBE I'LL JUST HAVE TO TAKE HIM WITH ME!
NOW, VILLAIN, FEEL THE WRATH OF FRANKENSTEIN-- EH?
FWOOOSH
DEADMAN?!
HEAD'S UP, GUYS!
NO!
I AM NOT MEANT FOR THIS PLANE! I AM THE ONE WHO WALKS BETWEEN WORLDS! THIS IS BLASPHEMY!
YEAH, YEAH...I'VE HEARD IT ALL BEFORE.
KRACK

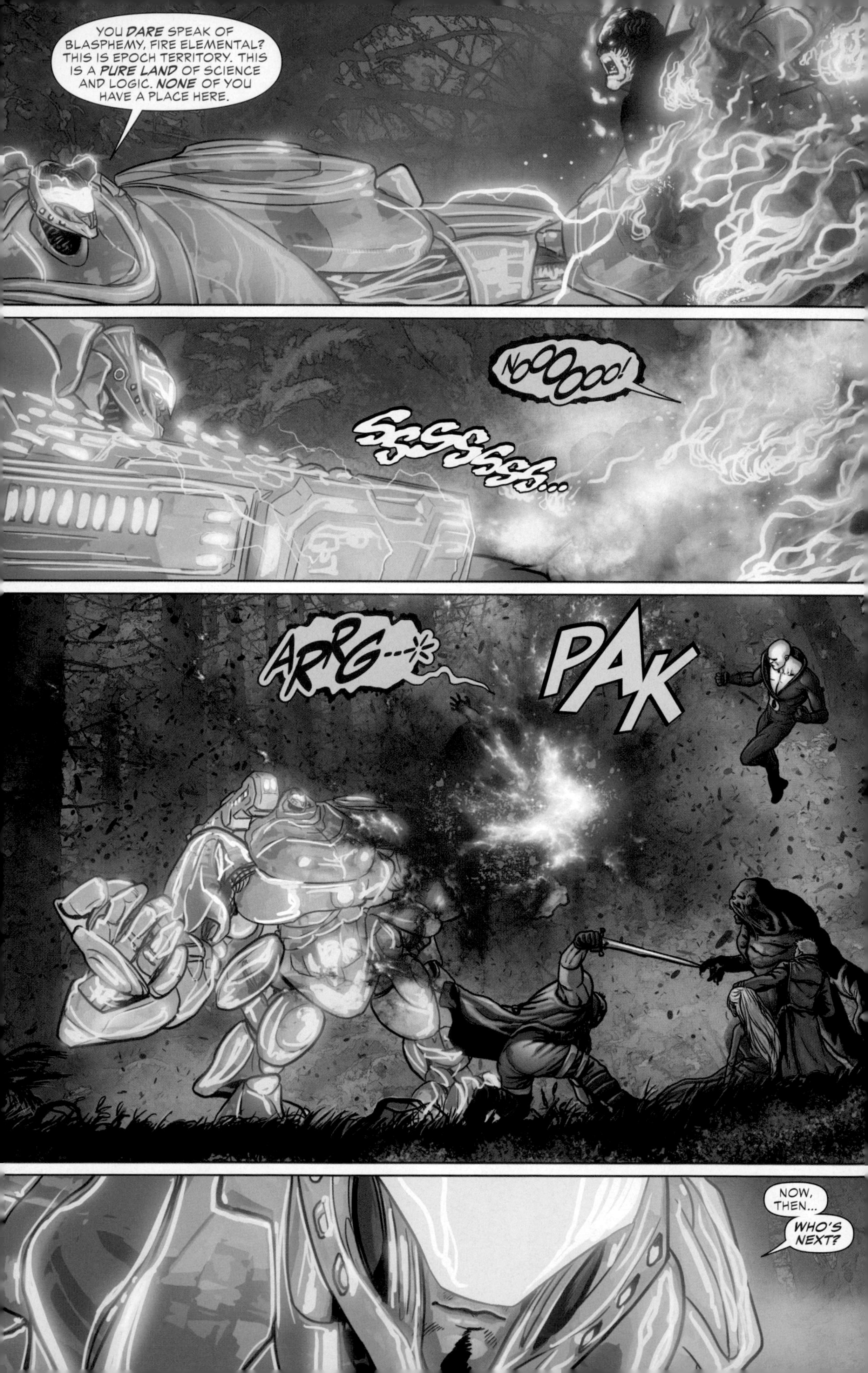
YOU **DARE** SPEAK OF BLASPHEMY, FIRE ELEMENTAL? THIS IS EPOCH TERRITORY. THIS IS A **PURE LAND** OF SCIENCE AND LOGIC. **NONE** OF YOU HAVE A PLACE HERE.
NOOOOOO!
SSSSSSS...
ARRG--*
PAK
NOW, THEN...
WHO'S NEXT?

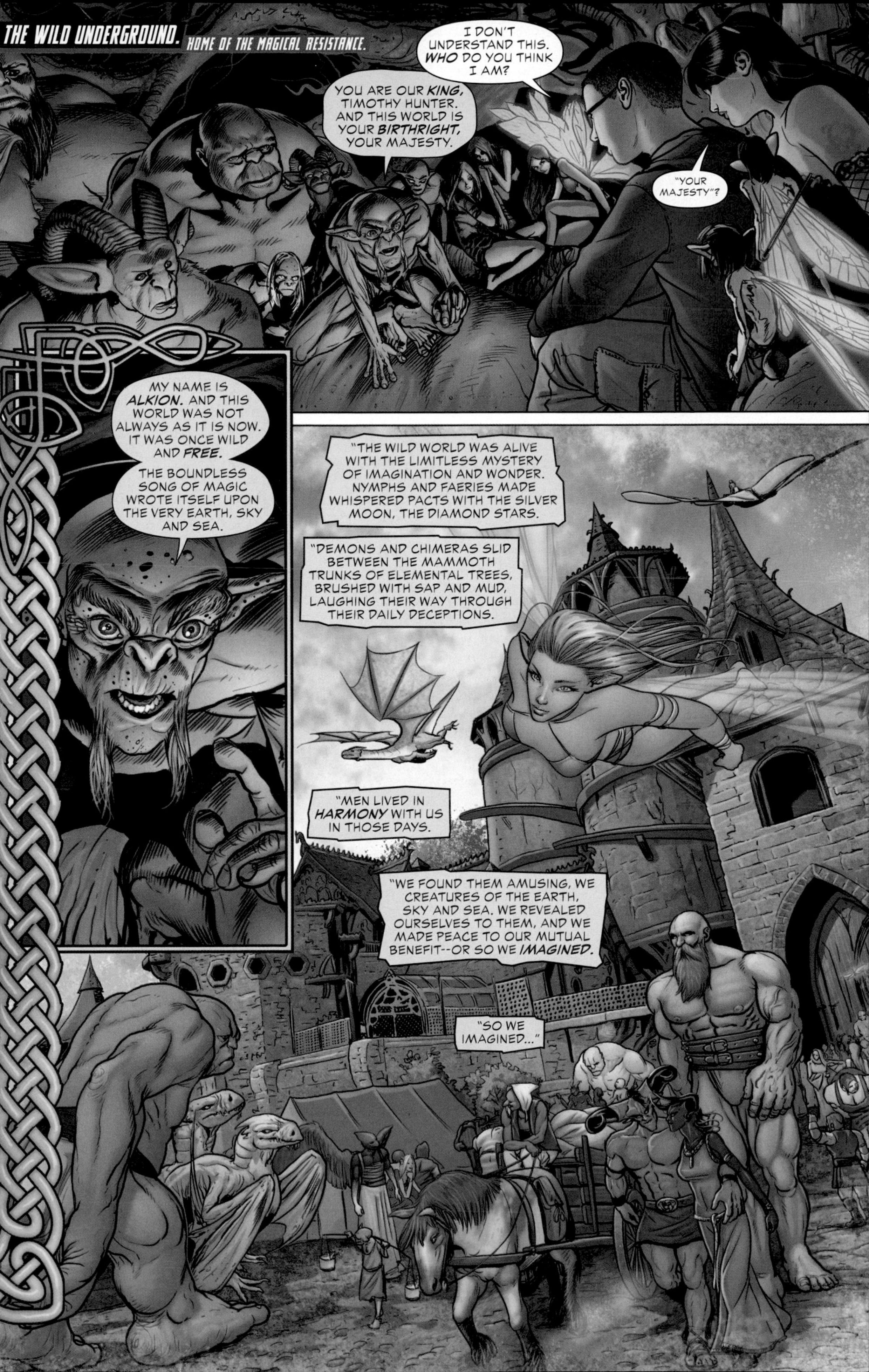
THE WILD UNDERGROUND. HOME OF THE MAGICAL RESISTANCE.
I DON'T UNDERSTAND THIS. WHO DO YOU THINK I AM?
YOU ARE OUR KING, TIMOTHY HUNTER. AND THIS WORLD IS YOUR BIRTHRIGHT, YOUR MAJESTY.
"YOUR MAJESTY"?
MY NAME IS ALKION. AND THIS WORLD WAS NOT ALWAYS AS IT IS NOW. IT WAS ONCE WILD AND FREE.
THE BOUNDLESS SONG OF MAGIC WROTE ITSELF UPON THE VERY EARTH, SKY AND SEA.
"THE WILD WORLD WAS ALIVE WITH THE LIMITLESS MYSTERY OF IMAGINATION AND WONDER. NYMPHS AND FAERIES MADE WHISPERED PACTS WITH THE SILVER MOON, THE DIAMOND STARS.
"DEMONS AND CHIMERAS SLID BETWEEN THE MAMMOTH TRUNKS OF ELEMENTAL TREES, BRUSHED WITH SAP AND MUD, LAUGHING THEIR WAY THROUGH THEIR DAILY DECEPTIONS.
"MEN LIVED IN HARMONY WITH US IN THOSE DAYS.
"WE FOUND THEM AMUSING, WE CREATURES OF THE EARTH, SKY AND SEA. WE REVEALED OURSELVES TO THEM, AND WE MADE PEACE TO OUR MUTUAL BENEFIT--OR SO WE IMAGINED.
"SO WE IMAGINED..."

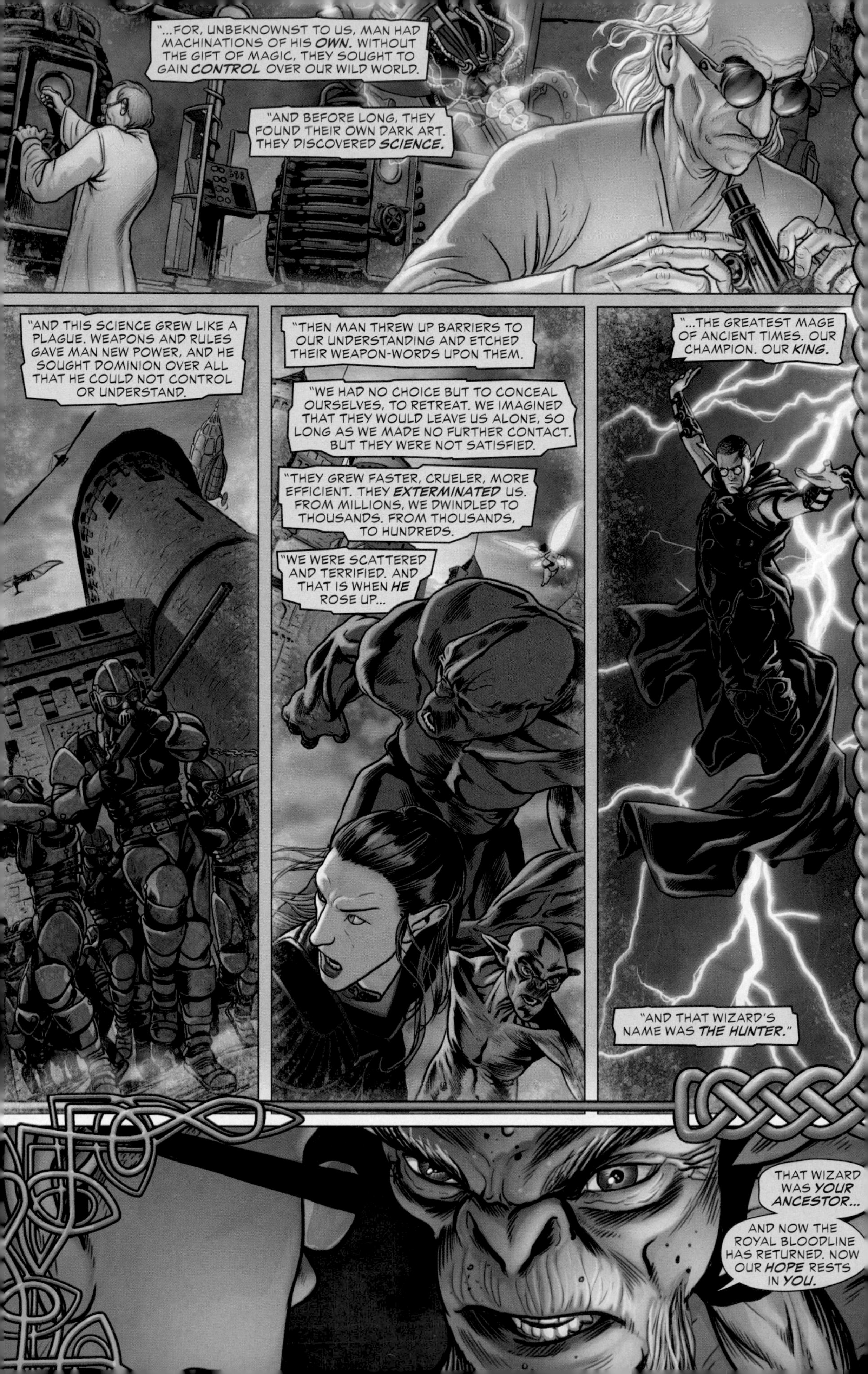
"...FOR, UNBEKNOWNST TO US, MAN HAD MACHINATIONS OF HIS OWN. WITHOUT THE GIFT OF MAGIC, THEY SOUGHT TO GAIN CONTROL OVER OUR WILD WORLD.
"AND BEFORE LONG, THEY FOUND THEIR OWN DARK ART. THEY DISCOVERED SCIENCE.
"AND THIS SCIENCE GREW LIKE A PLAGUE. WEAPONS AND RULES GAVE MAN NEW POWER, AND HE SOUGHT DOMINION OVER ALL THAT HE COULD NOT CONTROL OR UNDERSTAND.
"THEN MAN THREW UP BARRIERS TO OUR UNDERSTANDING AND ETCHED THEIR WEAPON-WORDS UPON THEM.
"WE HAD NO CHOICE BUT TO CONCEAL OURSELVES, TO RETREAT. WE IMAGINED THAT THEY WOULD LEAVE US ALONE, SO LONG AS WE MADE NO FURTHER CONTACT. BUT THEY WERE NOT SATISFIED.
"THEY GREW FASTER, CRUELER, MORE EFFICIENT. THEY EXTERMINATED US. FROM MILLIONS, WE DWINDLED TO THOUSANDS. FROM THOUSANDS, TO HUNDREDS.
"WE WERE SCATTERED AND TERRIFIED. AND THAT IS WHEN HE ROSE UP...
"...THE GREATEST MAGE OF ANCIENT TIMES. OUR CHAMPION. OUR KING.
"AND THAT WIZARD'S NAME WAS THE HUNTER."
THAT WIZARD WAS YOUR ANCESTOR...
AND NOW THE ROYAL BLOODLINE HAS RETURNED. NOW OUR HOPE RESTS IN YOU.

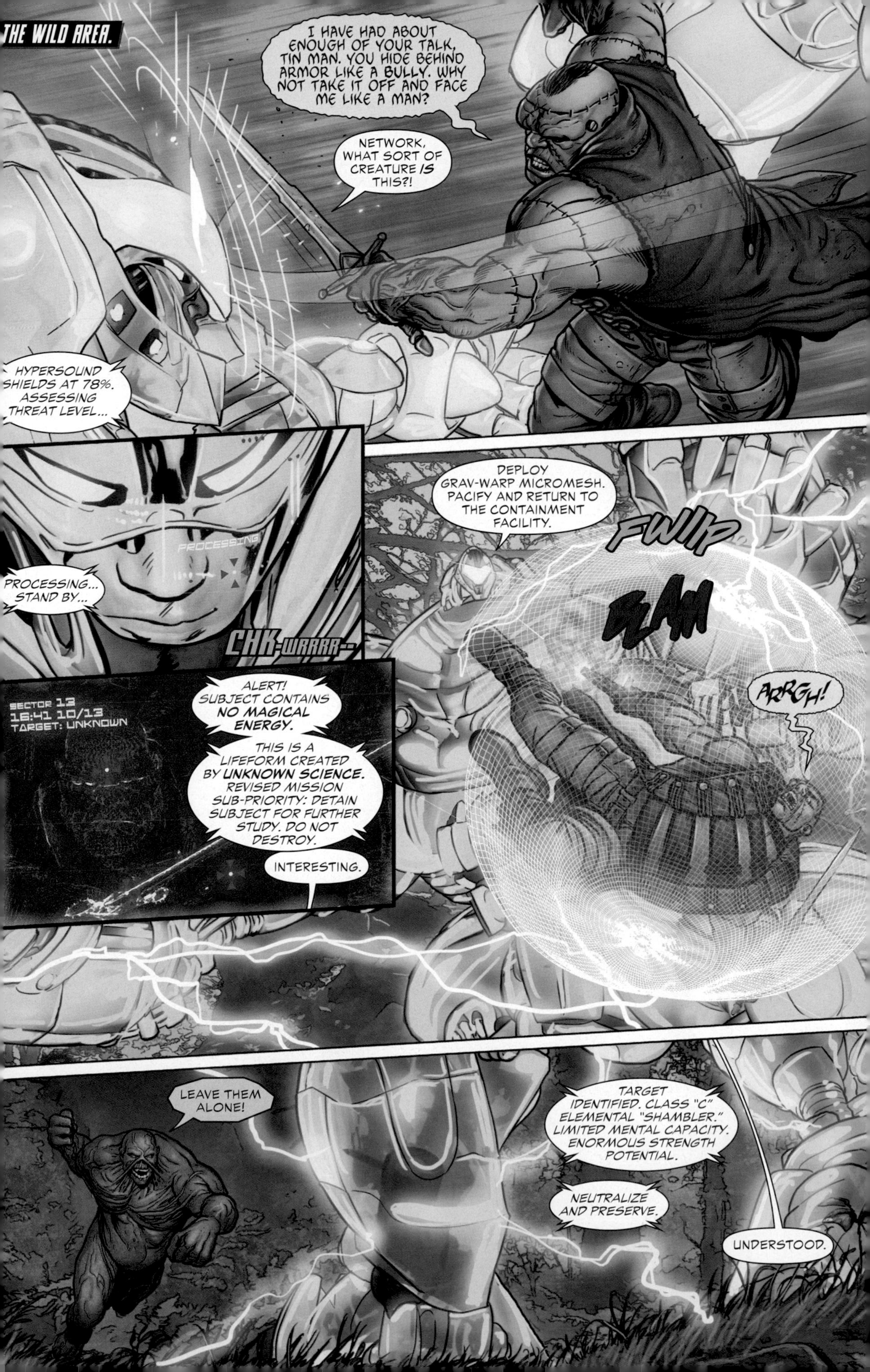
THE WILD AREA.
I HAVE HAD ABOUT ENOUGH OF YOUR TALK, TIN MAN. YOU HIDE BEHIND ARMOR LIKE A BULLY. WHY NOT TAKE IT OFF AND FACE ME LIKE A MAN?
NETWORK, WHAT SORT OF CREATURE IS THIS?!
HYPERSOUND SHIELDS AT 78%. ASSESSING THREAT LEVEL...
PROCESSING
PROCESSING... STAND BY...
CHK-WRRRR--
SECTOR 13
16:41 10/13
TARGET: UNKNOWN
ALERT! SUBJECT CONTAINS NO MAGICAL ENERGY.
THIS IS A LIFEFORM CREATED BY UNKNOWN SCIENCE. REVISED MISSION SUB-PRIORITY: DETAIN SUBJECT FOR FURTHER STUDY. DO NOT DESTROY.
INTERESTING.
DEPLOY GRAV-WARP MICROMESH. PACIFY AND RETURN TO THE CONTAINMENT FACILITY.
FWIIP
BLAM
ARRGH!
LEAVE THEM ALONE!
TARGET IDENTIFIED. CLASS "C" ELEMENTAL "SHAMBLER." LIMITED MENTAL CAPACITY. ENORMOUS STRENGTH POTENTIAL.
NEUTRALIZE AND PRESERVE.
UNDERSTOOD.

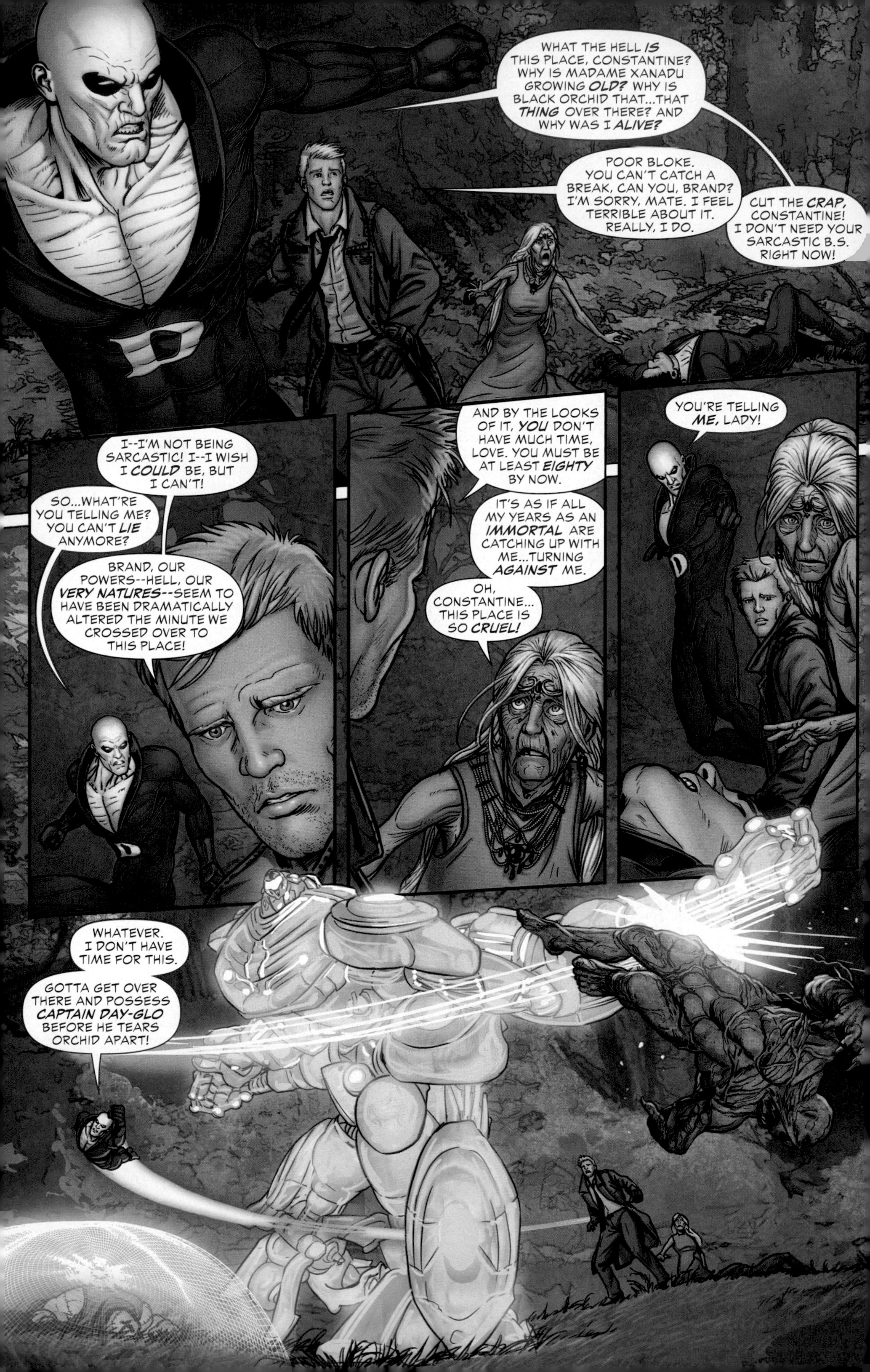
WHAT THE HELL IS THIS PLACE, CONSTANTINE? WHY IS MADAME XANADU GROWING OLD? WHY IS BLACK ORCHID THAT...THAT THING OVER THERE? AND WHY WAS I ALIVE?
POOR BLOKE. YOU CAN'T CATCH A BREAK, CAN YOU, BRAND? I'M SORRY, MATE. I FEEL TERRIBLE ABOUT IT. REALLY, I DO.
CUT THE CRAP, CONSTANTINE! I DON'T NEED YOUR SARCASTIC B.S. RIGHT NOW!
I--I'M NOT BEING SARCASTIC! I--I WISH I COULD BE, BUT I CAN'T!
SO...WHAT'RE YOU TELLING ME? YOU CAN'T LIE ANYMORE?
BRAND, OUR POWERS--HELL, OUR VERY NATURES--SEEM TO HAVE BEEN DRAMATICALLY ALTERED THE MINUTE WE CROSSED OVER TO THIS PLACE!
AND BY THE LOOKS OF IT, YOU DON'T HAVE MUCH TIME, LOVE. YOU MUST BE AT LEAST EIGHTY BY NOW.
IT'S AS IF ALL MY YEARS AS AN IMMORTAL ARE CATCHING UP WITH ME...TURNING AGAINST ME.
OH, CONSTANTINE... THIS PLACE IS SO CRUEL!
YOU'RE TELLING ME, LADY!
WHATEVER. I DON'T HAVE TIME FOR THIS.
GOTTA GET OVER THERE AND POSSESS CAPTAIN DAY-GLO BEFORE HE TEARS ORCHID APART!

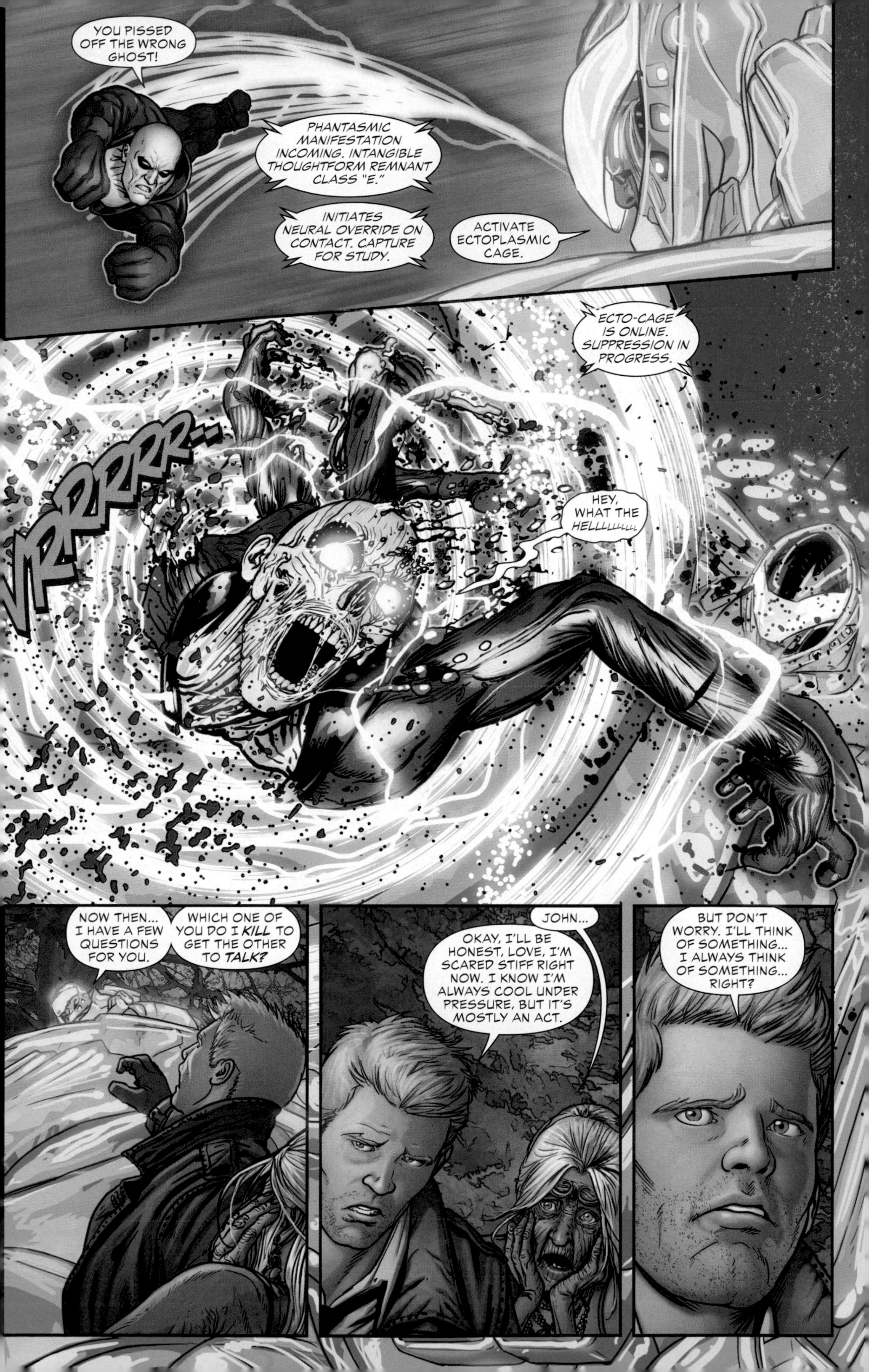
YOU PISSED OFF THE WRONG GHOST!
PHANTASMIC MANIFESTATION INCOMING. INTANGIBLE THOUGHTFORM REMNANT CLASS "E."
INITIATES NEURAL OVERRIDE ON CONTACT. CAPTURE FOR STUDY.
ACTIVATE ECTOPLASMIC CAGE.
ECTO-CAGE IS ONLINE. SUPPRESSION IN PROGRESS.
VRRRRR--
HEY, WHAT THE HELLLLLLLLL
NOW THEN... I HAVE A FEW QUESTIONS FOR YOU.
WHICH ONE OF YOU DO I KILL TO GET THE OTHER TO TALK?
JOHN...
OKAY, I'LL BE HONEST, LOVE, I'M SCARED STIFF RIGHT NOW. I KNOW I'M ALWAYS COOL UNDER PRESSURE, BUT IT'S MOSTLY AN ACT.
BUT DON'T WORRY. I'LL THINK OF SOMETHING... I ALWAYS THINK OF SOMETHING... RIGHT?

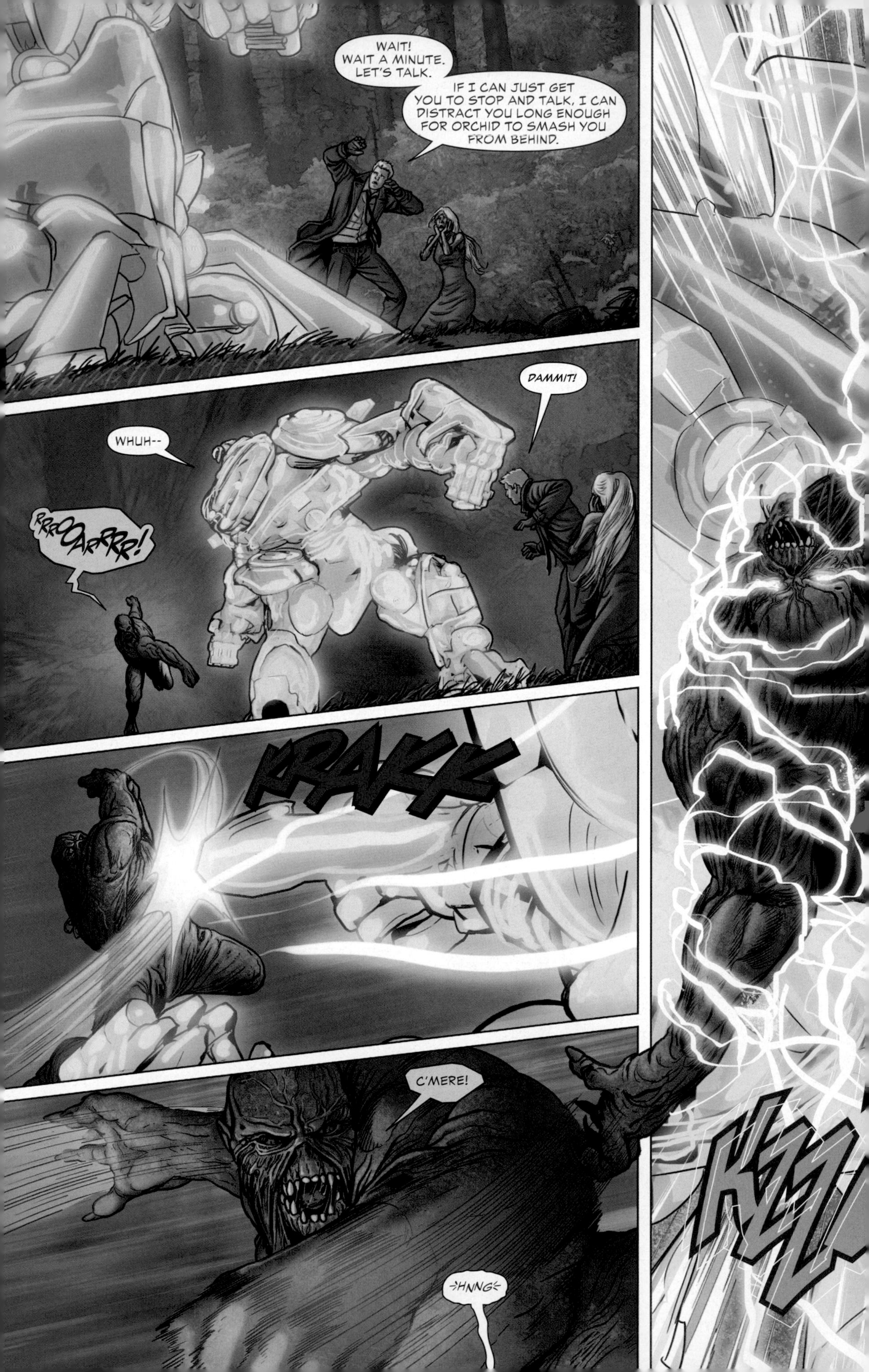
WAIT! WAIT A MINUTE. LET'S TALK.
IF I CAN JUST GET YOU TO STOP AND TALK, I CAN DISTRACT YOU LONG ENOUGH FOR ORCHID TO SMASH YOU FROM BEHIND.
DAMMIT!
WHUH--
RRROOARRRR!
KRAKK
C'MERE!
HNNG
KZZ

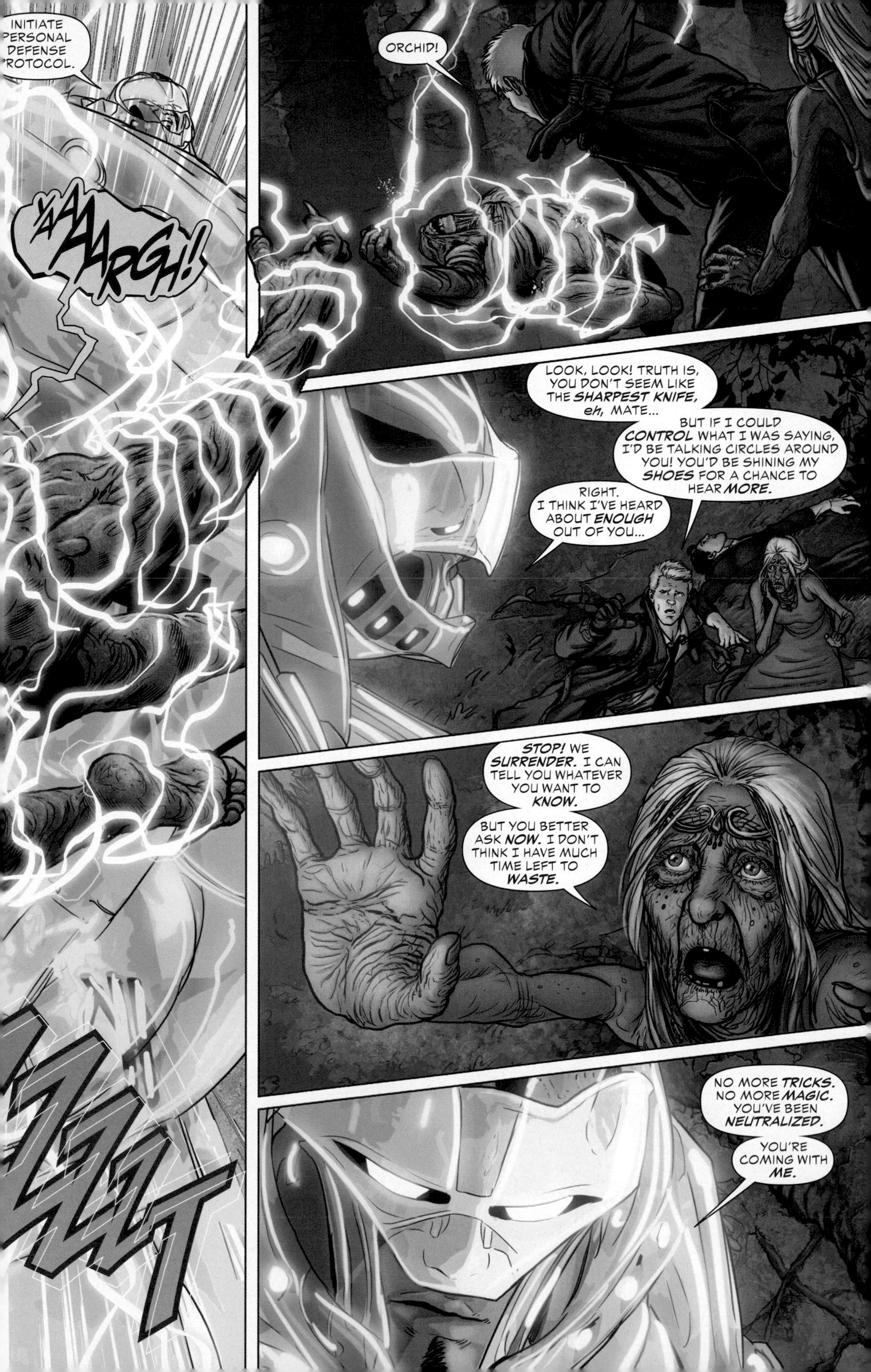
INITIATE PERSONAL DEFENSE PROTOCOL.
ORCHID!
YAAAAARGH!
LOOK, LOOK! TRUTH IS, YOU DON'T SEEM LIKE THE SHARPEST KNIFE, eh, MATE...
BUT IF I COULD CONTROL WHAT I WAS SAYING, I'D BE TALKING CIRCLES AROUND YOU! YOU'D BE SHINING MY SHOES FOR A CHANCE TO HEAR MORE.
RIGHT. I THINK I'VE HEARD ABOUT ENOUGH OUT OF YOU...
STOP! WE SURRENDER. I CAN TELL YOU WHATEVER YOU WANT TO KNOW.
BUT YOU BETTER ASK NOW. I DON'T THINK I HAVE MUCH TIME LEFT TO WASTE.
NO MORE TRICKS. NO MORE MAGIC. YOU'VE BEEN NEUTRALIZED.
YOU'RE COMING WITH ME.

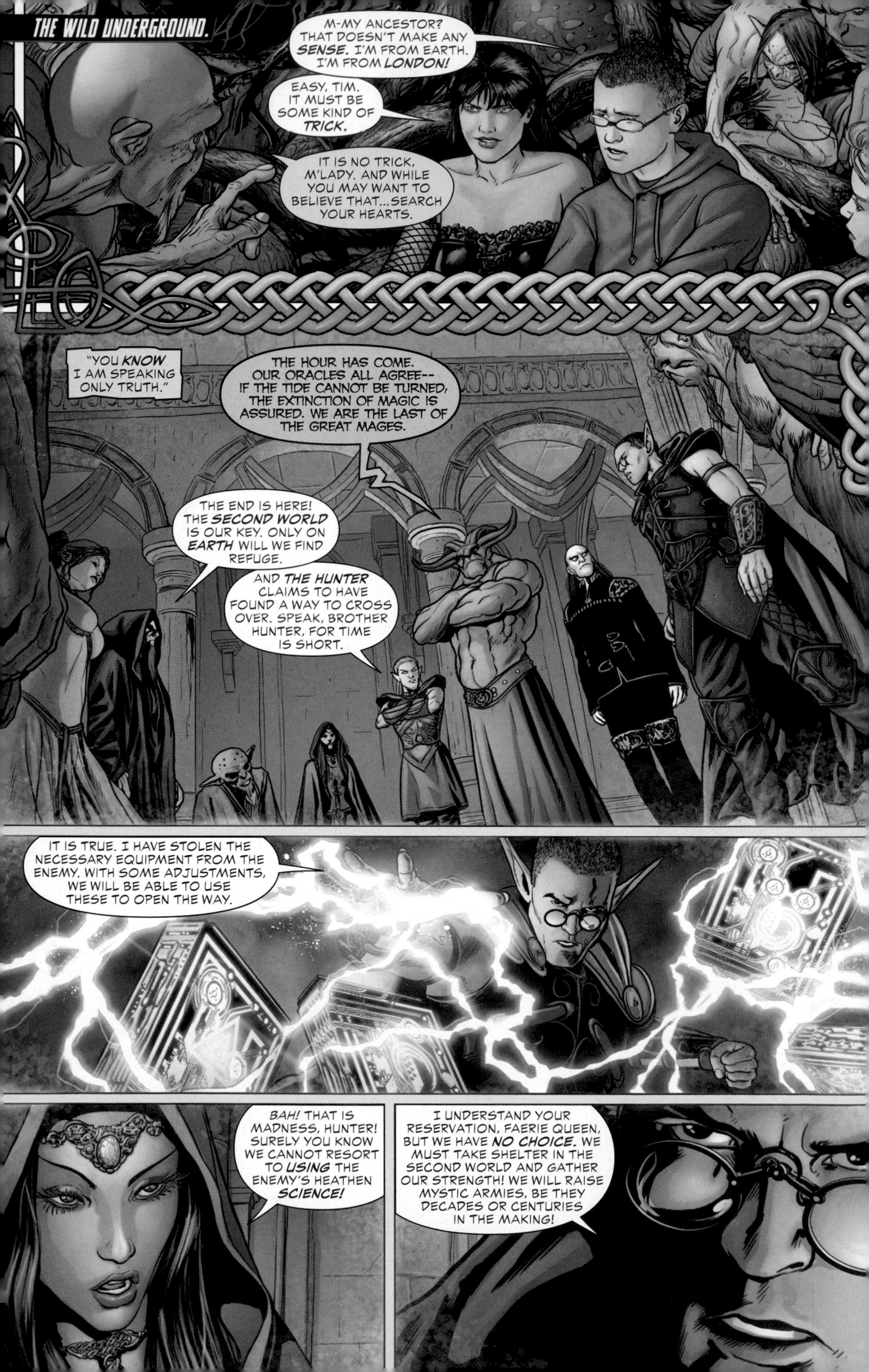
THE WILD UNDERGROUND.
M-MY ANCESTOR? THAT DOESN'T MAKE ANY SENSE. I'M FROM EARTH. I'M FROM LONDON!
EASY, TIM. IT MUST BE SOME KIND OF TRICK.
IT IS NO TRICK, M'LADY. AND WHILE YOU MAY WANT TO BELIEVE THAT...SEARCH YOUR HEARTS.
"YOU KNOW I AM SPEAKING ONLY TRUTH."
THE HOUR HAS COME. OUR ORACLES ALL AGREE-- IF THE TIDE CANNOT BE TURNED, THE EXTINCTION OF MAGIC IS ASSURED. WE ARE THE LAST OF THE GREAT MAGES.
THE END IS HERE! THE SECOND WORLD IS OUR KEY. ONLY ON EARTH WILL WE FIND REFUGE.
AND THE HUNTER CLAIMS TO HAVE FOUND A WAY TO CROSS OVER. SPEAK, BROTHER HUNTER, FOR TIME IS SHORT.
IT IS TRUE. I HAVE STOLEN THE NECESSARY EQUIPMENT FROM THE ENEMY. WITH SOME ADJUSTMENTS, WE WILL BE ABLE TO USE THESE TO OPEN THE WAY.
BAH! THAT IS MADNESS, HUNTER! SURELY YOU KNOW WE CANNOT RESORT TO USING THE ENEMY'S HEATHEN SCIENCE!
I UNDERSTAND YOUR RESERVATION, FAERIE QUEEN, BUT WE HAVE NO CHOICE. WE MUST TAKE SHELTER IN THE SECOND WORLD AND GATHER OUR STRENGTH! WE WILL RAISE MYSTIC ARMIES, BE THEY DECADES OR CENTURIES IN THE MAKING!

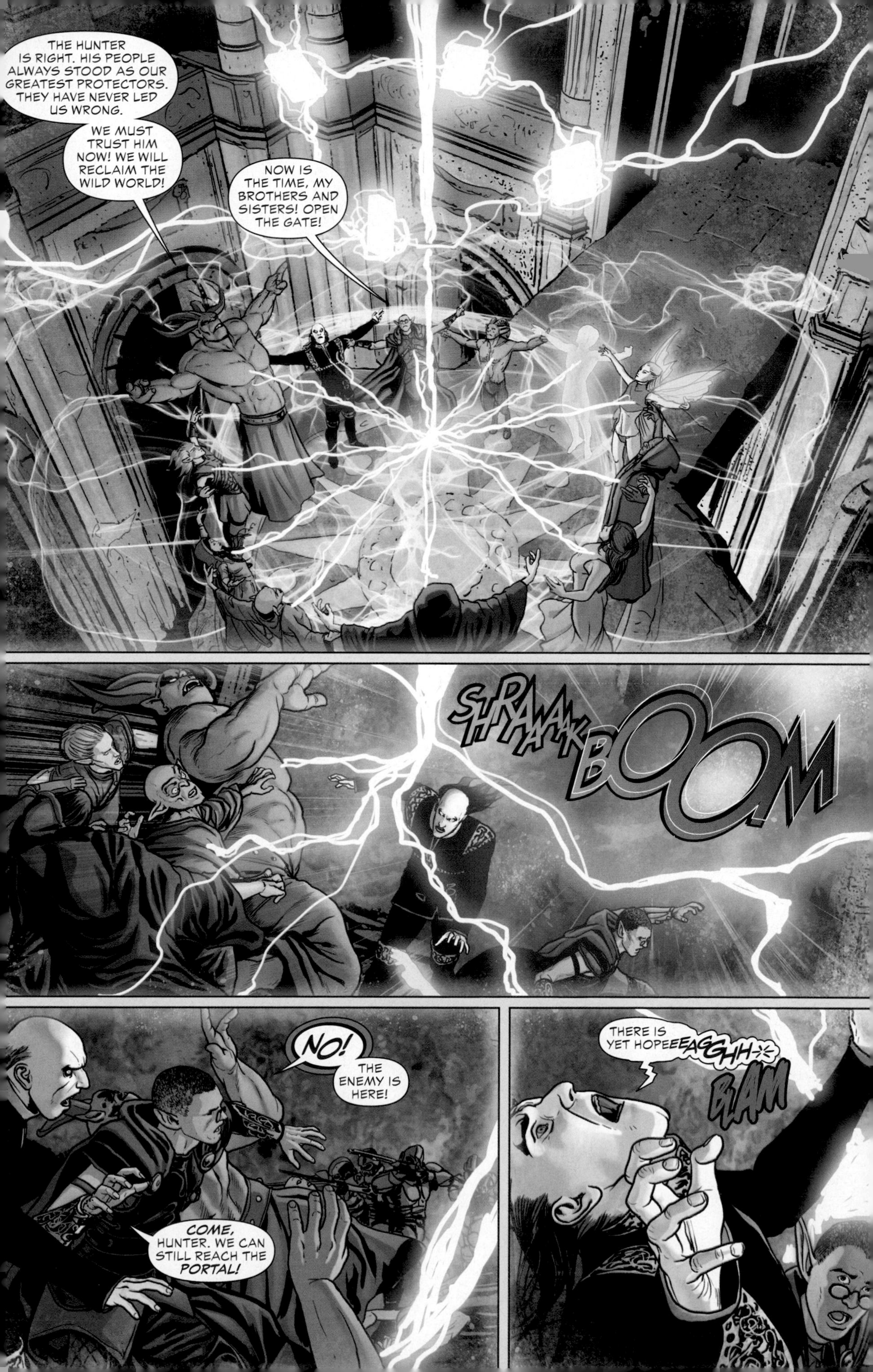
THE HUNTER IS RIGHT. HIS PEOPLE ALWAYS STOOD AS OUR GREATEST PROTECTORS. THEY HAVE NEVER LED US WRONG.
WE MUST TRUST HIM NOW! WE WILL RECLAIM THE WILD WORLD!
NOW IS THE TIME, MY BROTHERS AND SISTERS! OPEN THE GATE!
SHRAAAKBOOOM
NO!
THE ENEMY IS HERE!
COME, HUNTER. WE CAN STILL REACH THE PORTAL!
THERE IS YET HOPEEEEAGGHH
BLAM

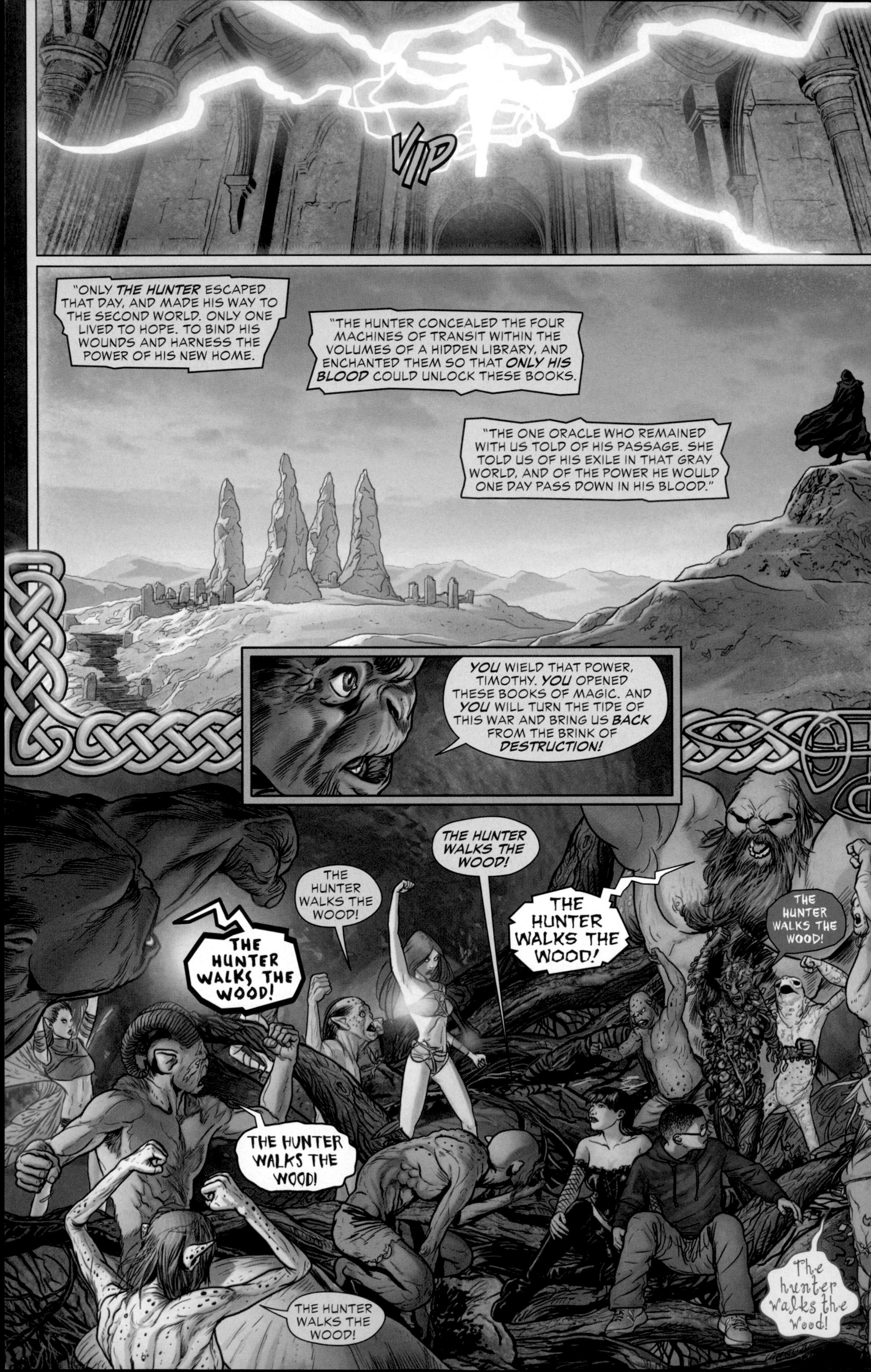
VIP
"ONLY THE HUNTER ESCAPED THAT DAY, AND MADE HIS WAY TO THE SECOND WORLD. ONLY ONE LIVED TO HOPE. TO BIND HIS WOUNDS AND HARNESS THE POWER OF HIS NEW HOME.
"THE HUNTER CONCEALED THE FOUR MACHINES OF TRANSIT WITHIN THE VOLUMES OF A HIDDEN LIBRARY, AND ENCHANTED THEM SO THAT ONLY HIS BLOOD COULD UNLOCK THESE BOOKS.
"THE ONE ORACLE WHO REMAINED WITH US TOLD OF HIS PASSAGE. SHE TOLD US OF HIS EXILE IN THAT GRAY WORLD, AND OF THE POWER HE WOULD ONE DAY PASS DOWN IN HIS BLOOD."
YOU WIELD THAT POWER, TIMOTHY. YOU OPENED THESE BOOKS OF MAGIC. AND YOU WILL TURN THE TIDE OF THIS WAR AND BRING US BACK FROM THE BRINK OF DESTRUCTION!
THE HUNTER WALKS THE WOOD!
THE HUNTER WALKS THE WOOD!
THE HUNTER WALKS THE WOOD!
THE HUNTER WALKS THE WOOD!
THE HUNTER WALKS THE WOOD!
THE HUNTER WALKS THE WOOD!
THE HUNTER WALKS THE WOOD!
The hunter walks the wood!

I--I HAVE A CONFESSION, XANADU. SEE, I HAVE A FEELING YOU'RE NOT GOING TO MAKE IT OUT OF THIS ONE *ALIVE*, SO I JUST WANTED TO SAY...

...I KNOW I ACT THE RIGHT BASTARD MOST OF THE TIME, BUT THE TRUTH IS, I ALWAYS REALLY *LIKED* YOU.

QUIT YOUR INCESSANT BABBLING, CONSTANTINE. WE NEED TO DEVISE AN EXIT STRATEGY. *NOW!*

IT'S...NO USE...TOO LATE.

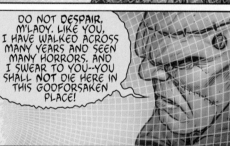

DO NOT *DESPAIR*, M'LADY. LIKE YOU, I HAVE WALKED ACROSS MANY YEARS AND SEEN MANY HORRORS. AND I SWEAR TO YOU--YOU SHALL NOT DIE HERE IN THIS GODFORSAKEN PLACE!

BE *QUIET*, ALL OF YOU, OR I'LL REMOVE YOUR BLASPHEMOUS TONGUES!

YOU ARE IN *EPOCH* NOW. I WILL NOT HEAR ANY MORE OF YOUR EVIL *WORDS*.

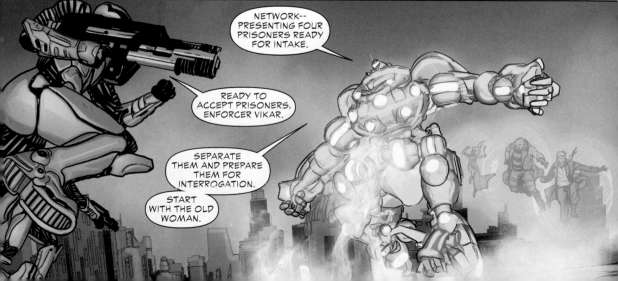

NETWORK-- PRESENTING FOUR PRISONERS READY FOR INTAKE.

READY TO ACCEPT PRISONERS, ENFORCER VIKAR.

SEPARATE THEM AND PREPARE THEM FOR INTERROGATION.

START WITH THE OLD WOMAN.

PROCESSING.

C-CONSTANTINE, HELP ME!

XANADU, HANG *TIGHT*, LOVE--I'LL THINK OF SOMETHING!

RRRRRRRL... MMBLLE

NETWORK! WHAT'S HAPPENING?

CONSTANTINE? IS THIS YOUR DOING?

IT'S NOT *ME*, FRANK!

RRRL

NETWORK, WHAT IS THE *SOURCE* OF THE EVENT? IS IT THE WORK OF MY PRISONERS?!

NEGATIVE. THIS IS NOT A LOCALIZED EVENT.

OH... THIS ISN'T GOOD.

RRRRRRU

NANDA PARBAT.

RRRRRRR RRRRR

PERIL! TELL ME THIS IS A *COINCIDENCE!* TELL ME YOUR DAMN PORTAL ISN'T CAUSING IT!

I WISH I COULD, COLONEL TREVOR! IT'S COMING FROM THE *OTHER SIDE!* WHEREVER THEY'VE GONE--THE PLACE IS SHAKING ITSELF *APART!*
AND THE EFFECT IS BLEEDING THROUGH OVER HERE! THIS IS BAD-- *VERY* BAD!

RRRRRRUM KRAKK

YAAAGH

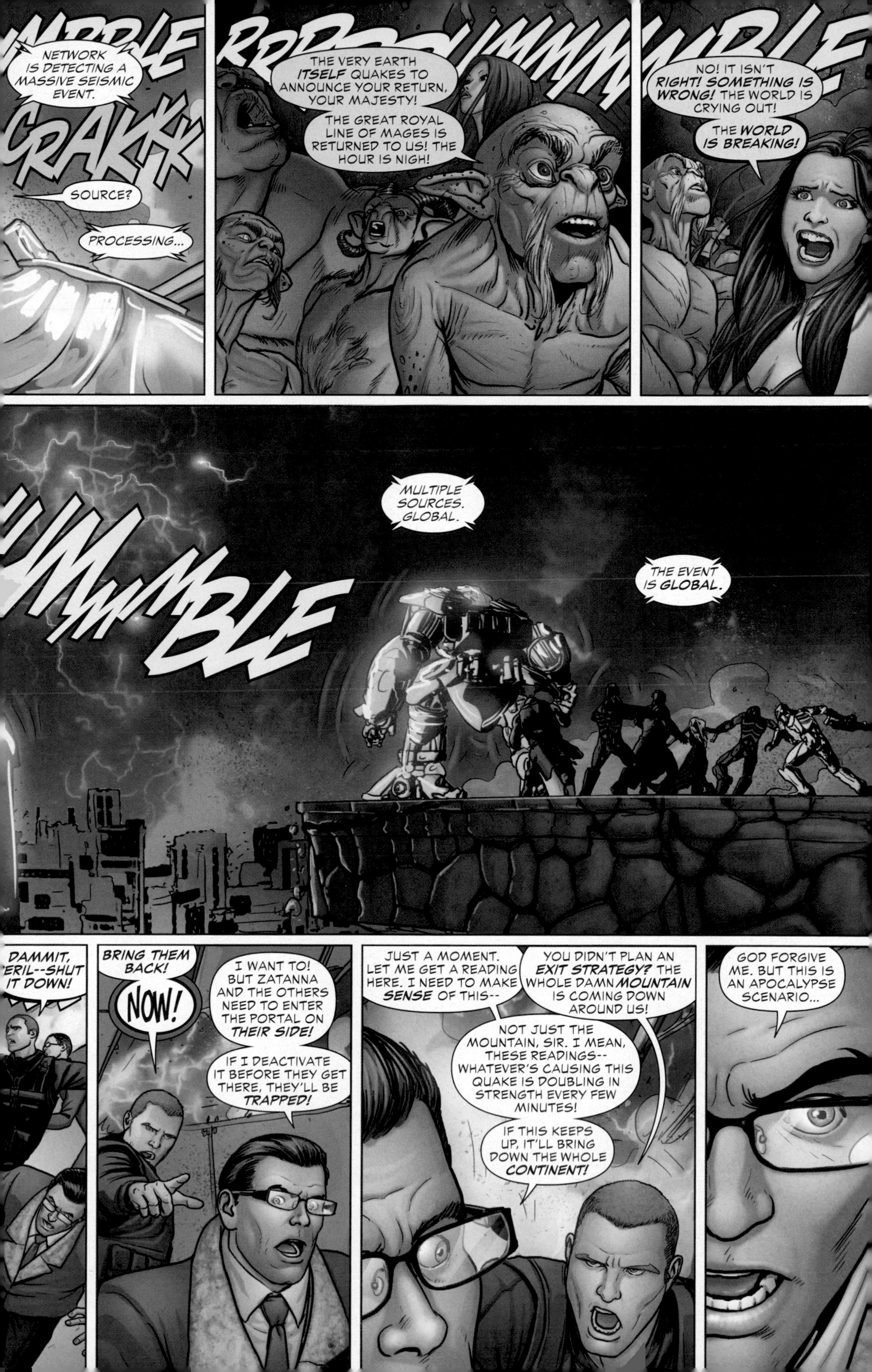

NETWORK IS DETECTING A MASSIVE SEISMIC EVENT.
CRAKK
SOURCE?
PROCESSING...
THE VERY EARTH ITSELF QUAKES TO ANNOUNCE YOUR RETURN, YOUR MAJESTY!
THE GREAT ROYAL LINE OF MAGES IS RETURNED TO US! THE HOUR IS NIGH!
NO! IT ISN'T RIGHT! SOMETHING IS WRONG! THE WORLD IS CRYING OUT!
THE WORLD IS BREAKING!
MULTIPLE SOURCES. GLOBAL.
THE EVENT IS GLOBAL.
DAMMIT, ERIL--SHUT IT DOWN!
BRING THEM BACK!
NOW!
I WANT TO! BUT ZATANNA AND THE OTHERS NEED TO ENTER THE PORTAL ON THEIR SIDE!
IF I DEACTIVATE IT BEFORE THEY GET THERE, THEY'LL BE TRAPPED!
JUST A MOMENT. LET ME GET A READING HERE. I NEED TO MAKE SENSE OF THIS--
YOU DIDN'T PLAN AN EXIT STRATEGY? THE WHOLE DAMN MOUNTAIN IS COMING DOWN AROUND US!
NOT JUST THE MOUNTAIN, SIR. I MEAN, THESE READINGS-- WHATEVER'S CAUSING THIS QUAKE IS DOUBLING IN STRENGTH EVERY FEW MINUTES!
IF THIS KEEPS UP, IT'LL BRING DOWN THE WHOLE CONTINENT!
GOD FORGIVE ME. BUT THIS IS AN APOCALYPSE SCENARIO...

...I'VE DOOMED US ALL!

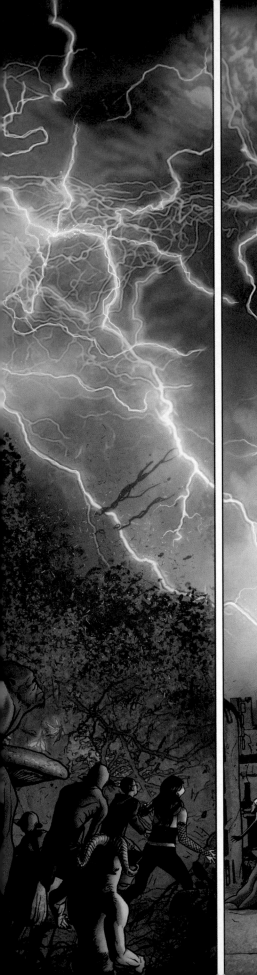

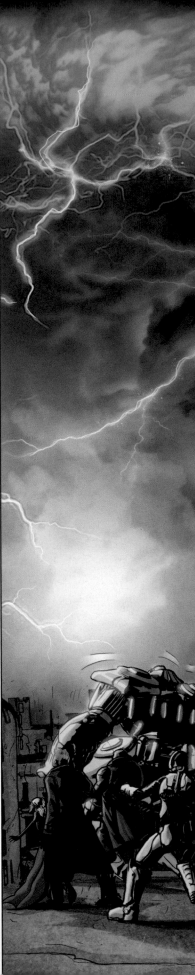

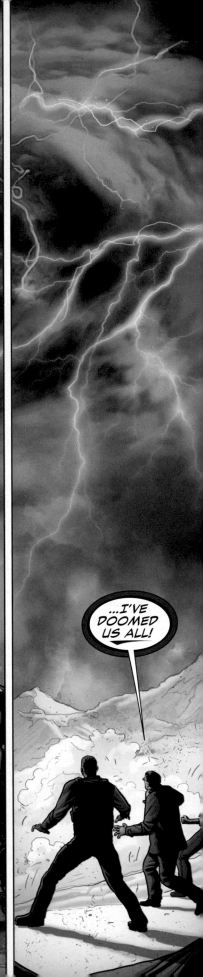

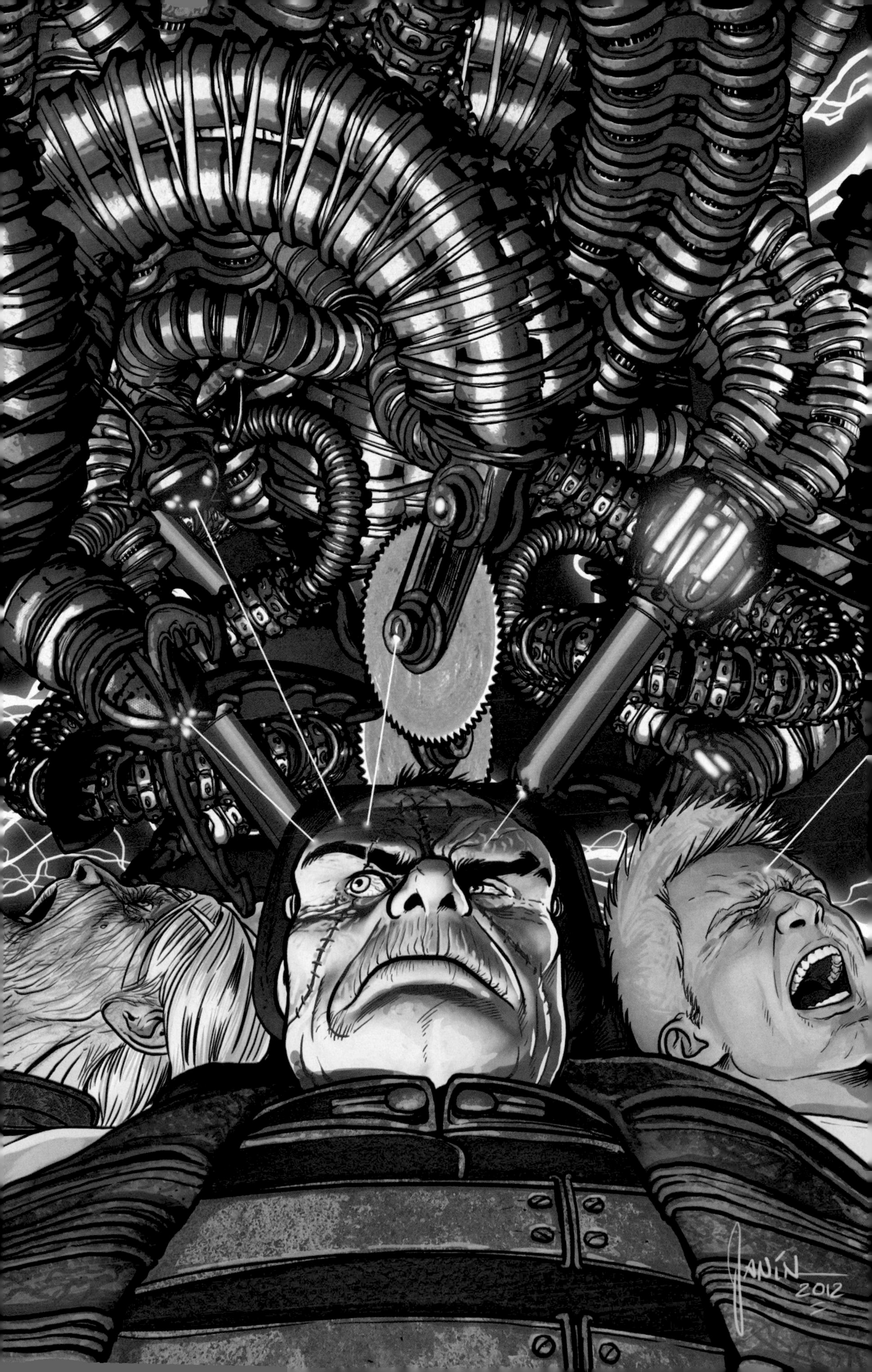
JANÍN
2012

THE DEATH OF MAGIC part three
PRISONERS OF EPOCH

JEFF LEMIRE
RAY FAWKES
writers

MIKEL JANIN
artist

MIKEL JANIN
cover artist

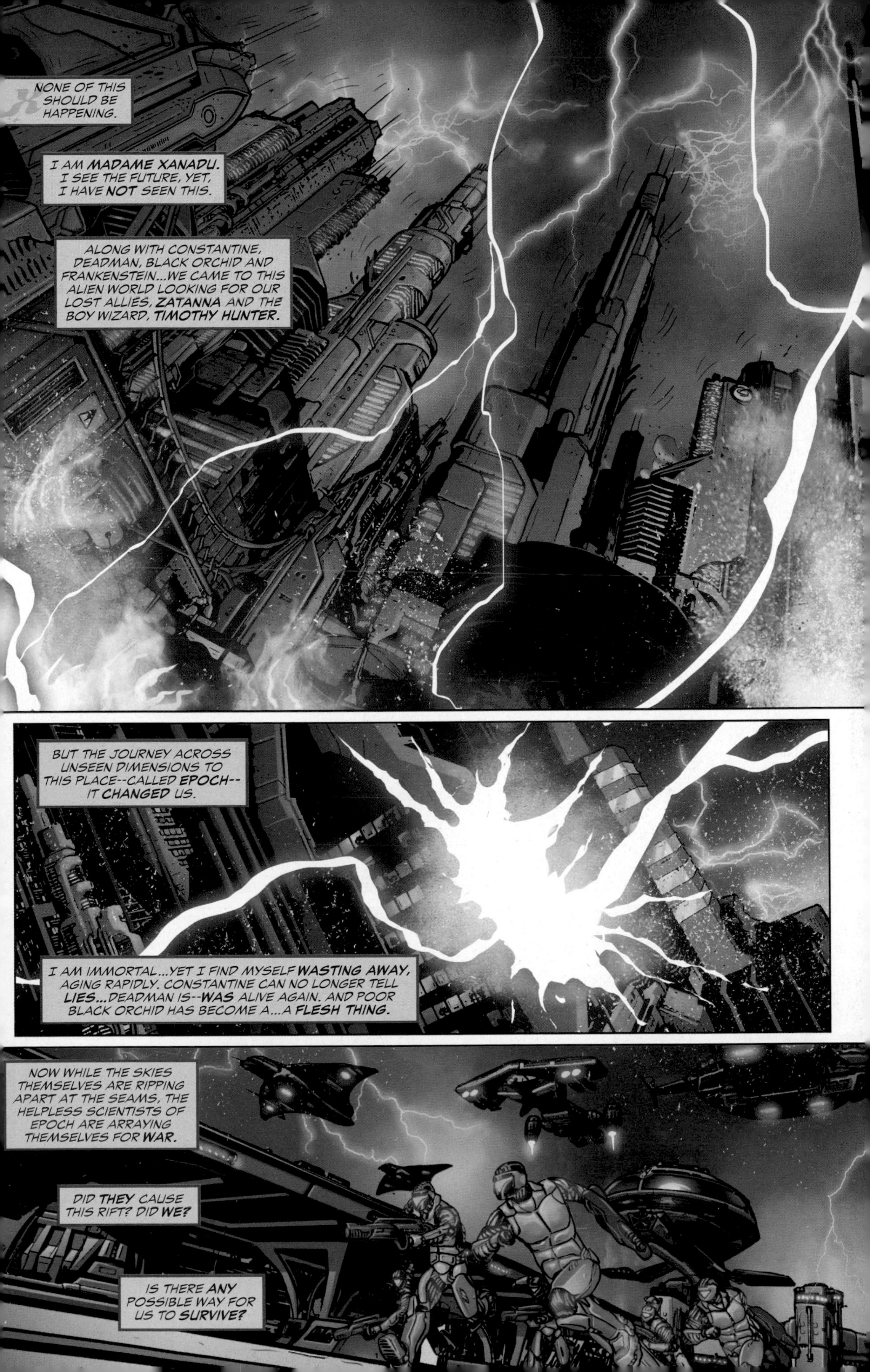
NONE OF THIS SHOULD BE HAPPENING.
I AM MADAME XANADU. I SEE THE FUTURE, YET, I HAVE NOT SEEN THIS.
ALONG WITH CONSTANTINE, DEADMAN, BLACK ORCHID AND FRANKENSTEIN...WE CAME TO THIS ALIEN WORLD LOOKING FOR OUR LOST ALLIES, ZATANNA AND THE BOY WIZARD, TIMOTHY HUNTER.
BUT THE JOURNEY ACROSS UNSEEN DIMENSIONS TO THIS PLACE--CALLED EPOCH--IT CHANGED US.
I AM IMMORTAL...YET I FIND MYSELF WASTING AWAY, AGING RAPIDLY. CONSTANTINE CAN NO LONGER TELL LIES...DEADMAN IS--WAS ALIVE AGAIN. AND POOR BLACK ORCHID HAS BECOME A...A FLESH THING.
NOW WHILE THE SKIES THEMSELVES ARE RIPPING APART AT THE SEAMS, THE HELPLESS SCIENTISTS OF EPOCH ARE ARRAYING THEMSELVES FOR WAR.
DID THEY CAUSE THIS RIFT? DID WE?
IS THERE ANY POSSIBLE WAY FOR US TO SURVIVE?

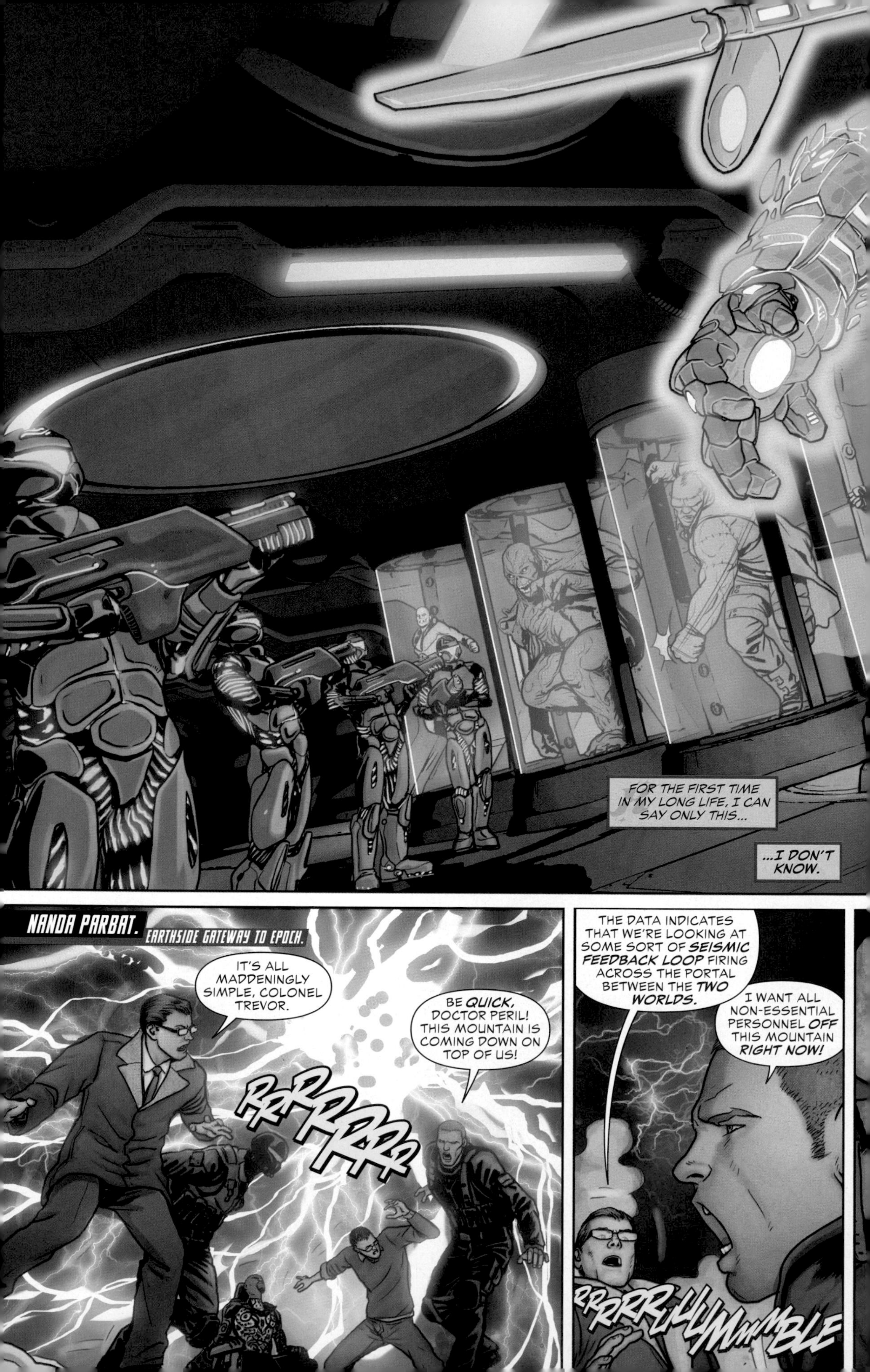

FOR THE FIRST TIME IN MY LONG LIFE, I CAN SAY ONLY THIS...
...I DON'T KNOW.
NANDA PARBAT.
EARTHSIDE GATEWAY TO EPOCH.
IT'S ALL MADDENINGLY SIMPLE, COLONEL TREVOR.
BE QUICK, DOCTOR PERIL! THIS MOUNTAIN IS COMING DOWN ON TOP OF US!
RRRRRRRR
THE DATA INDICATES THAT WE'RE LOOKING AT SOME SORT OF SEISMIC FEEDBACK LOOP FIRING ACROSS THE PORTAL BETWEEN THE TWO WORLDS.
I WANT ALL NON-ESSENTIAL PERSONNEL OFF THIS MOUNTAIN RIGHT NOW!
RRRRRUUMMMMBLE

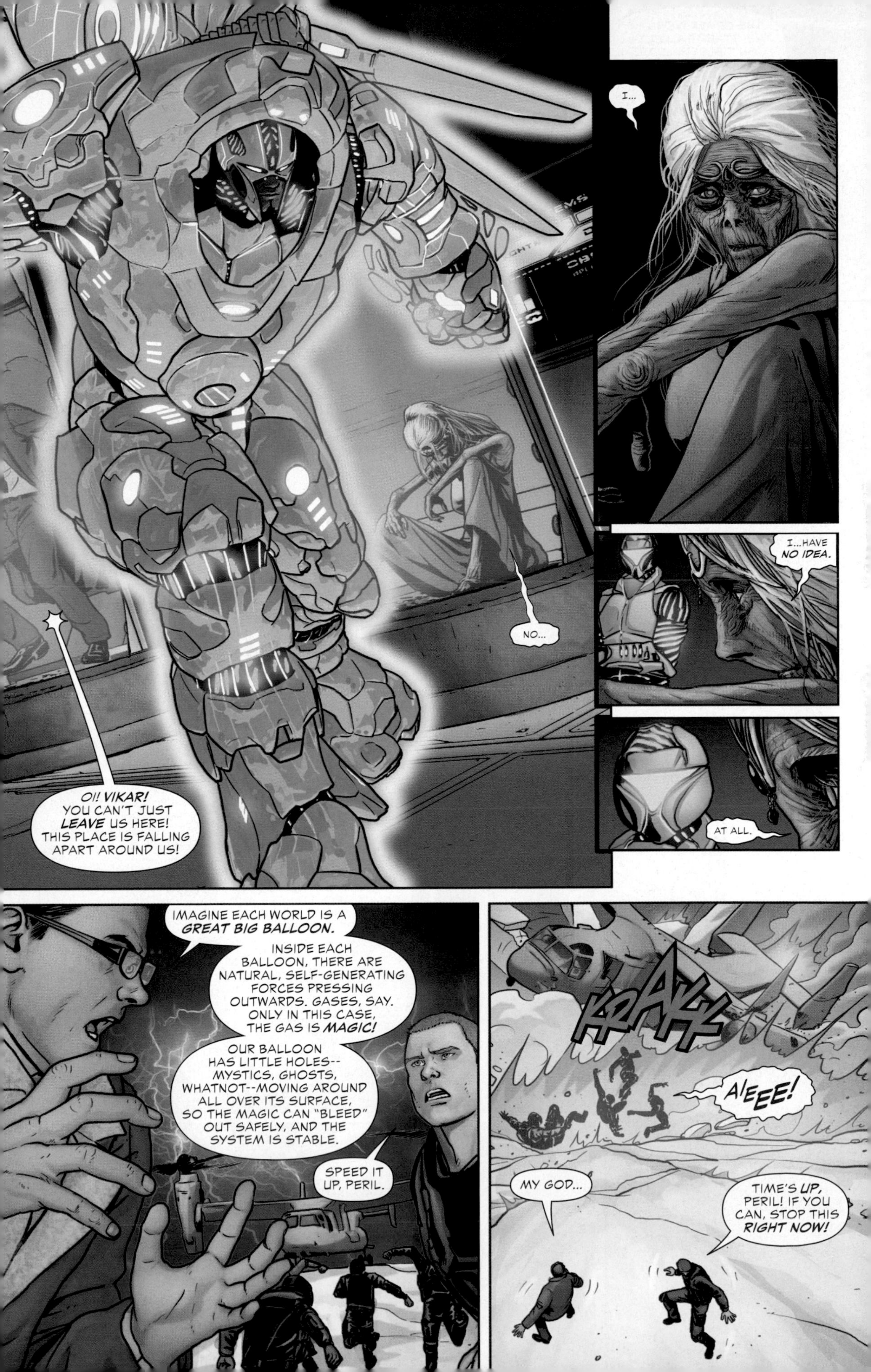
I...
NO...
OI! VIKAR! YOU CAN'T JUST LEAVE US HERE! THIS PLACE IS FALLING APART AROUND US!
I...HAVE NO IDEA.
AT ALL.
IMAGINE EACH WORLD IS A GREAT BIG BALLOON.
INSIDE EACH BALLOON, THERE ARE NATURAL, SELF-GENERATING FORCES PRESSING OUTWARDS. GASES, SAY. ONLY IN THIS CASE, THE GAS IS MAGIC!
OUR BALLOON HAS LITTLE HOLES--MYSTICS, GHOSTS, WHATNOT--MOVING AROUND ALL OVER ITS SURFACE, SO THE MAGIC CAN "BLEED" OUT SAFELY, AND THE SYSTEM IS STABLE.
SPEED IT UP, PERIL.
KRAKK
AIEEE!
MY GOD...
TIME'S UP, PERIL! IF YOU CAN, STOP THIS RIGHT NOW!

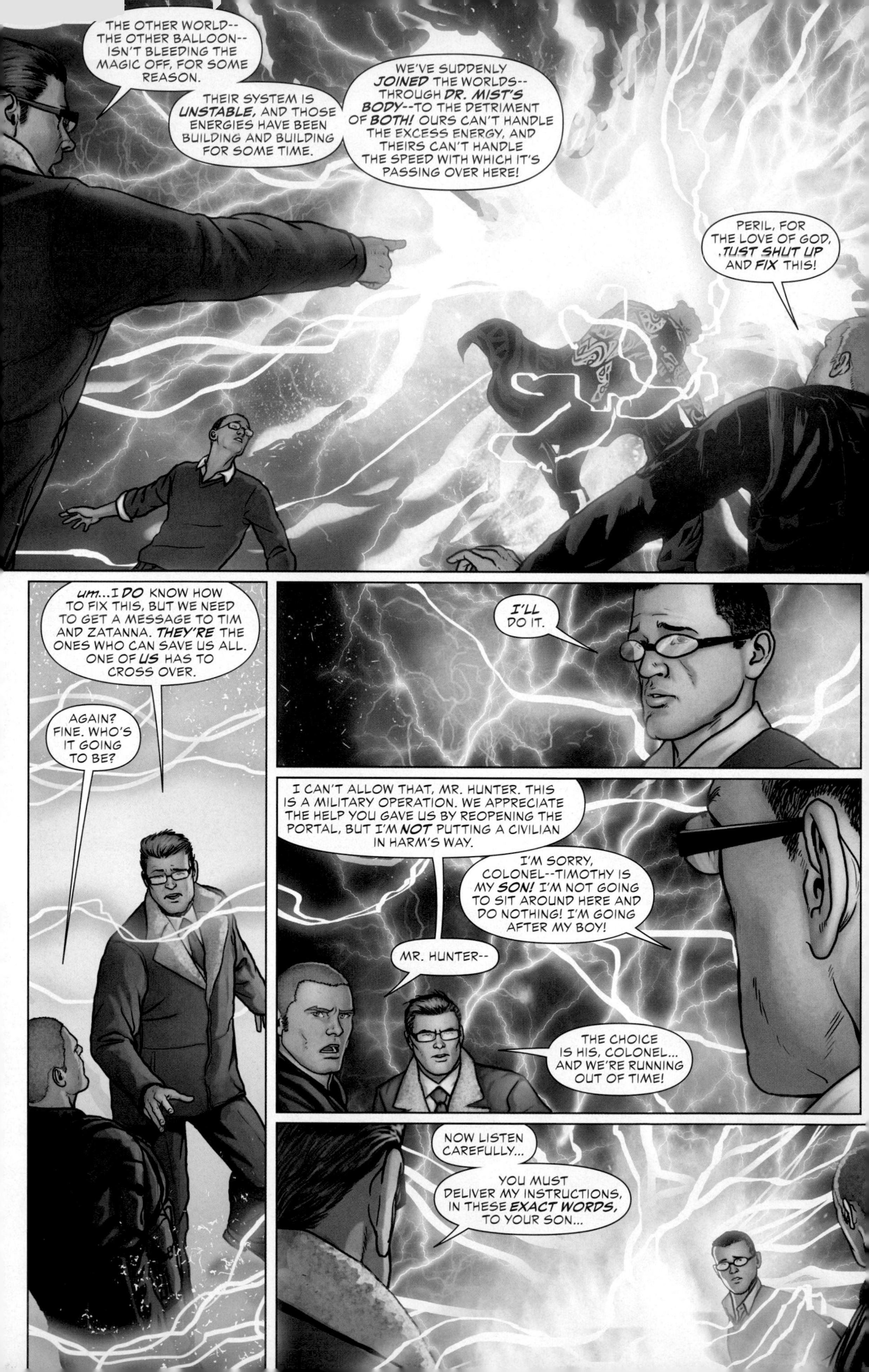
THE OTHER WORLD-- THE OTHER BALLOON-- ISN'T BLEEDING THE MAGIC OFF, FOR SOME REASON.
THEIR SYSTEM IS UNSTABLE, AND THOSE ENERGIES HAVE BEEN BUILDING AND BUILDING FOR SOME TIME.
WE'VE SUDDENLY JOINED THE WORLDS-- THROUGH DR. MIST'S BODY--TO THE DETRIMENT OF BOTH! OURS CAN'T HANDLE THE EXCESS ENERGY, AND THEIRS CAN'T HANDLE THE SPEED WITH WHICH IT'S PASSING OVER HERE!
PERIL, FOR THE LOVE OF GOD, JUST SHUT UP AND FIX THIS!
um...I DO KNOW HOW TO FIX THIS, BUT WE NEED TO GET A MESSAGE TO TIM AND ZATANNA. THEY'RE THE ONES WHO CAN SAVE US ALL. ONE OF US HAS TO CROSS OVER.
AGAIN? FINE. WHO'S IT GOING TO BE?
I'LL DO IT.
I CAN'T ALLOW THAT, MR. HUNTER. THIS IS A MILITARY OPERATION. WE APPRECIATE THE HELP YOU GAVE US BY REOPENING THE PORTAL, BUT I'M NOT PUTTING A CIVILIAN IN HARM'S WAY.
I'M SORRY, COLONEL--TIMOTHY IS MY SON! I'M NOT GOING TO SIT AROUND HERE AND DO NOTHING! I'M GOING AFTER MY BOY!
MR. HUNTER--
THE CHOICE IS HIS, COLONEL... AND WE'RE RUNNING OUT OF TIME!
NOW LISTEN CAREFULLY...
YOU MUST DELIVER MY INSTRUCTIONS, IN THESE EXACT WORDS, TO YOUR SON...

I DON'T GET IT, ZATANNA.

LOOK, TIM. THESE GUYS SAY YOU'RE THEIR LONG-LOST KING...

...BUT IF I NEEDED TO *MANIPULATE* A KID WITH INCREDIBLE POWER--WHO MAYBE FEELS A LITTLE WEIRD OR LONELY OR WHATEVER--I'D TELL HIM HE WAS THE "*CHOSEN ONE*"...

I'M JUST SAYING. DO WHAT YOU THINK IS RIGHT, BUT DON'T GET SUCKED INTO SOMETHING YOU DON'T WANT JUST BECAUSE OF A *STORY*.

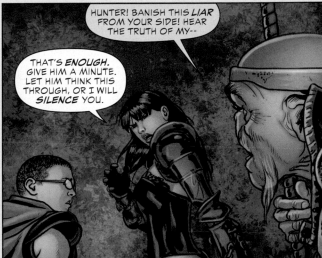

HUNTER! BANISH THIS *LIAR* FROM YOUR SIDE! HEAR THE TRUTH OF MY--

THAT'S *ENOUGH*. GIVE HIM A MINUTE. LET HIM THINK THIS THROUGH, OR I WILL *SILENCE* YOU.

WAIT!

A NETWORK ENFORCER!

NO...

...OUR *SPY*.

THERE'S SOMETHING YOU MUST SEE!

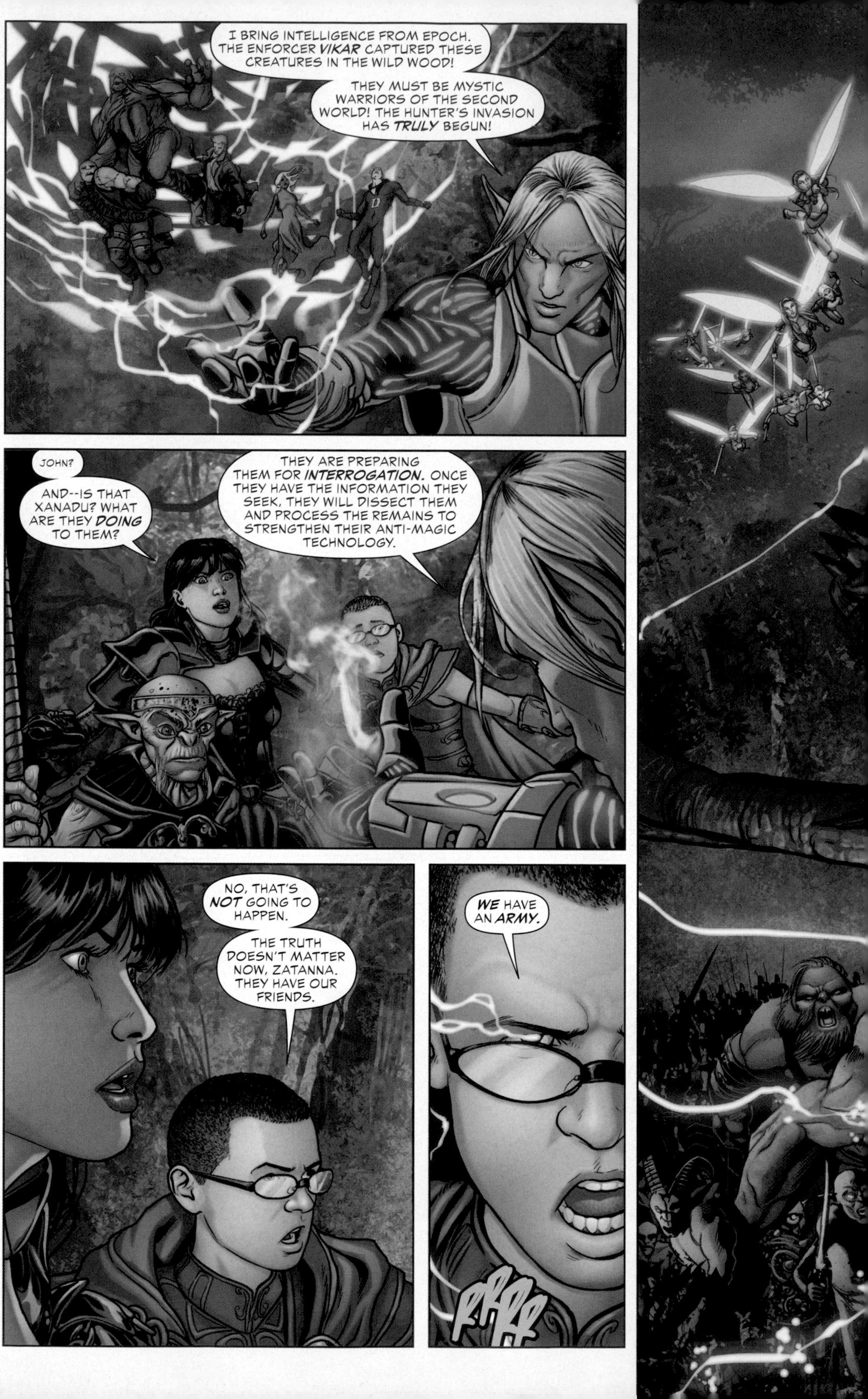
I BRING INTELLIGENCE FROM EPOCH. THE ENFORCER VIKAR CAPTURED THESE CREATURES IN THE WILD WOOD!
THEY MUST BE MYSTIC WARRIORS OF THE SECOND WORLD! THE HUNTER'S INVASION HAS TRULY BEGUN!
JOHN?
AND--IS THAT XANADU? WHAT ARE THEY DOING TO THEM?
THEY ARE PREPARING THEM FOR INTERROGATION. ONCE THEY HAVE THE INFORMATION THEY SEEK, THEY WILL DISSECT THEM AND PROCESS THE REMAINS TO STRENGTHEN THEIR ANTI-MAGIC TECHNOLOGY.
NO, THAT'S NOT GOING TO HAPPEN.
THE TRUTH DOESN'T MATTER NOW, ZATANNA. THEY HAVE OUR FRIENDS.
WE HAVE AN ARMY.
RRRR

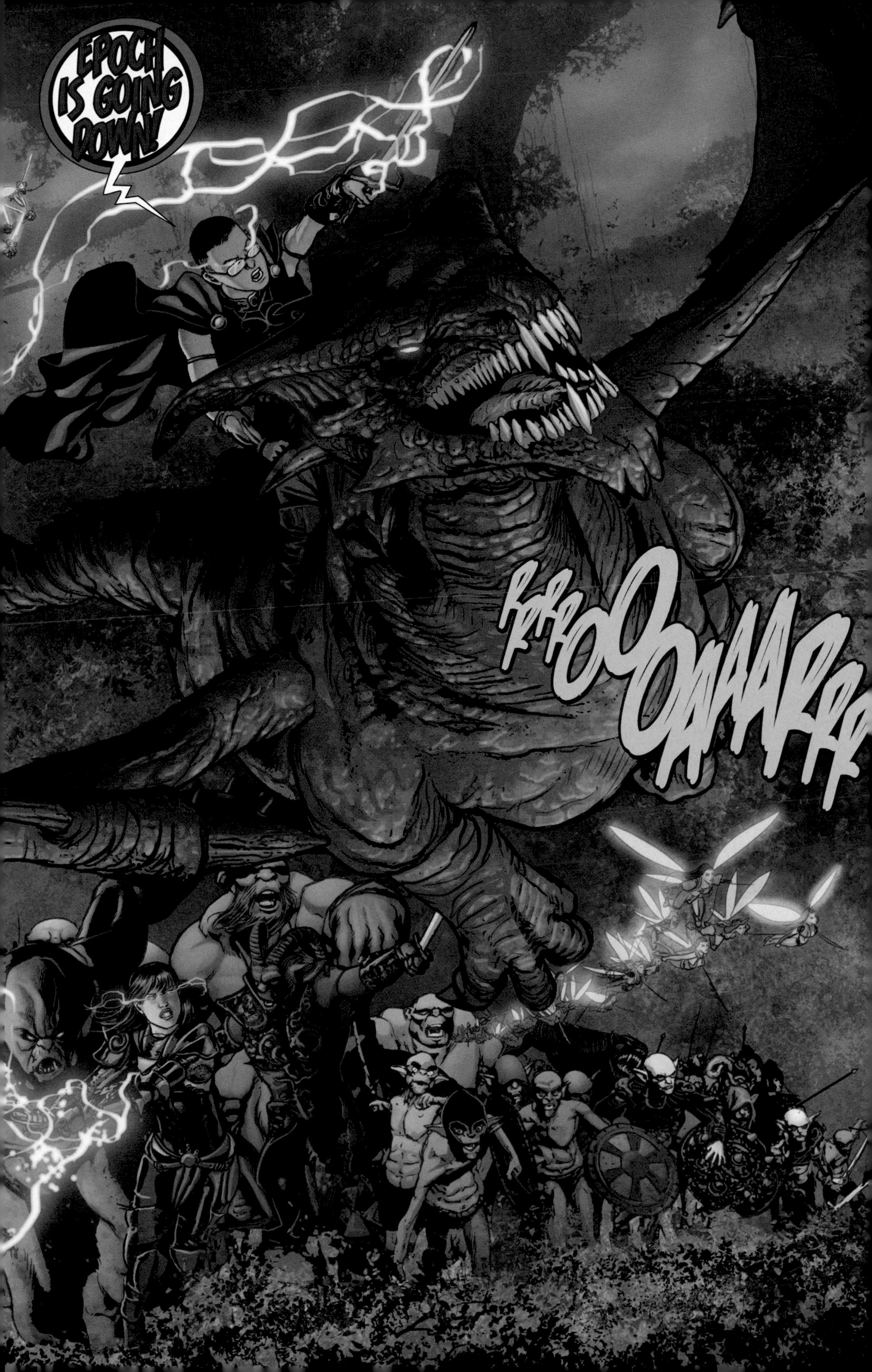
EPOCH IS GOING DOWN!
RRRROOOAAARRR

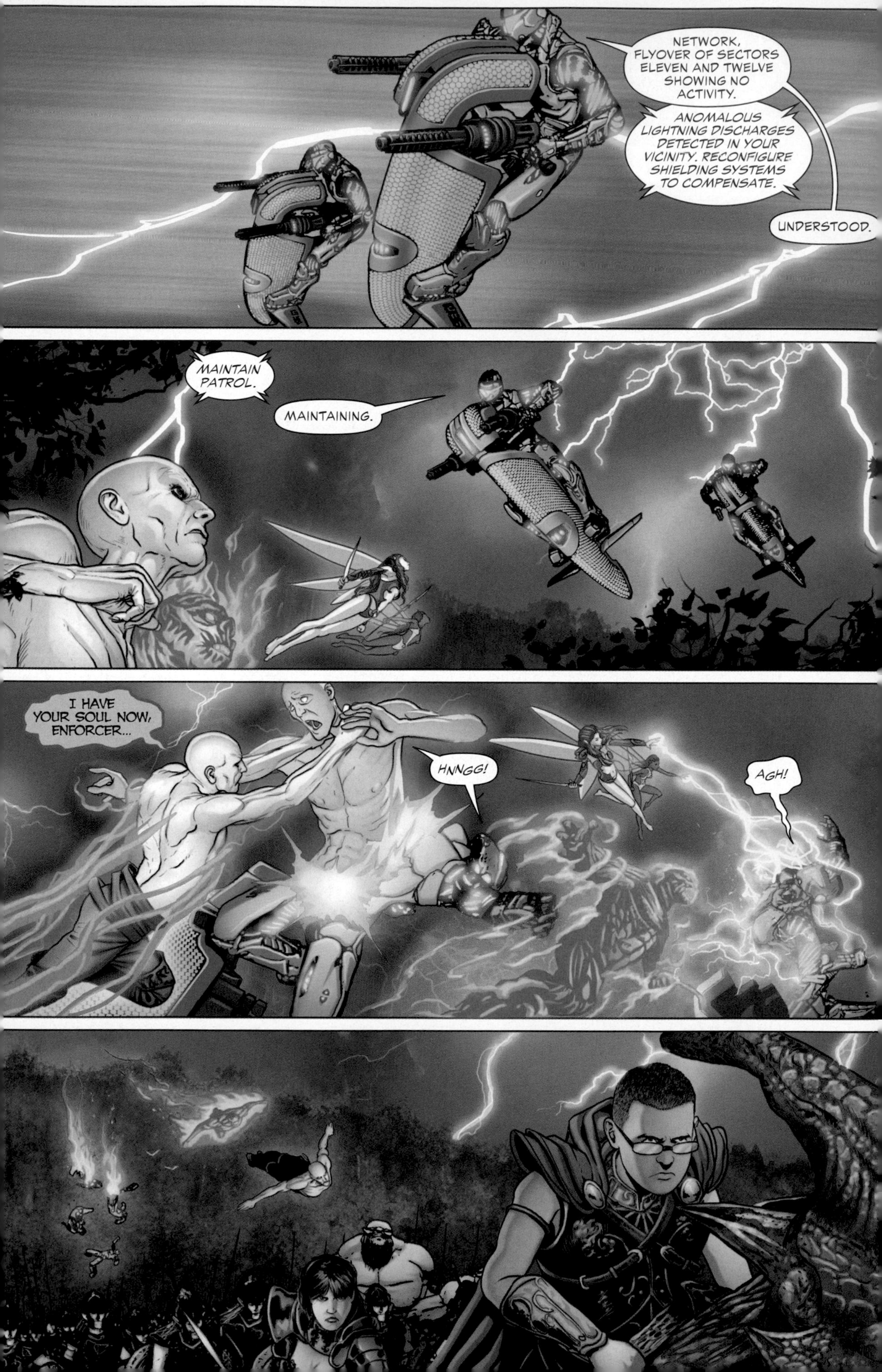
NETWORK, FLYOVER OF SECTORS ELEVEN AND TWELVE SHOWING NO ACTIVITY.
ANOMALOUS LIGHTNING DISCHARGES DETECTED IN YOUR VICINITY. RECONFIGURE SHIELDING SYSTEMS TO COMPENSATE.
UNDERSTOOD.
MAINTAIN PATROL.
MAINTAINING.
I HAVE YOUR SOUL NOW, ENFORCER...
HNNGG!
AGH!

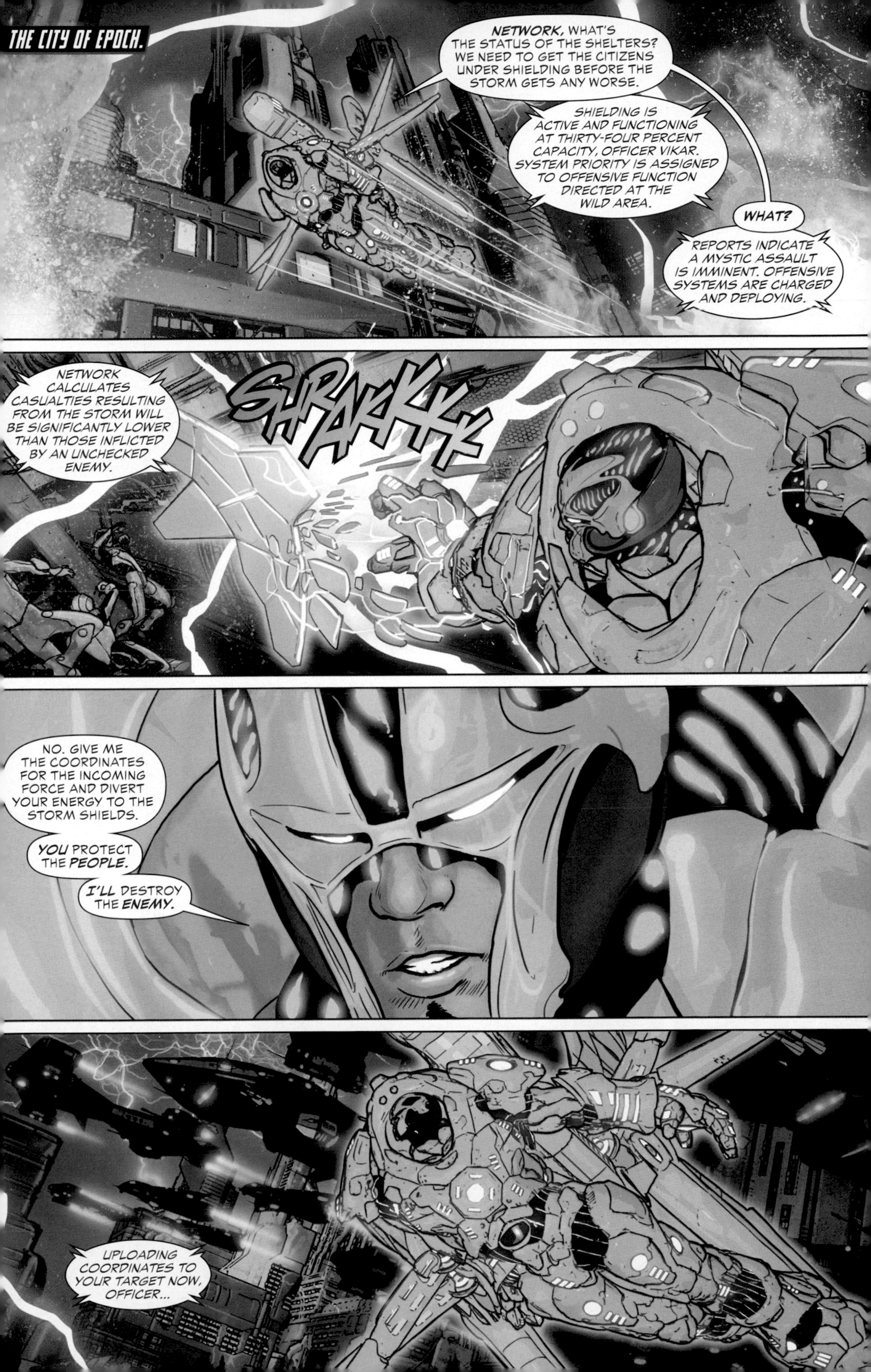
THE CITY OF EPOCH.
NETWORK, WHAT'S THE STATUS OF THE SHELTERS? WE NEED TO GET THE CITIZENS UNDER SHIELDING BEFORE THE STORM GETS ANY WORSE.
SHIELDING IS ACTIVE AND FUNCTIONING AT THIRTY-FOUR PERCENT CAPACITY, OFFICER VIKAR. SYSTEM PRIORITY IS ASSIGNED TO OFFENSIVE FUNCTION DIRECTED AT THE WILD AREA.
WHAT?
REPORTS INDICATE A MYSTIC ASSAULT IS IMMINENT. OFFENSIVE SYSTEMS ARE CHARGED AND DEPLOYING.
NETWORK CALCULATES CASUALTIES RESULTING FROM THE STORM WILL BE SIGNIFICANTLY LOWER THAN THOSE INFLICTED BY AN UNCHECKED ENEMY.
SHRAKKKK
NO. GIVE ME THE COORDINATES FOR THE INCOMING FORCE AND DIVERT YOUR ENERGY TO THE STORM SHIELDS.
YOU PROTECT THE PEOPLE.
I'LL DESTROY THE ENEMY.
UPLOADING COORDINATES TO YOUR TARGET NOW, OFFICER...

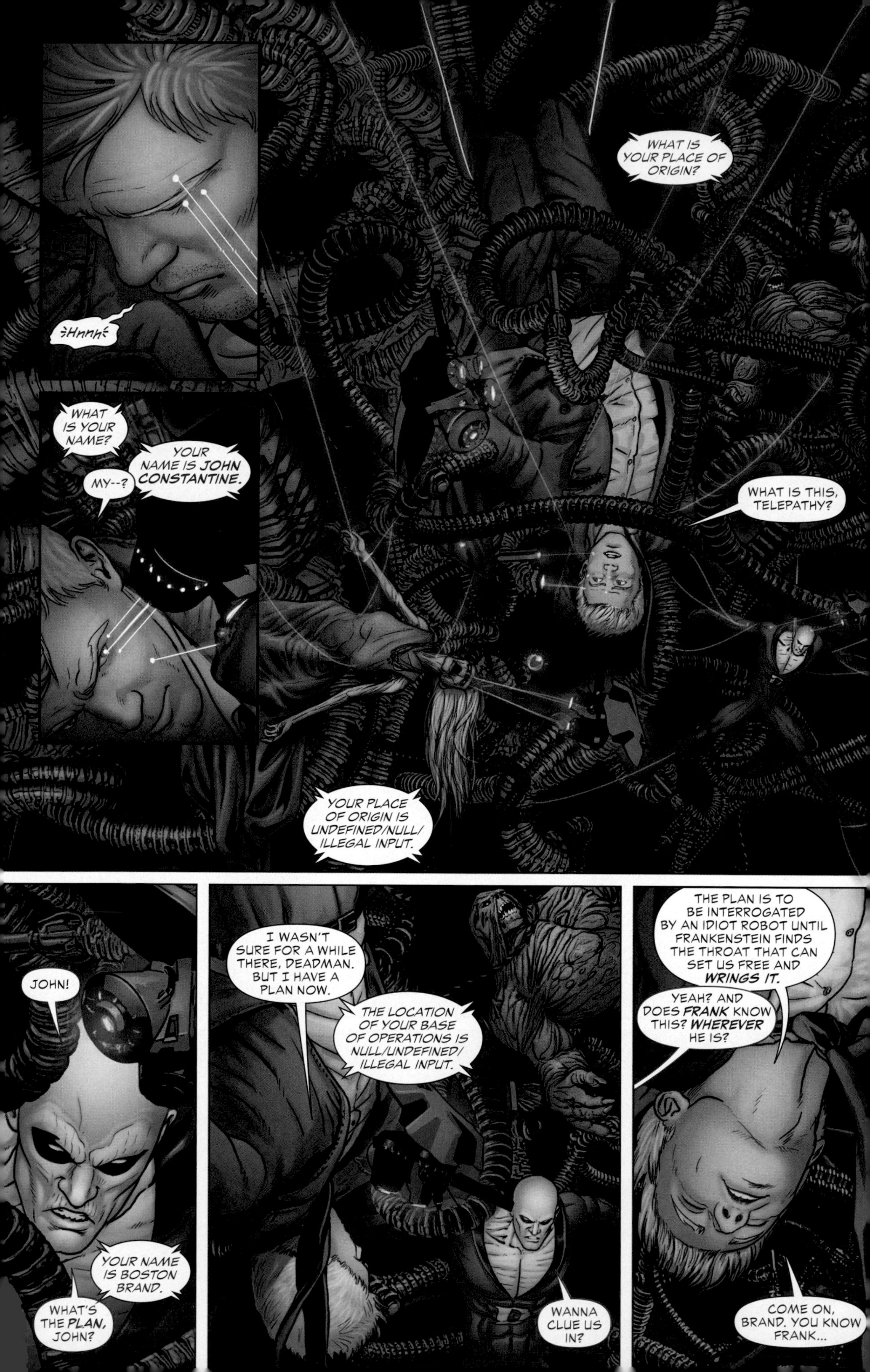

WHAT IS YOUR PLACE OF ORIGIN?
Hnnh
WHAT IS YOUR NAME?
MY--?
YOUR NAME IS JOHN CONSTANTINE.
WHAT IS THIS, TELEPATHY?
YOUR PLACE OF ORIGIN IS UNDEFINED/NULL/ ILLEGAL INPUT.
JOHN!
YOUR NAME IS BOSTON BRAND.
WHAT'S THE PLAN, JOHN?
I WASN'T SURE FOR A WHILE THERE, DEADMAN. BUT I HAVE A PLAN NOW.
THE LOCATION OF YOUR BASE OF OPERATIONS IS NULL/UNDEFINED/ ILLEGAL INPUT.
WANNA CLUE US IN?
THE PLAN IS TO BE INTERROGATED BY AN IDIOT ROBOT UNTIL FRANKENSTEIN FINDS THE THROAT THAT CAN SET US FREE AND WRINGS IT.
YEAH? AND DOES FRANK KNOW THIS? WHEREVER HE IS?
COME ON, BRAND. YOU KNOW FRANK...

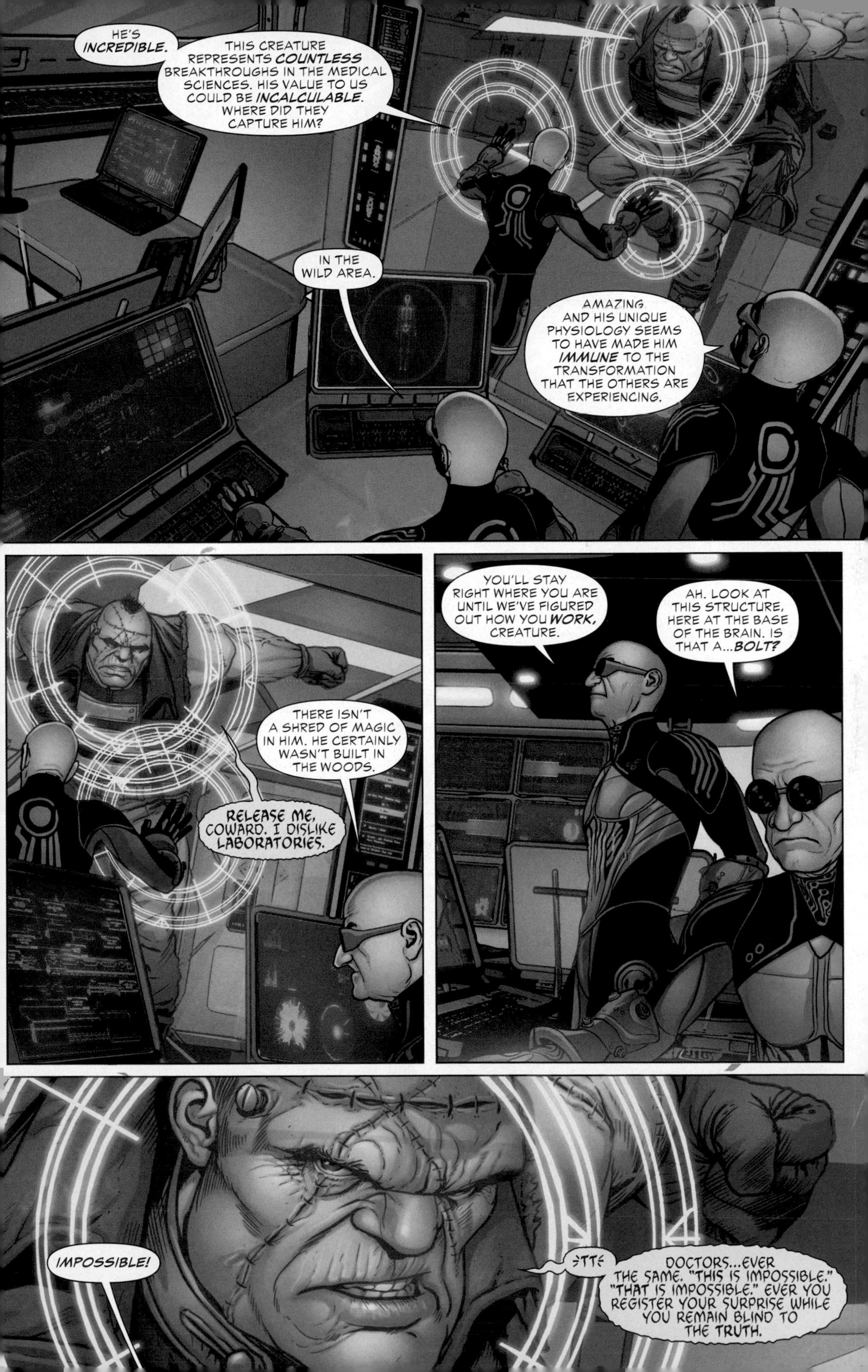
HE'S INCREDIBLE.
THIS CREATURE REPRESENTS COUNTLESS BREAKTHROUGHS IN THE MEDICAL SCIENCES. HIS VALUE TO US COULD BE INCALCULABLE. WHERE DID THEY CAPTURE HIM?
IN THE WILD AREA.
AMAZING AND HIS UNIQUE PHYSIOLOGY SEEMS TO HAVE MADE HIM IMMUNE TO THE TRANSFORMATION THAT THE OTHERS ARE EXPERIENCING.
THERE ISN'T A SHRED OF MAGIC IN HIM. HE CERTAINLY WASN'T BUILT IN THE WOODS.
RELEASE ME, COWARD. I DISLIKE LABORATORIES.
YOU'LL STAY RIGHT WHERE YOU ARE UNTIL WE'VE FIGURED OUT HOW YOU WORK, CREATURE.
AH. LOOK AT THIS STRUCTURE, HERE AT THE BASE OF THE BRAIN. IS THAT A...BOLT?
IMPOSSIBLE!
TT
DOCTORS...EVER THE SAME. "THIS IS IMPOSSIBLE." "THAT IS IMPOSSIBLE." EVER YOU REGISTER YOUR SURPRISE WHILE YOU REMAIN BLIND TO THE TRUTH.

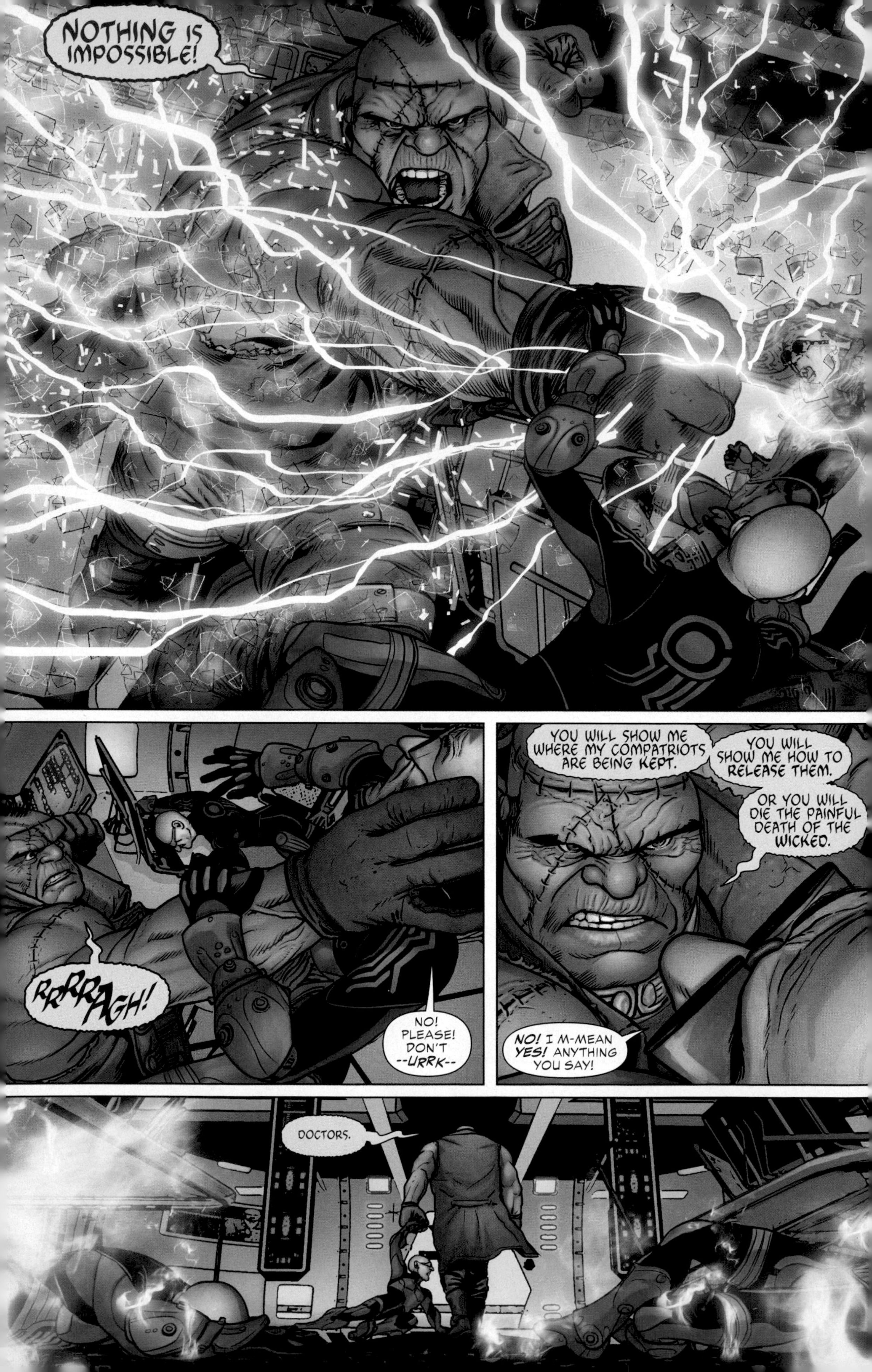
NOTHING IS IMPOSSIBLE!
RRRRAGH!
NO! PLEASE! DON'T --URRK--
YOU WILL SHOW ME WHERE MY COMPATRIOTS ARE BEING KEPT.
YOU WILL SHOW ME HOW TO RELEASE THEM.
OR YOU WILL DIE THE PAINFUL DEATH OF THE WICKED.
NO! I M-MEAN YES! ANYTHING YOU SAY!
DOCTORS.

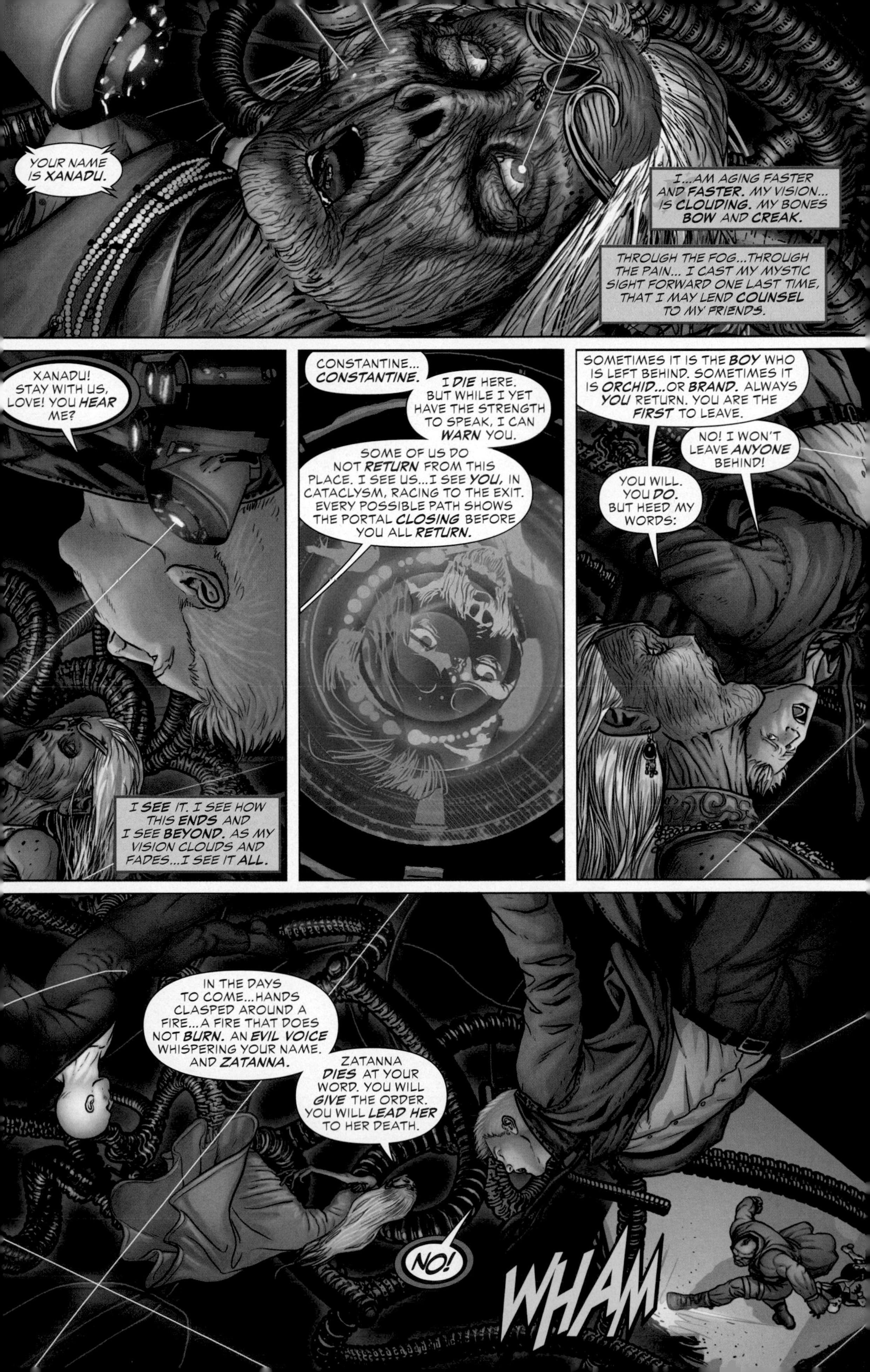
YOUR NAME IS XANADU.
I...AM AGING FASTER AND FASTER. MY VISION... IS CLOUDING. MY BONES BOW AND CREAK.
THROUGH THE FOG...THROUGH THE PAIN... I CAST MY MYSTIC SIGHT FORWARD ONE LAST TIME, THAT I MAY LEND COUNSEL TO MY FRIENDS.
XANADU! STAY WITH US, LOVE! YOU HEAR ME?
I SEE IT. I SEE HOW THIS ENDS AND I SEE BEYOND. AS MY VISION CLOUDS AND FADES...I SEE IT ALL.
CONSTANTINE... CONSTANTINE.
I DIE HERE. BUT WHILE I YET HAVE THE STRENGTH TO SPEAK, I CAN WARN YOU.
SOME OF US DO NOT RETURN FROM THIS PLACE. I SEE US...I SEE YOU, IN CATACLYSM, RACING TO THE EXIT. EVERY POSSIBLE PATH SHOWS THE PORTAL CLOSING BEFORE YOU ALL RETURN.
SOMETIMES IT IS THE BOY WHO IS LEFT BEHIND. SOMETIMES IT IS ORCHID...OR BRAND. ALWAYS YOU RETURN. YOU ARE THE FIRST TO LEAVE.
NO! I WON'T LEAVE ANYONE BEHIND!
YOU WILL. YOU DO. BUT HEED MY WORDS:
IN THE DAYS TO COME...HANDS CLASPED AROUND A FIRE...A FIRE THAT DOES NOT BURN. AN EVIL VOICE WHISPERING YOUR NAME. AND ZATANNA.
ZATANNA DIES AT YOUR WORD. YOU WILL GIVE THE ORDER. YOU WILL LEAD HER TO HER DEATH.
NO!
WHAM

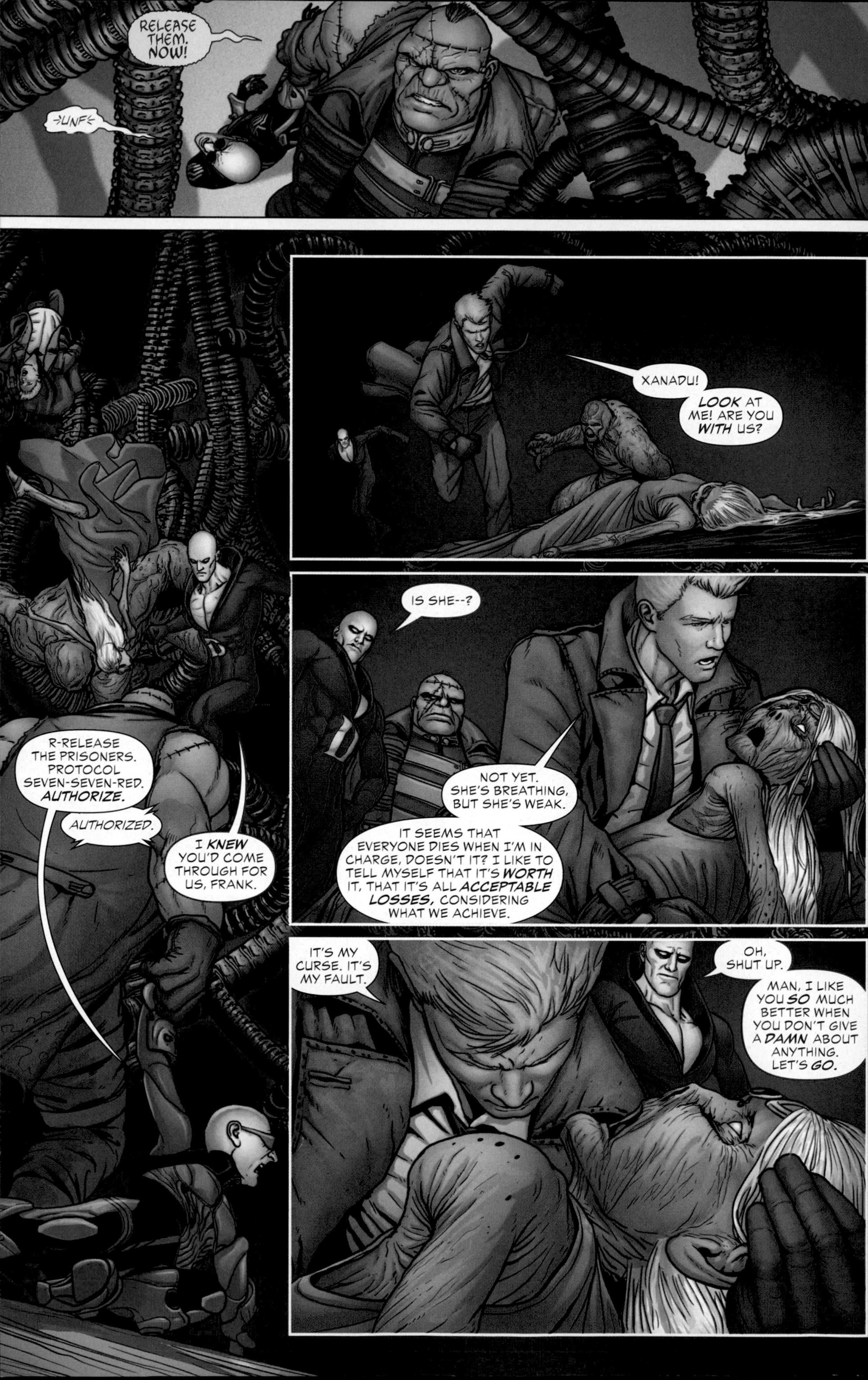
RELEASE THEM. NOW!
UNF
XANADU! LOOK AT ME! ARE YOU WITH US?
IS SHE--?
NOT YET. SHE'S BREATHING, BUT SHE'S WEAK.
IT SEEMS THAT EVERYONE DIES WHEN I'M IN CHARGE, DOESN'T IT? I LIKE TO TELL MYSELF THAT IT'S WORTH IT, THAT IT'S ALL ACCEPTABLE LOSSES, CONSIDERING WHAT WE ACHIEVE.
R-RELEASE THE PRISONERS. PROTOCOL SEVEN-SEVEN-RED. AUTHORIZE.
AUTHORIZED.
I KNEW YOU'D COME THROUGH FOR US, FRANK.
IT'S MY CURSE. IT'S MY FAULT.
OH, SHUT UP.
MAN, I LIKE YOU SO MUCH BETTER WHEN YOU DON'T GIVE A DAMN ABOUT ANYTHING. LET'S GO.

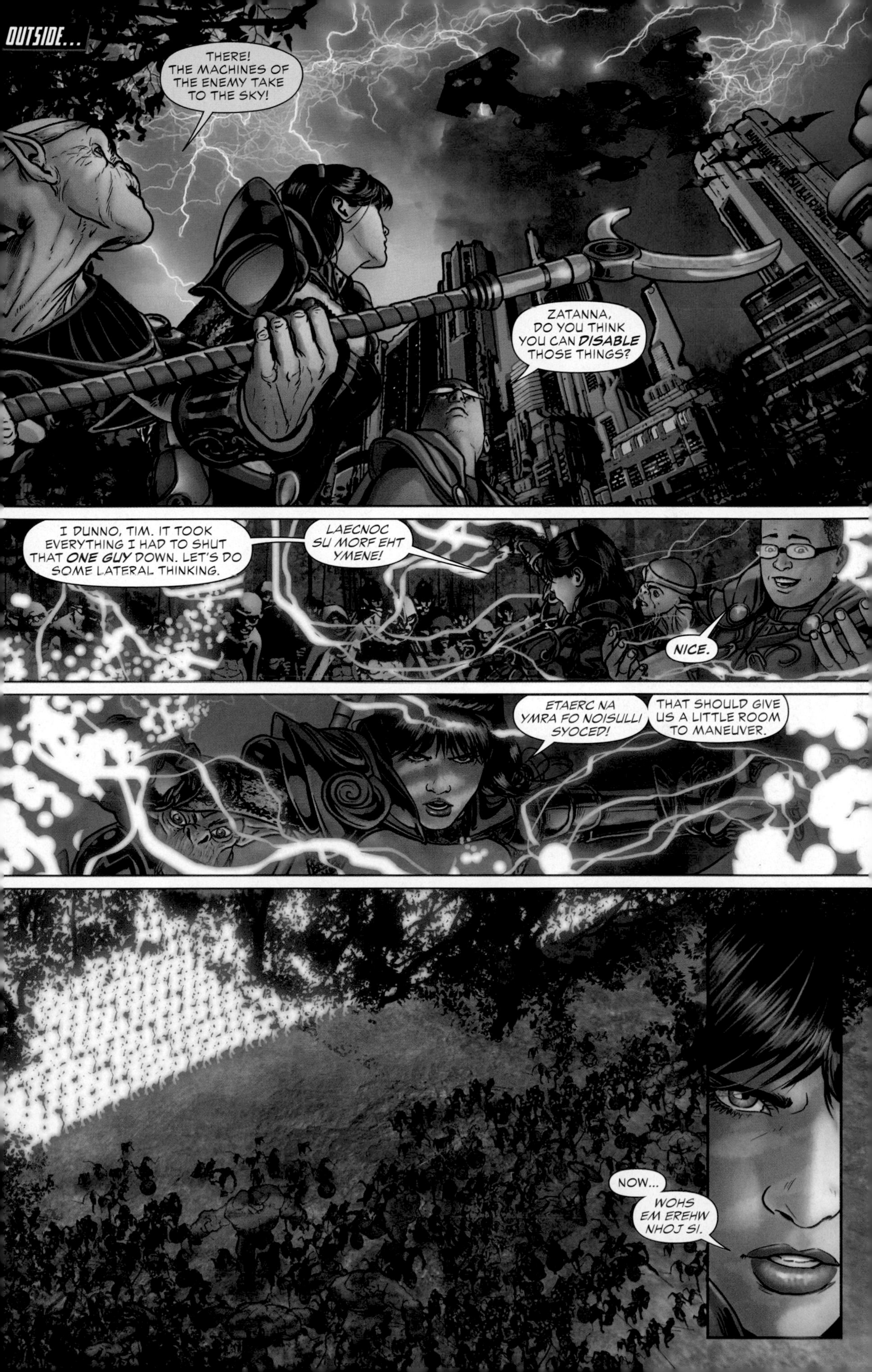
OUTSIDE...
THERE! THE MACHINES OF THE ENEMY TAKE TO THE SKY!
ZATANNA, DO YOU THINK YOU CAN DISABLE THOSE THINGS?
I DUNNO, TIM. IT TOOK EVERYTHING I HAD TO SHUT THAT ONE GUY DOWN. LET'S DO SOME LATERAL THINKING.
LAECNOC SU MORF EHT YMENE!
NICE.
ETAERC NA YMRA FO NOISULLI SYOCED!
THAT SHOULD GIVE US A LITTLE ROOM TO MANEUVER.
NOW...
WOHS EM EREHW NHOJ SI.

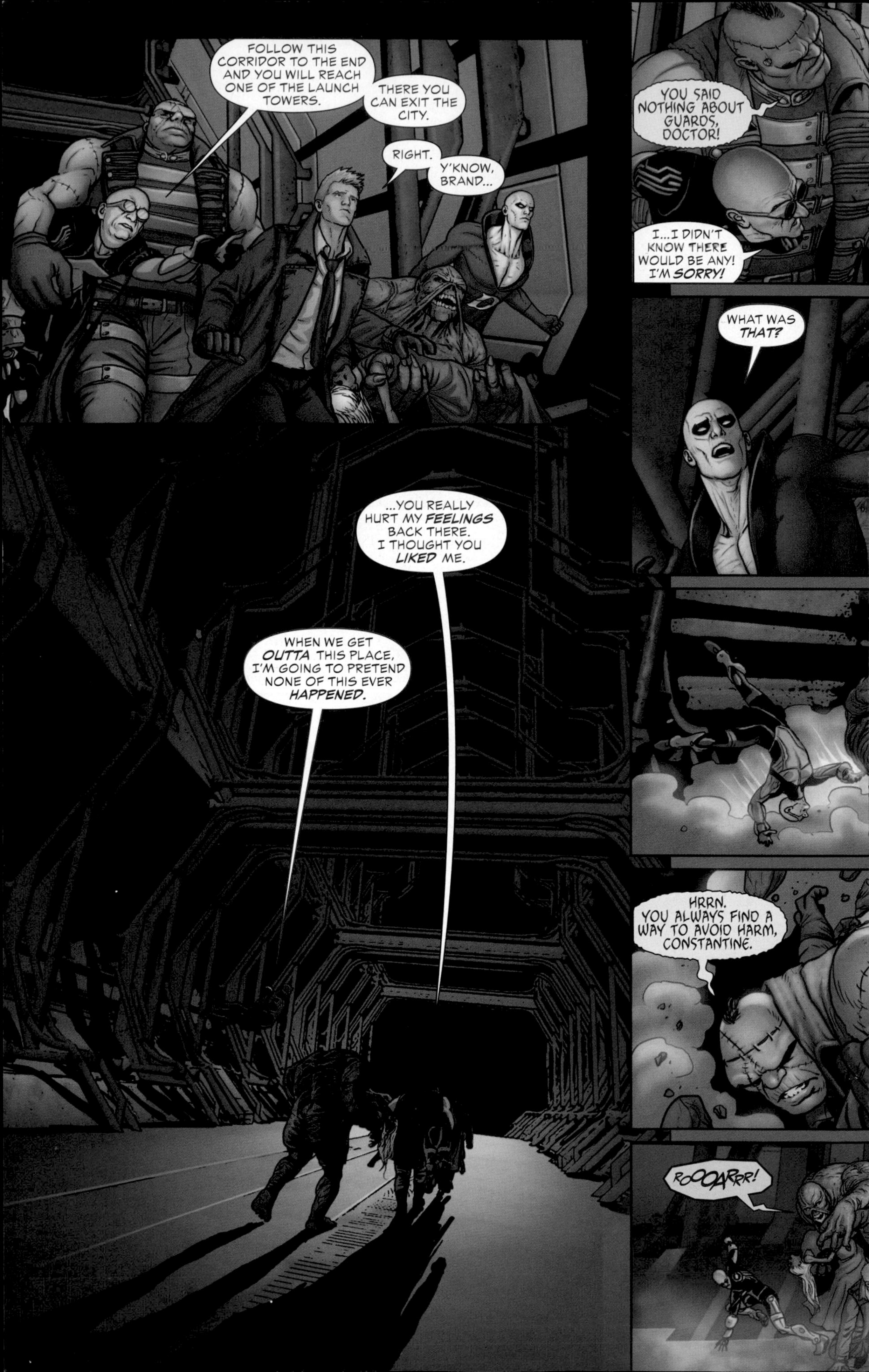
FOLLOW THIS CORRIDOR TO THE END AND YOU WILL REACH ONE OF THE LAUNCH TOWERS.
THERE YOU CAN EXIT THE CITY.
RIGHT.
Y'KNOW, BRAND...
...YOU REALLY HURT MY FEELINGS BACK THERE. I THOUGHT YOU LIKED ME.
WHEN WE GET OUTTA THIS PLACE, I'M GOING TO PRETEND NONE OF THIS EVER HAPPENED.
YOU SAID NOTHING ABOUT GUARDS, DOCTOR!
I...I DIDN'T KNOW THERE WOULD BE ANY! I'M SORRY!
WHAT WAS THAT?
HRRN. YOU ALWAYS FIND A WAY TO AVOID HARM, CONSTANTINE.
ROOOARRR!

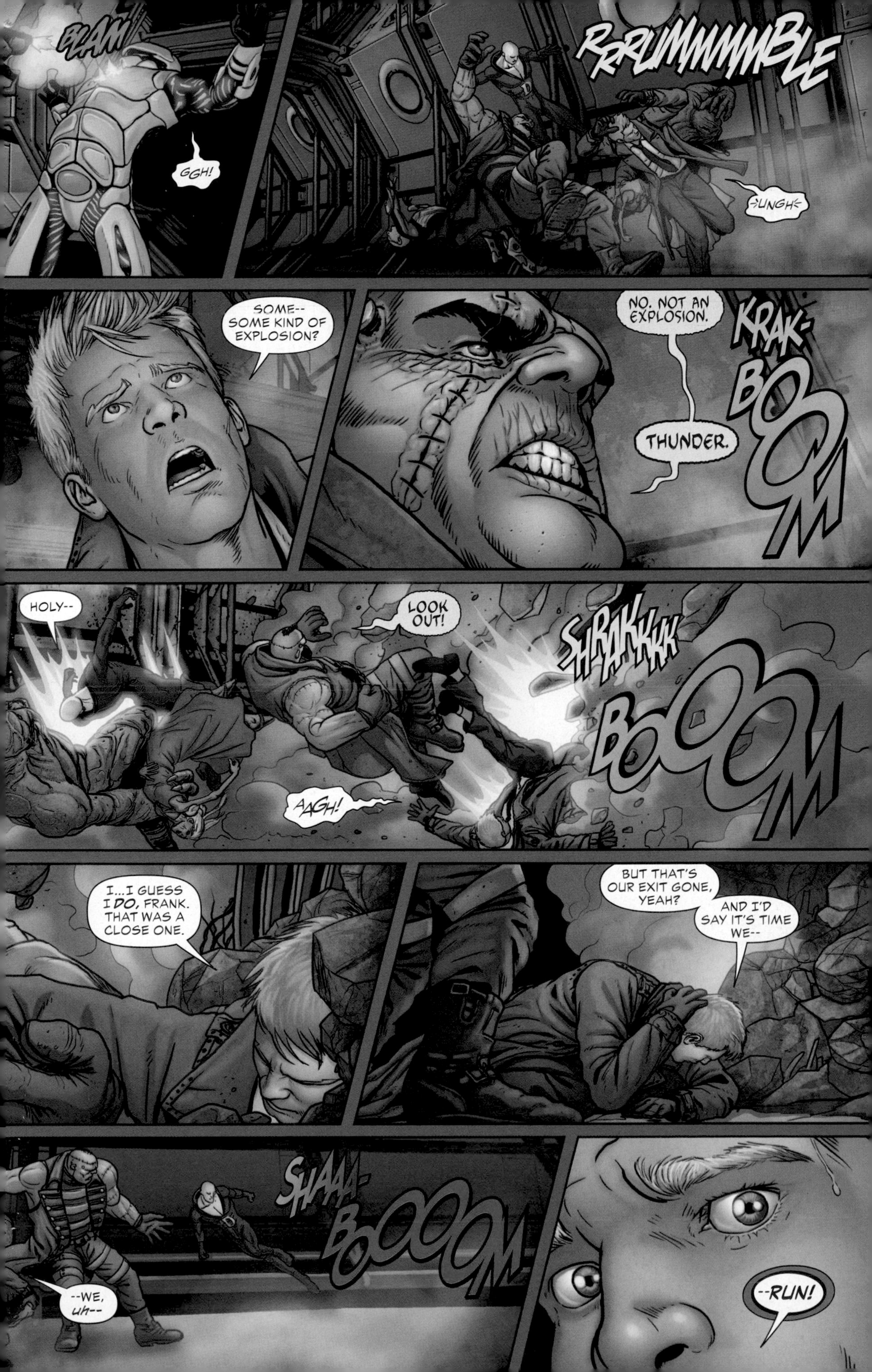
BLAM
GGH!
RRRUMMMMBLE
UNGH
SOME-- SOME KIND OF EXPLOSION?
NO. NOT AN EXPLOSION.
THUNDER.
KRAK-BOOM
HOLY--
LOOK OUT!
SHRAKKKK
BOOOM
AAGH!
I...I GUESS I DO, FRANK. THAT WAS A CLOSE ONE.
BUT THAT'S OUR EXIT GONE, YEAH?
AND I'D SAY IT'S TIME WE--
SHAAA-BOOOOM
--WE, UH--
--RUN!

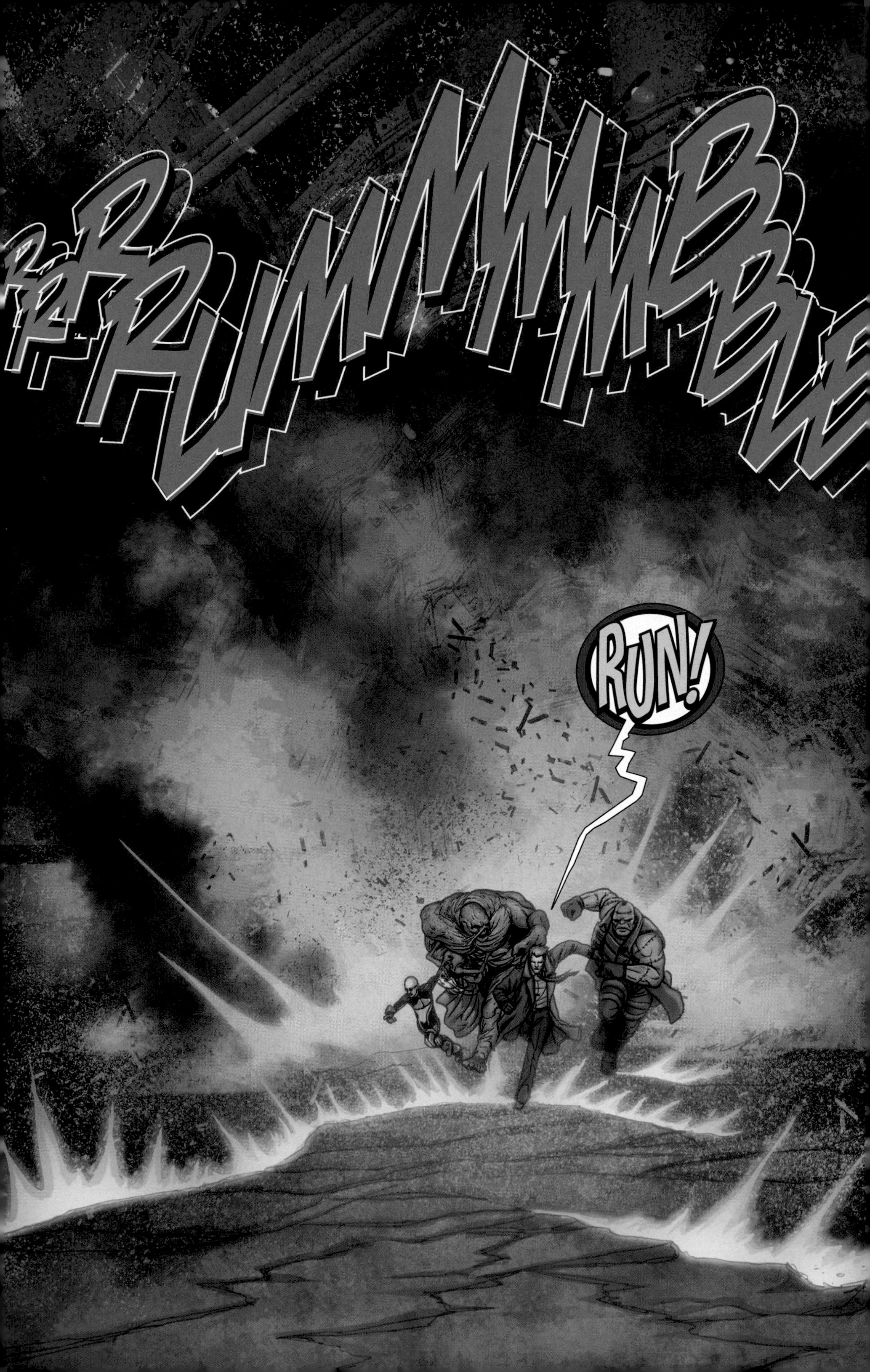
RRRUMMMMBBLE
RUN!

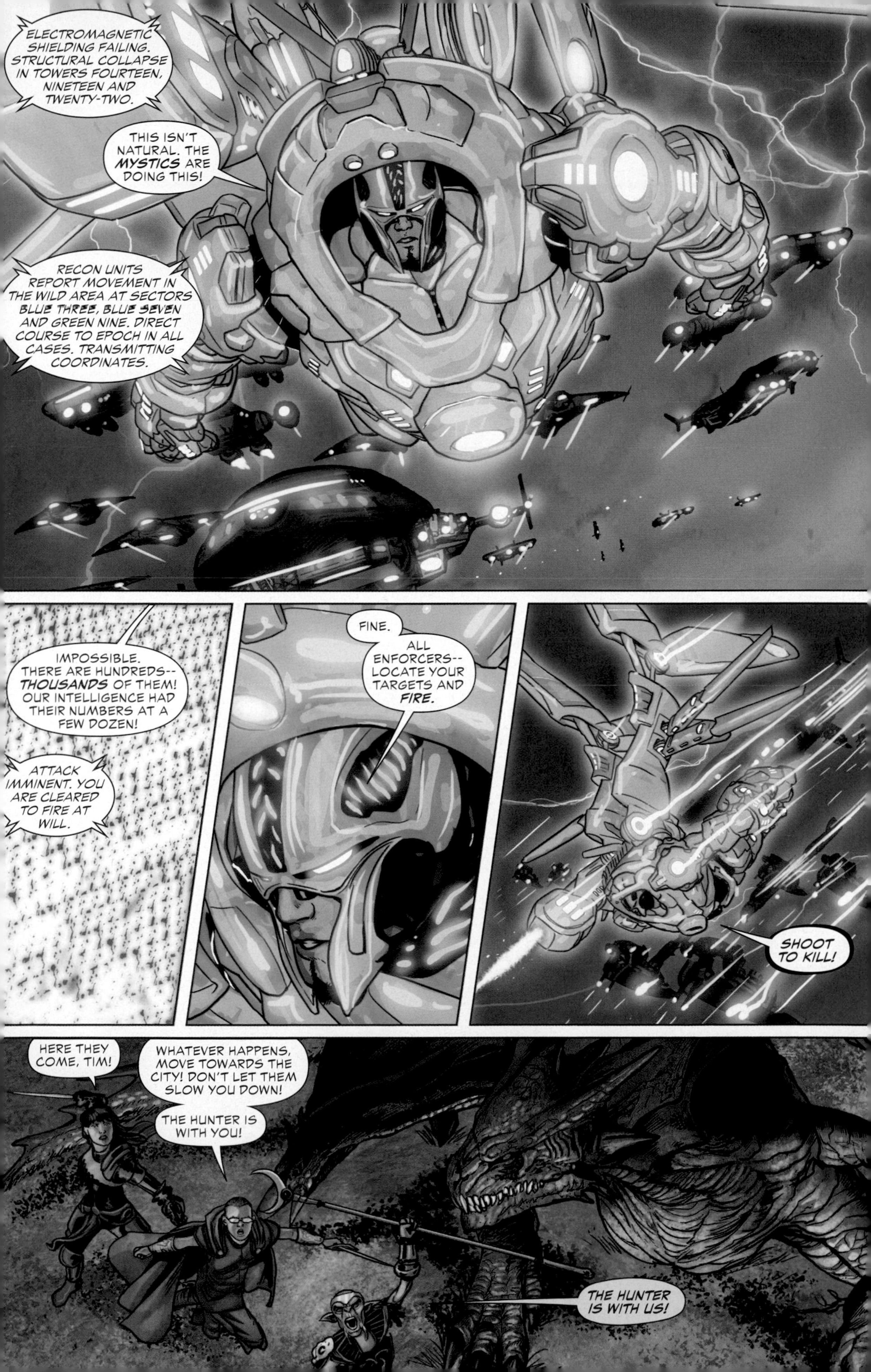
ELECTROMAGNETIC SHIELDING FAILING. STRUCTURAL COLLAPSE IN TOWERS FOURTEEN, NINETEEN AND TWENTY-TWO.
THIS ISN'T NATURAL. THE MYSTICS ARE DOING THIS!
RECON UNITS REPORT MOVEMENT IN THE WILD AREA AT SECTORS BLUE THREE, BLUE SEVEN AND GREEN NINE. DIRECT COURSE TO EPOCH IN ALL CASES. TRANSMITTING COORDINATES.
IMPOSSIBLE. THERE ARE HUNDREDS--THOUSANDS OF THEM! OUR INTELLIGENCE HAD THEIR NUMBERS AT A FEW DOZEN!
ATTACK IMMINENT. YOU ARE CLEARED TO FIRE AT WILL.
FINE.
ALL ENFORCERS--LOCATE YOUR TARGETS AND FIRE.
SHOOT TO KILL!
HERE THEY COME, TIM!
WHATEVER HAPPENS, MOVE TOWARDS THE CITY! DON'T LET THEM SLOW YOU DOWN!
THE HUNTER IS WITH YOU!
THE HUNTER IS WITH US!

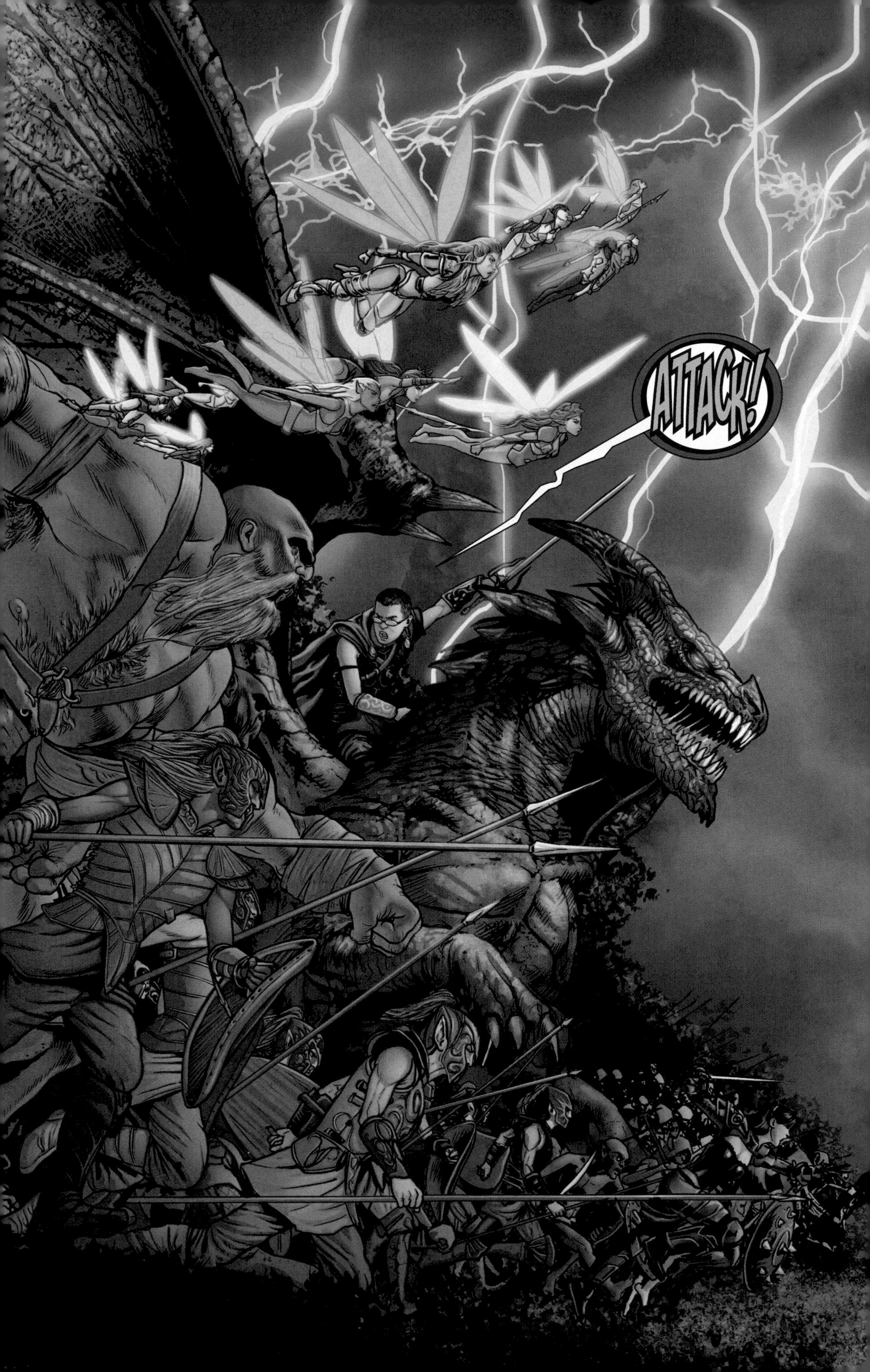
ATTACK!

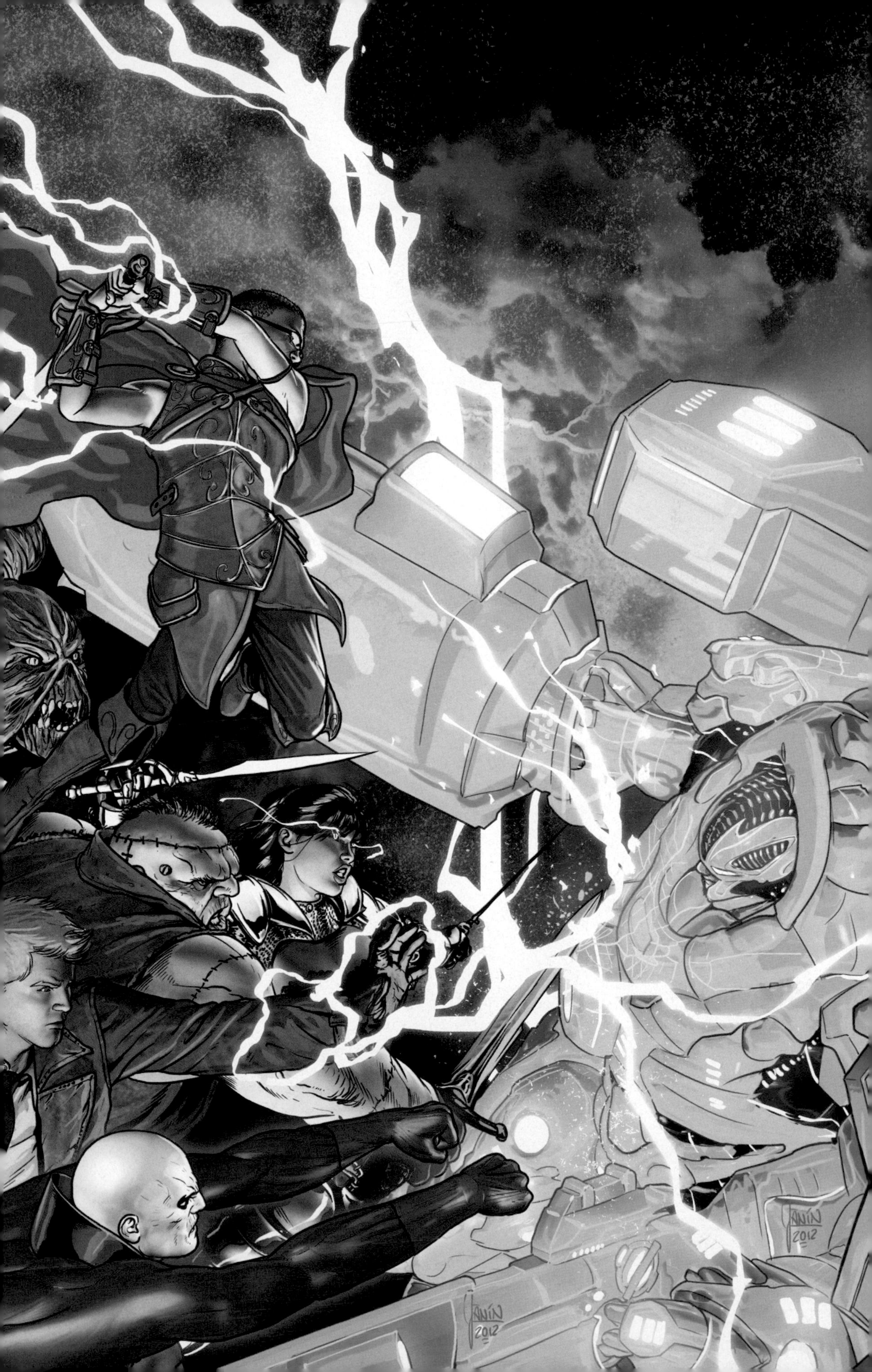
Janín 2012
Janín 2012

THE DEATH OF MAGIC part four
THE LAST STAND

RAY FAWKES
JEFF LEMIRE
writers

MIKEL JANIN
artist

MIKEL JANIN
cover artist

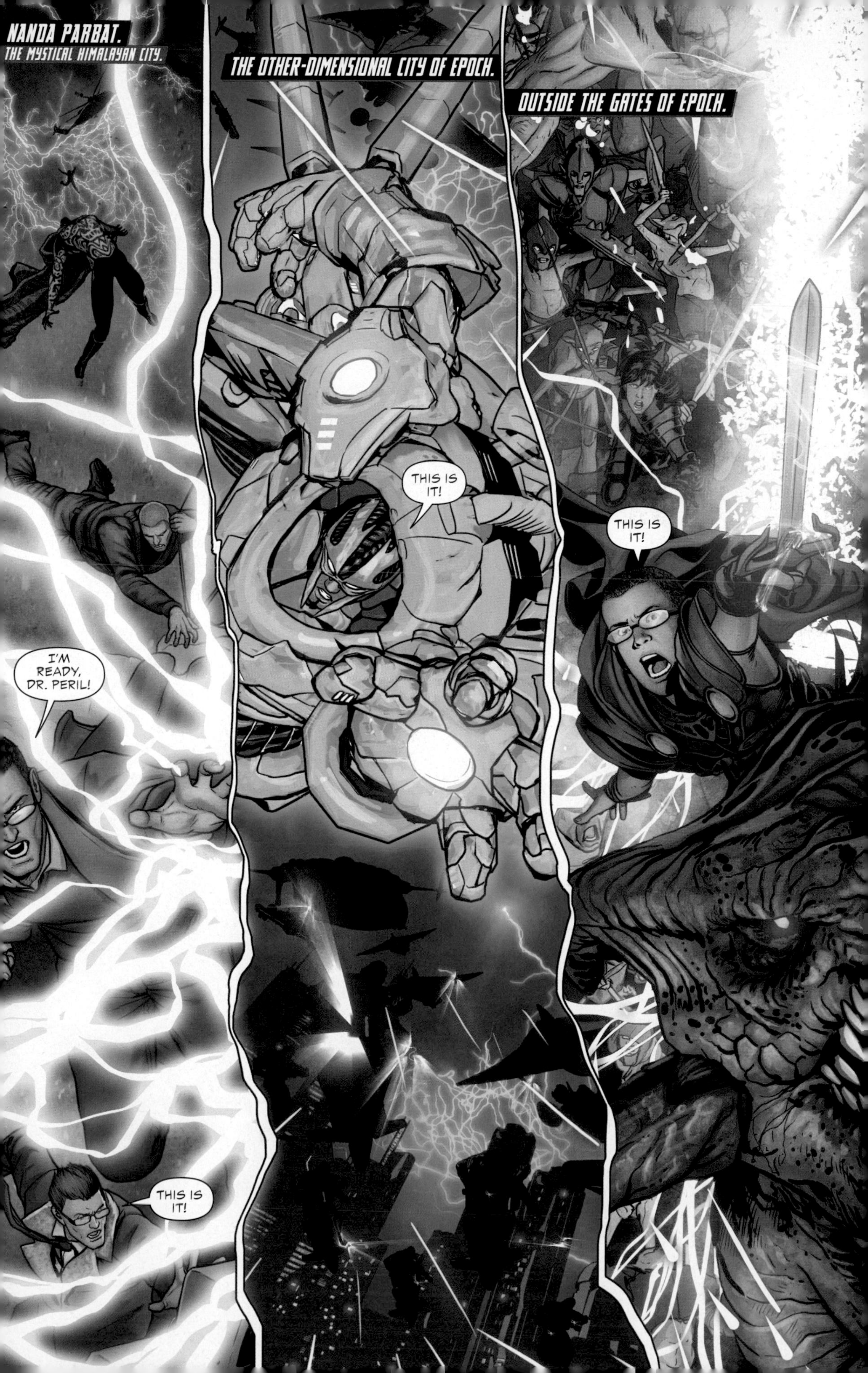
NANDA PARBAT.
THE MYSTICAL HIMALAYAN CITY.
I'M READY, DR. PERIL!
THIS IS IT!
THE OTHER-DIMENSIONAL CITY OF EPOCH.
THIS IS IT!
OUTSIDE THE GATES OF EPOCH.
THIS IS IT!

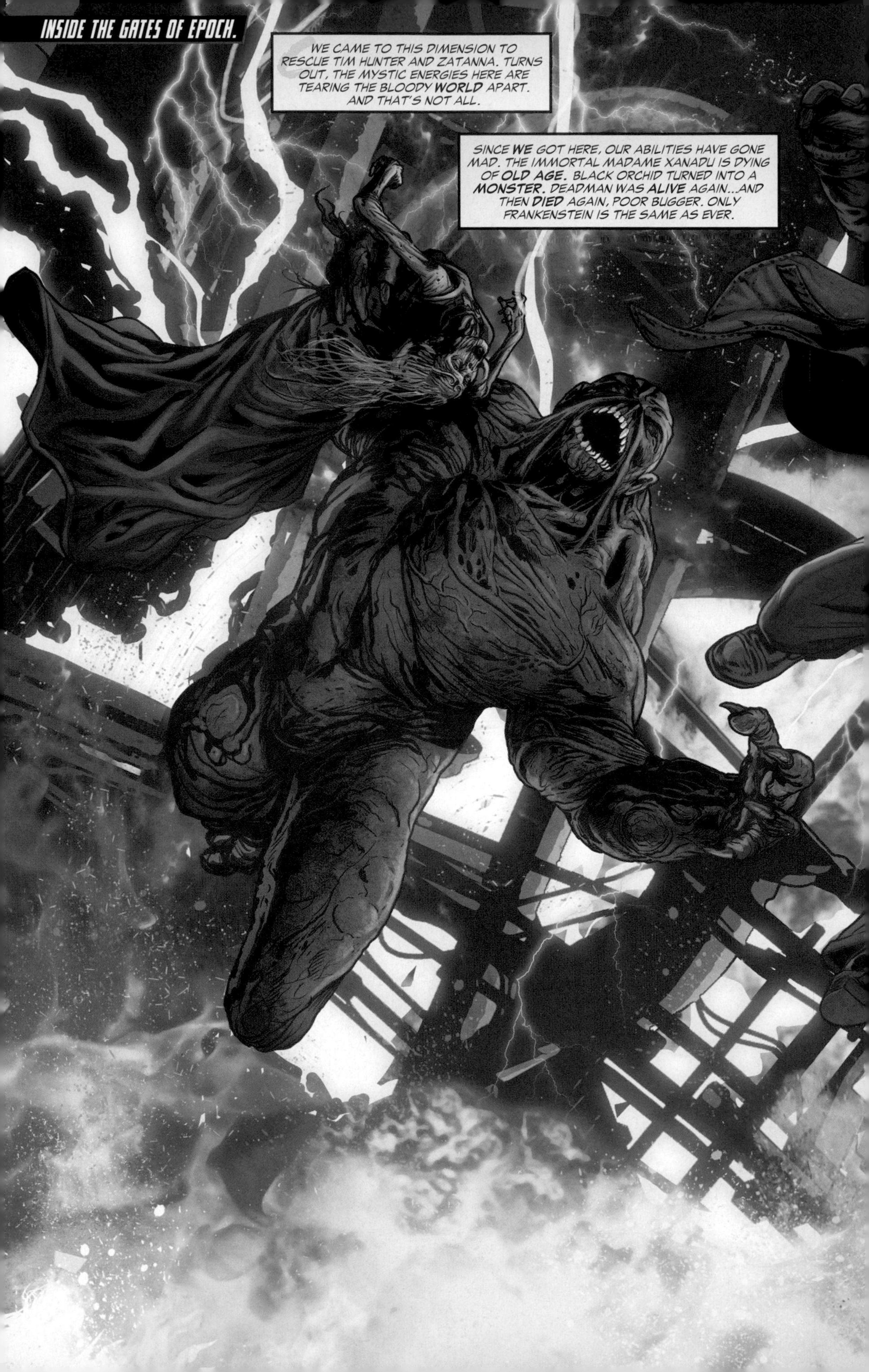
INSIDE THE GATES OF EPOCH.
WE CAME TO THIS DIMENSION TO RESCUE TIM HUNTER AND ZATANNA. TURNS OUT, THE MYSTIC ENERGIES HERE ARE TEARING THE BLOODY WORLD APART. AND THAT'S NOT ALL.
SINCE WE GOT HERE, OUR ABILITIES HAVE GONE MAD. THE IMMORTAL MADAME XANADU IS DYING OF OLD AGE. BLACK ORCHID TURNED INTO A MONSTER. DEADMAN WAS ALIVE AGAIN...AND THEN DIED AGAIN, POOR BUGGER. ONLY FRANKENSTEIN IS THE SAME AS EVER.

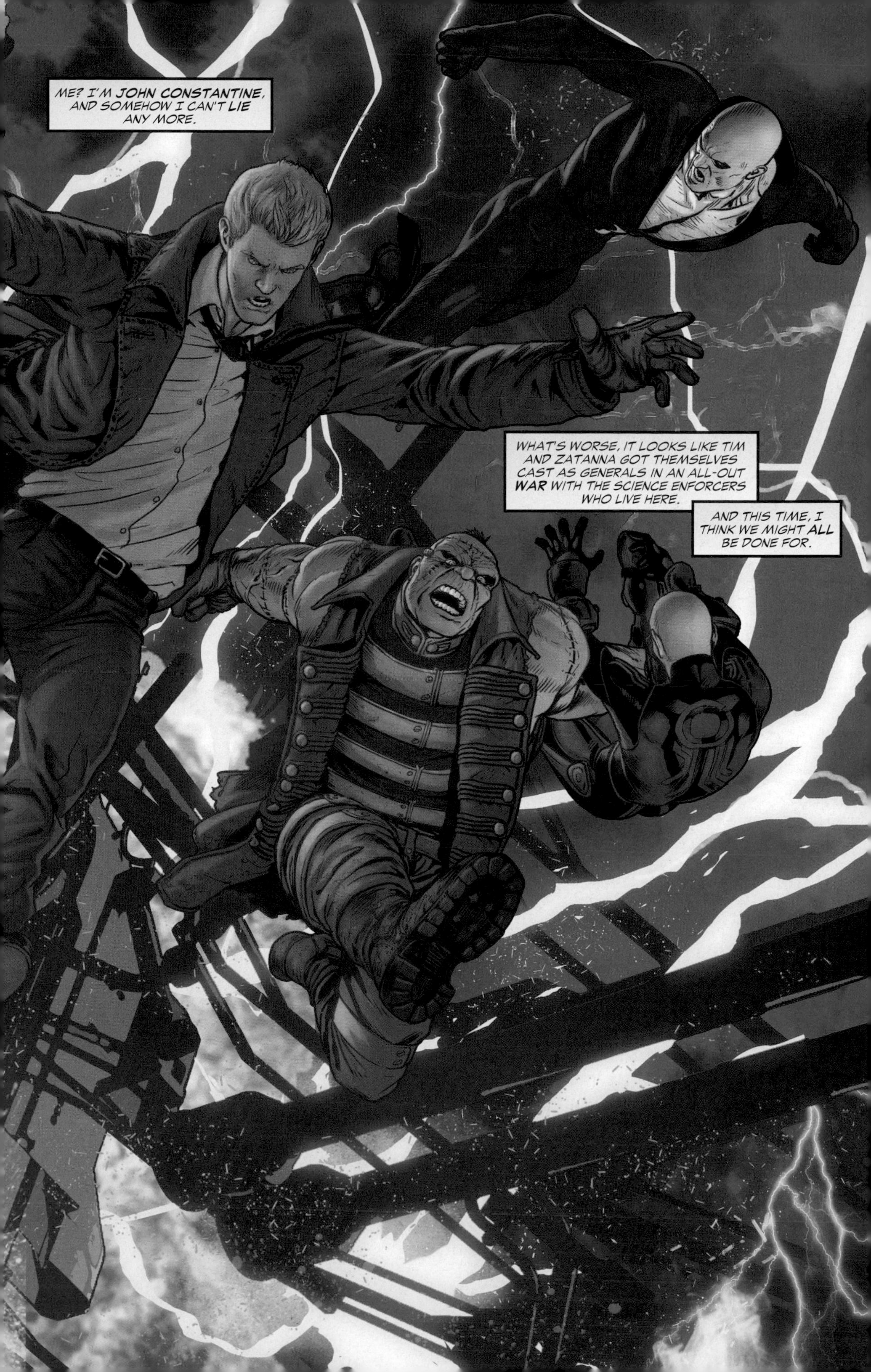
ME? I'M JOHN CONSTANTINE, AND SOMEHOW I CAN'T LIE ANY MORE.
WHAT'S WORSE, IT LOOKS LIKE TIM AND ZATANNA GOT THEMSELVES CAST AS GENERALS IN AN ALL-OUT WAR WITH THE SCIENCE ENFORCERS WHO LIVE HERE.
AND THIS TIME, I THINK WE MIGHT ALL BE DONE FOR.

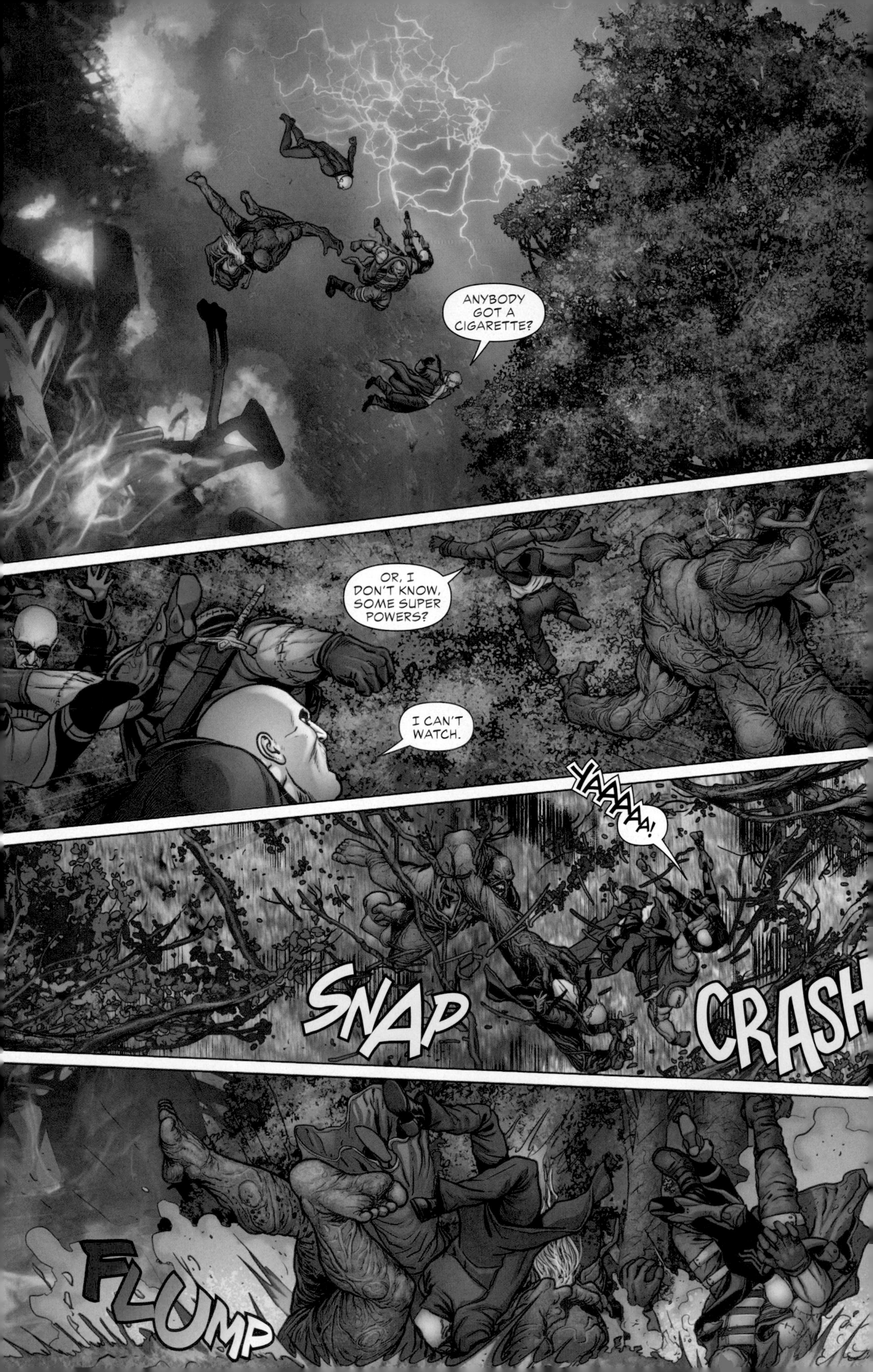
ANYBODY GOT A CIGARETTE?
OR, I DON'T KNOW, SOME SUPER POWERS?
I CAN'T WATCH.
YAAAAAA!
SNAP
CRASH
FLUMP

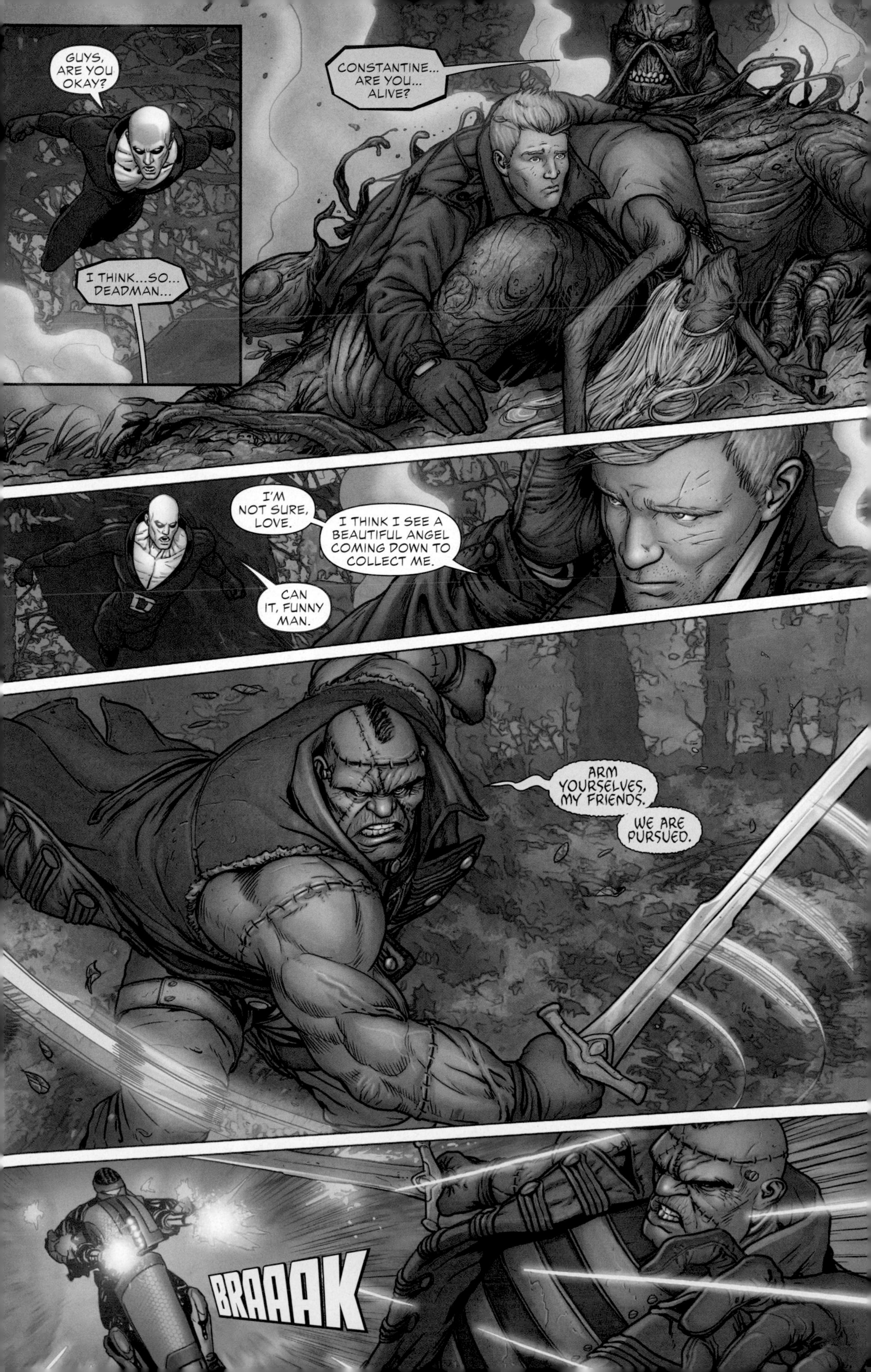
GUYS, ARE YOU OKAY?
CONSTANTINE... ARE YOU... ALIVE?
I THINK...SO... DEADMAN...
I'M NOT SURE, LOVE.
I THINK I SEE A BEAUTIFUL ANGEL COMING DOWN TO COLLECT ME.
CAN IT, FUNNY MAN.
ARM YOURSELVES, MY FRIENDS.
WE ARE PURSUED.
BRAAAK

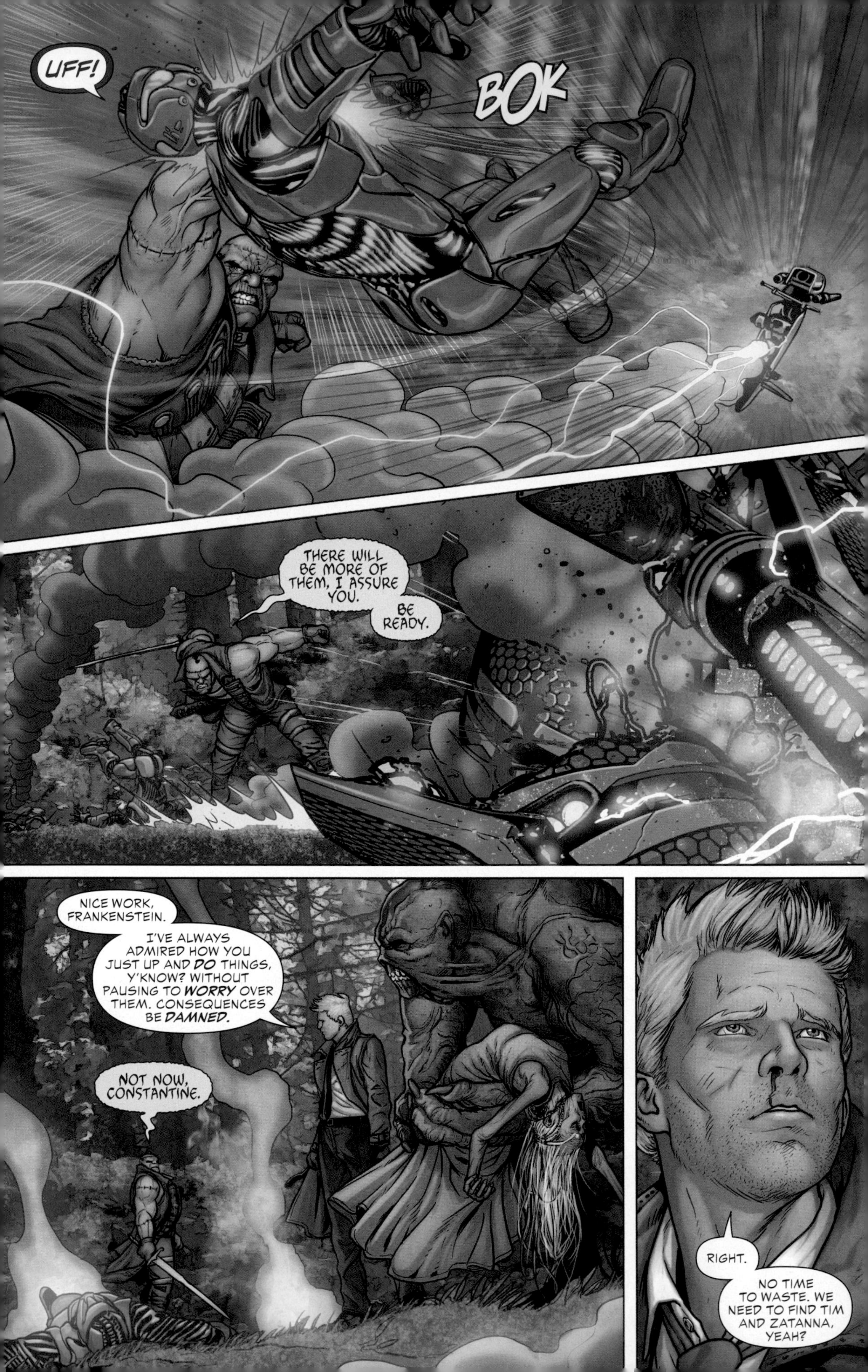
UFF!
BOK
THERE WILL BE MORE OF THEM, I ASSURE YOU.
BE READY.
NICE WORK, FRANKENSTEIN.
I'VE ALWAYS ADMIRED HOW YOU JUST UP AND *DO* THINGS, Y'KNOW? WITHOUT PAUSING TO *WORRY* OVER THEM. CONSEQUENCES BE *DAMNED.*
NOT NOW, CONSTANTINE.
RIGHT.
NO TIME TO WASTE. WE NEED TO FIND TIM AND ZATANNA, YEAH?

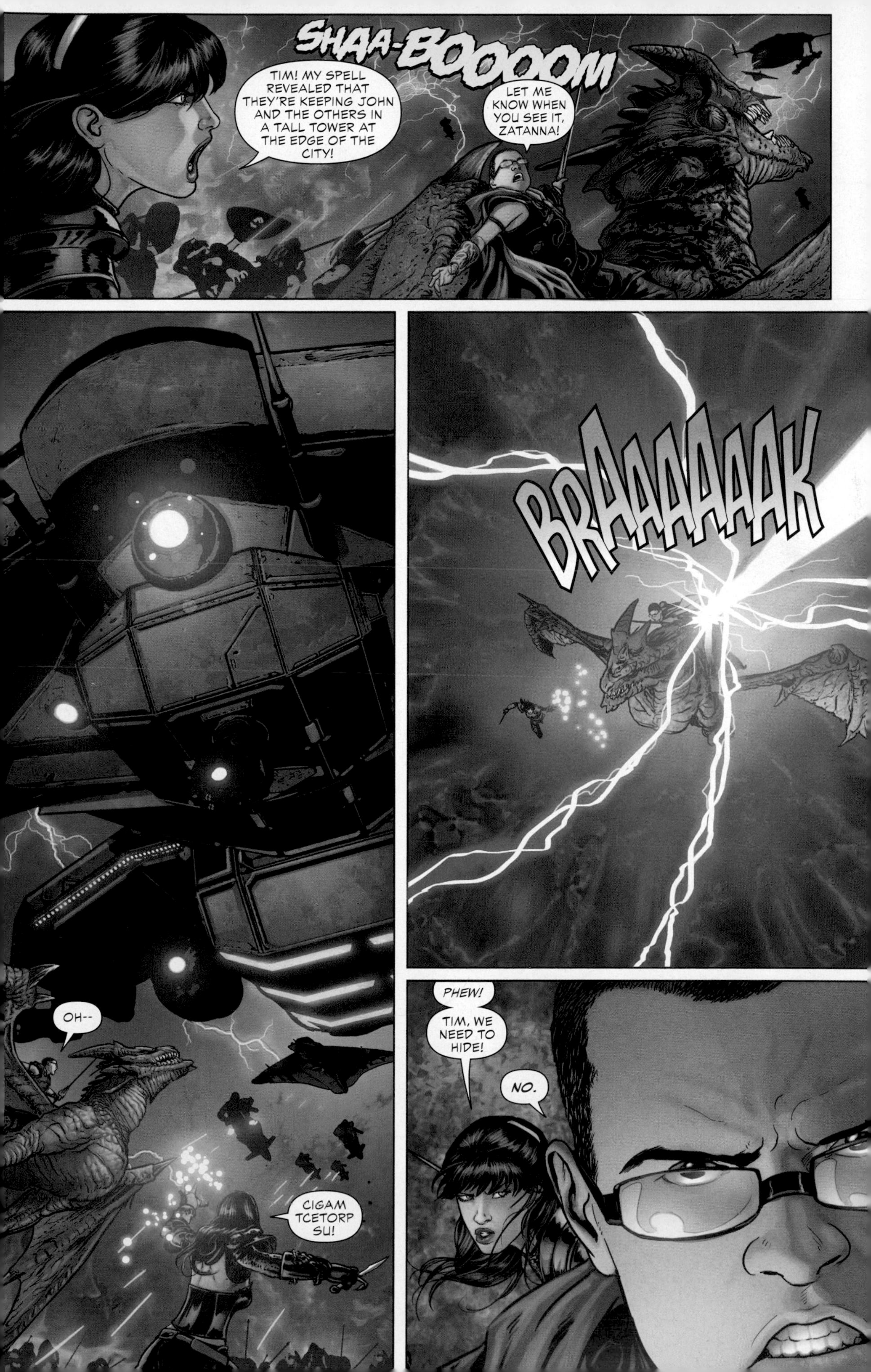
SHAA-BOOOOOM
TIM! MY SPELL REVEALED THAT THEY'RE KEEPING JOHN AND THE OTHERS IN A TALL TOWER AT THE EDGE OF THE CITY!
LET ME KNOW WHEN YOU SEE IT, ZATANNA!
OH--
CIGAM TCETORP SU!
BRAAAAAAK
PHEW!
TIM, WE NEED TO HIDE!
NO.

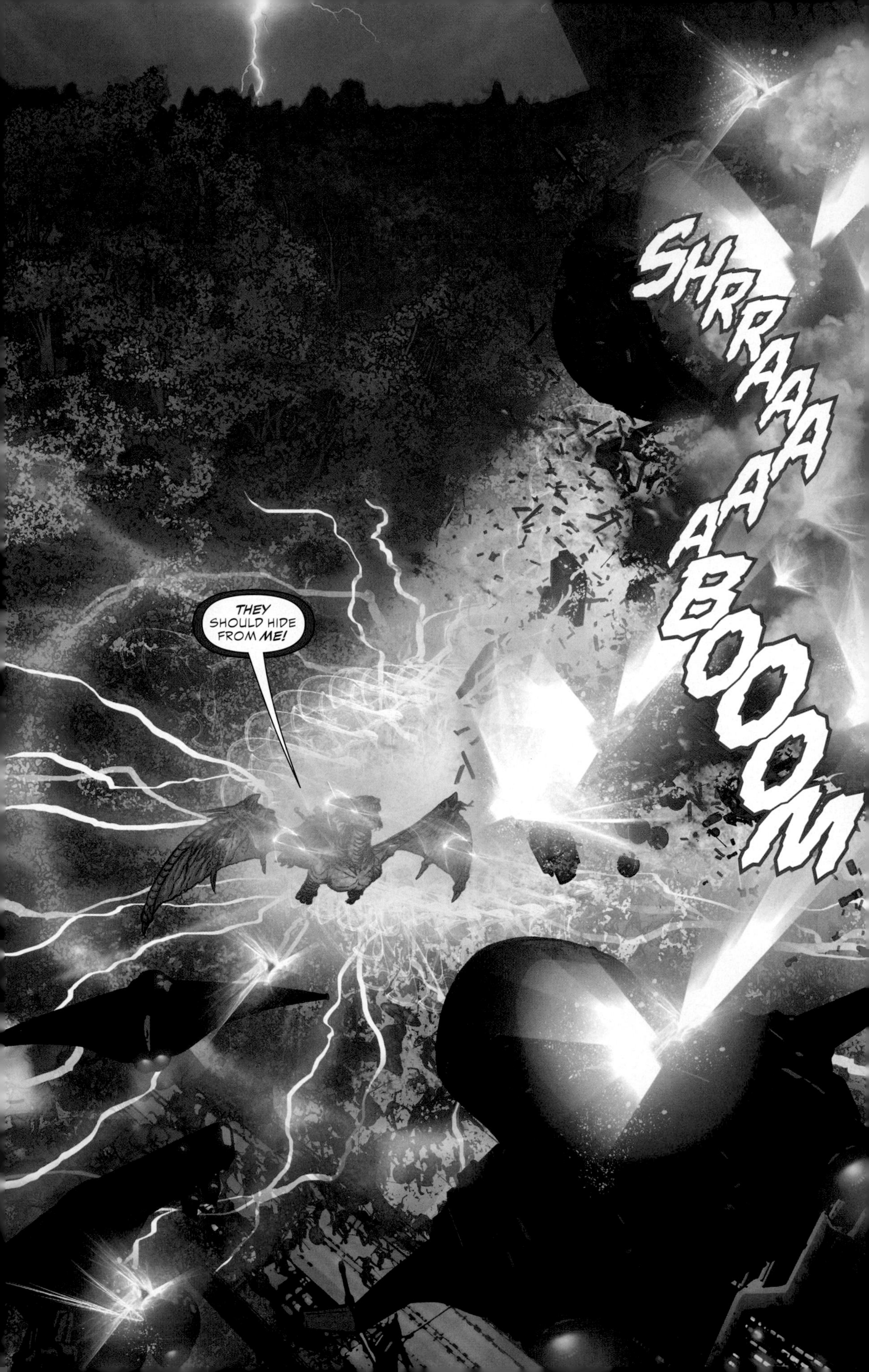
THEY SHOULD HIDE FROM ME!
SHRRAAAAABOOOOM

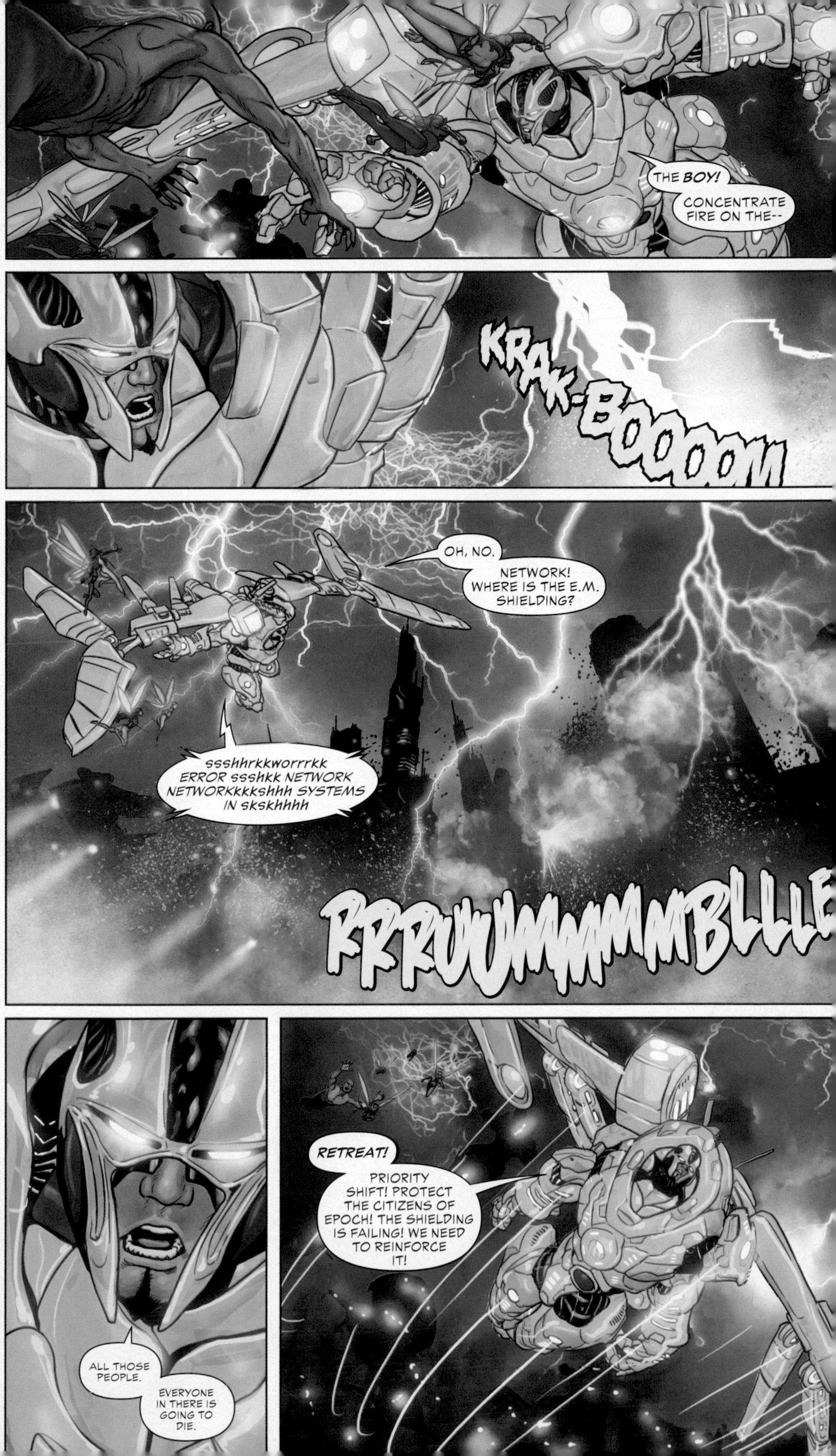

THE BOY!
CONCENTRATE FIRE ON THE--
KRAK-BOOOOOM
OH, NO.
NETWORK! WHERE IS THE E.M. SHIELDING?
ssshhrkkworrrkk ERROR ssshkk NETWORK NETWORKkkkshhh SYSTEMS IN skskhhhhh
RRRUUMMMMMBLLLE
ALL THOSE PEOPLE.
EVERYONE IN THERE IS GOING TO DIE.
RETREAT!
PRIORITY SHIFT! PROTECT THE CITIZENS OF EPOCH! THE SHIELDING IS FAILING! WE NEED TO REINFORCE IT!

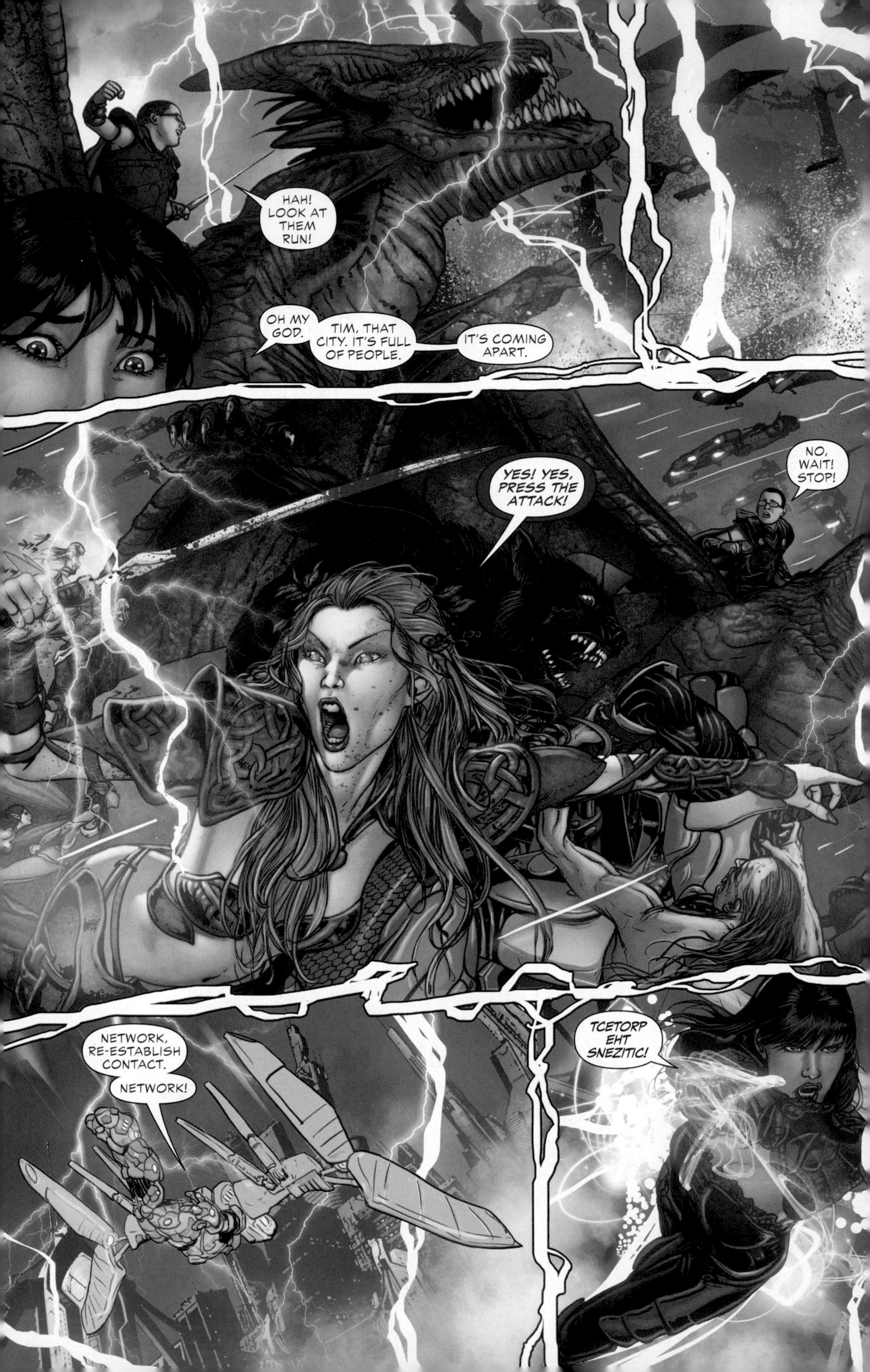
HAH! LOOK AT THEM RUN!
OH MY GOD.
TIM, THAT CITY. IT'S FULL OF PEOPLE.
IT'S COMING APART.
YES! YES, PRESS THE ATTACK!
NO, WAIT! STOP!
NETWORK, RE-ESTABLISH CONTACT.
NETWORK!
TCETORP EHT SNEZITIC!

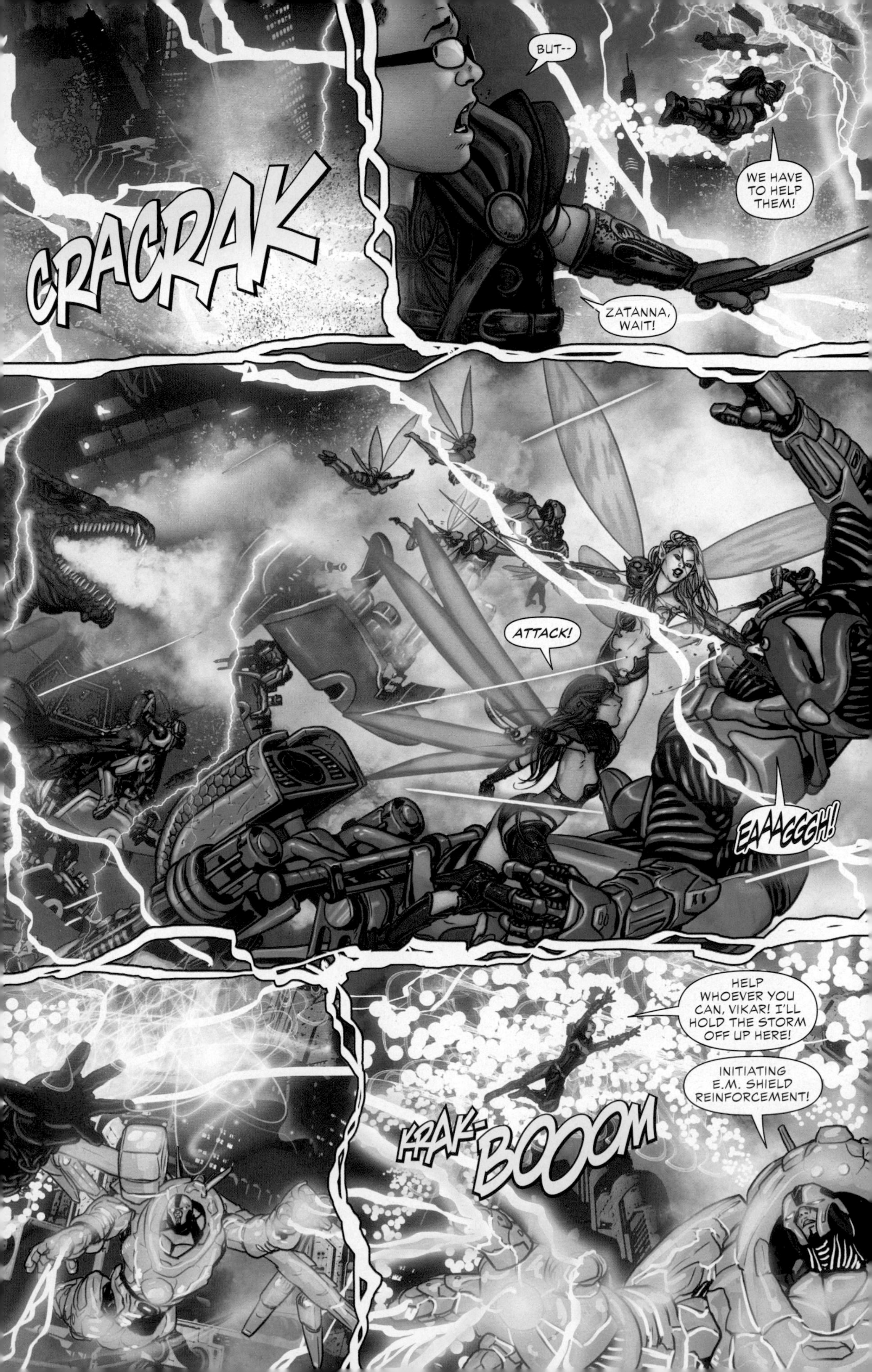
CRACRAK
BUT--
WE HAVE TO HELP THEM!
ZATANNA, WAIT!
ATTACK!
EAAAGGH!
HELP WHOEVER YOU CAN, VIKAR! I'LL HOLD THE STORM OFF UP HERE!
INITIATING E.M. SHIELD REINFORCEMENT!
KRAK-BOOOOM

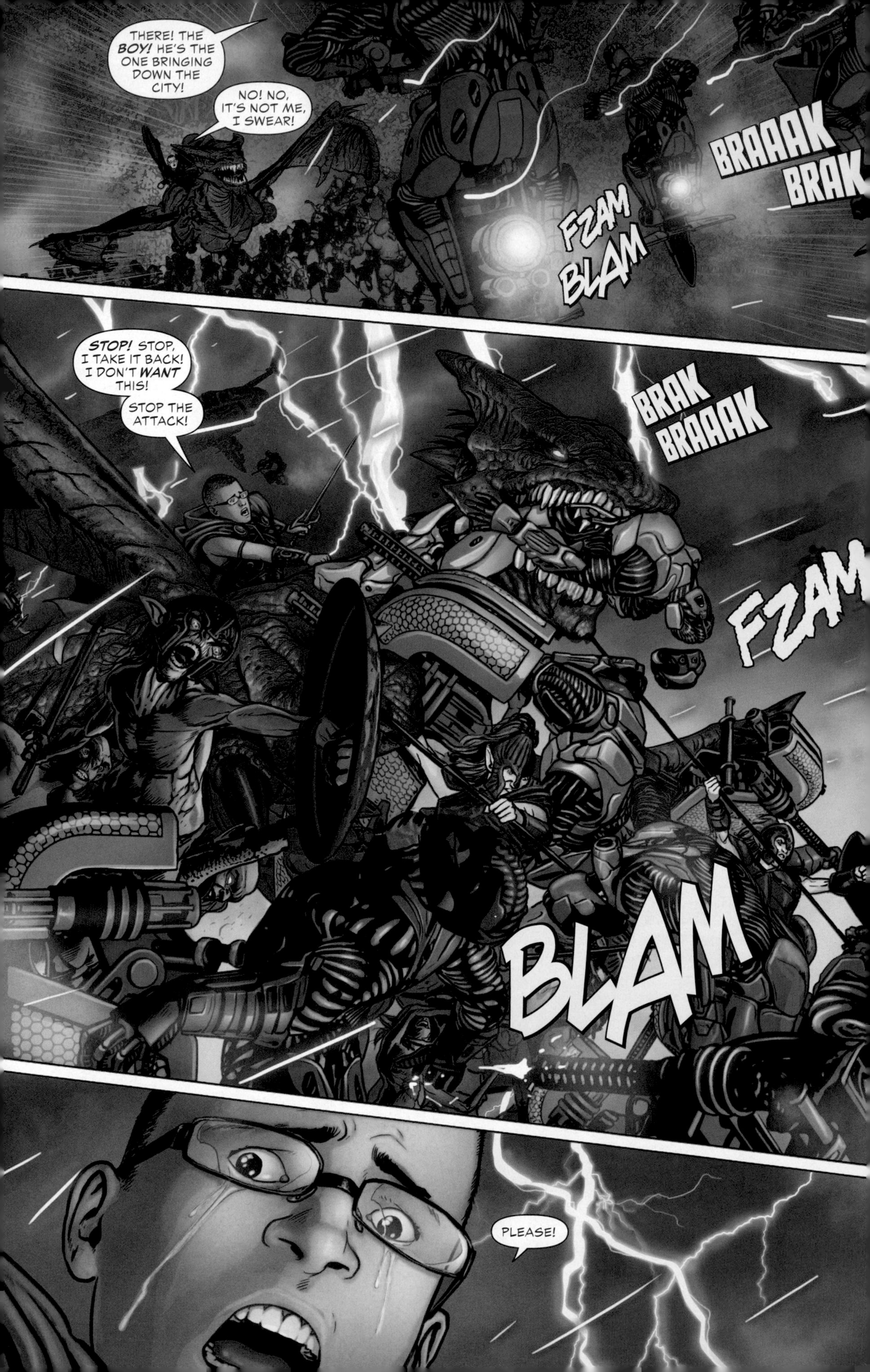
THERE! THE BOY! HE'S THE ONE BRINGING DOWN THE CITY!
NO! NO, IT'S NOT ME, I SWEAR!
FZAM BLAM
BRAAAK BRAK
STOP! STOP, I TAKE IT BACK! I DON'T WANT THIS!
STOP THE ATTACK!
BRAK BRAAAK
FZAM
BLAM
PLEASE!

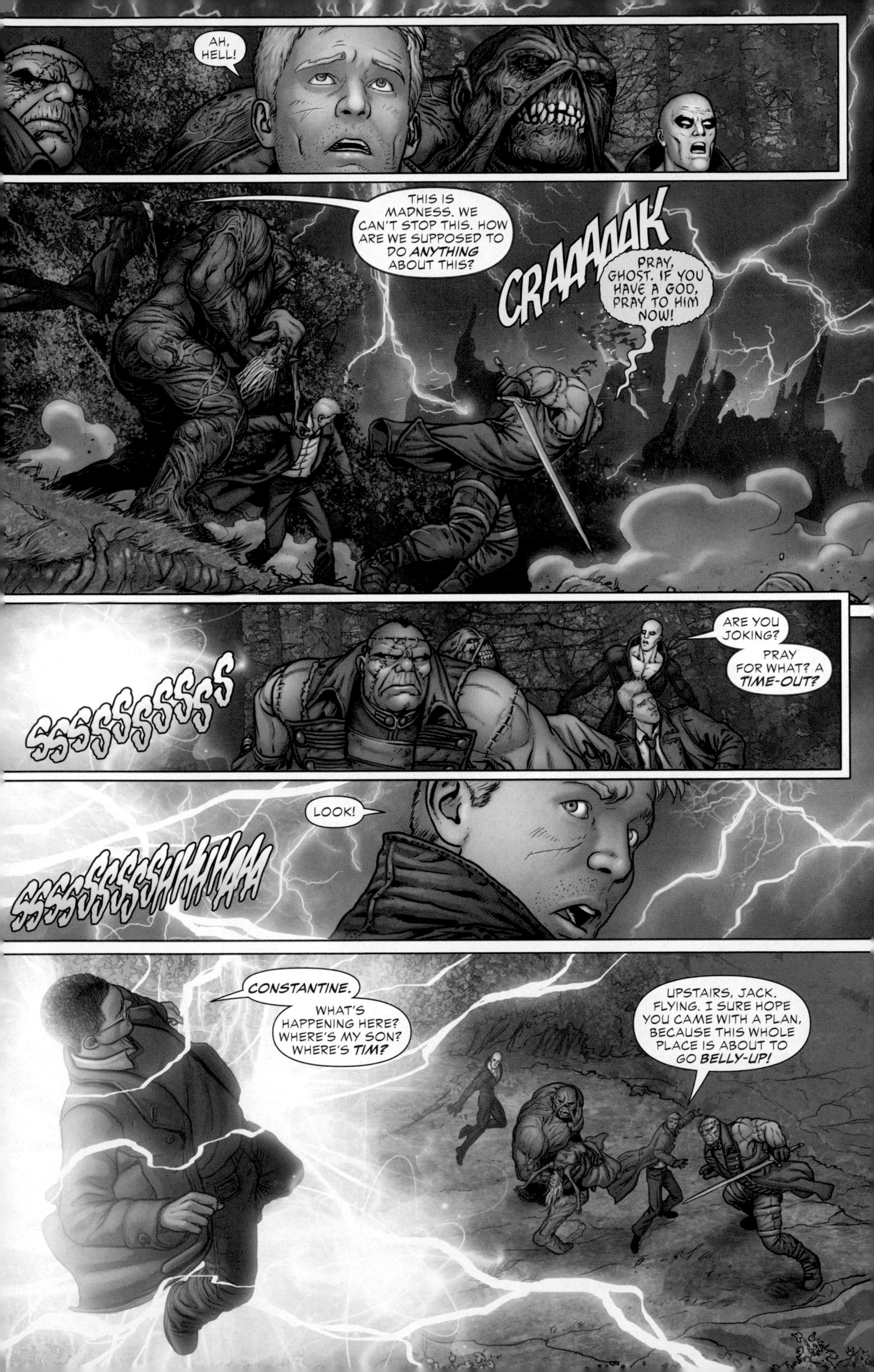
AH, HELL!
THIS IS MADNESS. WE CAN'T STOP THIS. HOW ARE WE SUPPOSED TO DO ANYTHING ABOUT THIS?
CRAAAAAK
PRAY, GHOST. IF YOU HAVE A GOD, PRAY TO HIM NOW!
SSSSSSSSSSS
ARE YOU JOKING?
PRAY FOR WHAT? A TIME-OUT?
LOOK!
SSSSSSSSSSHHHHAAA
CONSTANTINE.
WHAT'S HAPPENING HERE? WHERE'S MY SON? WHERE'S TIM?
UPSTAIRS, JACK. FLYING. I SURE HOPE YOU CAME WITH A PLAN, BECAUSE THIS WHOLE PLACE IS ABOUT TO GO BELLY-UP!

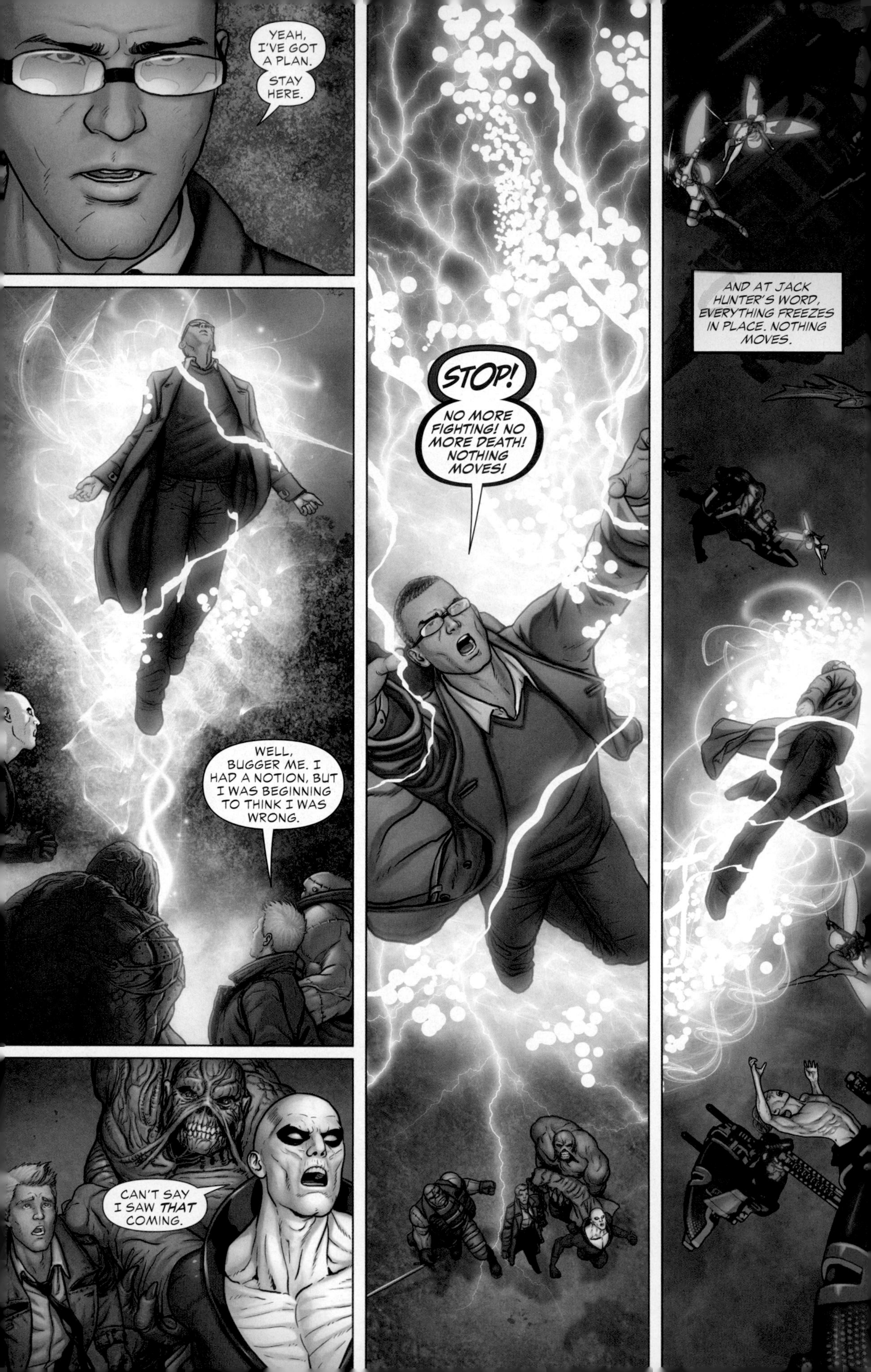
YEAH, I'VE GOT A PLAN.
STAY HERE.
WELL, BUGGER ME. I HAD A NOTION, BUT I WAS BEGINNING TO THINK I WAS WRONG.
CAN'T SAY I SAW *THAT* COMING.
STOP!
NO MORE FIGHTING! NO MORE DEATH! NOTHING MOVES!
AND AT JACK HUNTER'S WORD, EVERYTHING FREEZES IN PLACE. NOTHING MOVES.

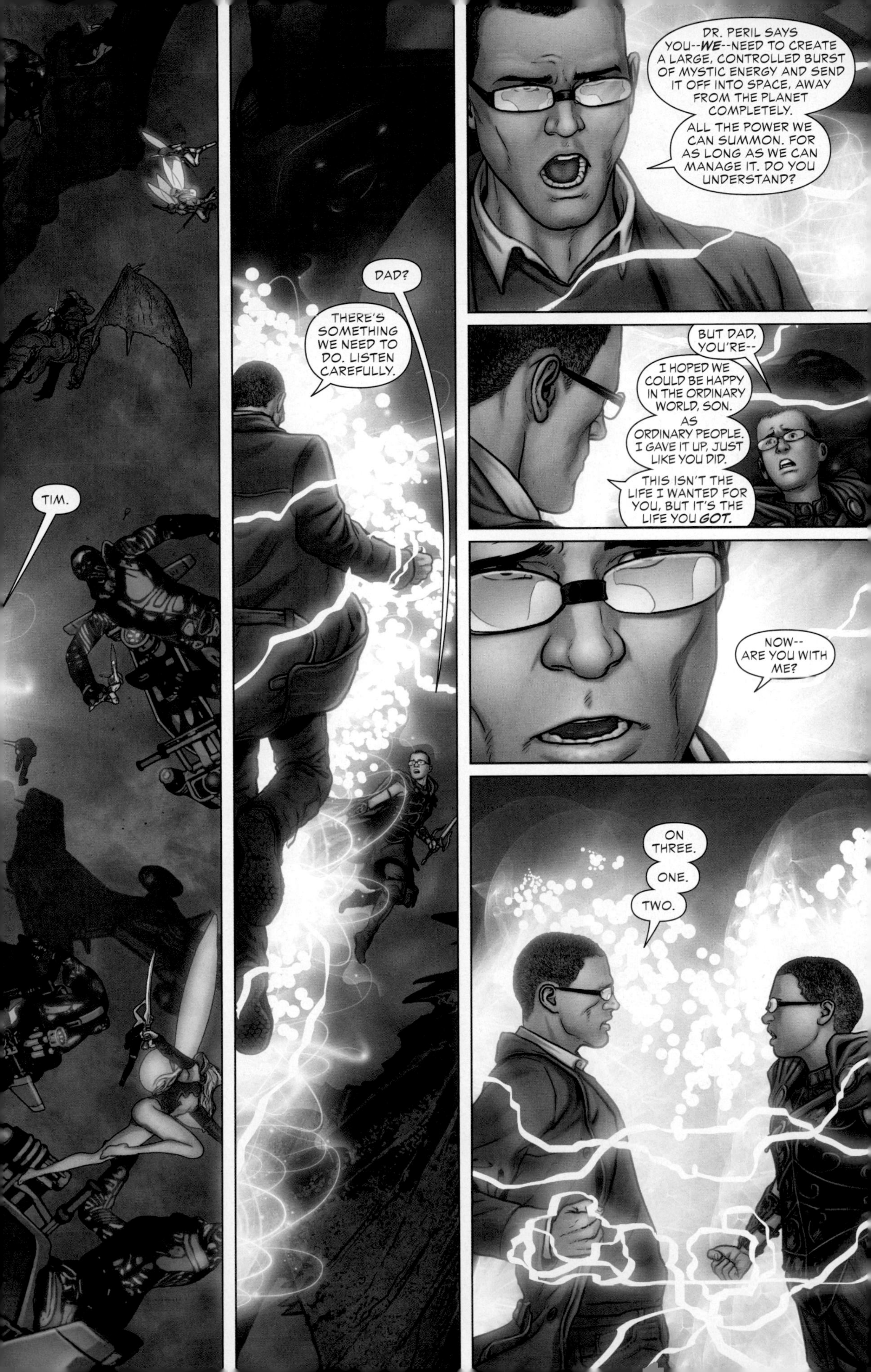
TIM.
DAD?
THERE'S SOMETHING WE NEED TO DO. LISTEN CAREFULLY.
DR. PERIL SAYS YOU--WE--NEED TO CREATE A LARGE, CONTROLLED BURST OF MYSTIC ENERGY AND SEND IT OFF INTO SPACE, AWAY FROM THE PLANET COMPLETELY.
ALL THE POWER WE CAN SUMMON. FOR AS LONG AS WE CAN MANAGE IT. DO YOU UNDERSTAND?
BUT DAD, YOU'RE--
I HOPED WE COULD BE HAPPY IN THE ORDINARY WORLD, SON.
AS ORDINARY PEOPLE. I GAVE IT UP, JUST LIKE YOU DID.
THIS ISN'T THE LIFE I WANTED FOR YOU, BUT IT'S THE LIFE YOU GOT.
NOW-- ARE YOU WITH ME?
ON THREE.
ONE.
TWO.

"THREE."

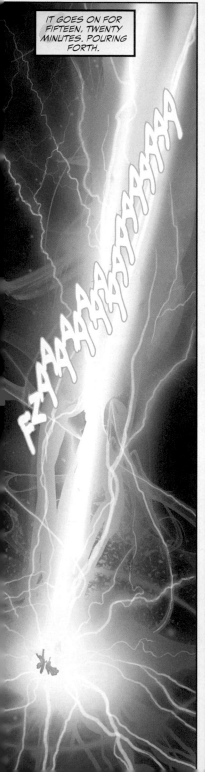

IT GOES ON FOR FIFTEEN, TWENTY MINUTES. POURING FORTH.

RAAAAAAAAAAAAAAAAA

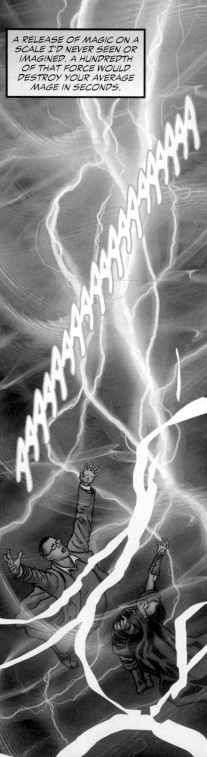

A RELEASE OF MAGIC ON A SCALE I'D NEVER SEEN OR IMAGINED. A HUNDREDTH OF THAT FORCE WOULD DESTROY YOUR AVERAGE MAGE IN SECONDS.

AAAAAAAAAAAAAAAAAAAAA

THERE. THAT OUGHT TO DO IT.

DAD!

YOU CAN ALL COME DOWN FROM THERE WHEN YOU'RE READY TO STOP FIGHTING.

BUT DAD, HOW DID YOU--

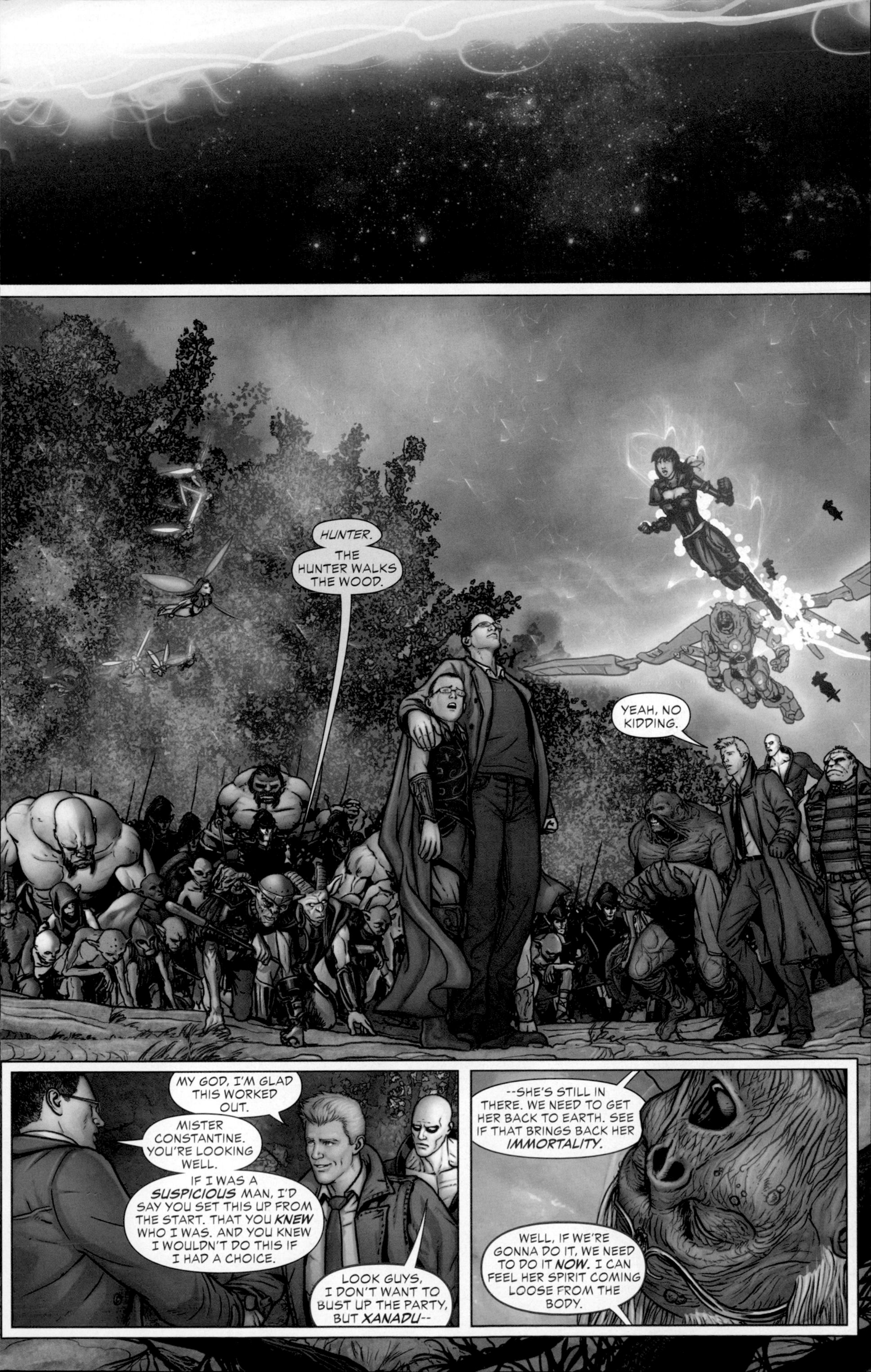
HUNTER. THE HUNTER WALKS THE WOOD.
YEAH, NO KIDDING.
MY GOD, I'M GLAD THIS WORKED OUT.
MISTER CONSTANTINE. YOU'RE LOOKING WELL.
IF I WAS A SUSPICIOUS MAN, I'D SAY YOU SET THIS UP FROM THE START. THAT YOU KNEW WHO I WAS. AND YOU KNEW I WOULDN'T DO THIS IF I HAD A CHOICE.
LOOK GUYS, I DON'T WANT TO BUST UP THE PARTY, BUT XANADU--
--SHE'S STILL IN THERE. WE NEED TO GET HER BACK TO EARTH. SEE IF THAT BRINGS BACK HER IMMORTALITY.
WELL, IF WE'RE GONNA DO IT, WE NEED TO DO IT NOW. I CAN FEEL HER SPIRIT COMING LOOSE FROM THE BODY.

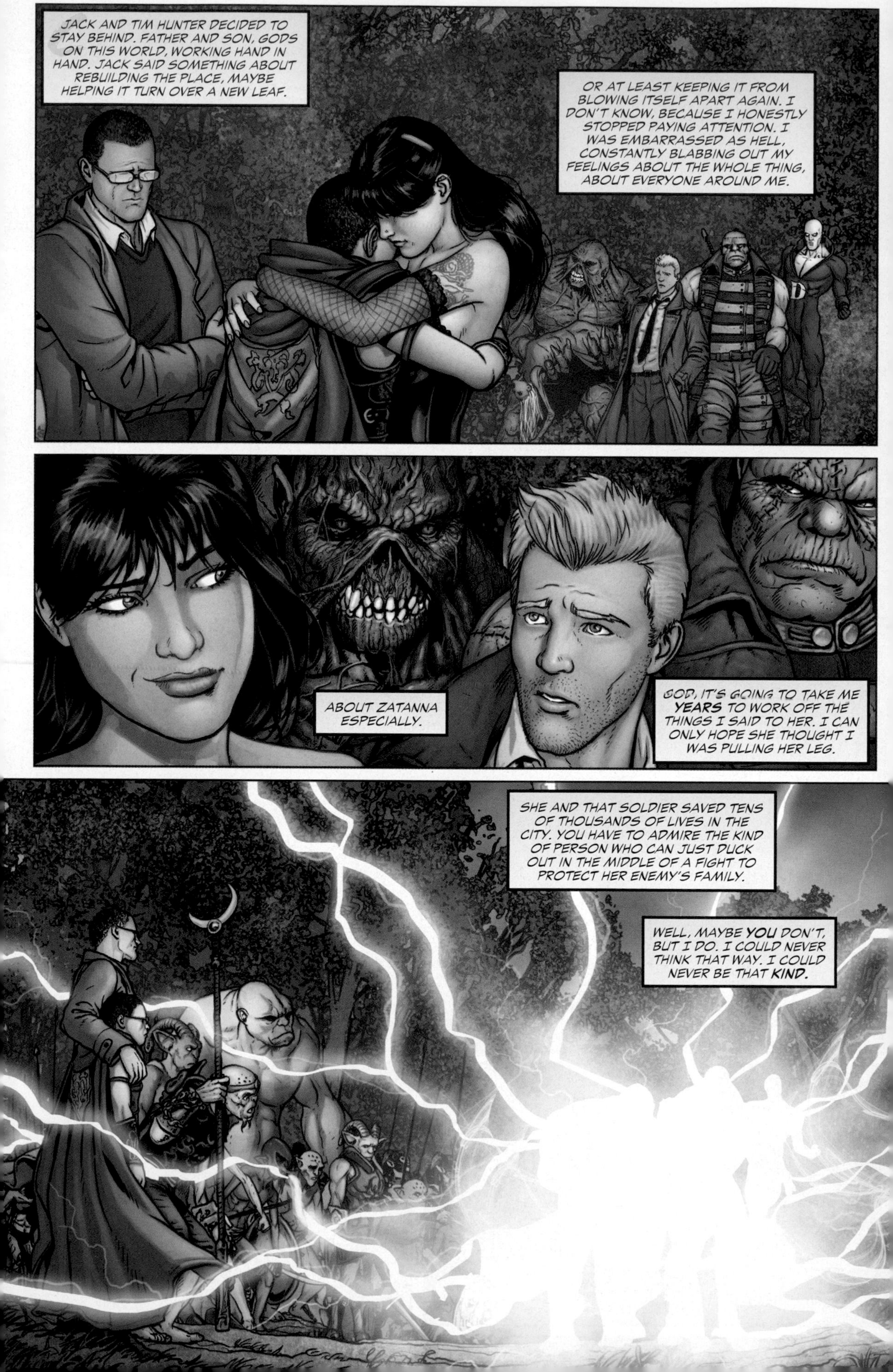
JACK AND TIM HUNTER DECIDED TO STAY BEHIND. FATHER AND SON, GODS ON THIS WORLD, WORKING HAND IN HAND. JACK SAID SOMETHING ABOUT REBUILDING THE PLACE, MAYBE HELPING IT TURN OVER A NEW LEAF.
OR AT LEAST KEEPING IT FROM BLOWING ITSELF APART AGAIN. I DON'T KNOW, BECAUSE I HONESTLY STOPPED PAYING ATTENTION. I WAS EMBARRASSED AS HELL, CONSTANTLY BLABBING OUT MY FEELINGS ABOUT THE WHOLE THING, ABOUT EVERYONE AROUND ME.
ABOUT ZATANNA ESPECIALLY.
GOD, IT'S GOING TO TAKE ME YEARS TO WORK OFF THE THINGS I SAID TO HER. I CAN ONLY HOPE SHE THOUGHT I WAS PULLING HER LEG.
SHE AND THAT SOLDIER SAVED TENS OF THOUSANDS OF LIVES IN THE CITY. YOU HAVE TO ADMIRE THE KIND OF PERSON WHO CAN JUST DUCK OUT IN THE MIDDLE OF A FIGHT TO PROTECT HER ENEMY'S FAMILY.
WELL, MAYBE YOU DON'T, BUT I DO. I COULD NEVER THINK THAT WAY. I COULD NEVER BE THAT KIND.

ANYWAY, THAT'S HOW IT ALL WRAPPED UP, PERIL. CATASTROPHE AVERTED. WAR ENDED. CITY SAVED.

AND HERE I AM, BACK TO MESELF AS THEY SAY, AND ONLY A COUPLE OF THINGS LEFT TO DO BEFORE THIS BUSINESS IS ALL TIED UP IN A NEAT LITTLE BOW.

NOT THAT I DON'T HAVE A MILLION OTHER QUESTIONS, BUT WHAT DO YOU MEAN BY THAT? WHAT DO YOU STILL HAVE TO DO?

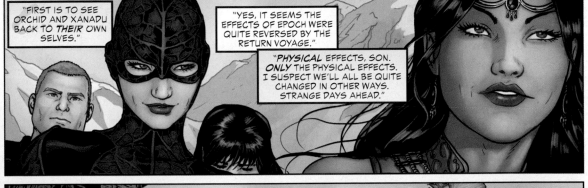

"FIRST IS TO SEE ORCHID AND XANADU BACK TO *THEIR* OWN SELVES."

"YES, IT SEEMS THE EFFECTS OF EPOCH WERE QUITE REVERSED BY THE RETURN VOYAGE."

"*PHYSICAL* EFFECTS, SON. *ONLY* THE PHYSICAL EFFECTS. I SUSPECT WE'LL ALL BE QUITE CHANGED IN OTHER WAYS. STRANGE DAYS AHEAD."

HERE COMES THE SECOND THING.

JOHN. I JUST WANT TO SAY--

YOU DON'T HAVE TO SAY ANYTHING.

SORRY, ZEE, BUT I REALLY DO.

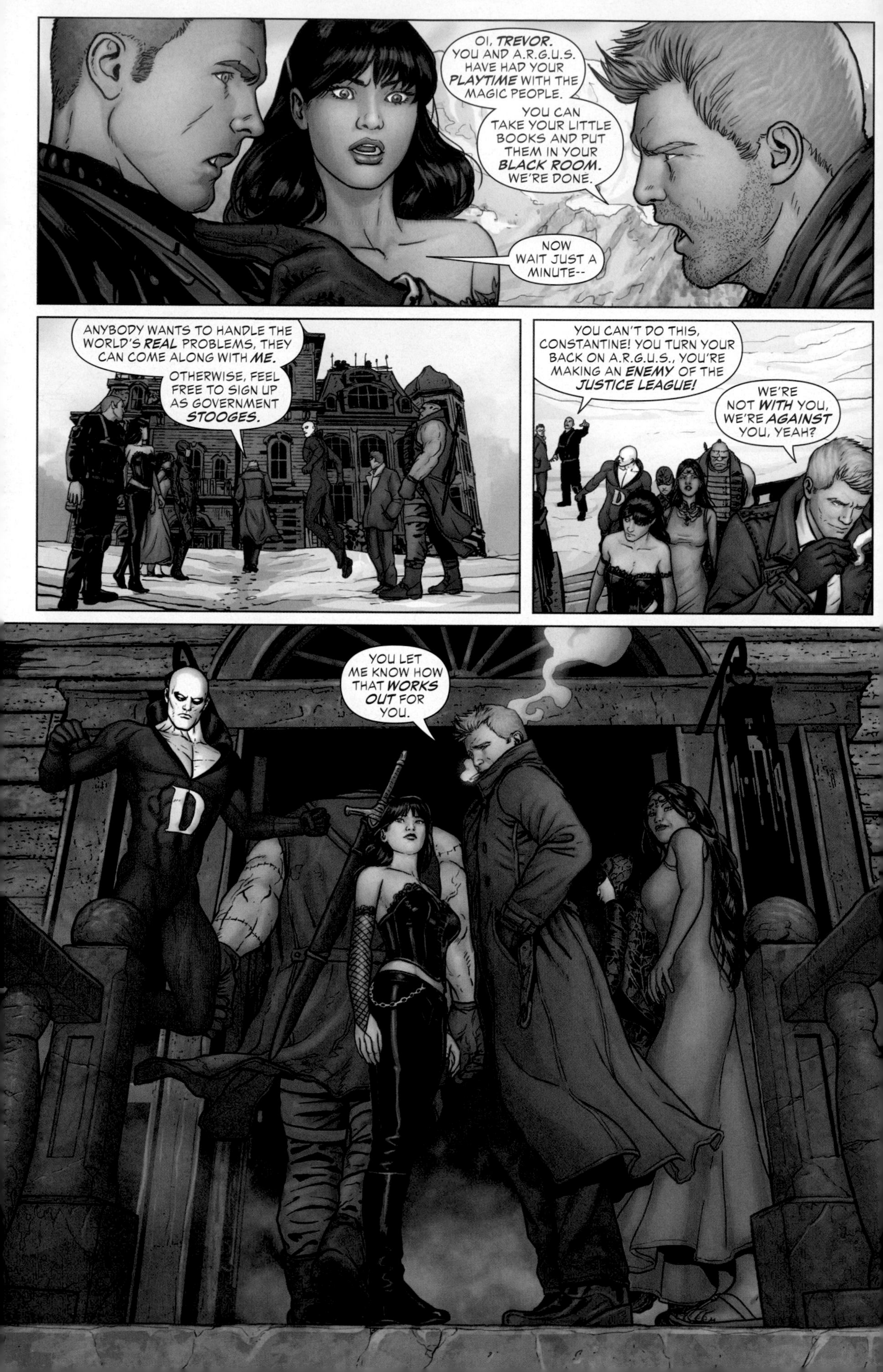
OI, TREVOR. YOU AND A.R.G.U.S. HAVE HAD YOUR PLAYTIME WITH THE MAGIC PEOPLE.
YOU CAN TAKE YOUR LITTLE BOOKS AND PUT THEM IN YOUR BLACK ROOM. WE'RE DONE.
NOW WAIT JUST A MINUTE--
ANYBODY WANTS TO HANDLE THE WORLD'S REAL PROBLEMS, THEY CAN COME ALONG WITH ME.
OTHERWISE, FEEL FREE TO SIGN UP AS GOVERNMENT STOOGES.
YOU CAN'T DO THIS, CONSTANTINE! YOU TURN YOUR BACK ON A.R.G.U.S., YOU'RE MAKING AN ENEMY OF THE JUSTICE LEAGUE!
WE'RE NOT WITH YOU, WE'RE AGAINST YOU, YEAH?
YOU LET ME KNOW HOW THAT WORKS OUT FOR YOU.

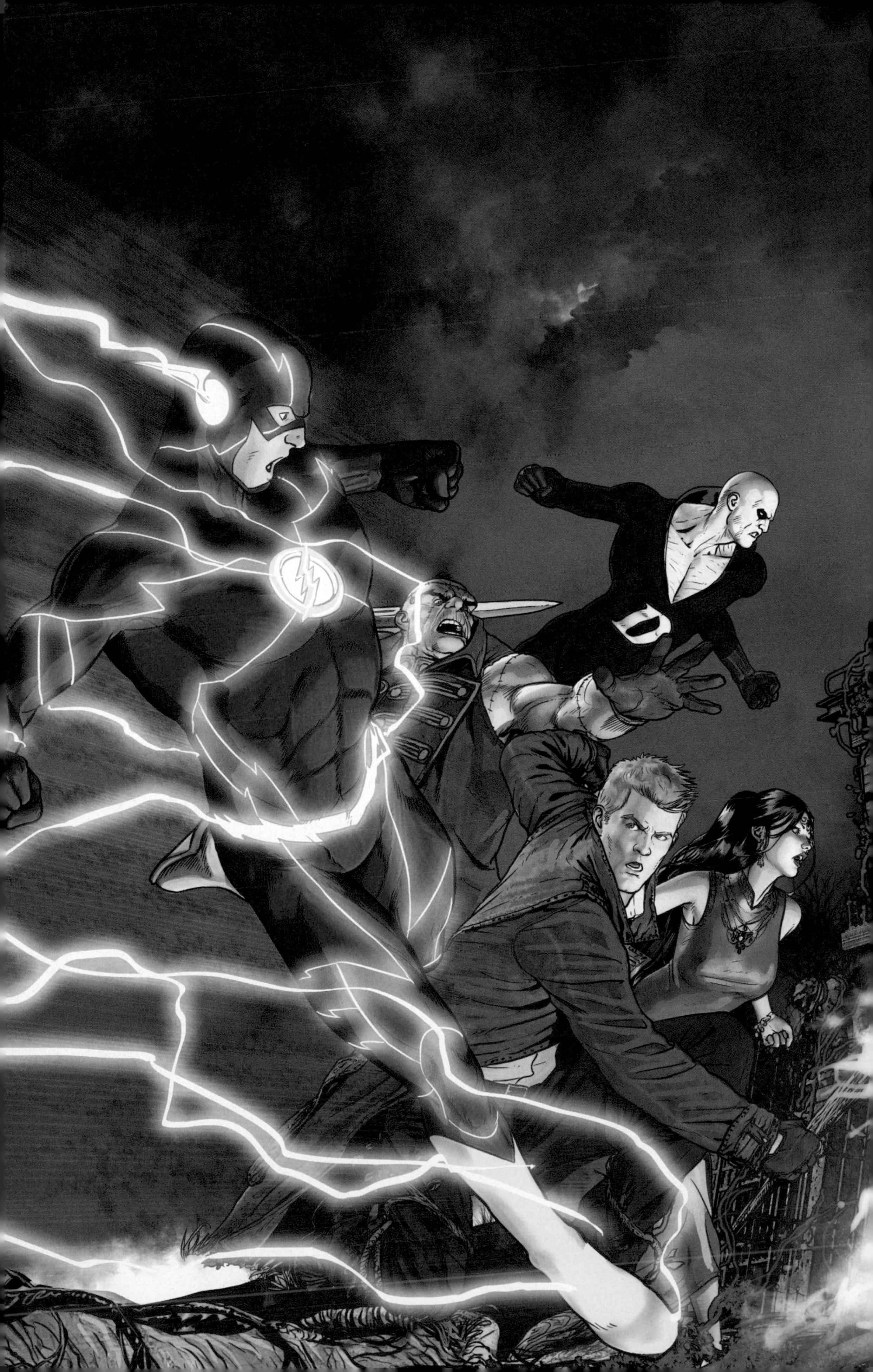

HORROR CITY part one
HOUSE OF MISERY

JEFF LEMIRE
RAY FAWKES
writers

MIKEL JANIN
layouts

VICENTE CIFUENTES
finishes

MIKEL JANIN
cover artist

SWAMP THING created by LEN WEIN & BERNIE WRIGHTSON

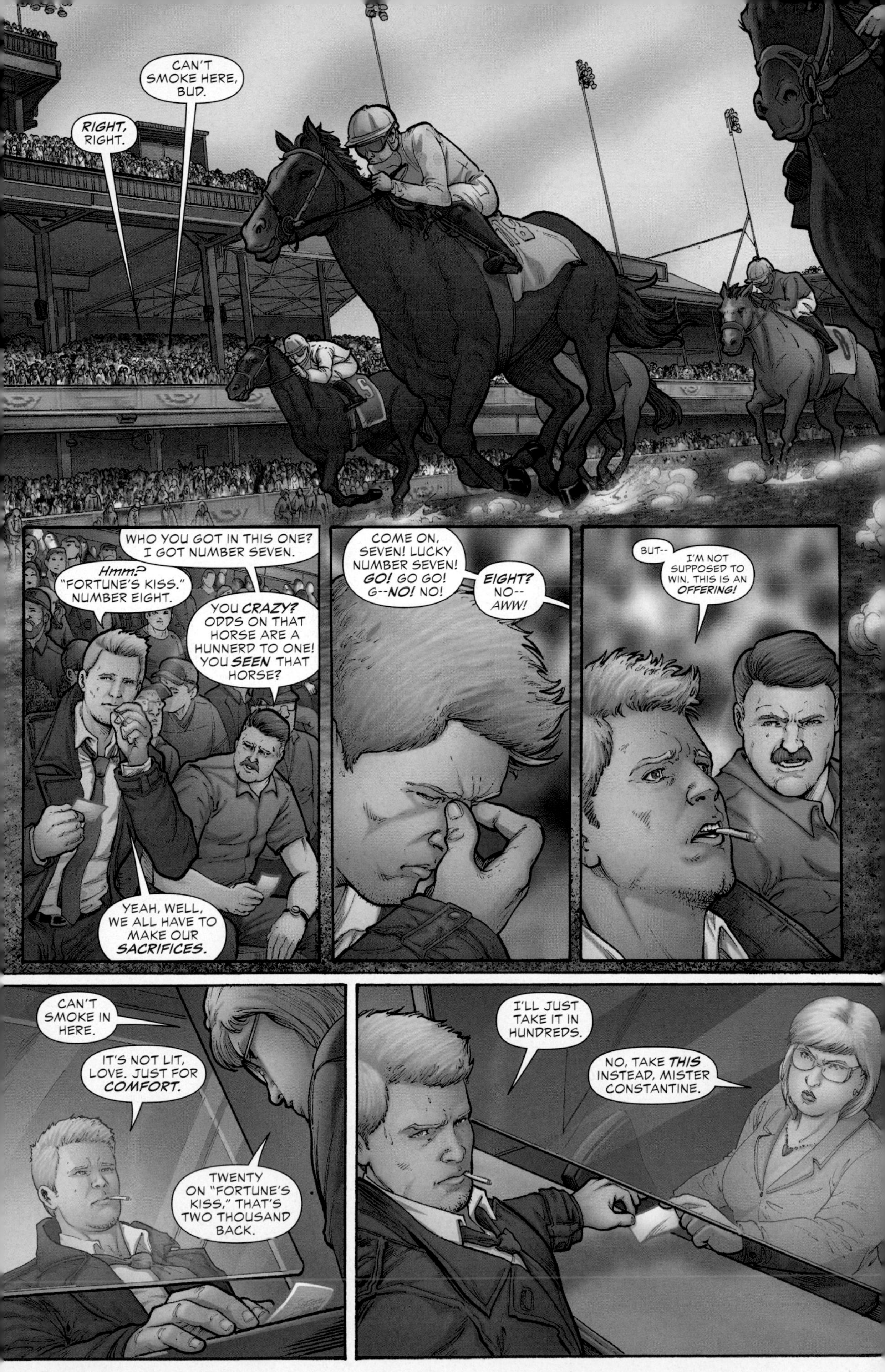
CAN'T SMOKE HERE, BUD.
RIGHT, RIGHT.
WHO YOU GOT IN THIS ONE? I GOT NUMBER SEVEN.
Hmm? "FORTUNE'S KISS." NUMBER EIGHT.
YOU CRAZY? ODDS ON THAT HORSE ARE A HUNNERD TO ONE! YOU SEEN THAT HORSE?
YEAH, WELL, WE ALL HAVE TO MAKE OUR SACRIFICES.
COME ON, SEVEN! LUCKY NUMBER SEVEN! GO! GO GO! G--NO! NO!
EIGHT? NO-- AWW!
BUT--
I'M NOT SUPPOSED TO WIN. THIS IS AN OFFERING!
CAN'T SMOKE IN HERE.
IT'S NOT LIT, LOVE. JUST FOR COMFORT.
TWENTY ON "FORTUNE'S KISS," THAT'S TWO THOUSAND BACK.
I'LL JUST TAKE IT IN HUNDREDS.
NO, TAKE THIS INSTEAD, MISTER CONSTANTINE.

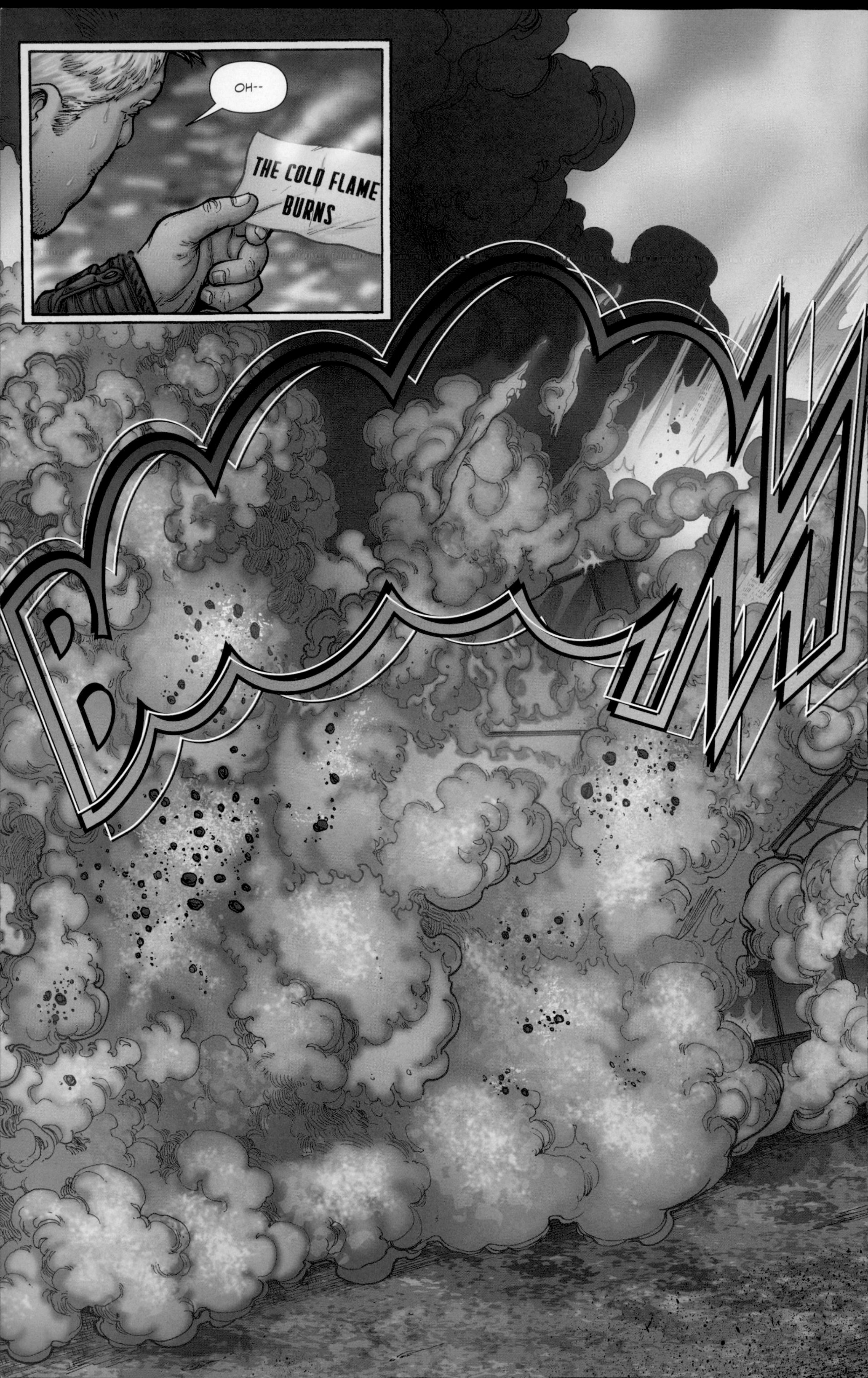
OH--
THE COLD FLAME BURNS
BOOOM

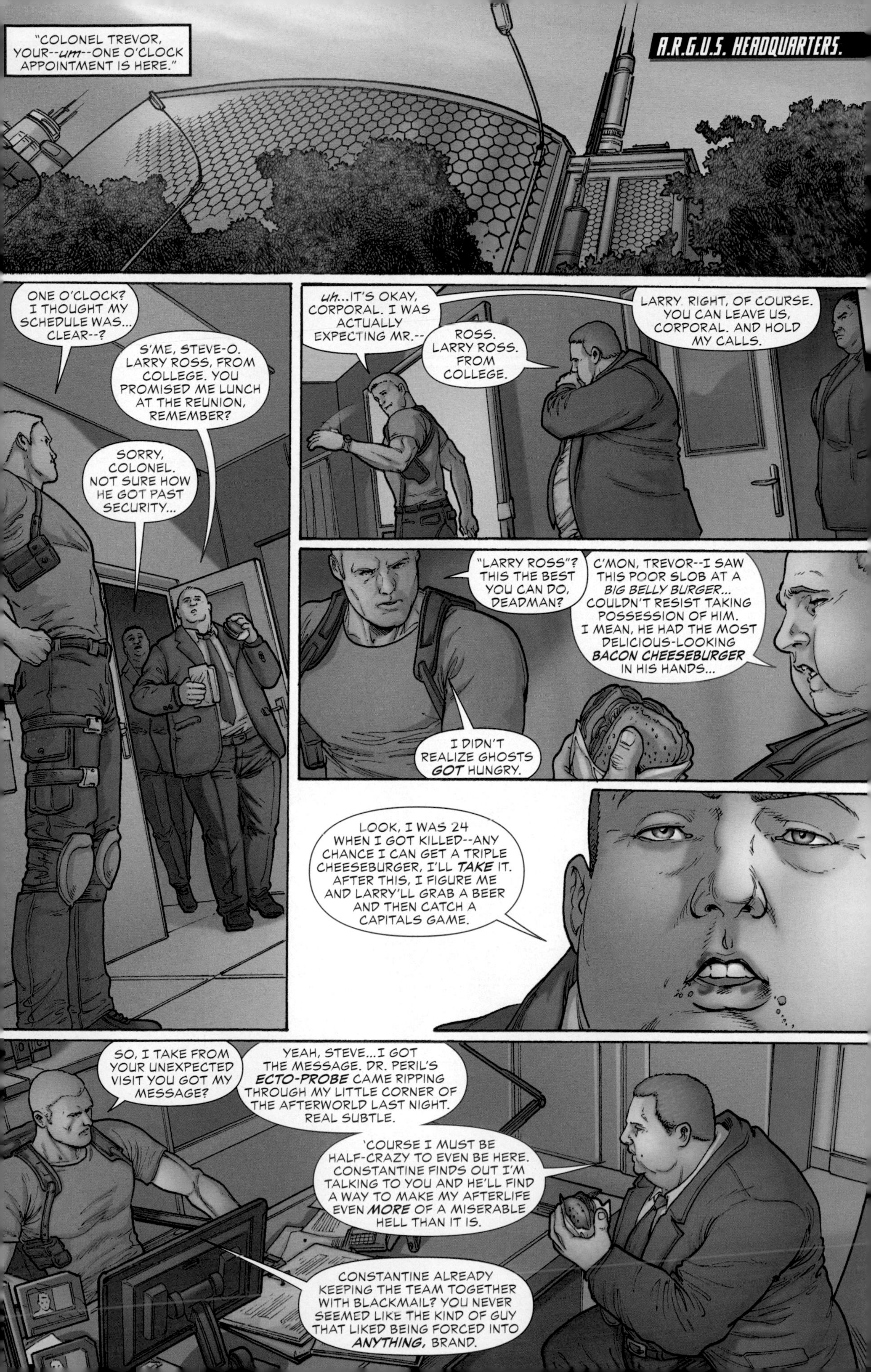
"COLONEL TREVOR, YOUR--*UM*--ONE O'CLOCK APPOINTMENT IS HERE."
A.R.G.U.S. HEADQUARTERS.
ONE O'CLOCK? I THOUGHT MY SCHEDULE WAS... CLEAR--?
S'ME, STEVE-O. LARRY ROSS, FROM COLLEGE. YOU PROMISED ME LUNCH AT THE REUNION, REMEMBER?
SORRY, COLONEL. NOT SURE HOW HE GOT PAST SECURITY...
UH...IT'S OKAY, CORPORAL. I WAS ACTUALLY EXPECTING MR.--
ROSS. LARRY ROSS. FROM COLLEGE.
LARRY. RIGHT, OF COURSE. YOU CAN LEAVE US, CORPORAL. AND HOLD MY CALLS.
"LARRY ROSS"? THIS THE BEST YOU CAN DO, DEADMAN?
C'MON, TREVOR--I SAW THIS POOR SLOB AT A *BIG BELLY BURGER*... COULDN'T RESIST TAKING POSSESSION OF HIM. I MEAN, HE HAD THE MOST DELICIOUS-LOOKING *BACON CHEESEBURGER* IN HIS HANDS...
I DIDN'T REALIZE GHOSTS *GOT* HUNGRY.
LOOK, I WAS 24 WHEN I GOT KILLED--ANY CHANCE I CAN GET A TRIPLE CHEESEBURGER, I'LL *TAKE* IT. AFTER THIS, I FIGURE ME AND LARRY'LL GRAB A BEER AND THEN CATCH A CAPITALS GAME.
SO, I TAKE FROM YOUR UNEXPECTED VISIT YOU GOT MY MESSAGE?
YEAH, STEVE...I GOT THE MESSAGE. DR. PERIL'S *ECTO-PROBE* CAME RIPPING THROUGH MY LITTLE CORNER OF THE AFTERWORLD LAST NIGHT. REAL SUBTLE.
'COURSE I MUST BE HALF-CRAZY TO EVEN BE HERE. CONSTANTINE FINDS OUT I'M TALKING TO YOU AND HE'LL FIND A WAY TO MAKE MY AFTERLIFE EVEN *MORE* OF A MISERABLE HELL THAN IT IS.
CONSTANTINE ALREADY KEEPING THE TEAM TOGETHER WITH BLACKMAIL? YOU NEVER SEEMED LIKE THE KIND OF GUY THAT LIKED BEING FORCED INTO *ANYTHING*, BRAND.

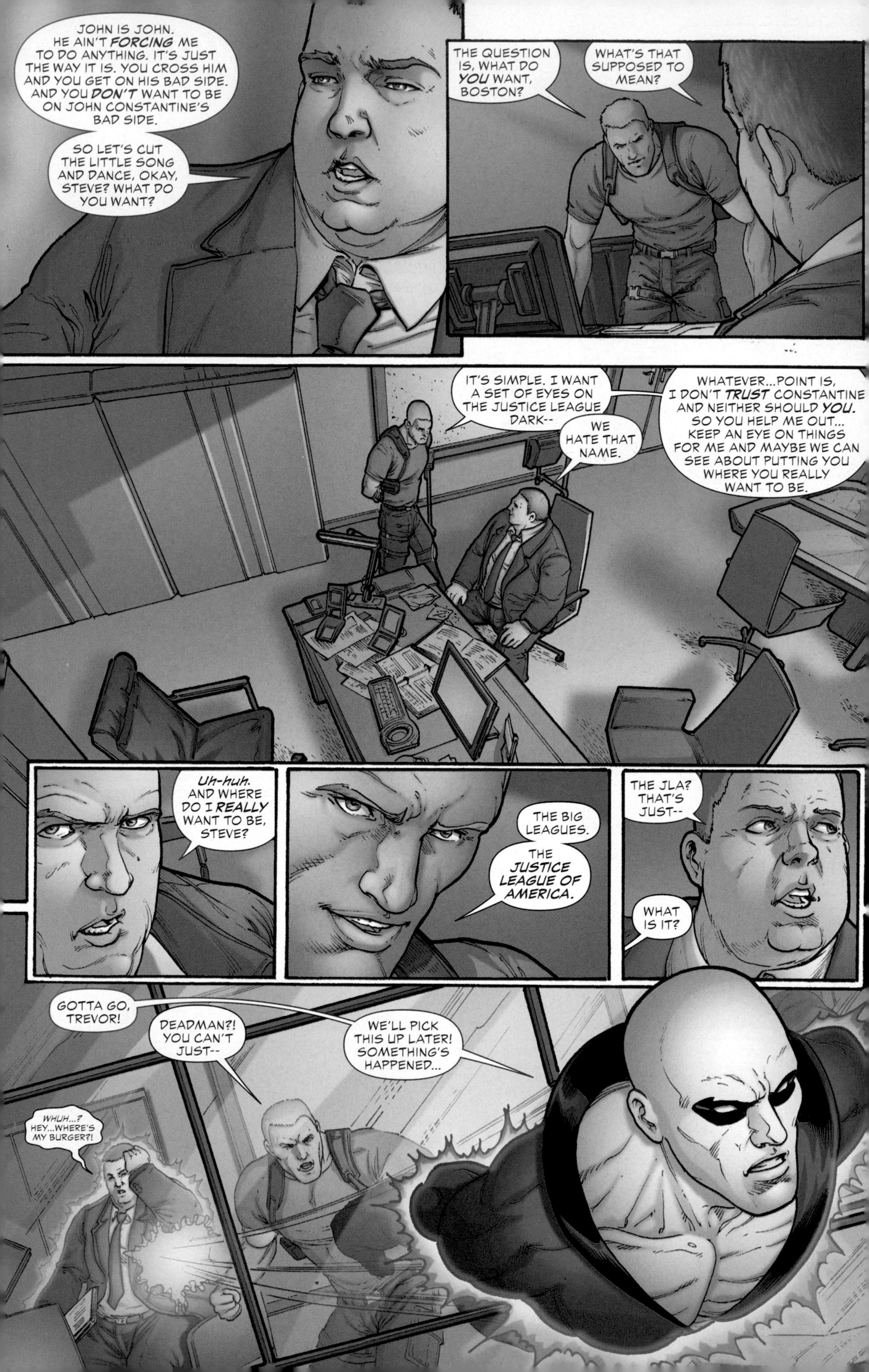
JOHN IS JOHN. HE AIN'T *FORCING* ME TO DO ANYTHING. IT'S JUST THE WAY IT IS. YOU CROSS HIM AND YOU GET ON HIS BAD SIDE. AND YOU *DON'T* WANT TO BE ON JOHN CONSTANTINE'S BAD SIDE.
SO LET'S CUT THE LITTLE SONG AND DANCE, OKAY, STEVE? WHAT DO YOU WANT?
THE QUESTION IS, WHAT DO *YOU* WANT, BOSTON?
WHAT'S THAT SUPPOSED TO MEAN?
IT'S SIMPLE. I WANT A SET OF EYES ON THE JUSTICE LEAGUE DARK--
WE HATE THAT NAME.
WHATEVER...POINT IS, I DON'T *TRUST* CONSTANTINE AND NEITHER SHOULD *YOU.* SO YOU HELP ME OUT... KEEP AN EYE ON THINGS FOR ME AND MAYBE WE CAN SEE ABOUT PUTTING YOU WHERE YOU REALLY WANT TO BE.
Uh-huh. AND WHERE DO I *REALLY* WANT TO BE, STEVE?
THE BIG LEAGUES.
THE *JUSTICE LEAGUE OF AMERICA.*
THE JLA? THAT'S JUST--
WHAT IS IT?
GOTTA GO, TREVOR!
WE'LL PICK THIS UP LATER! SOMETHING'S HAPPENED...
DEADMAN?! YOU CAN'T JUST--
WHUH...? HEY...WHERE'S MY BURGER?!

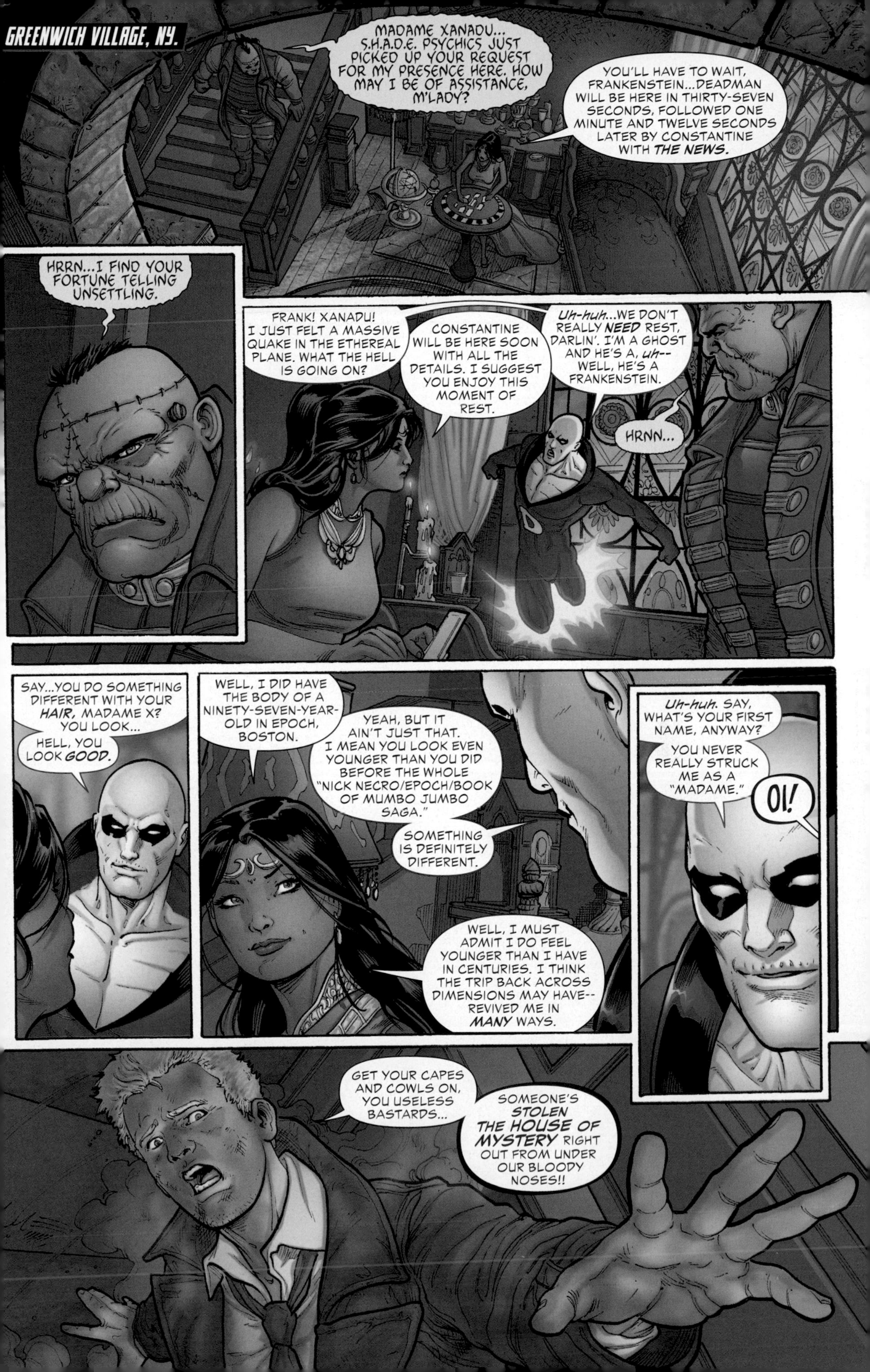
GREENWICH VILLAGE, NY.
MADAME XANADU... S.H.A.D.E. PSYCHICS JUST PICKED UP YOUR REQUEST FOR MY PRESENCE HERE. HOW MAY I BE OF ASSISTANCE, M'LADY?
YOU'LL HAVE TO WAIT, FRANKENSTEIN...DEADMAN WILL BE HERE IN THIRTY-SEVEN SECONDS, FOLLOWED ONE MINUTE AND TWELVE SECONDS LATER BY CONSTANTINE WITH *THE NEWS.*
HRRN...I FIND YOUR FORTUNE TELLING UNSETTLING.
FRANK! XANADU! I JUST FELT A MASSIVE QUAKE IN THE ETHEREAL PLANE. WHAT THE HELL IS GOING ON?
CONSTANTINE WILL BE HERE SOON WITH ALL THE DETAILS. I SUGGEST YOU ENJOY THIS MOMENT OF REST.
Uh-huh...WE DON'T REALLY *NEED* REST, DARLIN'. I'M A GHOST AND HE'S A, *uh*-- WELL, HE'S A FRANKENSTEIN.
HRNN...
SAY...YOU DO SOMETHING DIFFERENT WITH YOUR *HAIR*, MADAME X? YOU LOOK...
HELL, YOU LOOK *GOOD*.
WELL, I DID HAVE THE BODY OF A NINETY-SEVEN-YEAR-OLD IN EPOCH, BOSTON.
YEAH, BUT IT AIN'T JUST THAT. I MEAN YOU LOOK EVEN YOUNGER THAN YOU DID BEFORE THE WHOLE "NICK NECRO/EPOCH/BOOK OF MUMBO JUMBO SAGA."
SOMETHING IS DEFINITELY DIFFERENT.
WELL, I MUST ADMIT I DO FEEL YOUNGER THAN I HAVE IN CENTURIES. I THINK THE TRIP BACK ACROSS DIMENSIONS MAY HAVE-- REVIVED ME IN *MANY* WAYS.
Uh-huh. SAY, WHAT'S YOUR FIRST NAME, ANYWAY?
YOU NEVER REALLY STRUCK ME AS A "MADAME."
OI!
GET YOUR CAPES AND COWLS ON, YOU USELESS BASTARDS...
SOMEONE'S *STOLEN THE HOUSE OF MYSTERY* RIGHT OUT FROM UNDER OUR BLOODY NOSES!!

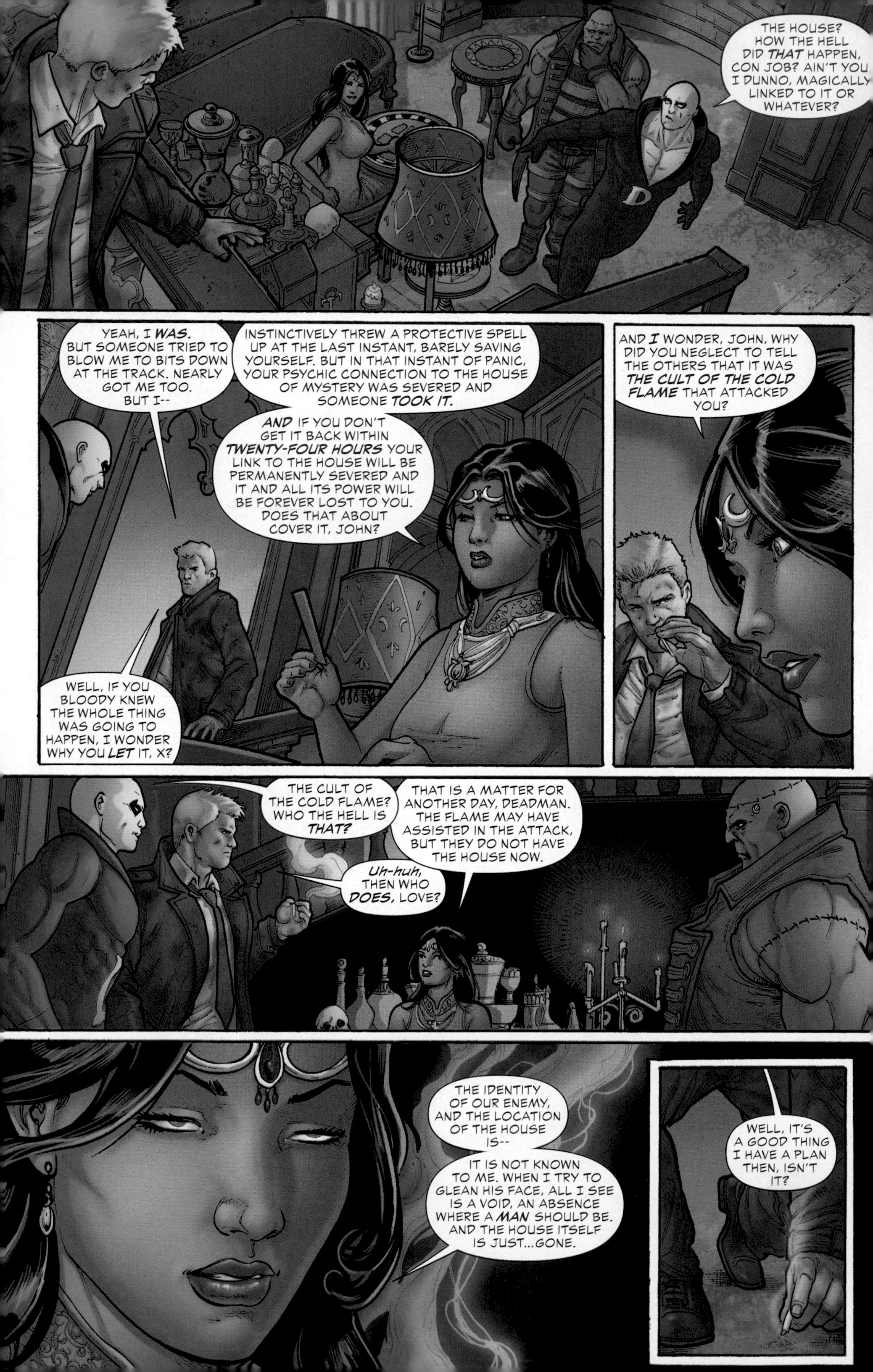
THE HOUSE? HOW THE HELL DID THAT HAPPEN, CON JOB? AIN'T YOU I DUNNO, MAGICALLY LINKED TO IT OR WHATEVER?
YEAH, I WAS. BUT SOMEONE TRIED TO BLOW ME TO BITS DOWN AT THE TRACK. NEARLY GOT ME TOO. BUT I--
INSTINCTIVELY THREW A PROTECTIVE SPELL UP AT THE LAST INSTANT, BARELY SAVING YOURSELF. BUT IN THAT INSTANT OF PANIC, YOUR PSYCHIC CONNECTION TO THE HOUSE OF MYSTERY WAS SEVERED AND SOMEONE TOOK IT.
AND IF YOU DON'T GET IT BACK WITHIN TWENTY-FOUR HOURS YOUR LINK TO THE HOUSE WILL BE PERMANENTLY SEVERED AND IT AND ALL ITS POWER WILL BE FOREVER LOST TO YOU. DOES THAT ABOUT COVER IT, JOHN?
WELL, IF YOU BLOODY KNEW THE WHOLE THING WAS GOING TO HAPPEN, I WONDER WHY YOU LET IT, X?
AND I WONDER, JOHN, WHY DID YOU NEGLECT TO TELL THE OTHERS THAT IT WAS THE CULT OF THE COLD FLAME THAT ATTACKED YOU?
THE CULT OF THE COLD FLAME? WHO THE HELL IS THAT?
THAT IS A MATTER FOR ANOTHER DAY, DEADMAN. THE FLAME MAY HAVE ASSISTED IN THE ATTACK, BUT THEY DO NOT HAVE THE HOUSE NOW.
Uh-huh, THEN WHO DOES, LOVE?
THE IDENTITY OF OUR ENEMY, AND THE LOCATION OF THE HOUSE IS--
IT IS NOT KNOWN TO ME. WHEN I TRY TO GLEAN HIS FACE, ALL I SEE IS A VOID, AN ABSENCE WHERE A MAN SHOULD BE. AND THE HOUSE ITSELF IS JUST...GONE.
WELL, IT'S A GOOD THING I HAVE A PLAN THEN, ISN'T IT?

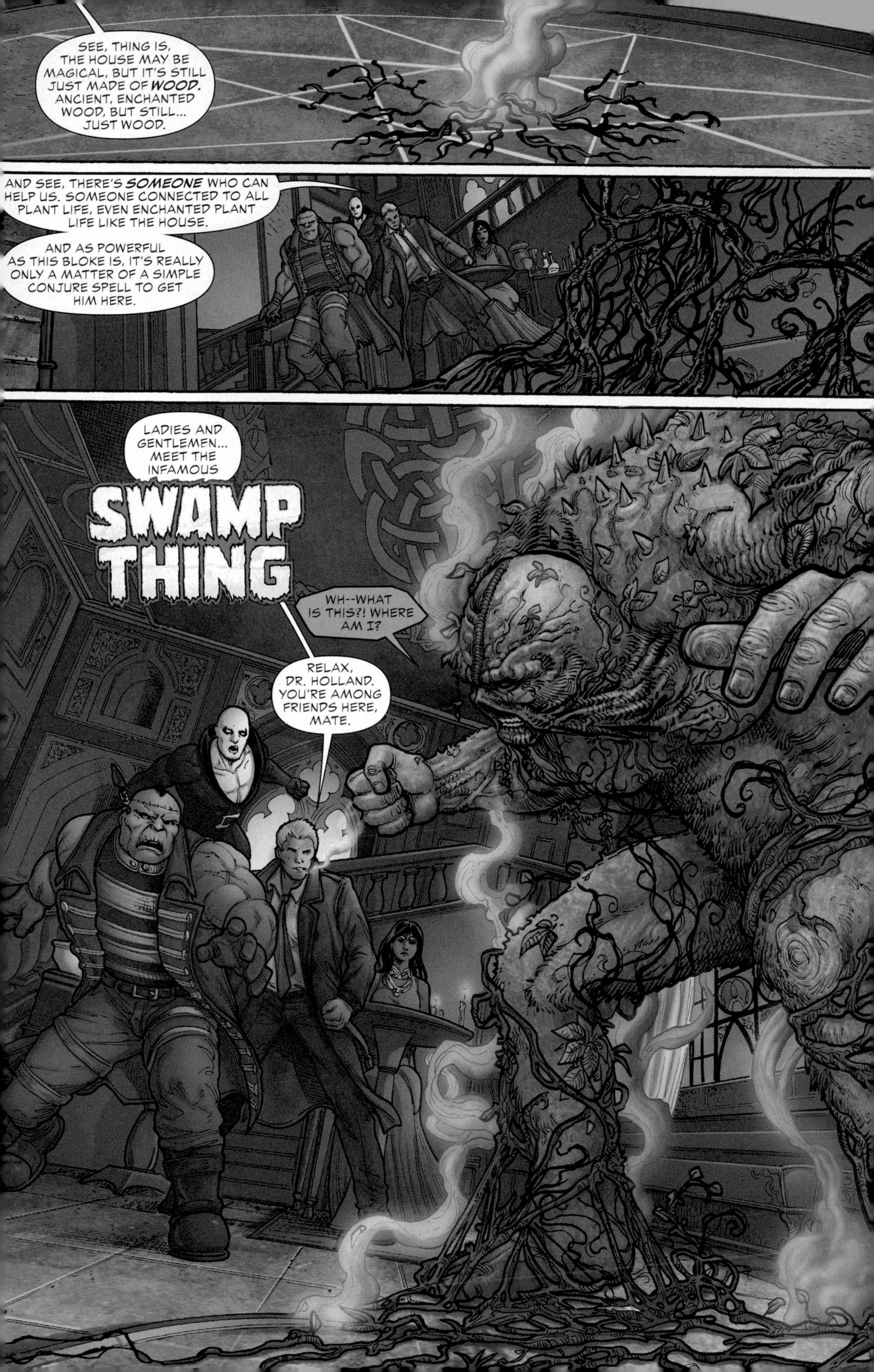
SEE, THING IS, THE HOUSE MAY BE MAGICAL, BUT IT'S STILL JUST MADE OF WOOD. ANCIENT, ENCHANTED WOOD, BUT STILL... JUST WOOD.
AND SEE, THERE'S SOMEONE WHO CAN HELP US. SOMEONE CONNECTED TO ALL PLANT LIFE, EVEN ENCHANTED PLANT LIFE LIKE THE HOUSE.
AND AS POWERFUL AS THIS BLOKE IS, IT'S REALLY ONLY A MATTER OF A SIMPLE CONJURE SPELL TO GET HIM HERE.
LADIES AND GENTLEMEN... MEET THE INFAMOUS
SWAMP THING
WH--WHAT IS THIS?! WHERE AM I?
RELAX, DR. HOLLAND. YOU'RE AMONG FRIENDS HERE, MATE.

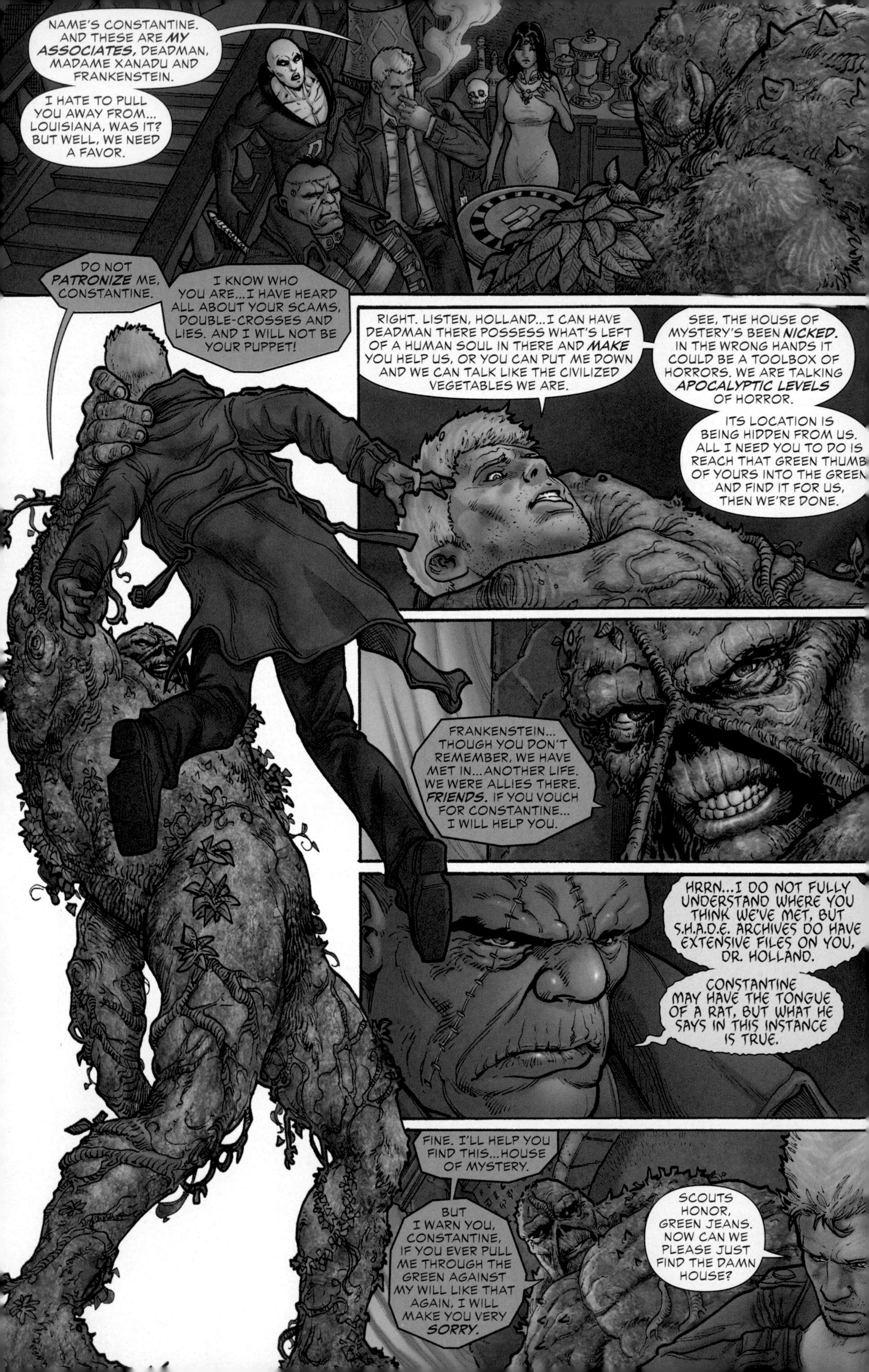
NAME'S CONSTANTINE. AND THESE ARE MY ASSOCIATES, DEADMAN, MADAME XANADU AND FRANKENSTEIN.
I HATE TO PULL YOU AWAY FROM... LOUISIANA, WAS IT? BUT WELL, WE NEED A FAVOR.
DO NOT PATRONIZE ME, CONSTANTINE.
I KNOW WHO YOU ARE...I HAVE HEARD ALL ABOUT YOUR SCAMS, DOUBLE-CROSSES AND LIES. AND I WILL NOT BE YOUR PUPPET!
RIGHT. LISTEN, HOLLAND...I CAN HAVE DEADMAN THERE POSSESS WHAT'S LEFT OF A HUMAN SOUL IN THERE AND MAKE YOU HELP US, OR YOU CAN PUT ME DOWN AND WE CAN TALK LIKE THE CIVILIZED VEGETABLES WE ARE.
SEE, THE HOUSE OF MYSTERY'S BEEN NICKED. IN THE WRONG HANDS IT COULD BE A TOOLBOX OF HORRORS. WE ARE TALKING APOCALYPTIC LEVELS OF HORROR.
ITS LOCATION IS BEING HIDDEN FROM US. ALL I NEED YOU TO DO IS REACH THAT GREEN THUMB OF YOURS INTO THE GREEN AND FIND IT FOR US, THEN WE'RE DONE.
FRANKENSTEIN... THOUGH YOU DON'T REMEMBER, WE HAVE MET IN...ANOTHER LIFE. WE WERE ALLIES THERE. FRIENDS. IF YOU VOUCH FOR CONSTANTINE... I WILL HELP YOU.
HRRN...I DO NOT FULLY UNDERSTAND WHERE YOU THINK WE'VE MET, BUT S.H.A.D.E. ARCHIVES DO HAVE EXTENSIVE FILES ON YOU, DR. HOLLAND.
CONSTANTINE MAY HAVE THE TONGUE OF A RAT, BUT WHAT HE SAYS IN THIS INSTANCE IS TRUE.
FINE. I'LL HELP YOU FIND THIS...HOUSE OF MYSTERY.
BUT I WARN YOU, CONSTANTINE, IF YOU EVER PULL ME THROUGH THE GREEN AGAINST MY WILL LIKE THAT AGAIN, I WILL MAKE YOU VERY SORRY.
SCOUTS HONOR, GREEN JEANS. NOW CAN WE PLEASE JUST FIND THE DAMN HOUSE?

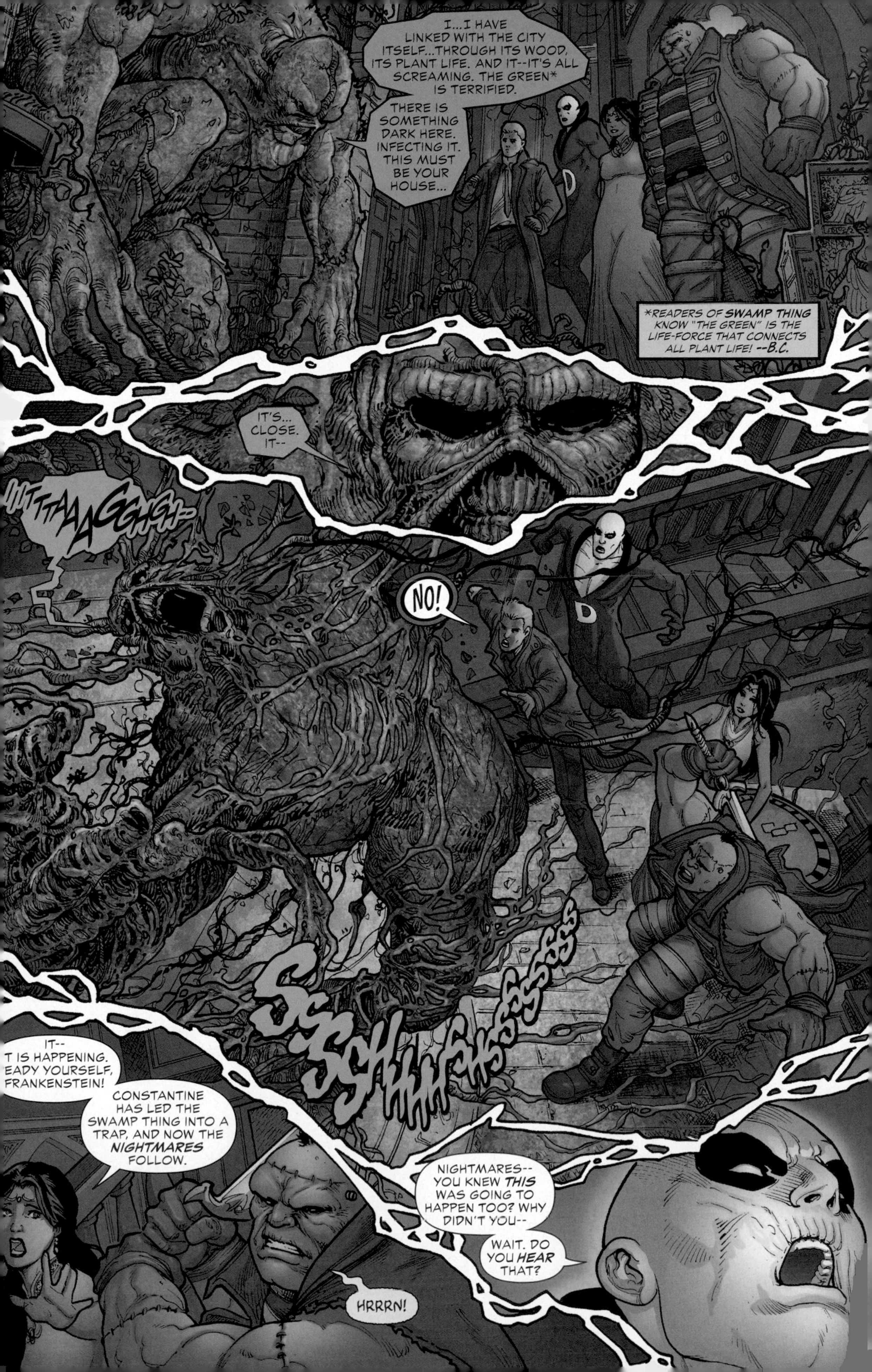
I...I HAVE LINKED WITH THE CITY ITSELF...THROUGH ITS WOOD, ITS PLANT LIFE. AND IT--IT'S ALL SCREAMING. THE GREEN* IS TERRIFIED.
THERE IS SOMETHING DARK HERE. INFECTING IT. THIS MUST BE YOUR HOUSE...
*READERS OF SWAMP THING KNOW "THE GREEN" IS THE LIFE-FORCE THAT CONNECTS ALL PLANT LIFE! --B.C.
IT'S... CLOSE. IT--
UUTTAAAGGHGH--
NO!
SSSGHHHHSSSSSSSS
IT-- T IS HAPPENING. EADY YOURSELF, FRANKENSTEIN!
CONSTANTINE HAS LED THE SWAMP THING INTO A TRAP, AND NOW THE NIGHTMARES FOLLOW.
NIGHTMARES-- YOU KNEW THIS WAS GOING TO HAPPEN TOO? WHY DIDN'T YOU--
WAIT. DO YOU HEAR THAT?
HRRRN!

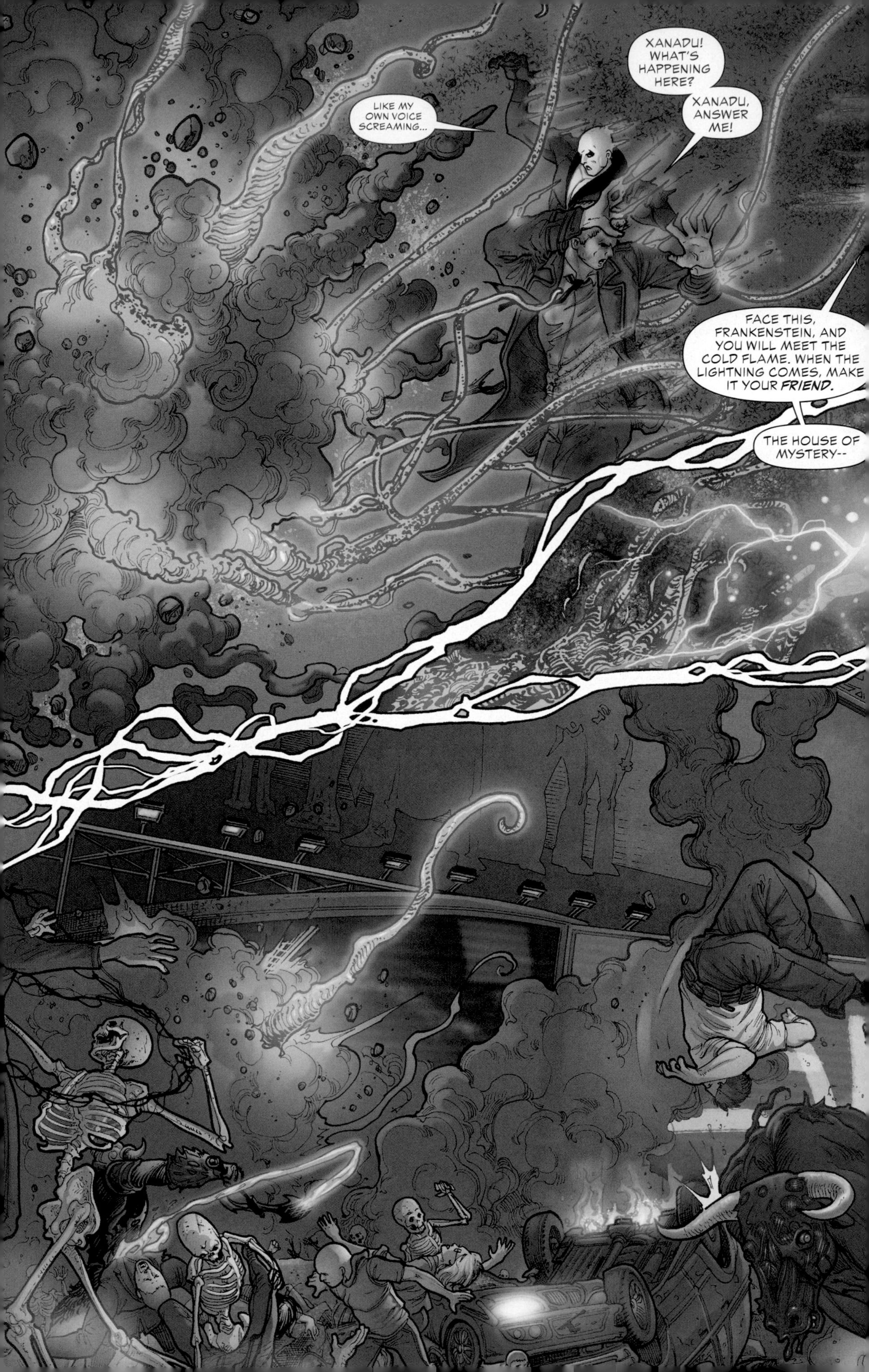

LIKE MY OWN VOICE SCREAMING...
XANADU! WHAT'S HAPPENING HERE?
XANADU, ANSWER ME!
FACE THIS, FRANKENSTEIN, AND YOU WILL MEET THE COLD FLAME. WHEN THE LIGHTNING COMES, MAKE IT YOUR ***FRIEND.***
THE HOUSE OF MYSTERY--

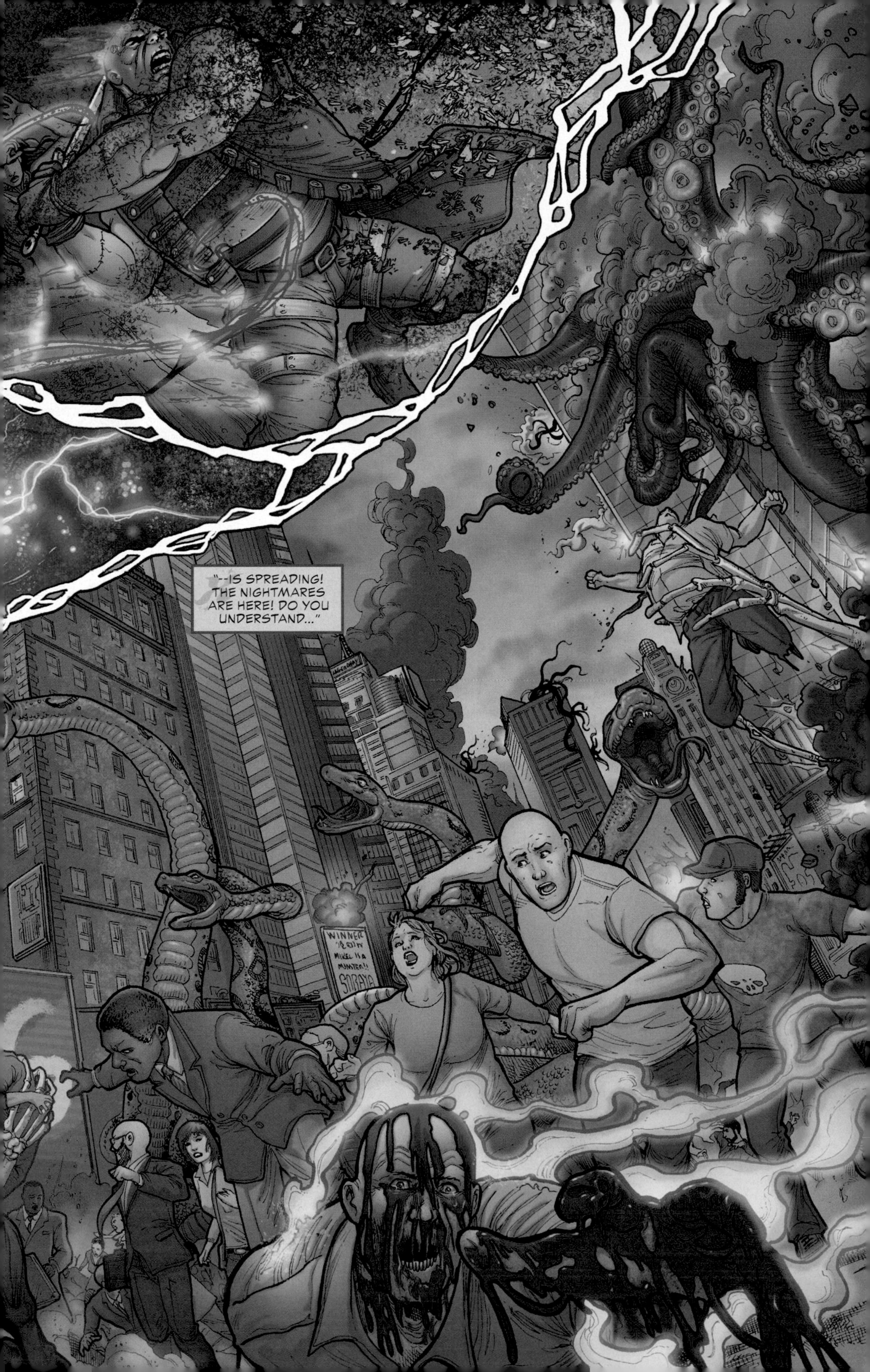
"--IS SPREADING! THE NIGHTMARES ARE HERE! DO YOU UNDERSTAND..."
WINNER
SORAYA

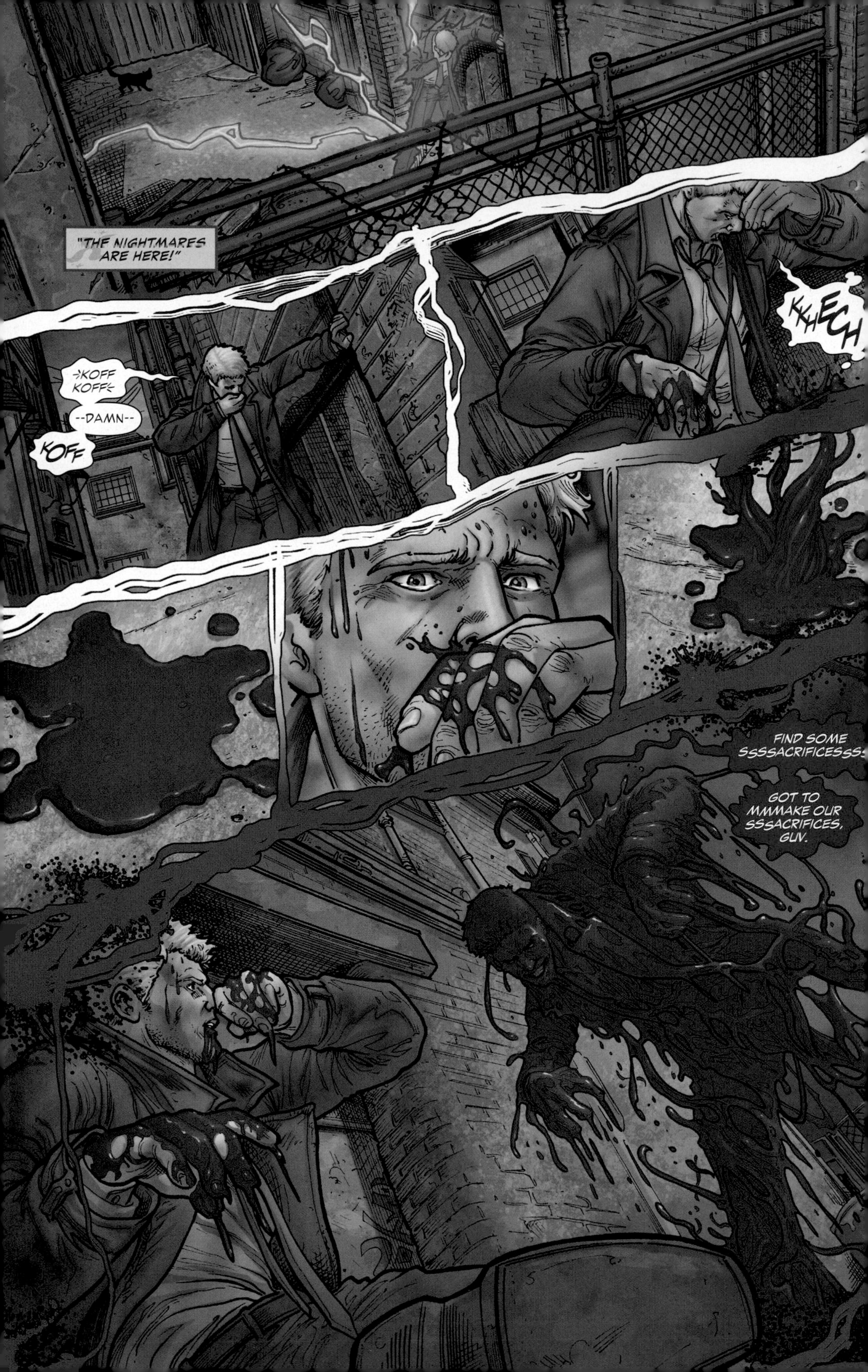
"THE NIGHTMARES ARE HERE!"
KKHECH
KOFF KOFF
--DAMN--
KOFF
FIND SOME SSSSACRIFICESSSS
GOT TO MMMAKE OUR SSSACRIFICES, GUV.

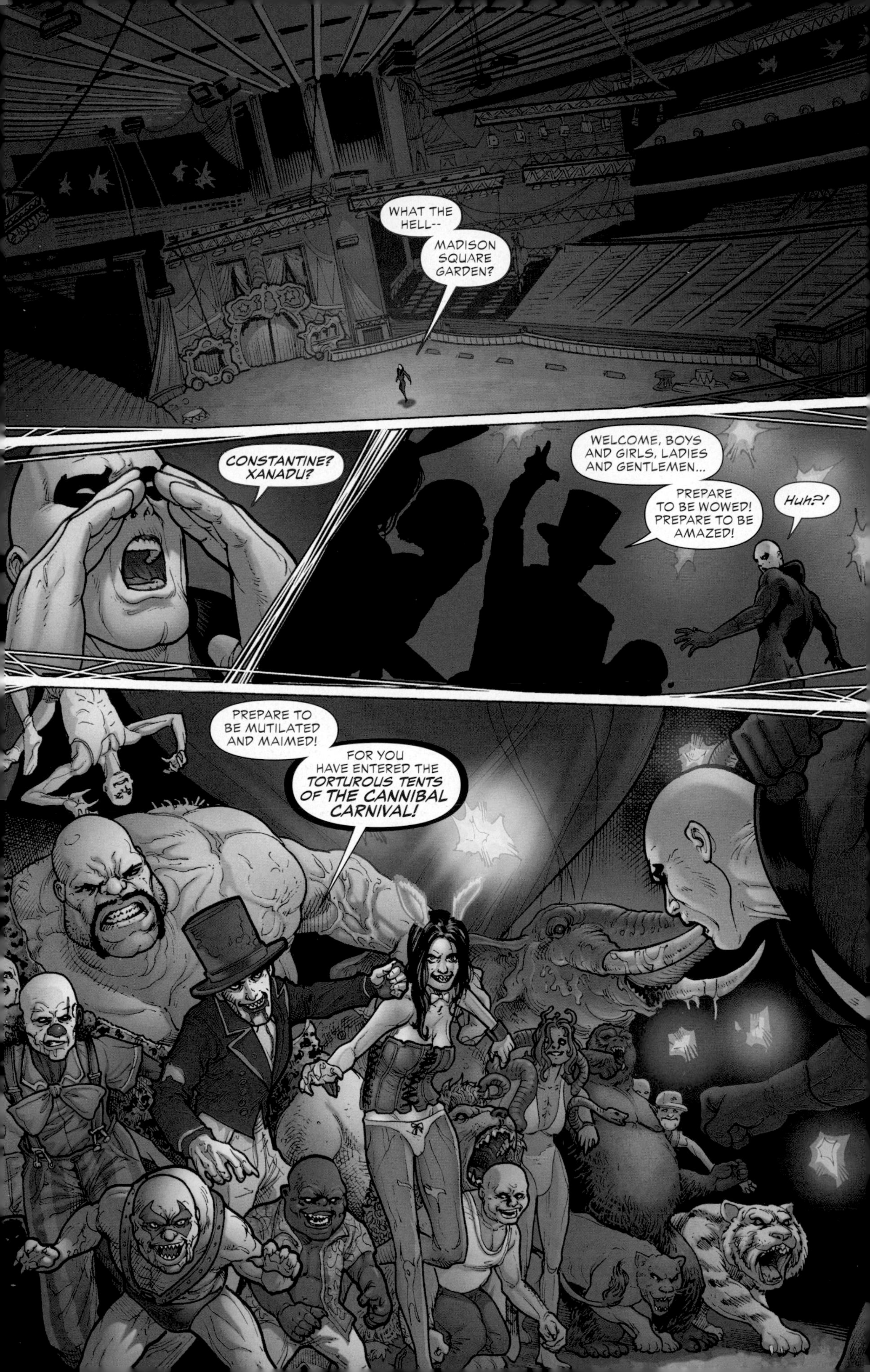
WHAT THE HELL--
MADISON SQUARE GARDEN?
CONSTANTINE? XANADU?
WELCOME, BOYS AND GIRLS, LADIES AND GENTLEMEN...
PREPARE TO BE WOWED! PREPARE TO BE AMAZED!
Huh?!
PREPARE TO BE MUTILATED AND MAIMED!
FOR YOU HAVE ENTERED THE TORTUROUS TENTS OF THE CANNIBAL CARNIVAL!

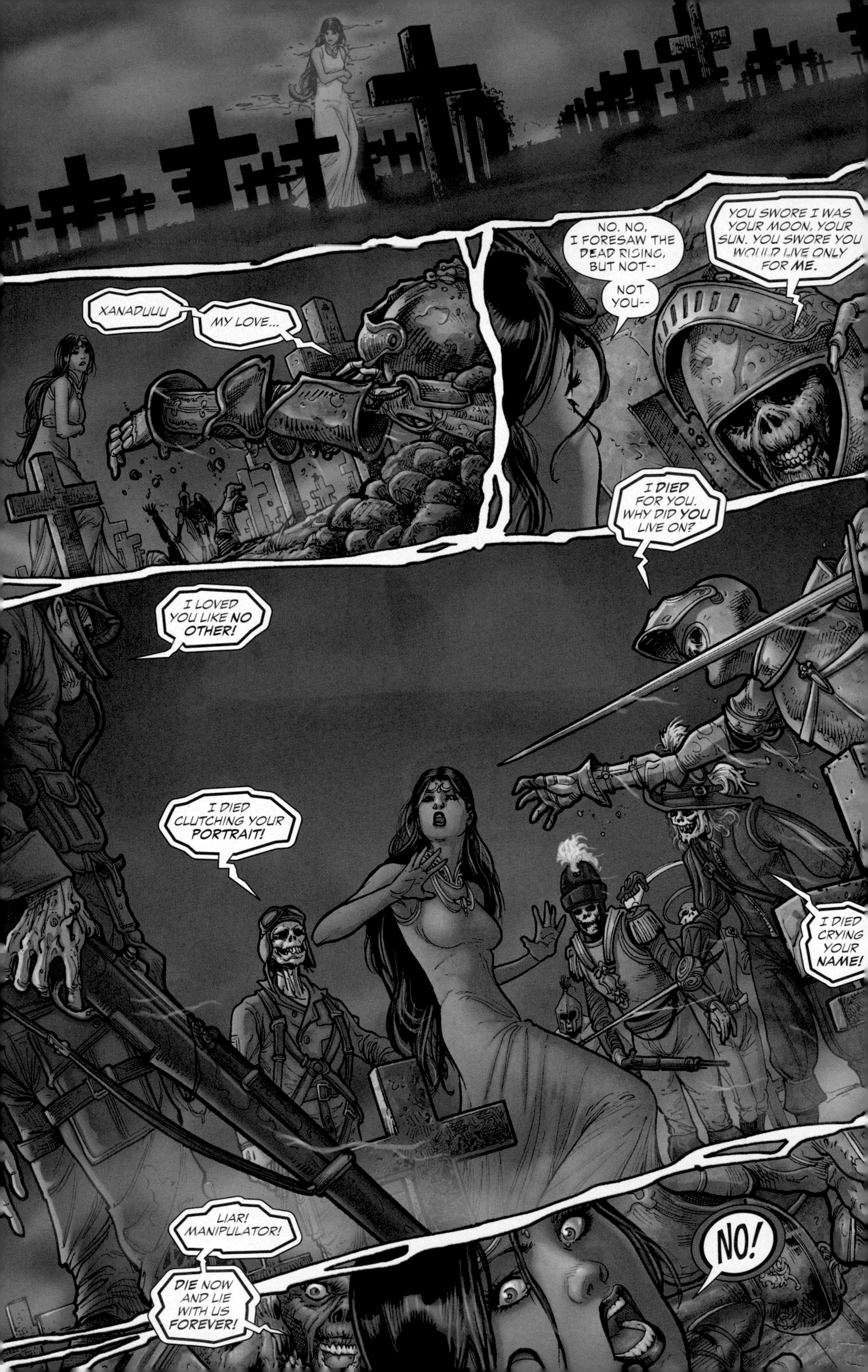
XANADUUU
MY LOVE...
NO. NO, I FORESAW THE DEAD RISING, BUT NOT--
NOT YOU--
YOU SWORE I WAS YOUR MOON, YOUR SUN. YOU SWORE YOU WOULD LIVE ONLY FOR ME.
I DIED FOR YOU. WHY DID YOU LIVE ON?
I LOVED YOU LIKE NO OTHER!
I DIED CLUTCHING YOUR PORTRAIT!
I DIED CRYING YOUR NAME!
LIAR! MANIPULATOR!
DIE NOW AND LIE WITH US FOREVER!
NO!

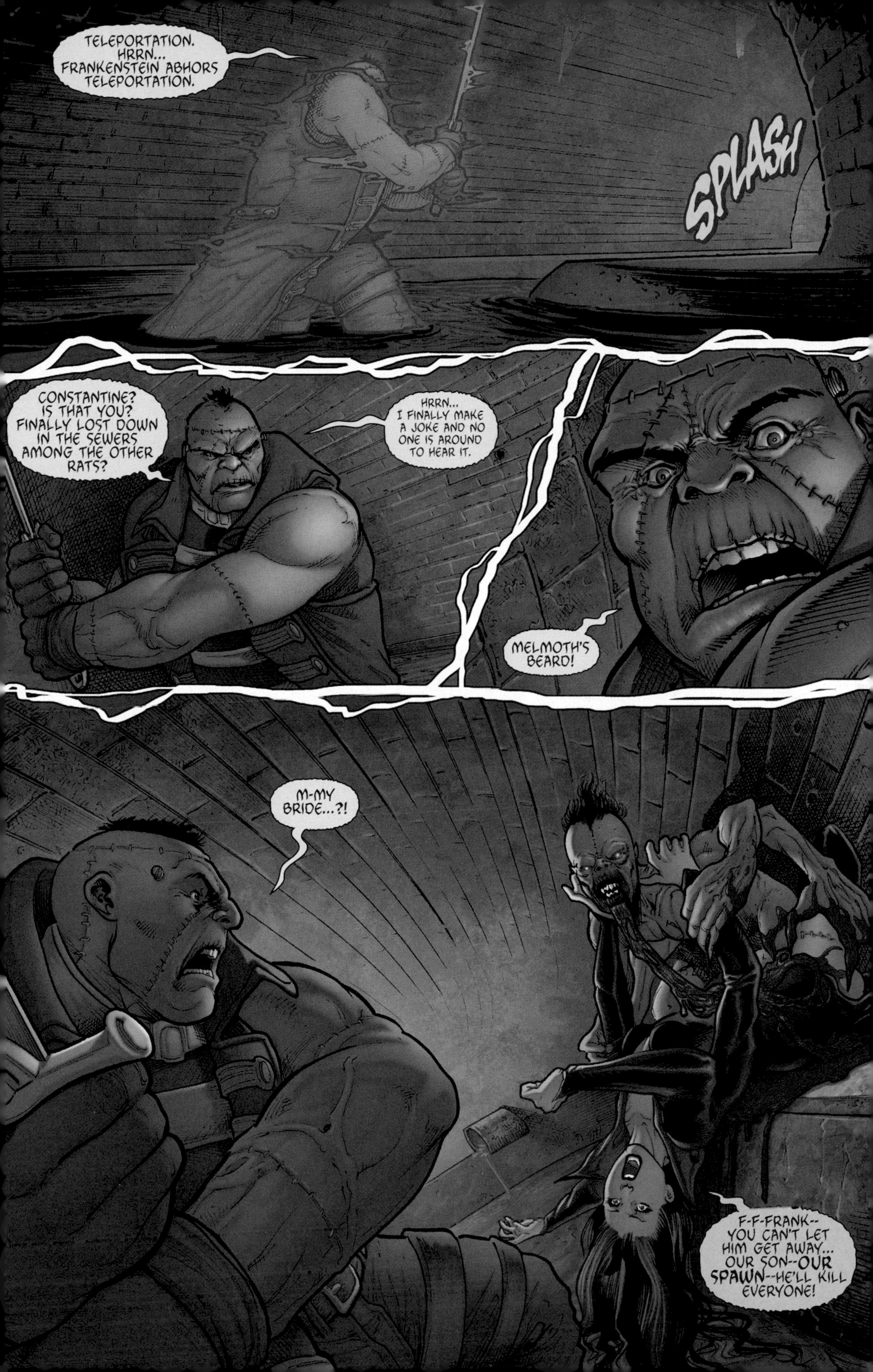

TELEPORTATION. HRRN... FRANKENSTEIN ABHORS TELEPORTATION.
SPLASH
CONSTANTINE? IS THAT YOU? FINALLY LOST DOWN IN THE SEWERS AMONG THE OTHER RATS?
HRRN... I FINALLY MAKE A JOKE AND NO ONE IS AROUND TO HEAR IT.
MELMOTH'S BEARD!
M-MY BRIDE...?!
F-F-FRANK-- YOU CAN'T LET HIM GET AWAY... OUR SON--**OUR SPAWN**--HE'LL KILL EVERYONE!

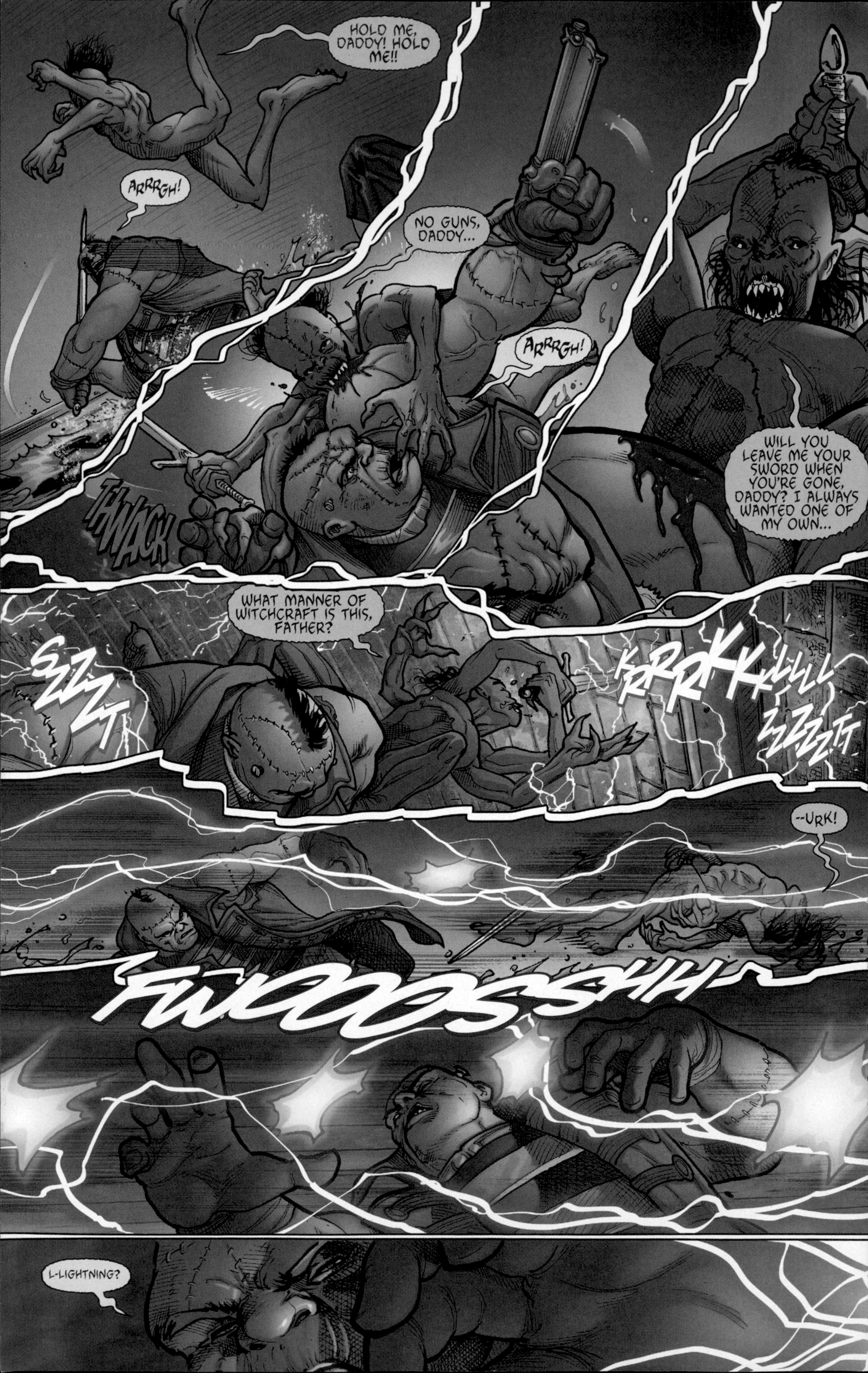
HOLD ME, DADDY! HOLD ME!!
ARRRGH!
NO GUNS, DADDY...
ARRRGH!
WILL YOU LEAVE ME YOUR SWORD WHEN YOU'RE GONE, DADDY? I ALWAYS WANTED ONE OF MY OWN...
THWACK
WHAT MANNER OF WITCHCRAFT IS THIS, FATHER?
SZZZT
KRRRKKKLLLL ZZZZZTT
--URK!
FWOOOSSHH
L-LIGHTNING?

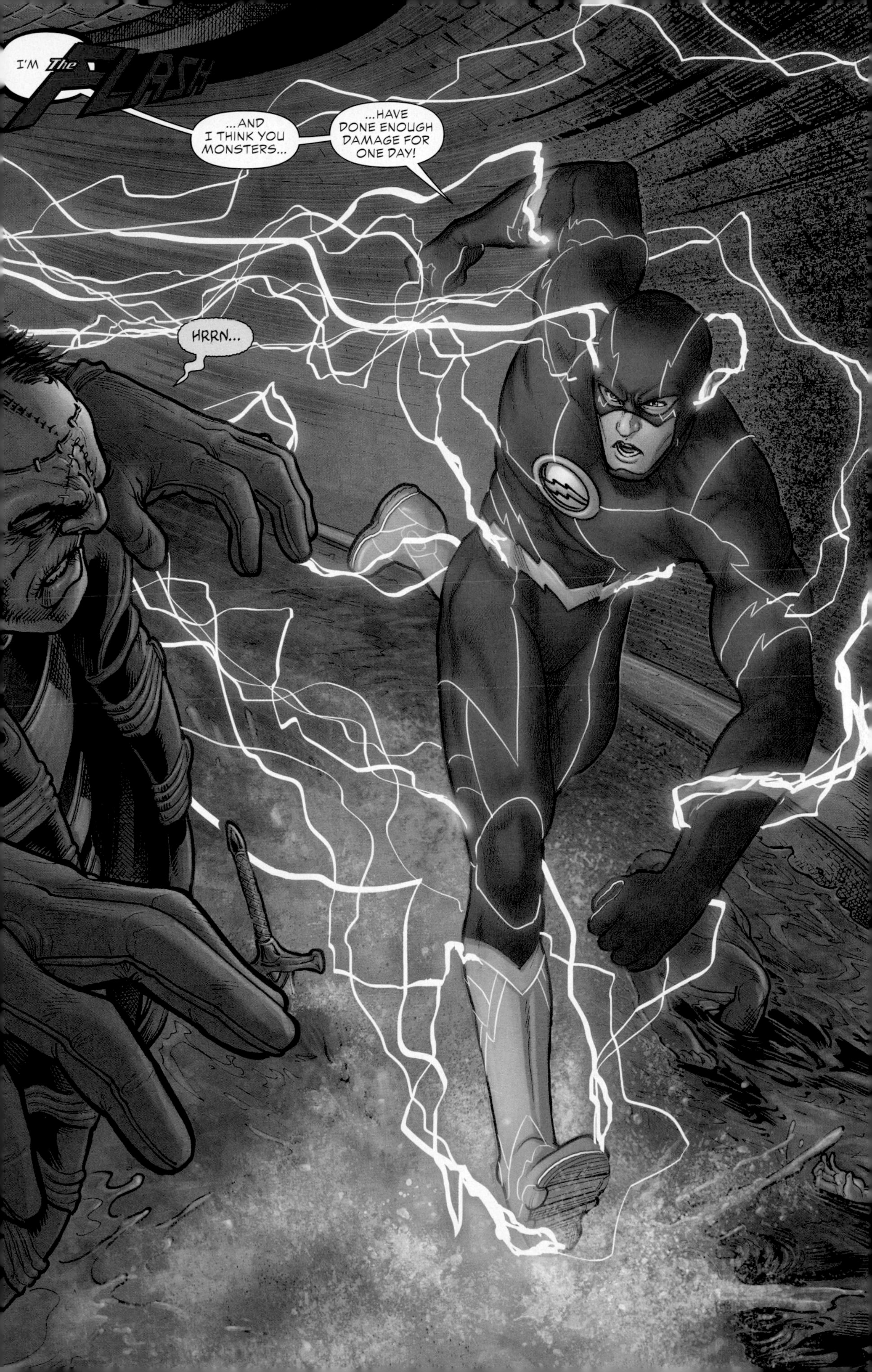
I'M The FLASH
...AND I THINK YOU MONSTERS...
...HAVE DONE ENOUGH DAMAGE FOR ONE DAY!
HRRN...

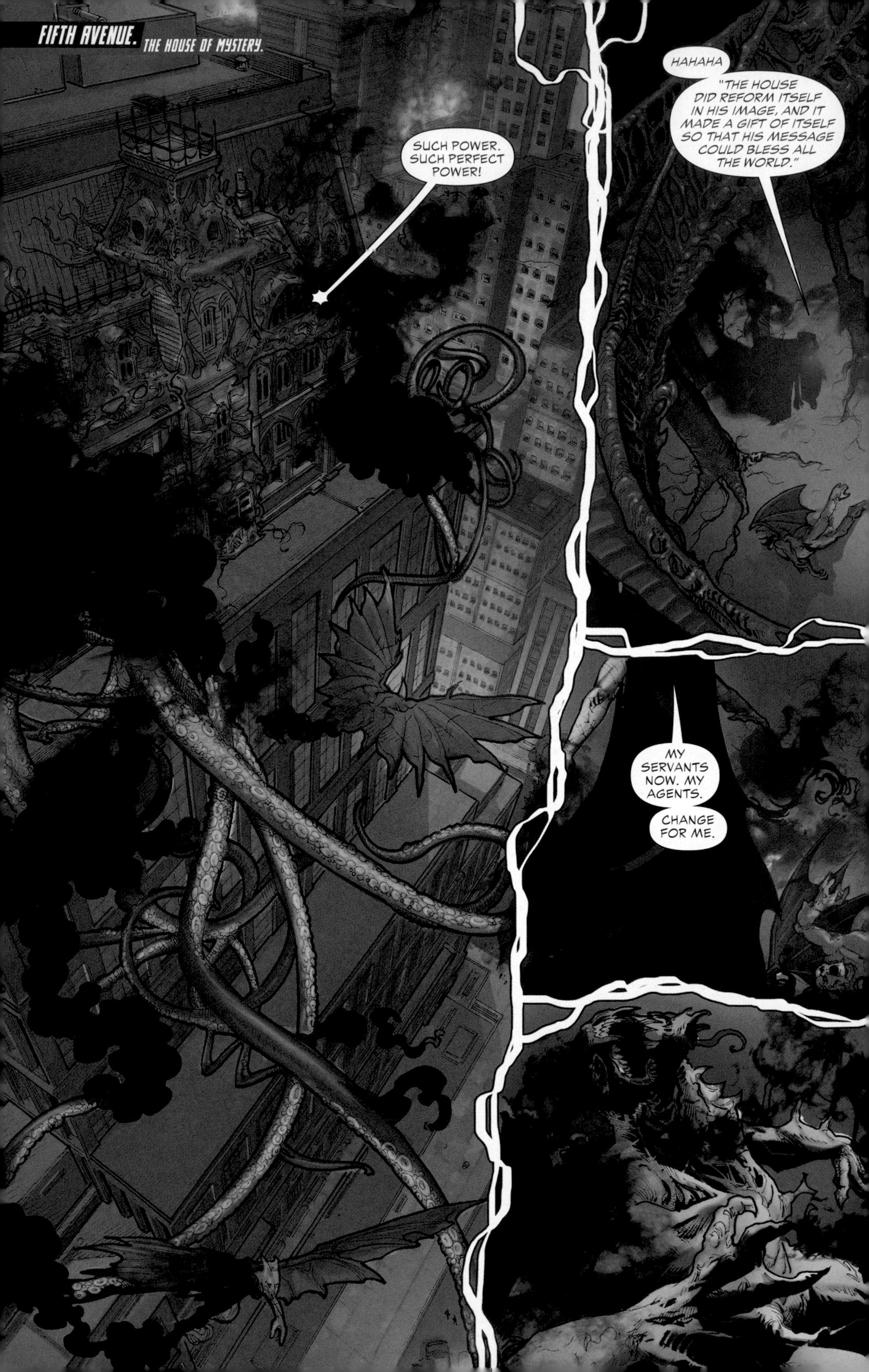

FIFTH AVENUE. THE HOUSE OF MYSTERY.
SUCH POWER. SUCH PERFECT POWER!
HAHAHA
"THE HOUSE DID REFORM ITSELF IN HIS IMAGE, AND IT MADE A GIFT OF ITSELF SO THAT HIS MESSAGE COULD BLESS ALL THE WORLD."
MY SERVANTS NOW. MY AGENTS.
CHANGE FOR ME.

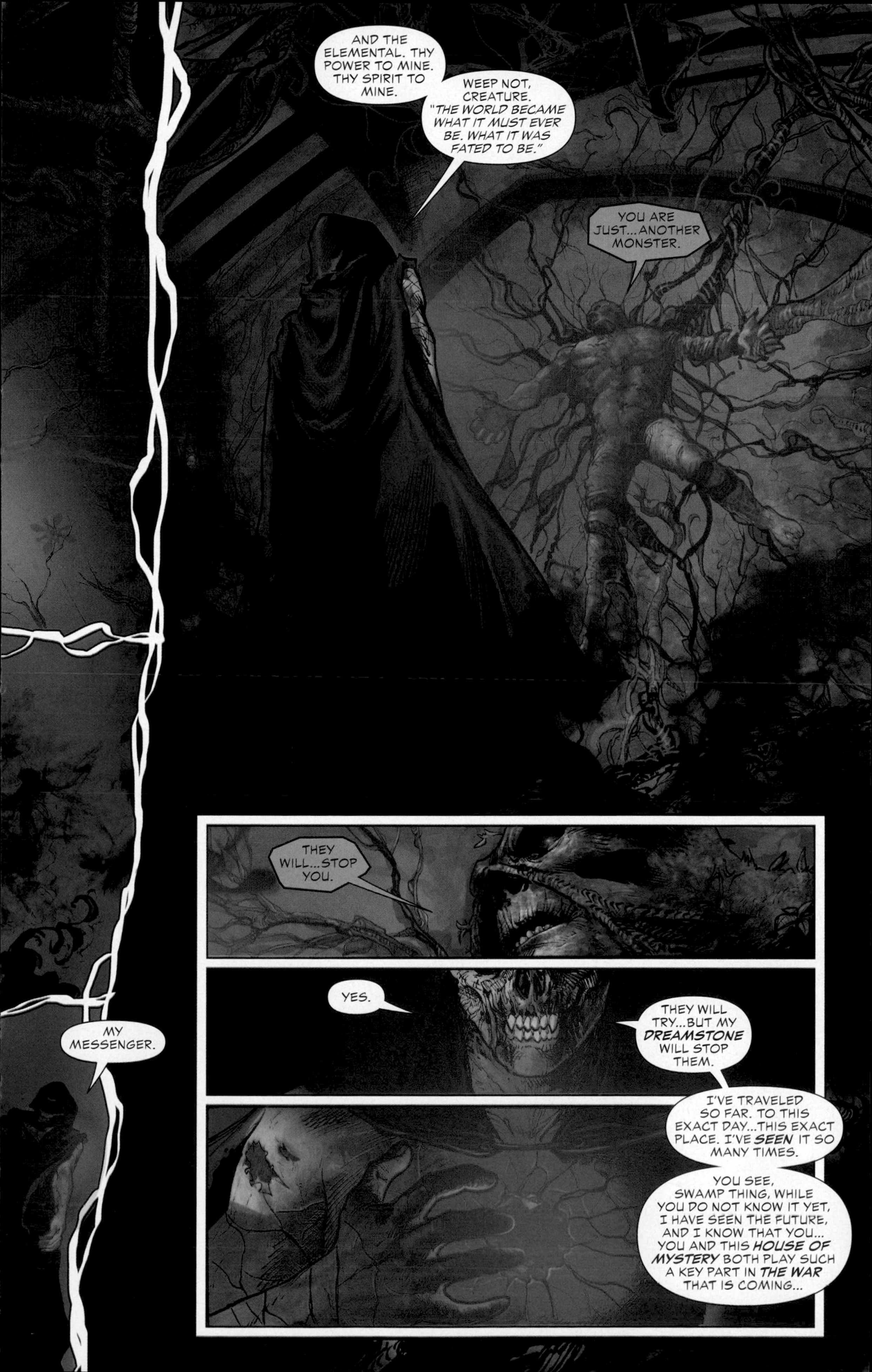
AND THE ELEMENTAL. THY POWER TO MINE. THY SPIRIT TO MINE.
WEEP NOT, CREATURE. "*THE WORLD BECAME WHAT IT MUST EVER BE. WHAT IT WAS FATED TO BE.*"
YOU ARE JUST...ANOTHER MONSTER.
THEY WILL...STOP YOU.
YES.
THEY WILL TRY...BUT MY ***DREAMSTONE*** WILL STOP THEM.
MY MESSENGER.
I'VE TRAVELED SO FAR. TO THIS EXACT DAY...THIS EXACT PLACE. I'VE ***SEEN*** IT SO MANY TIMES.
YOU SEE, SWAMP THING, WHILE YOU DO NOT KNOW IT YET, I HAVE SEEN THE FUTURE, AND I KNOW THAT YOU... YOU AND THIS ***HOUSE OF MYSTERY*** BOTH PLAY SUCH A KEY PART IN ***THE WAR*** THAT IS COMING...

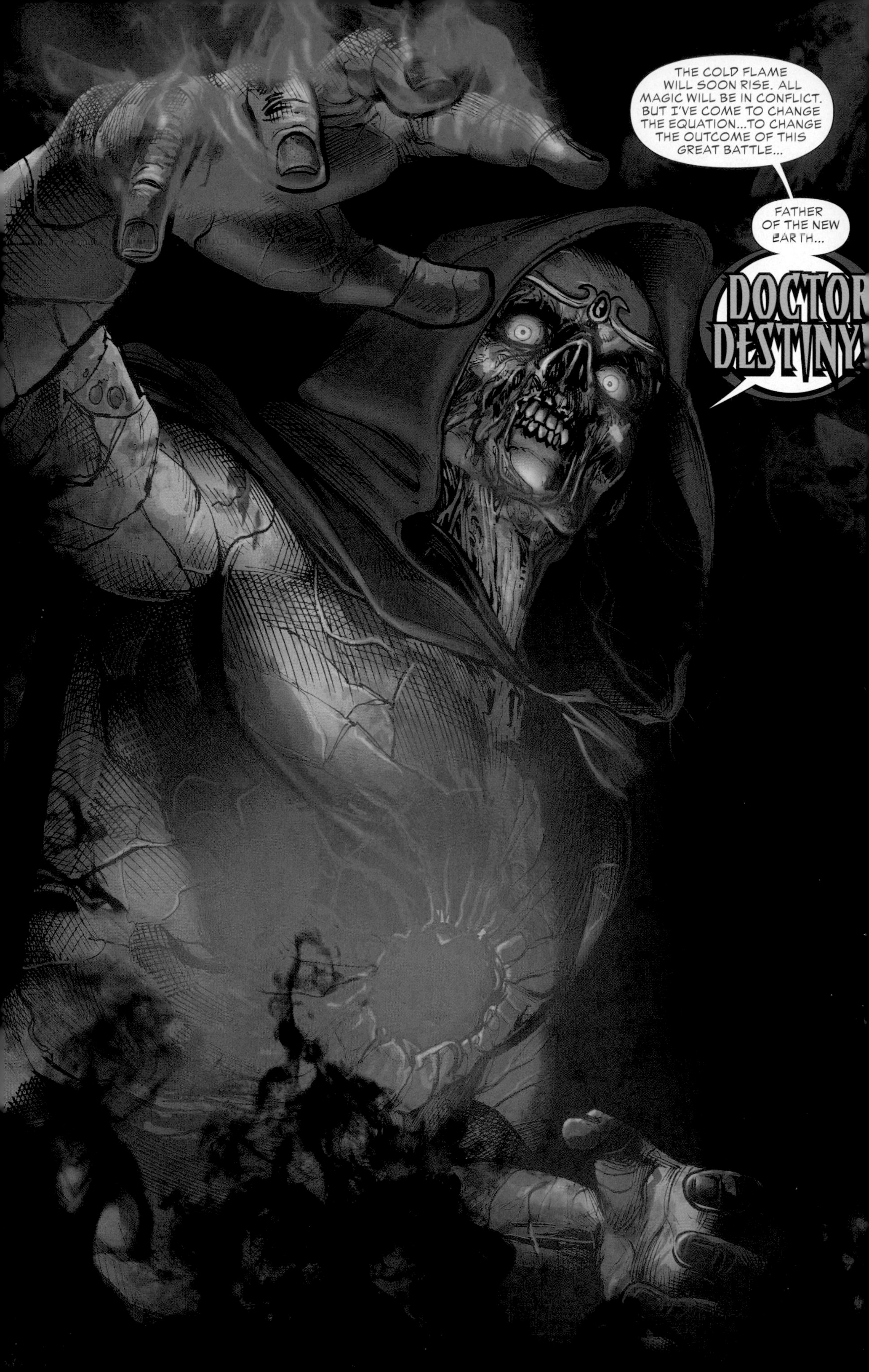
THE COLD FLAME WILL SOON RISE. ALL MAGIC WILL BE IN CONFLICT. BUT I'VE COME TO CHANGE THE EQUATION...TO CHANGE THE OUTCOME OF THIS GREAT BATTLE...
FATHER OF THE NEW EARTH...
DOCTOR DESTINY!

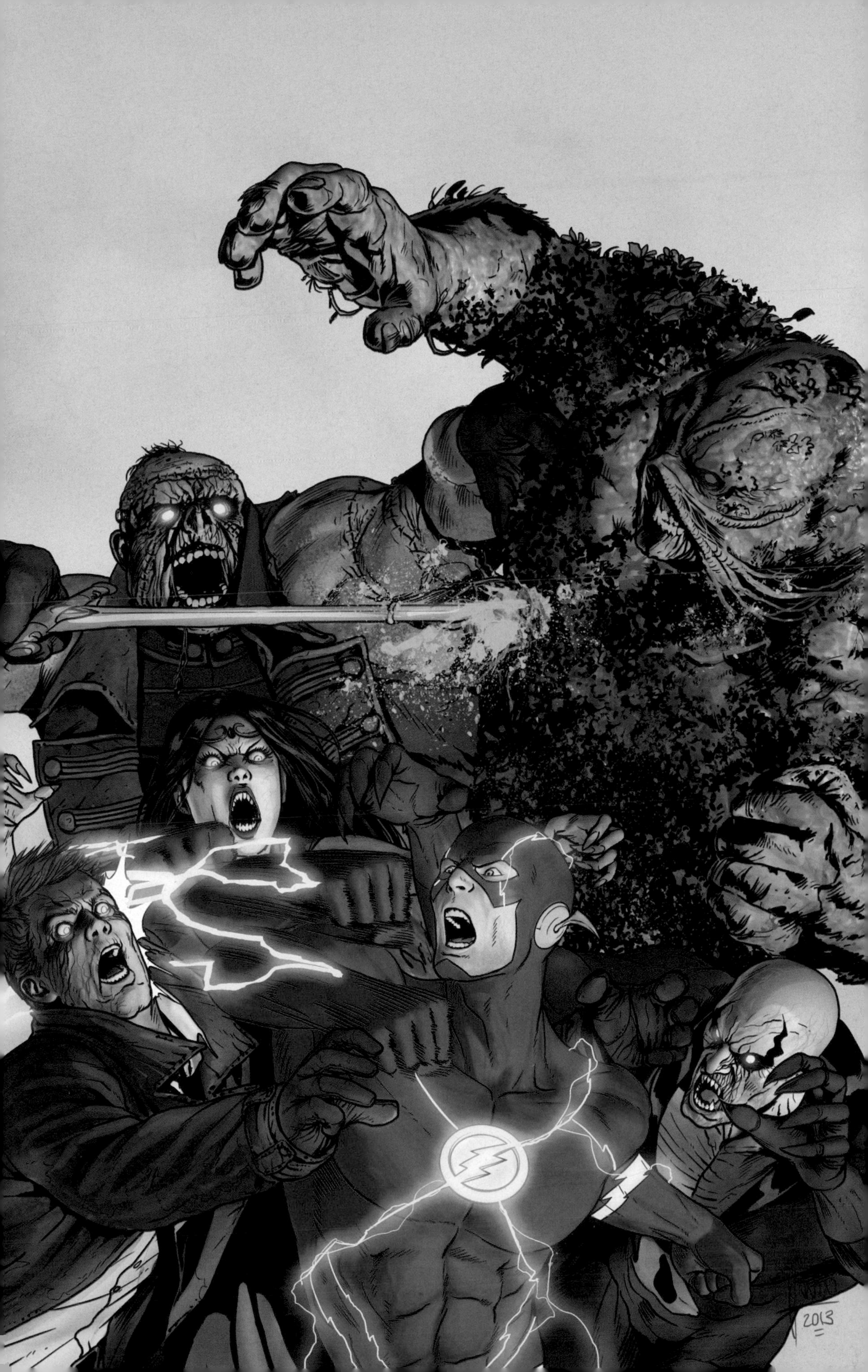
2013

HORROR CITY part two
THE NIGHTMARE GOSPEL

RAY FAWKES
JEFF LEMIRE
writers

MIKEL JANIN
layouts

VICENTE CIFUENTES
finishes

MIKEL JANIN
cover artist

SWAMP THING created by LEN WEIN & BERNIE WRIGHTSON

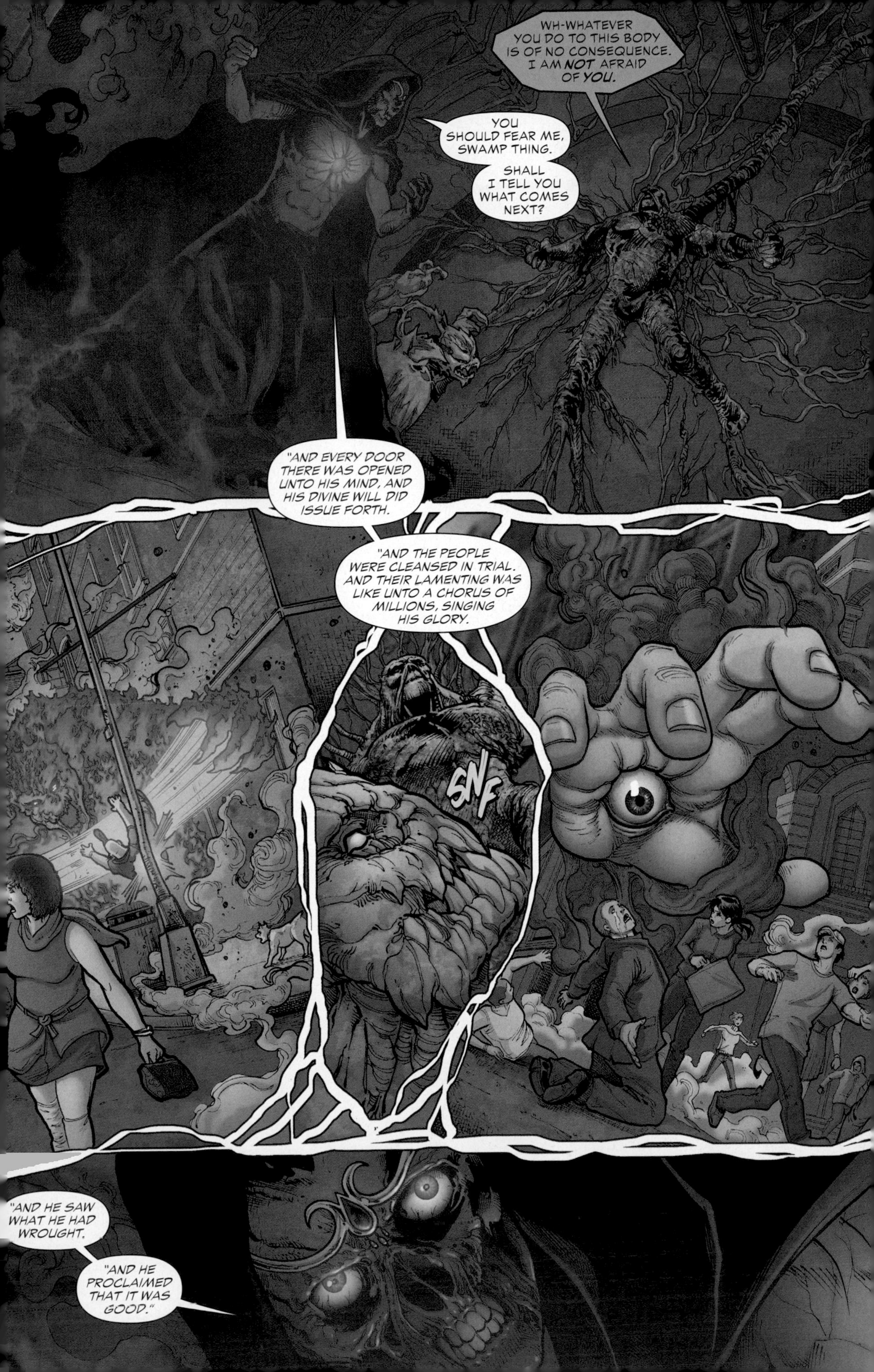
WH-WHATEVER YOU DO TO THIS BODY IS OF NO CONSEQUENCE. I AM NOT AFRAID OF YOU.
YOU SHOULD FEAR ME, SWAMP THING.
SHALL I TELL YOU WHAT COMES NEXT?
"AND EVERY DOOR THERE WAS OPENED UNTO HIS MIND, AND HIS DIVINE WILL DID ISSUE FORTH.
"AND THE PEOPLE WERE CLEANSED IN TRIAL. AND THEIR LAMENTING WAS LIKE UNTO A CHORUS OF MILLIONS, SINGING HIS GLORY.
SNF
"AND HE SAW WHAT HE HAD WROUGHT.
"AND HE PROCLAIMED THAT IT WAS GOOD."

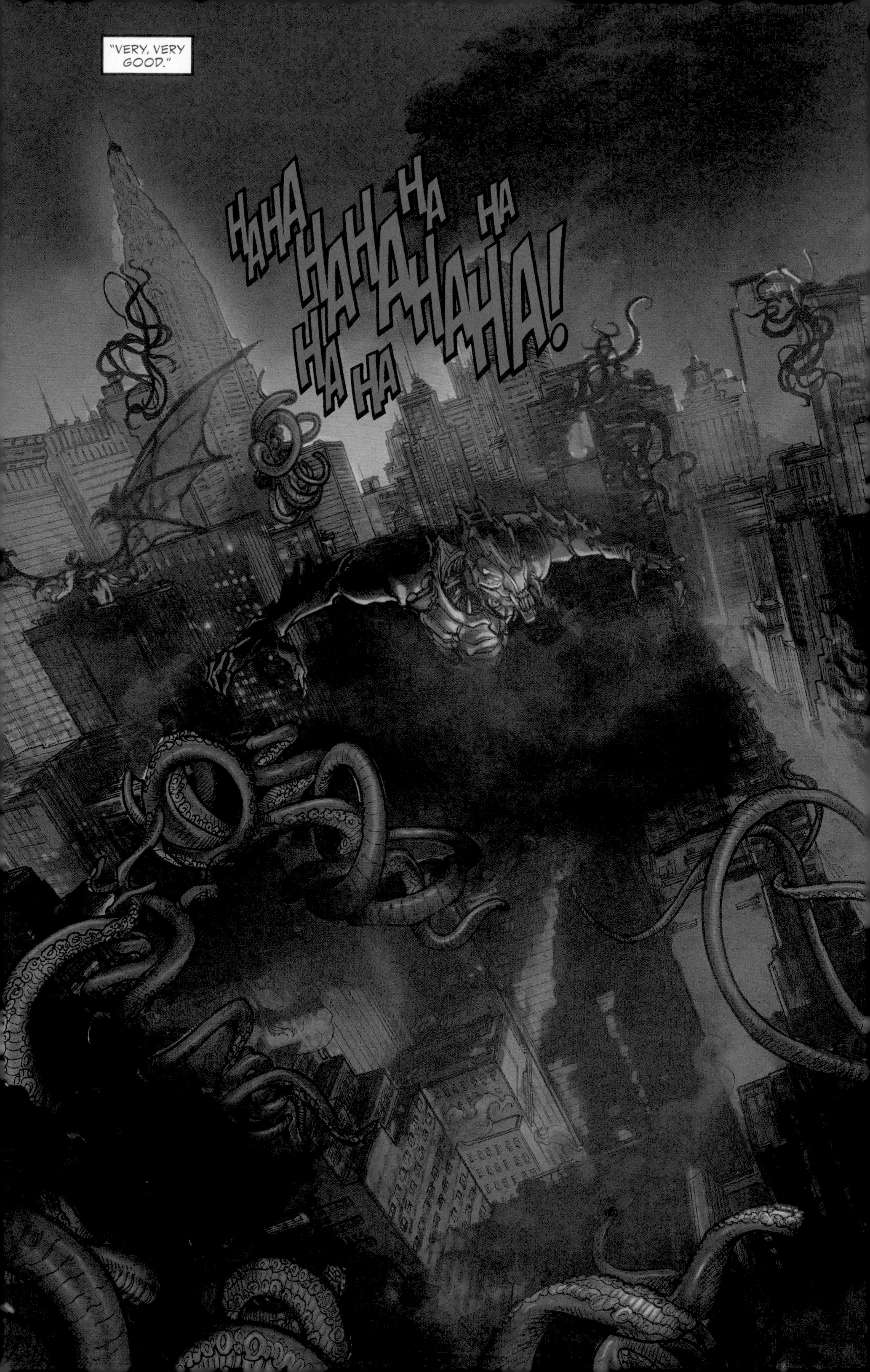
"VERY, VERY GOOD."
HAHA HAHAHA HA HA HA HAHAHAHA HA HAHAHA!

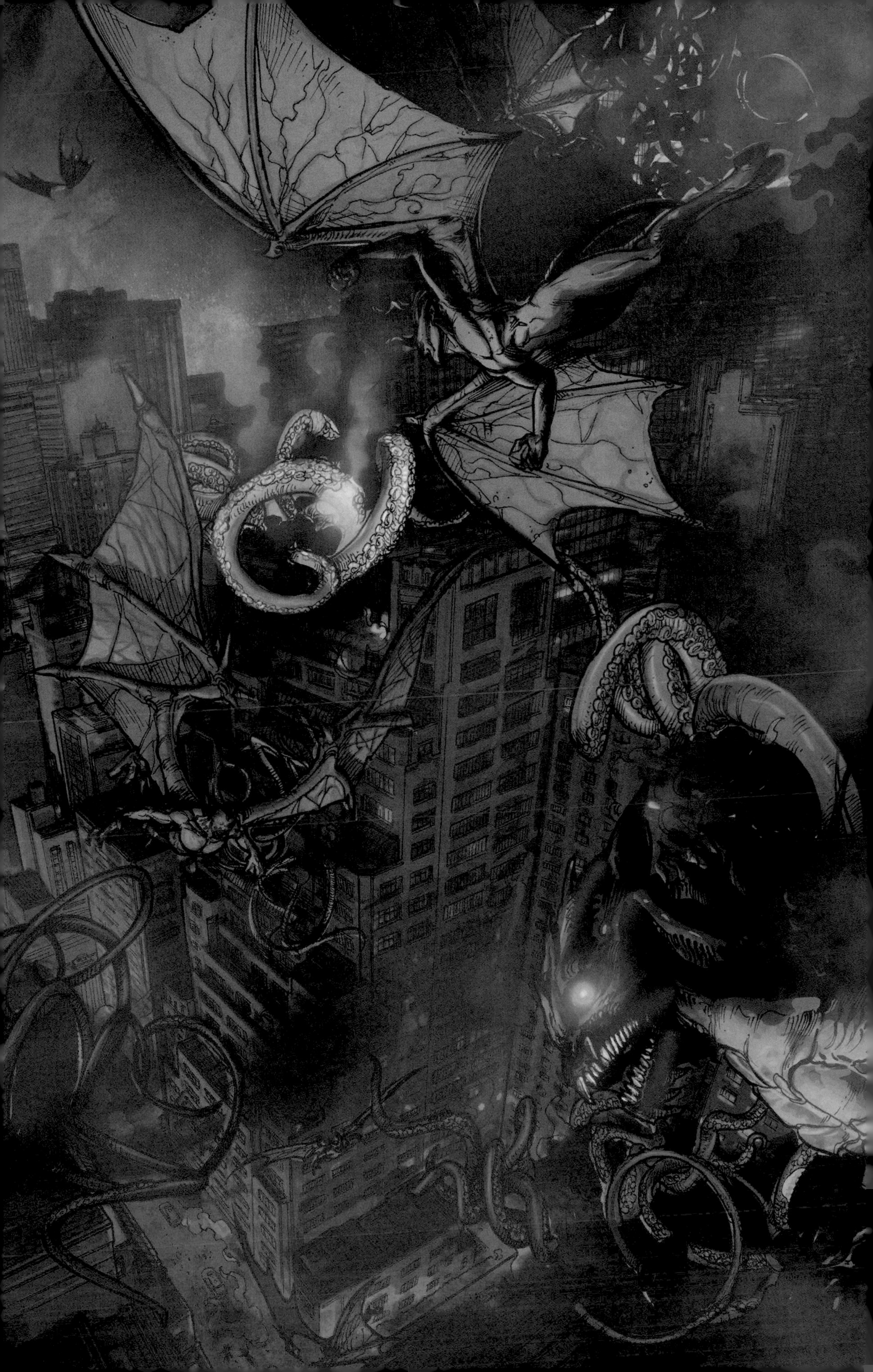

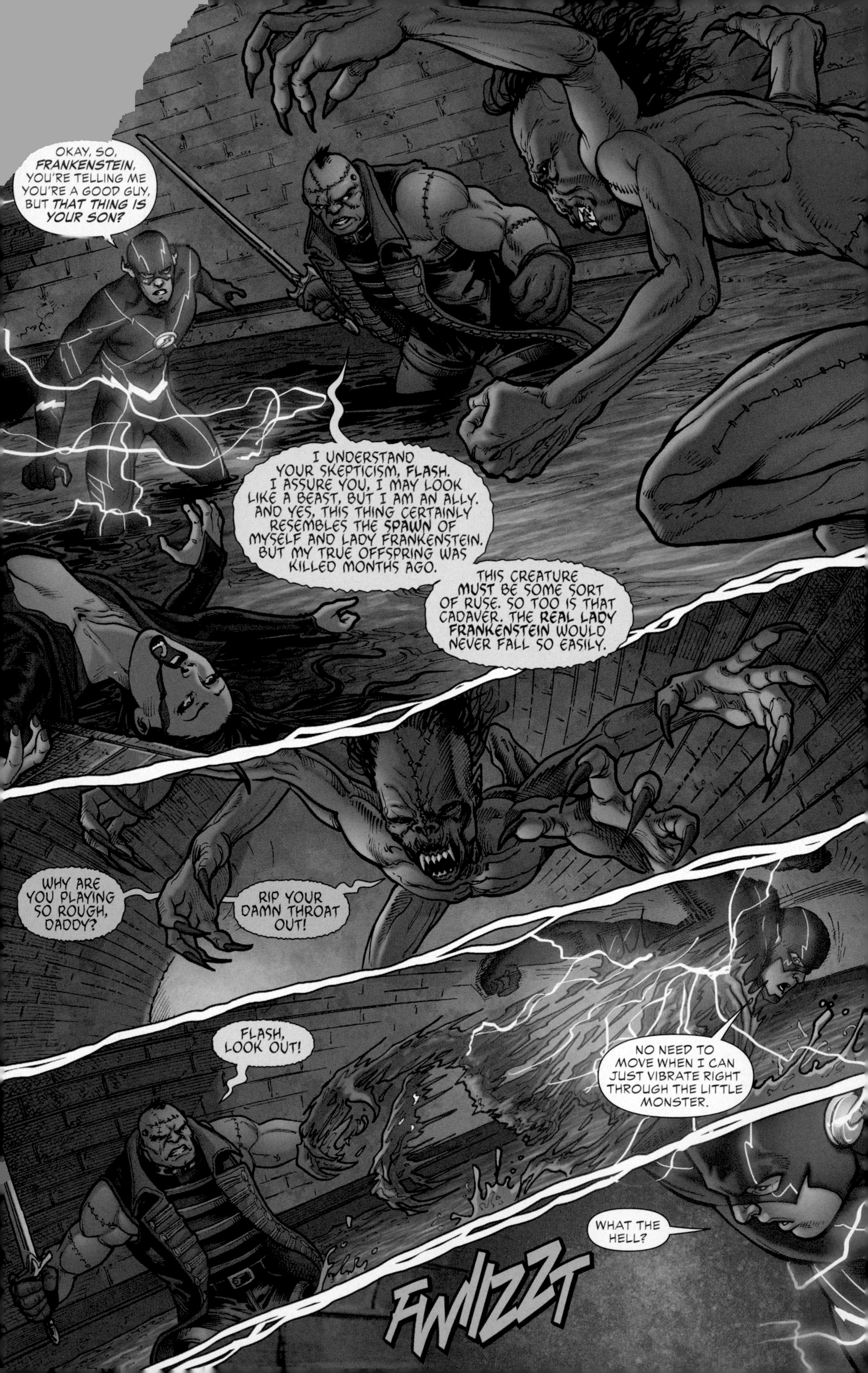
OKAY, SO, FRANKENSTEIN, YOU'RE TELLING ME YOU'RE A GOOD GUY, BUT THAT THING IS YOUR SON?
I UNDERSTAND YOUR SKEPTICISM, FLASH. I ASSURE YOU, I MAY LOOK LIKE A BEAST, BUT I AM AN ALLY. AND YES, THIS THING CERTAINLY RESEMBLES THE SPAWN OF MYSELF AND LADY FRANKENSTEIN. BUT MY TRUE OFFSPRING WAS KILLED MONTHS AGO.
THIS CREATURE MUST BE SOME SORT OF RUSE. SO TOO IS THAT CADAVER. THE REAL LADY FRANKENSTEIN WOULD NEVER FALL SO EASILY.
WHY ARE YOU PLAYING SO ROUGH, DADDY?
RIP YOUR DAMN THROAT OUT!
FLASH, LOOK OUT!
NO NEED TO MOVE WHEN I CAN JUST VIBRATE RIGHT THROUGH THE LITTLE MONSTER.
WHAT THE HELL?
FWIZZZT

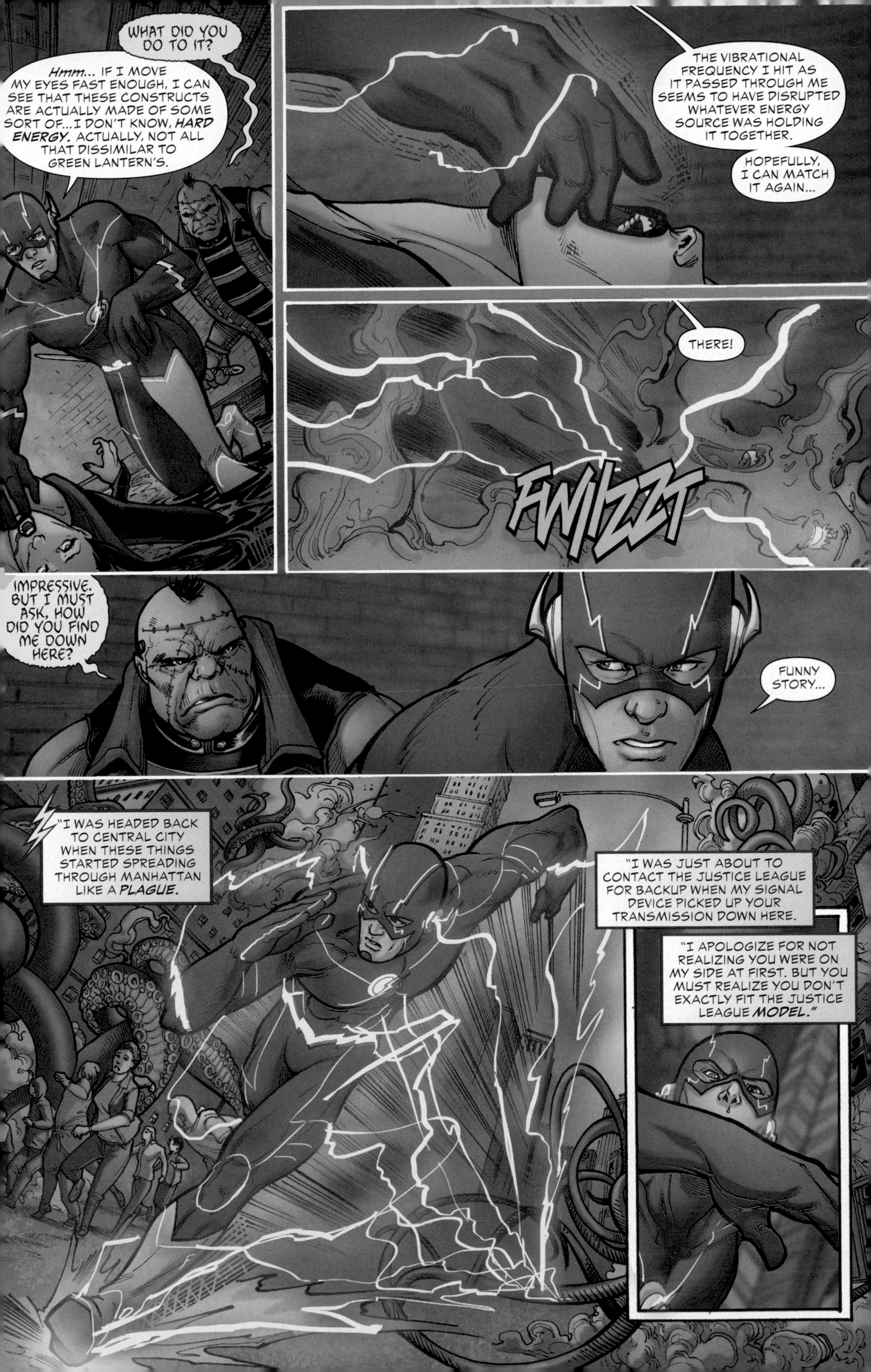
WHAT DID YOU DO TO IT?
Hmm... IF I MOVE MY EYES FAST ENOUGH, I CAN SEE THAT THESE CONSTRUCTS ARE ACTUALLY MADE OF SOME SORT OF...I DON'T KNOW, ***HARD ENERGY.*** ACTUALLY, NOT ALL THAT DISSIMILAR TO GREEN LANTERN'S.
THE VIBRATIONAL FREQUENCY I HIT AS IT PASSED THROUGH ME SEEMS TO HAVE DISRUPTED WHATEVER ENERGY SOURCE WAS HOLDING IT TOGETHER.
HOPEFULLY, I CAN MATCH IT AGAIN...
THERE!
FWIZZT
IMPRESSIVE. BUT I MUST ASK, HOW DID YOU FIND ME DOWN HERE?
FUNNY STORY...
"I WAS HEADED BACK TO CENTRAL CITY WHEN THESE THINGS STARTED SPREADING THROUGH MANHATTAN LIKE A ***PLAGUE.***
"I WAS JUST ABOUT TO CONTACT THE JUSTICE LEAGUE FOR BACKUP WHEN MY SIGNAL DEVICE PICKED UP YOUR TRANSMISSION DOWN HERE.
"I APOLOGIZE FOR NOT REALIZING YOU WERE ON MY SIDE AT FIRST. BUT YOU MUST REALIZE YOU DON'T EXACTLY FIT THE JUSTICE LEAGUE ***MODEL.***"

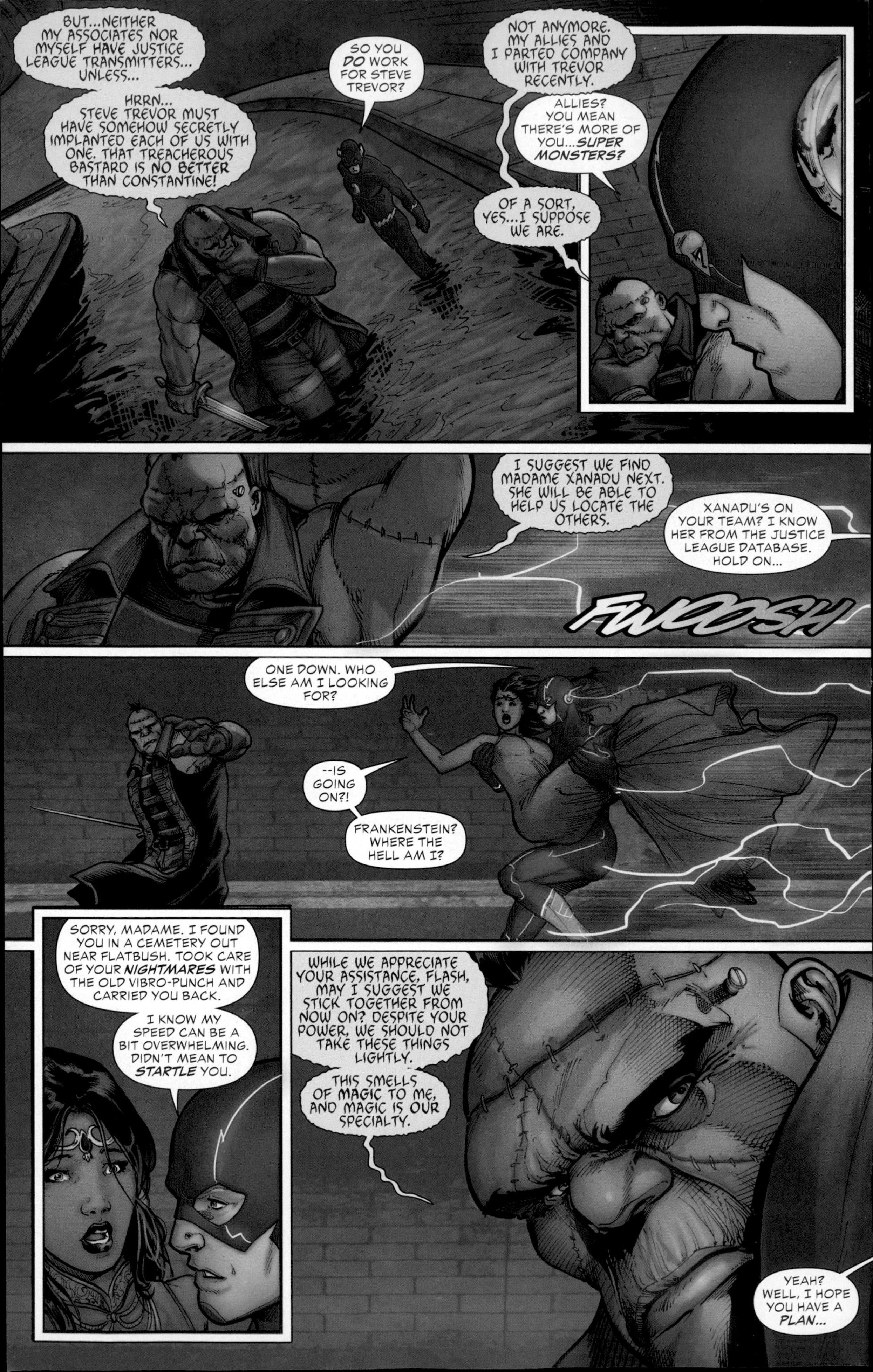
BUT...NEITHER MY ASSOCIATES NOR MYSELF HAVE JUSTICE LEAGUE TRANSMITTERS... UNLESS...
HRRN... STEVE TREVOR MUST HAVE SOMEHOW SECRETLY IMPLANTED EACH OF US WITH ONE. THAT TREACHEROUS BASTARD IS NO BETTER THAN CONSTANTINE!
SO YOU DO WORK FOR STEVE TREVOR?
NOT ANYMORE. MY ALLIES AND I PARTED COMPANY WITH TREVOR RECENTLY.
ALLIES? YOU MEAN THERE'S MORE OF YOU...SUPER MONSTERS?
OF A SORT, YES...I SUPPOSE WE ARE.
I SUGGEST WE FIND MADAME XANADU NEXT. SHE WILL BE ABLE TO HELP US LOCATE THE OTHERS.
XANADU'S ON YOUR TEAM? I KNOW HER FROM THE JUSTICE LEAGUE DATABASE. HOLD ON...
FWOOSH
ONE DOWN. WHO ELSE AM I LOOKING FOR?
FRANKENSTEIN? WHERE THE HELL AM I?
--IS GOING ON?!
SORRY, MADAME. I FOUND YOU IN A CEMETERY OUT NEAR FLATBUSH. TOOK CARE OF YOUR NIGHTMARES WITH THE OLD VIBRO-PUNCH AND CARRIED YOU BACK.
I KNOW MY SPEED CAN BE A BIT OVERWHELMING. DIDN'T MEAN TO STARTLE YOU.
WHILE WE APPRECIATE YOUR ASSISTANCE, FLASH, MAY I SUGGEST WE STICK TOGETHER FROM NOW ON? DESPITE YOUR POWER, WE SHOULD NOT TAKE THESE THINGS LIGHTLY.
THIS SMELLS OF MAGIC TO ME, AND MAGIC IS OUR SPECIALTY.
YEAH? WELL, I HOPE YOU HAVE A PLAN...

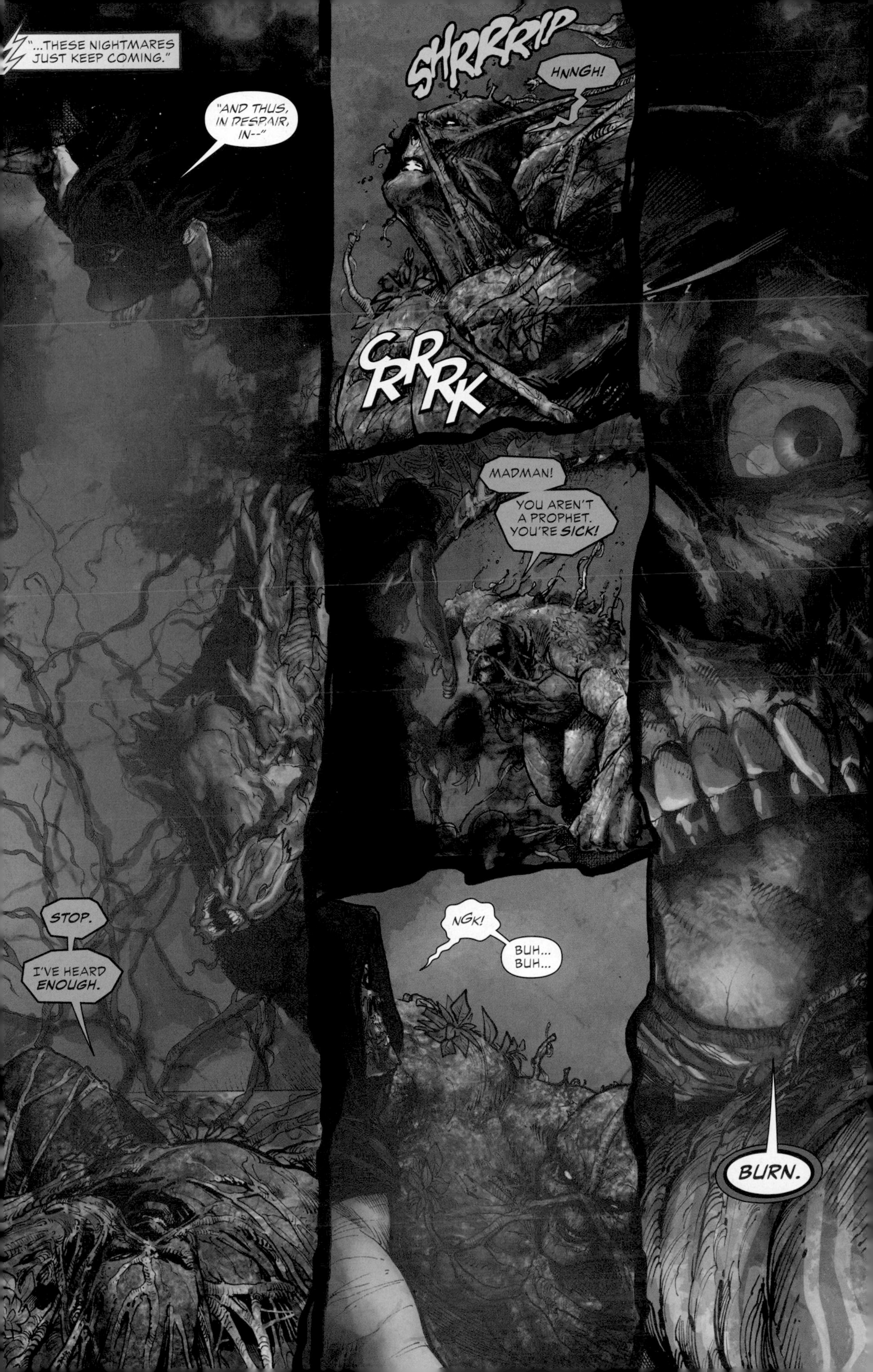
"...THESE NIGHTMARES JUST KEEP COMING."
"AND THUS, IN DESPAIR, IN--"
SHRRRIP
HNNGH!
CRRRK
MADMAN!
YOU AREN'T A PROPHET. YOU'RE SICK!
STOP.
I'VE HEARD ENOUGH.
NGK!
BUH... BUH...
BURN.

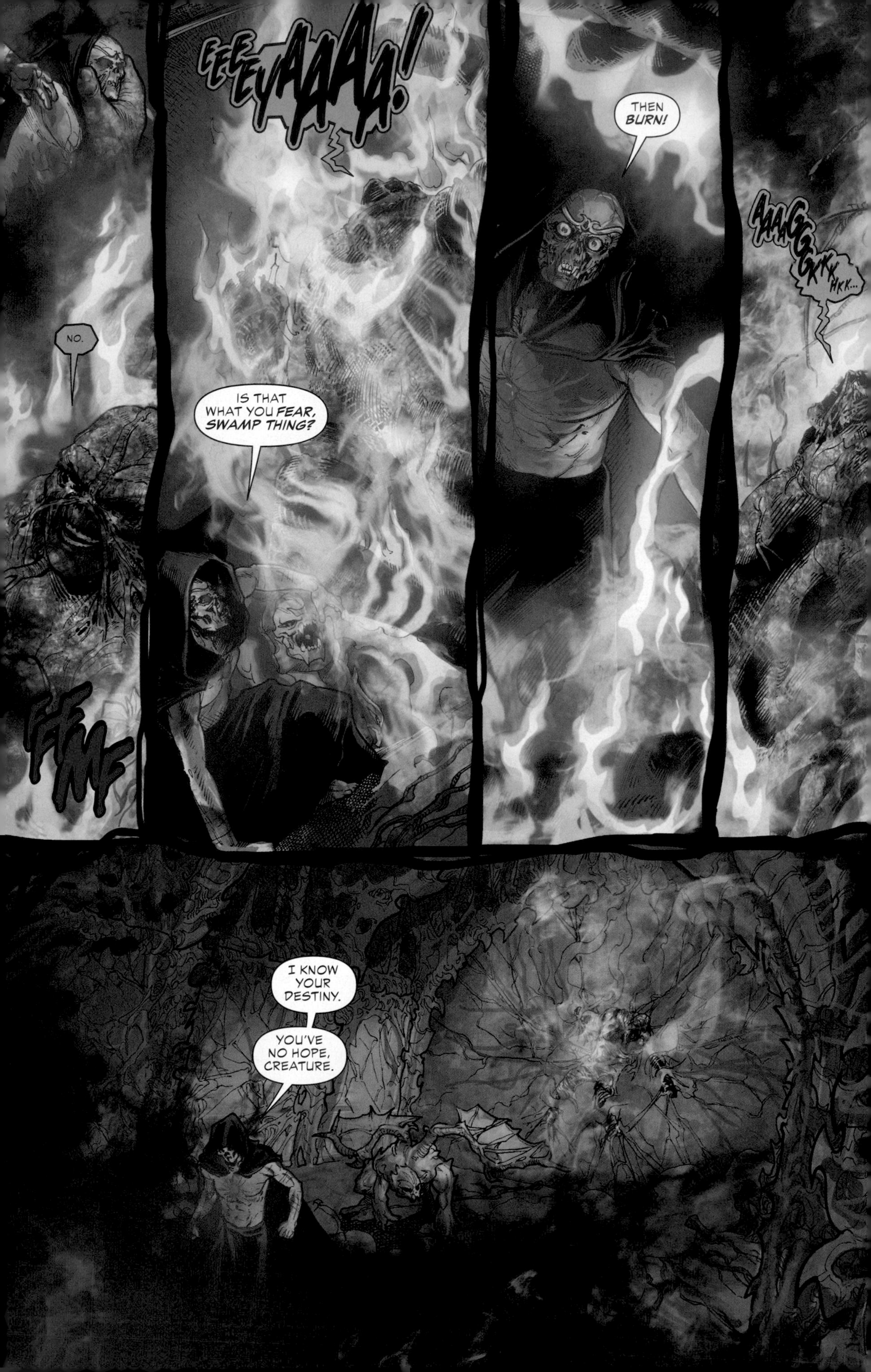

EEEEYAAAAA!
NO.
IS THAT WHAT YOU FEAR, SWAMP THING?
THEN BURN!
AAAAGGGKKKHKK...
FFFMF
I KNOW YOUR DESTINY.
YOU'VE NO HOPE, CREATURE.

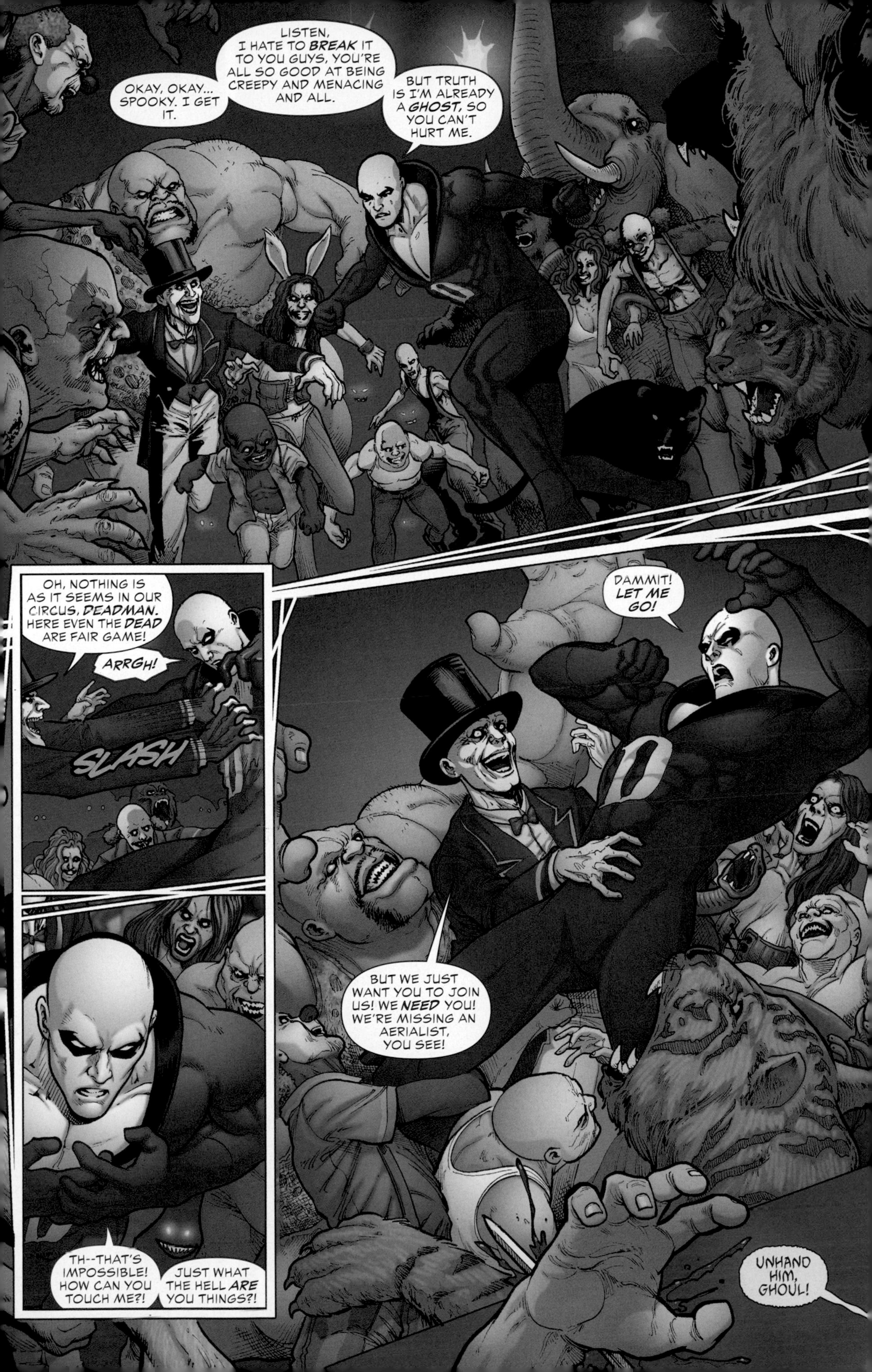
OKAY, OKAY... SPOOKY. I GET IT.
LISTEN, I HATE TO BREAK IT TO YOU GUYS, YOU'RE ALL SO GOOD AT BEING CREEPY AND MENACING AND ALL.
BUT TRUTH IS I'M ALREADY A GHOST, SO YOU CAN'T HURT ME.
OH, NOTHING IS AS IT SEEMS IN OUR CIRCUS, DEADMAN. HERE EVEN THE DEAD ARE FAIR GAME!
ARRGH!
SLASH
TH--THAT'S IMPOSSIBLE! HOW CAN YOU TOUCH ME?!
JUST WHAT THE HELL ARE YOU THINGS?!
DAMMIT! LET ME GO!
BUT WE JUST WANT YOU TO JOIN US! WE NEED YOU! WE'RE MISSING AN AERIALIST, YOU SEE!
UNHAND HIM, GHOUL!

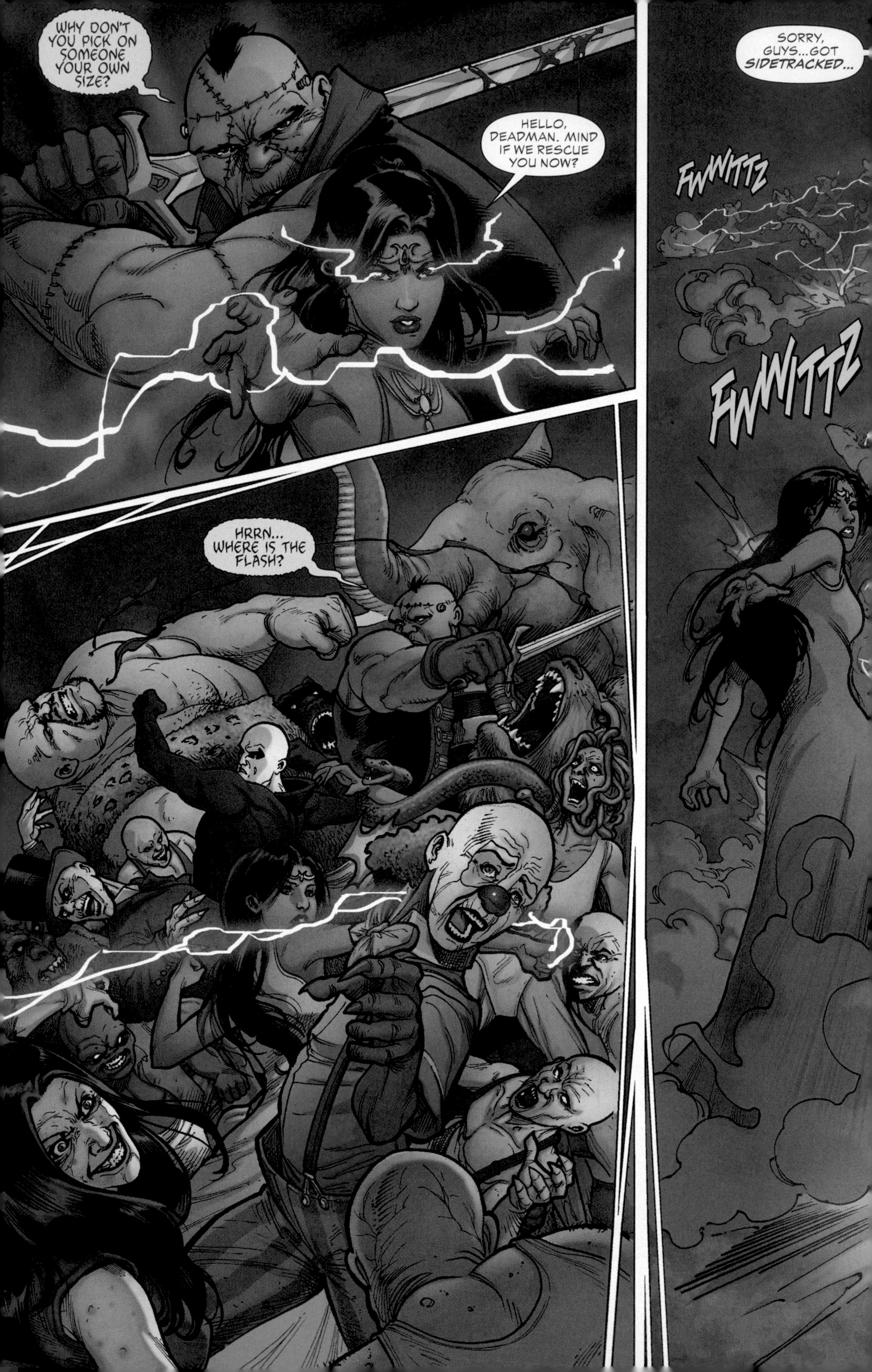
WHY DON'T YOU PICK ON SOMEONE YOUR OWN SIZE?
HELLO, DEADMAN. MIND IF WE RESCUE YOU NOW?
HRRN... WHERE IS THE FLASH?
SORRY, GUYS...GOT SIDETRACKED...
FWWITTZ
FWWITTZ

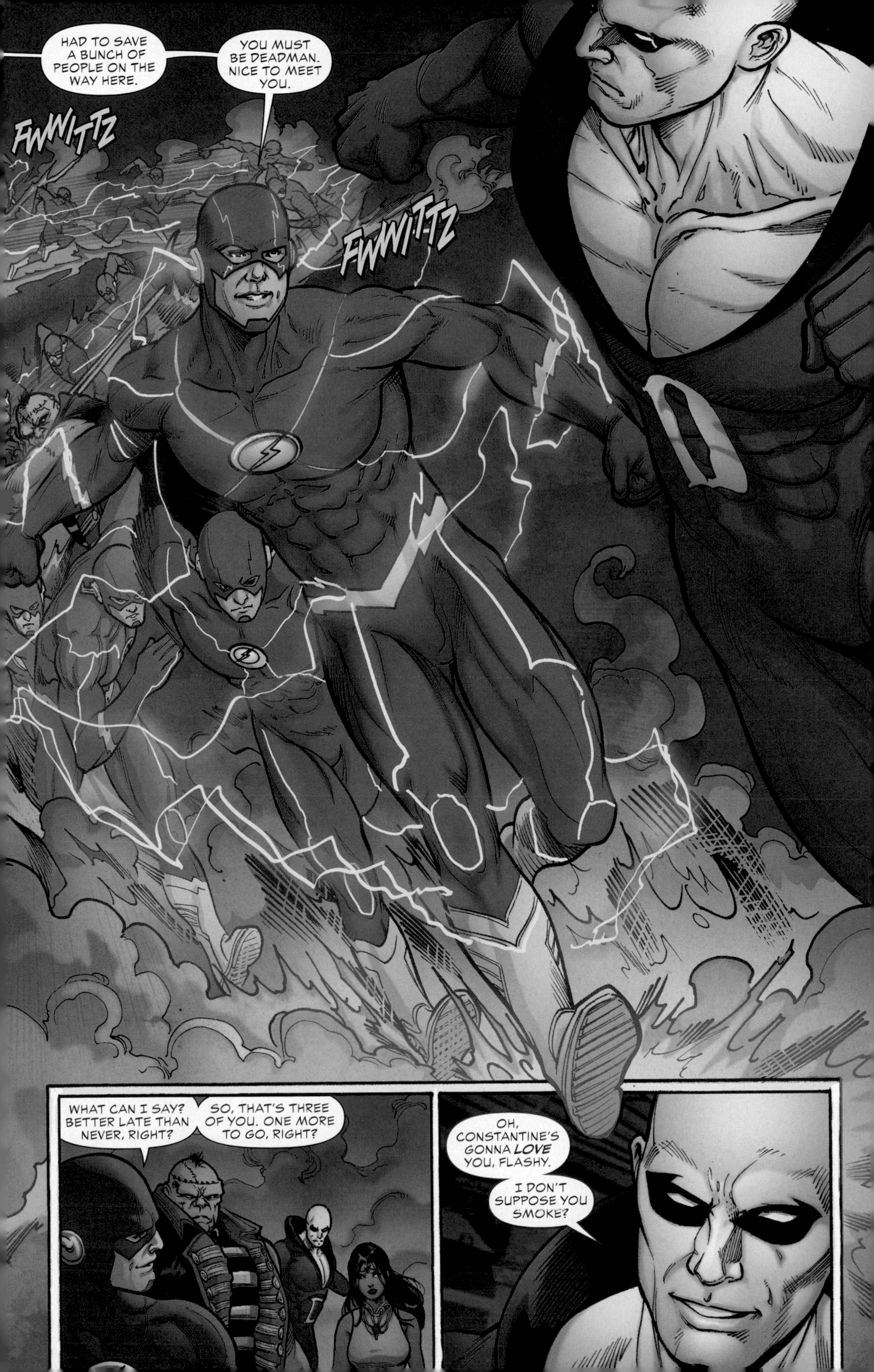
HAD TO SAVE A BUNCH OF PEOPLE ON THE WAY HERE.
YOU MUST BE DEADMAN. NICE TO MEET YOU.
FWWITTZ
FWWITTZ
WHAT CAN I SAY? BETTER LATE THAN NEVER, RIGHT?
SO, THAT'S THREE OF YOU. ONE MORE TO GO, RIGHT?
OH, CONSTANTINE'S GONNA LOVE YOU, FLASHY.
I DON'T SUPPOSE YOU SMOKE?

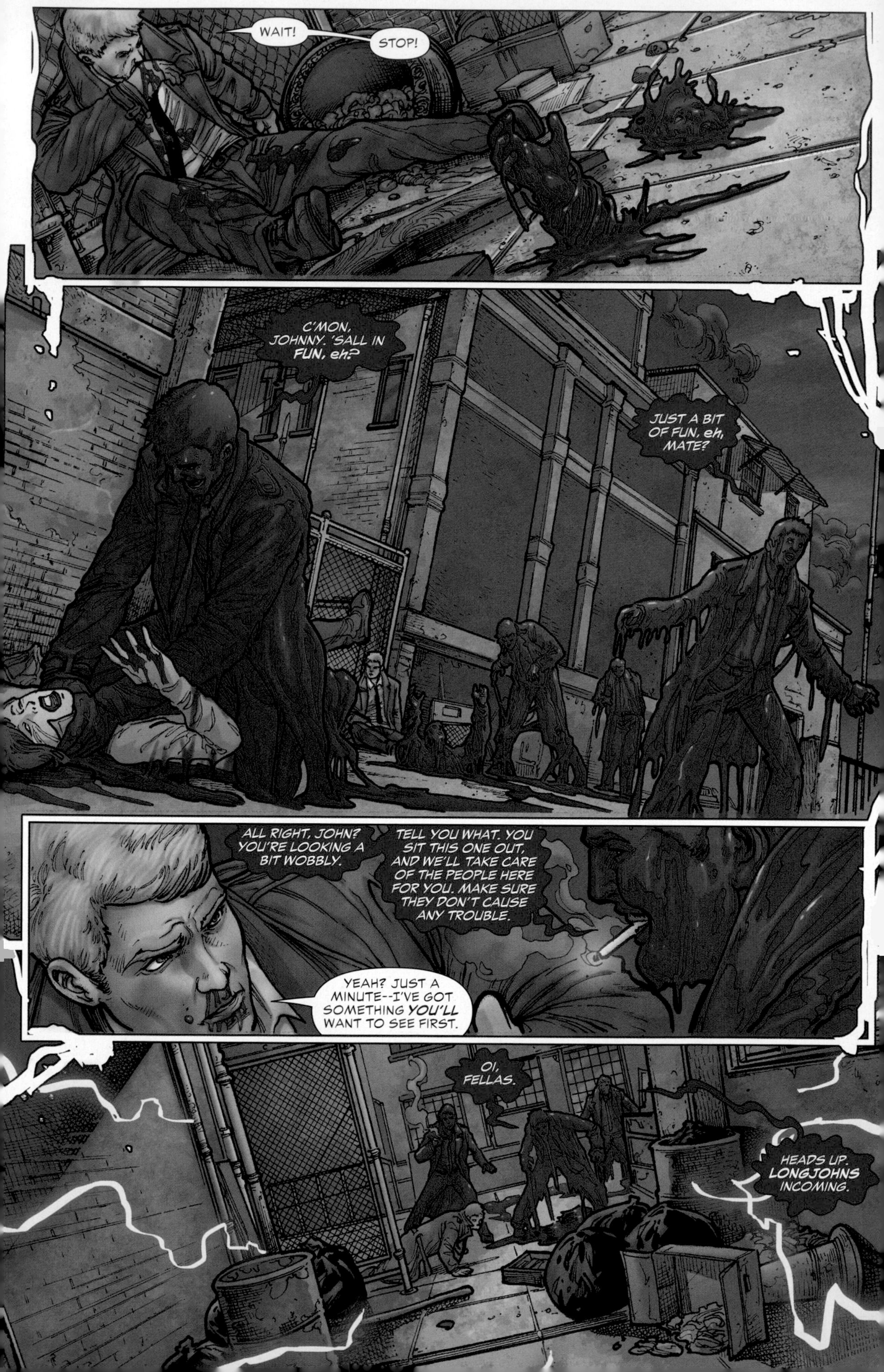
WAIT!
STOP!
C'MON, JOHNNY. 'SALL IN FUN, eh?
JUST A BIT OF FUN, eh, MATE?
ALL RIGHT, JOHN? YOU'RE LOOKING A BIT WOBBLY.
TELL YOU WHAT. YOU SIT THIS ONE OUT, AND WE'LL TAKE CARE OF THE PEOPLE HERE FOR YOU. MAKE SURE THEY DON'T CAUSE ANY TROUBLE.
YEAH? JUST A MINUTE--I'VE GOT SOMETHING YOU'LL WANT TO SEE FIRST.
OI, FELLAS.
HEADS UP. LONGJOHNS INCOMING.

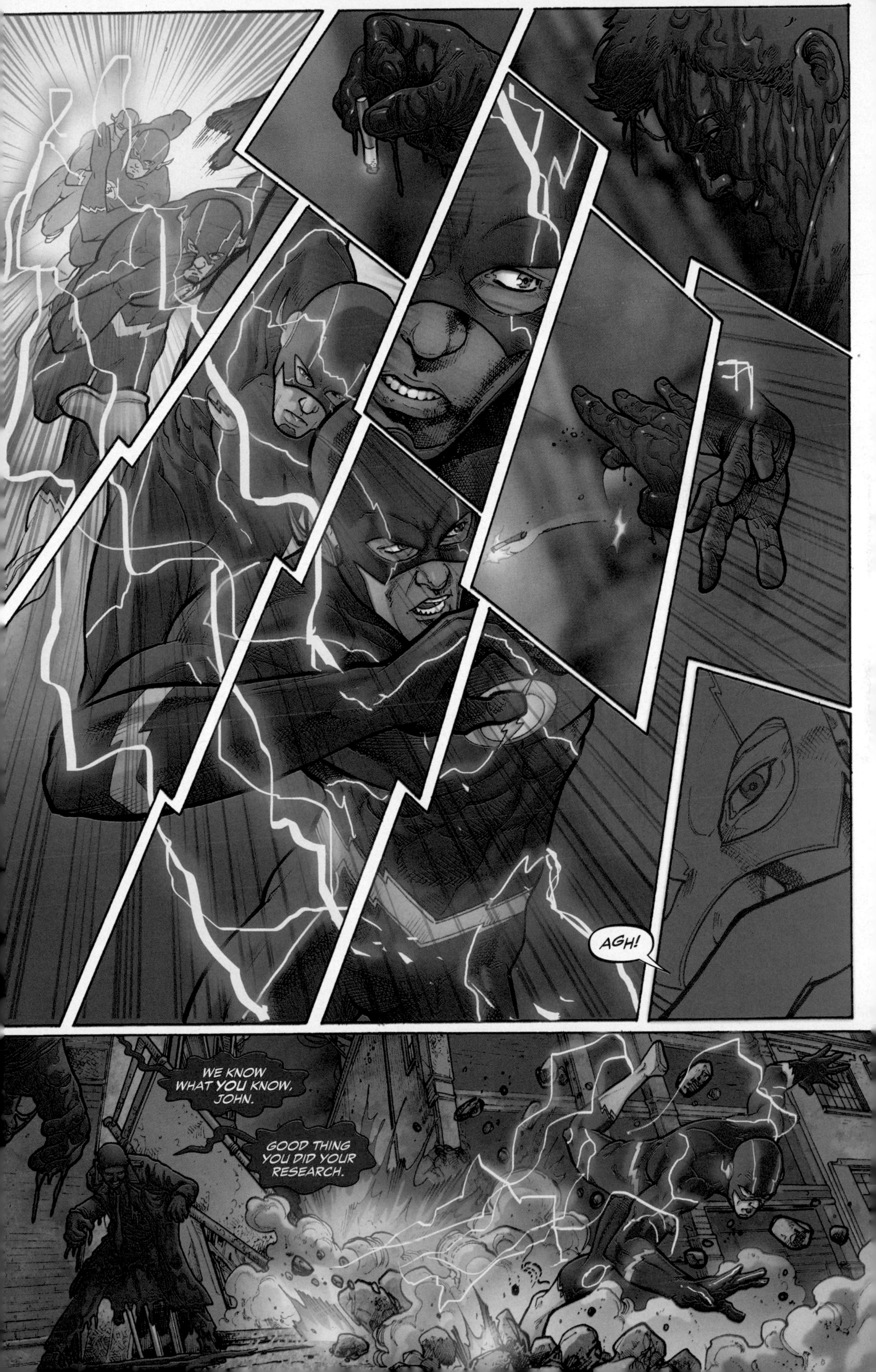
AGH!
WE KNOW WHAT YOU KNOW, JOHN.
GOOD THING YOU DID YOUR RESEARCH.

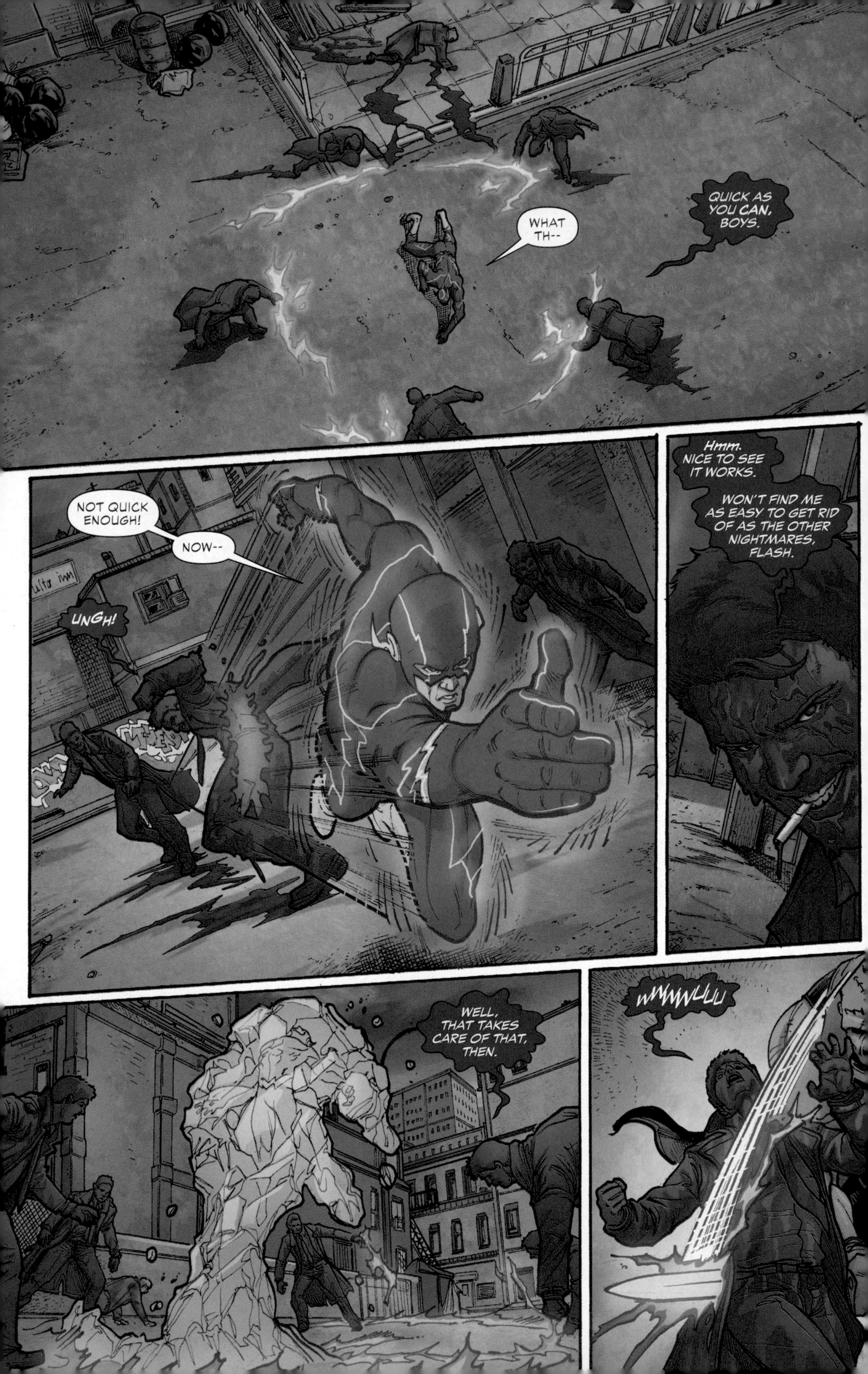
WHAT TH--
QUICK AS YOU CAN, BOYS.
NOT QUICK ENOUGH!
NOW--
UNGH!
Hmm. NICE TO SEE IT WORKS.
WON'T FIND ME AS EASY TO GET RID OF AS THE OTHER NIGHTMARES, FLASH.
WELL, THAT TAKES CARE OF THAT, THEN.
WMMWUUU

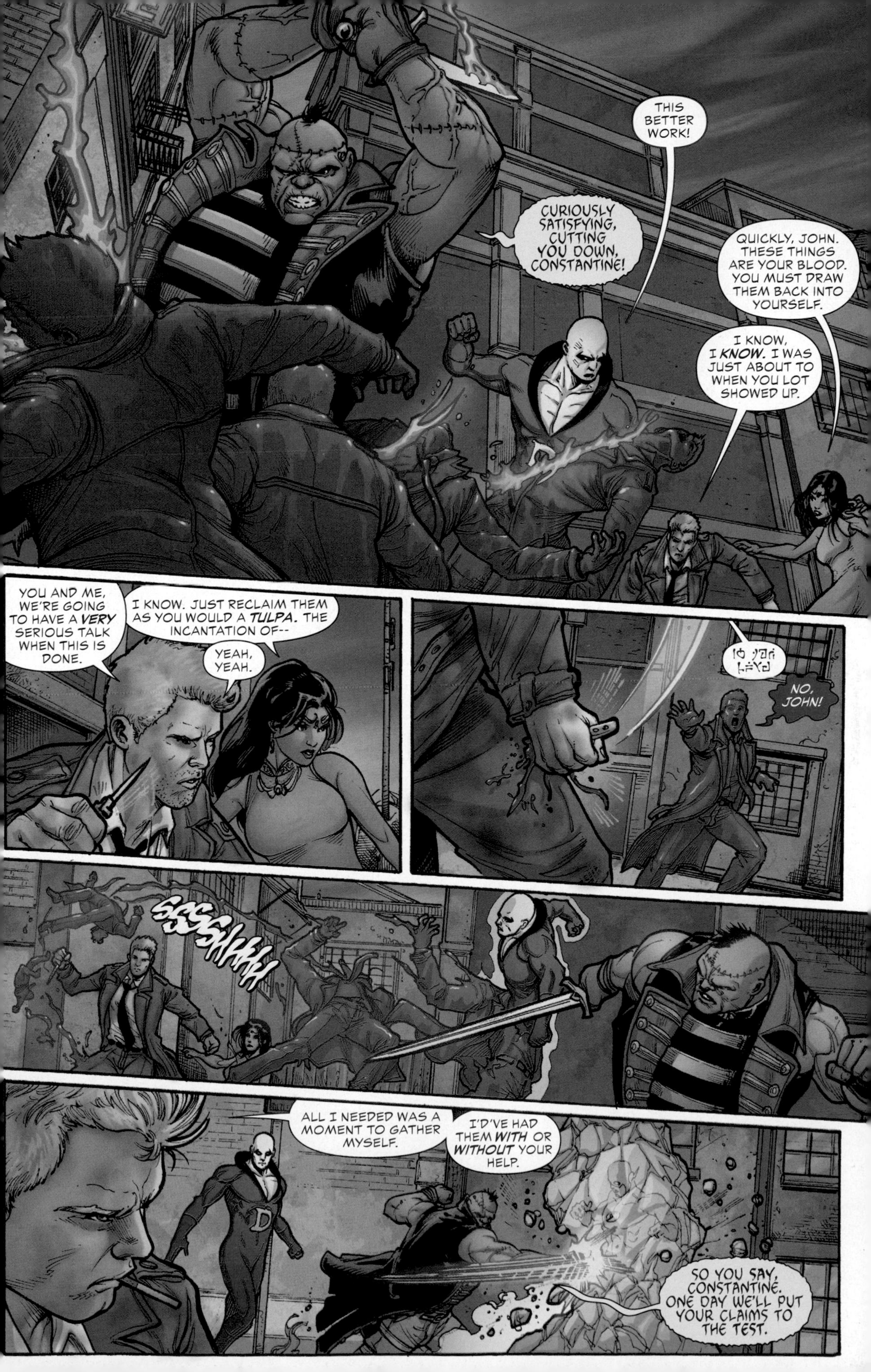
THIS BETTER WORK!
CURIOUSLY SATISFYING, CUTTING YOU DOWN, CONSTANTINE!
QUICKLY, JOHN. THESE THINGS ARE YOUR BLOOD. YOU MUST DRAW THEM BACK INTO YOURSELF.
I KNOW, I KNOW. I WAS JUST ABOUT TO WHEN YOU LOT SHOWED UP.
YOU AND ME, WE'RE GOING TO HAVE A VERY SERIOUS TALK WHEN THIS IS DONE.
I KNOW. JUST RECLAIM THEM AS YOU WOULD A TULPA. THE INCANTATION OF--
YEAH, YEAH.
NO, JOHN!
SSSSHHHH
ALL I NEEDED WAS A MOMENT TO GATHER MYSELF.
I'D'VE HAD THEM WITH OR WITHOUT YOUR HELP.
SO YOU SAY, CONSTANTINE. ONE DAY WE'LL PUT YOUR CLAIMS TO THE TEST.

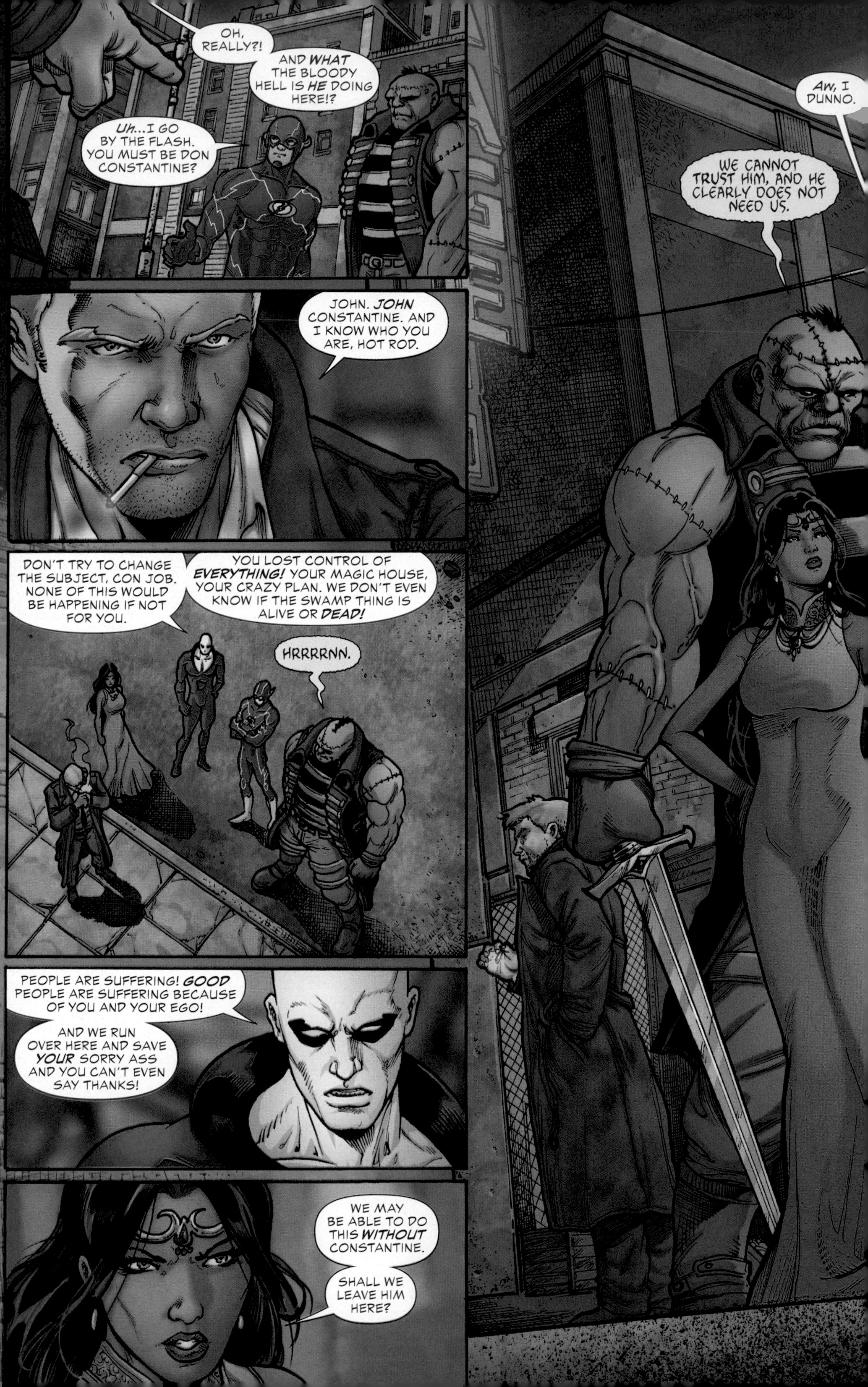
OH, REALLY?!
AND WHAT THE BLOODY HELL IS HE DOING HERE!?
Uh...I GO BY THE FLASH. YOU MUST BE DON CONSTANTINE?
JOHN. JOHN CONSTANTINE. AND I KNOW WHO YOU ARE, HOT ROD.
DON'T TRY TO CHANGE THE SUBJECT, CON JOB. NONE OF THIS WOULD BE HAPPENING IF NOT FOR YOU.
YOU LOST CONTROL OF EVERYTHING! YOUR MAGIC HOUSE, YOUR CRAZY PLAN. WE DON'T EVEN KNOW IF THE SWAMP THING IS ALIVE OR DEAD!
HRRRRNN.
PEOPLE ARE SUFFERING! GOOD PEOPLE ARE SUFFERING BECAUSE OF YOU AND YOUR EGO!
AND WE RUN OVER HERE AND SAVE YOUR SORRY ASS AND YOU CAN'T EVEN SAY THANKS!
WE MAY BE ABLE TO DO THIS WITHOUT CONSTANTINE.
SHALL WE LEAVE HIM HERE?
Aw, I DUNNO.
WE CANNOT TRUST HIM, AND HE CLEARLY DOES NOT NEED US.

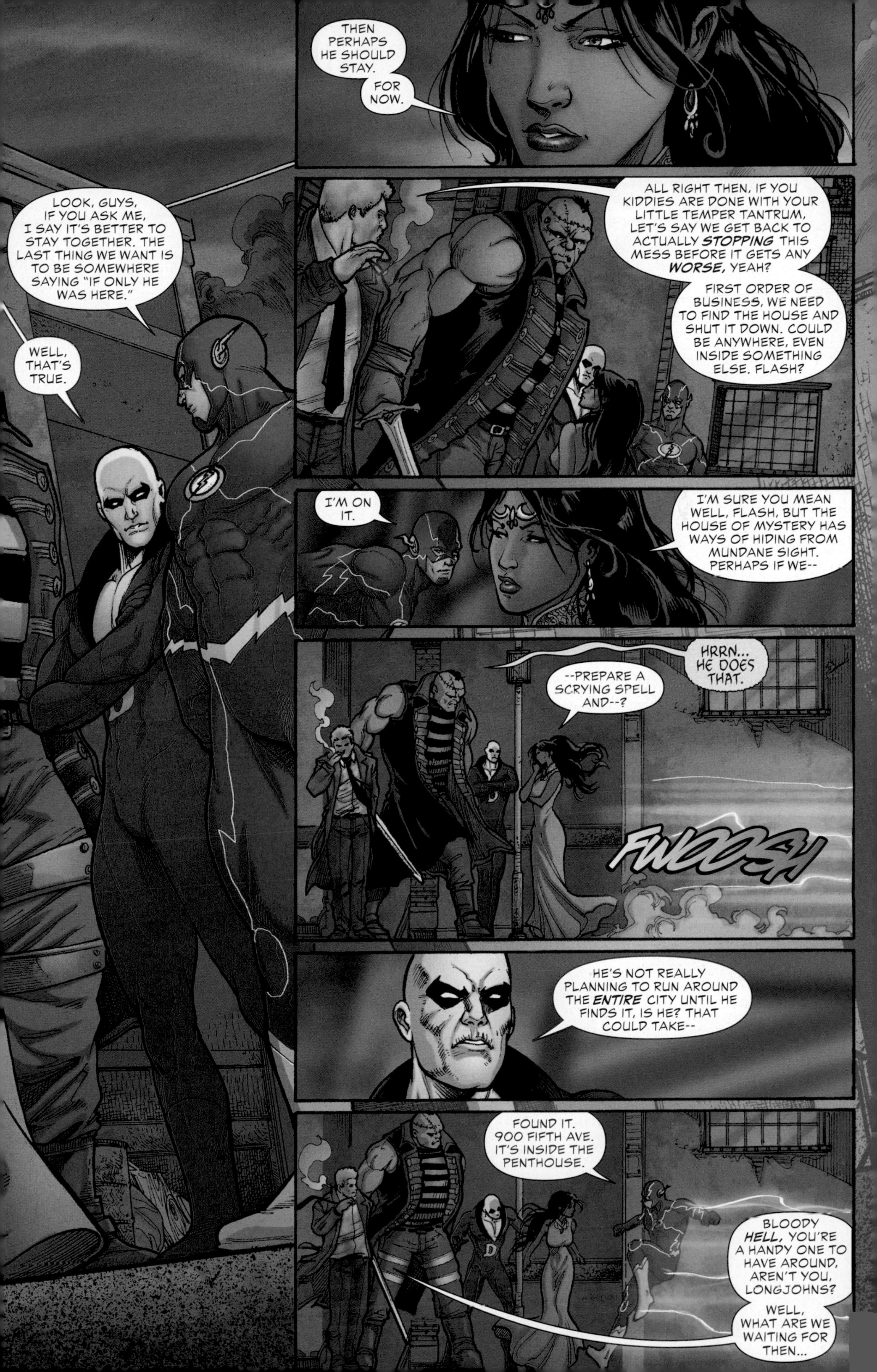
THEN PERHAPS HE SHOULD STAY.
FOR NOW.
LOOK, GUYS, IF YOU ASK ME, I SAY IT'S BETTER TO STAY TOGETHER. THE LAST THING WE WANT IS TO BE SOMEWHERE SAYING "IF ONLY HE WAS HERE."
WELL, THAT'S TRUE.
ALL RIGHT THEN, IF YOU KIDDIES ARE DONE WITH YOUR LITTLE TEMPER TANTRUM, LET'S SAY WE GET BACK TO ACTUALLY STOPPING THIS MESS BEFORE IT GETS ANY WORSE, YEAH?
FIRST ORDER OF BUSINESS, WE NEED TO FIND THE HOUSE AND SHUT IT DOWN. COULD BE ANYWHERE, EVEN INSIDE SOMETHING ELSE. FLASH?
I'M ON IT.
I'M SURE YOU MEAN WELL, FLASH, BUT THE HOUSE OF MYSTERY HAS WAYS OF HIDING FROM MUNDANE SIGHT. PERHAPS IF WE--
--PREPARE A SCRYING SPELL AND--?
HRRN... HE DOES THAT.
FWOOSH
HE'S NOT REALLY PLANNING TO RUN AROUND THE ENTIRE CITY UNTIL HE FINDS IT, IS HE? THAT COULD TAKE--
FOUND IT. 900 FIFTH AVE. IT'S INSIDE THE PENTHOUSE.
BLOODY HELL, YOU'RE A HANDY ONE TO HAVE AROUND, AREN'T YOU, LONGJOHNS?
WELL, WHAT ARE WE WAITING FOR THEN...

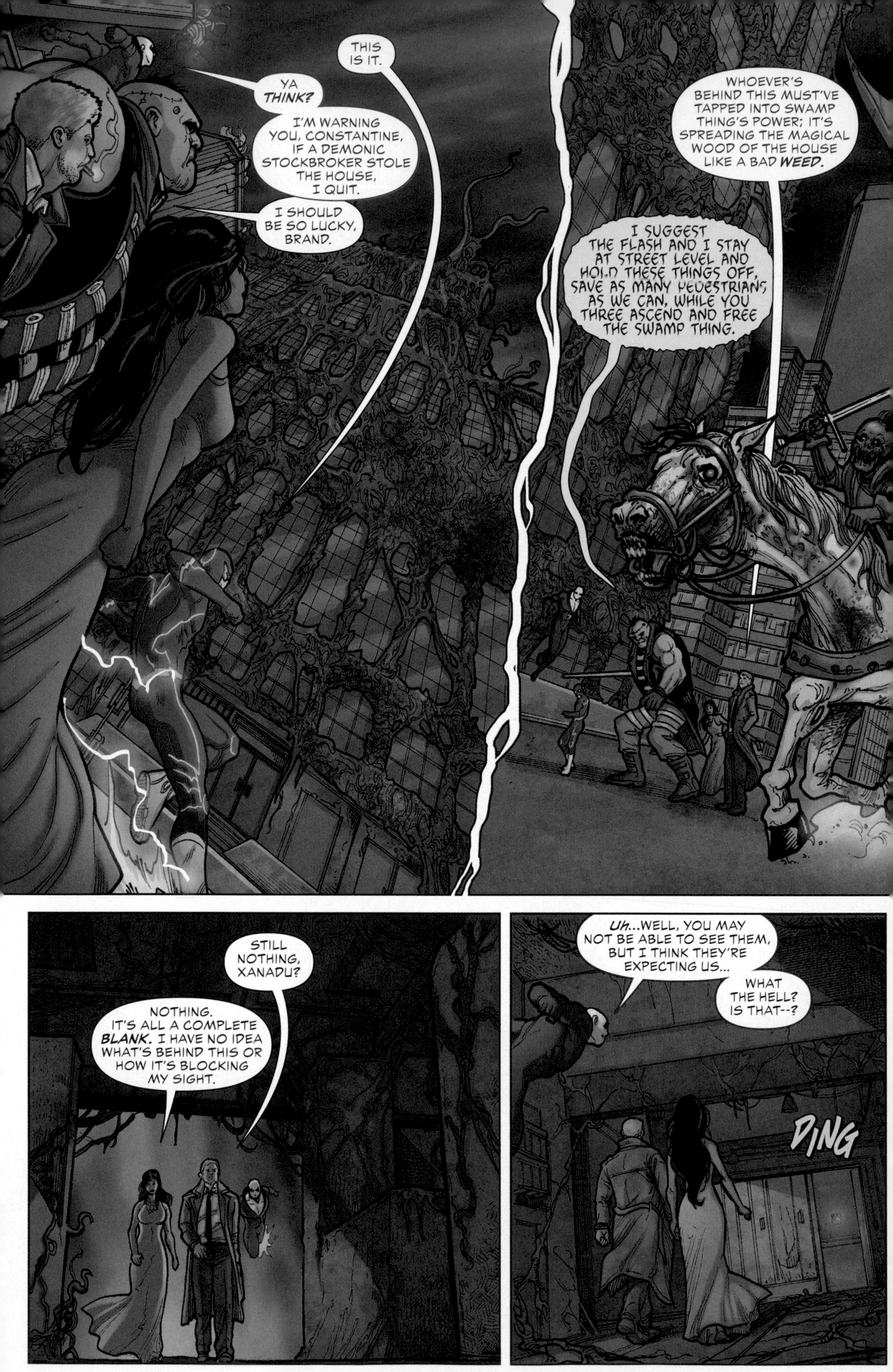
THIS IS IT.
YA THINK?
I'M WARNING YOU, CONSTANTINE, IF A DEMONIC STOCKBROKER STOLE THE HOUSE, I QUIT.
I SHOULD BE SO LUCKY, BRAND.
WHOEVER'S BEHIND THIS MUST'VE TAPPED INTO SWAMP THING'S POWER; IT'S SPREADING THE MAGICAL WOOD OF THE HOUSE LIKE A BAD WEED.
I SUGGEST THE FLASH AND I STAY AT STREET LEVEL AND HOLD THESE THINGS OFF, SAVE AS MANY PEDESTRIANS AS WE CAN, WHILE YOU THREE ASCEND AND FREE THE SWAMP THING.
STILL NOTHING, XANADU?
NOTHING. IT'S ALL A COMPLETE BLANK. I HAVE NO IDEA WHAT'S BEHIND THIS OR HOW IT'S BLOCKING MY SIGHT.
Uh...WELL, YOU MAY NOT BE ABLE TO SEE THEM, BUT I THINK THEY'RE EXPECTING US...
WHAT THE HELL? IS THAT--?
DING

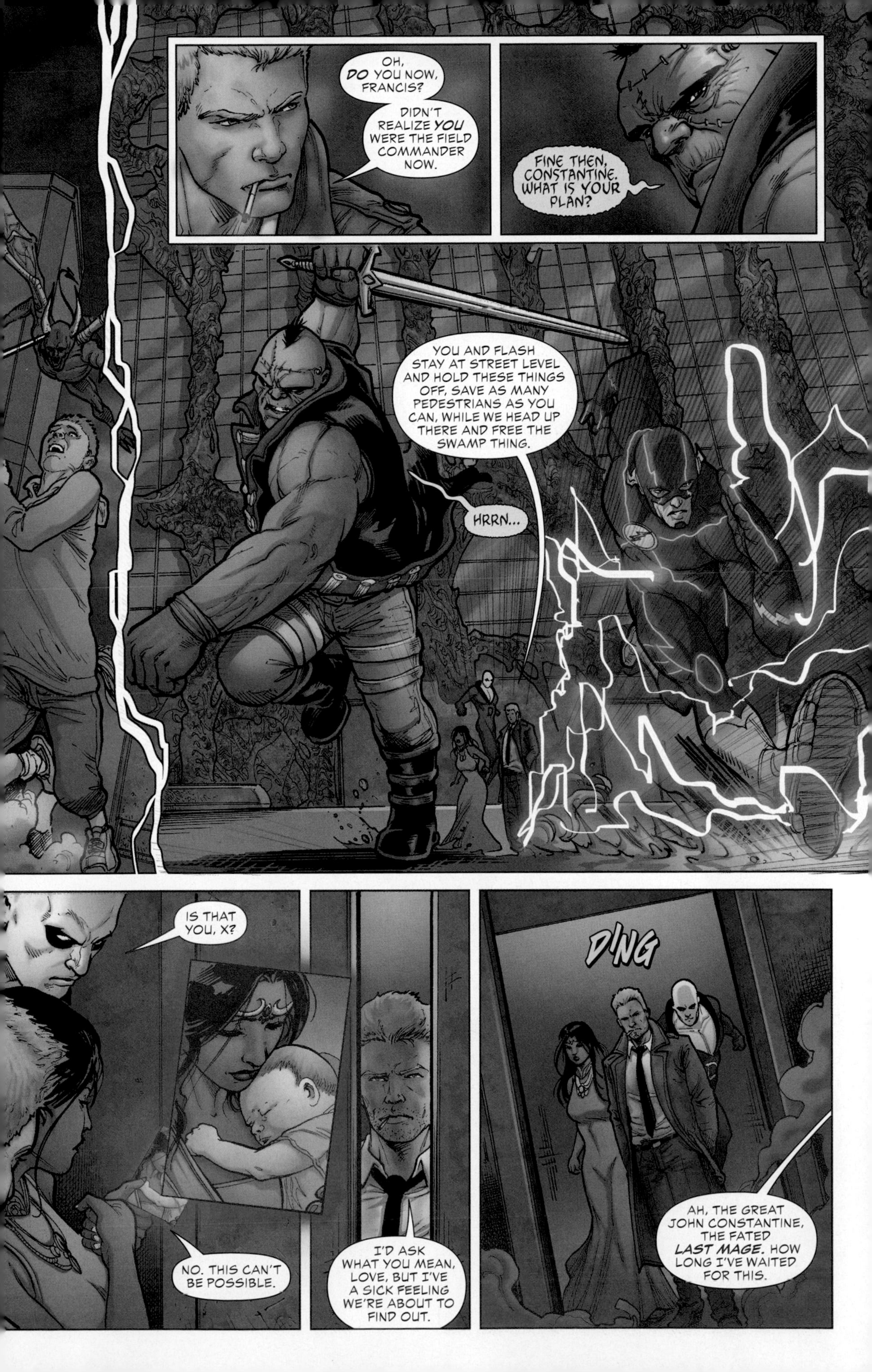
OH, DO YOU NOW, FRANCIS?
DIDN'T REALIZE YOU WERE THE FIELD COMMANDER NOW.
FINE THEN, CONSTANTINE. WHAT IS YOUR PLAN?
YOU AND FLASH STAY AT STREET LEVEL AND HOLD THESE THINGS OFF, SAVE AS MANY PEDESTRIANS AS YOU CAN, WHILE WE HEAD UP THERE AND FREE THE SWAMP THING.
HRRN...
IS THAT YOU, X?
NO. THIS CAN'T BE POSSIBLE.
I'D ASK WHAT YOU MEAN, LOVE, BUT I'VE A SICK FEELING WE'RE ABOUT TO FIND OUT.
DING
AH, THE GREAT JOHN CONSTANTINE, THE FATED LAST MAGE. HOW LONG I'VE WAITED FOR THIS.

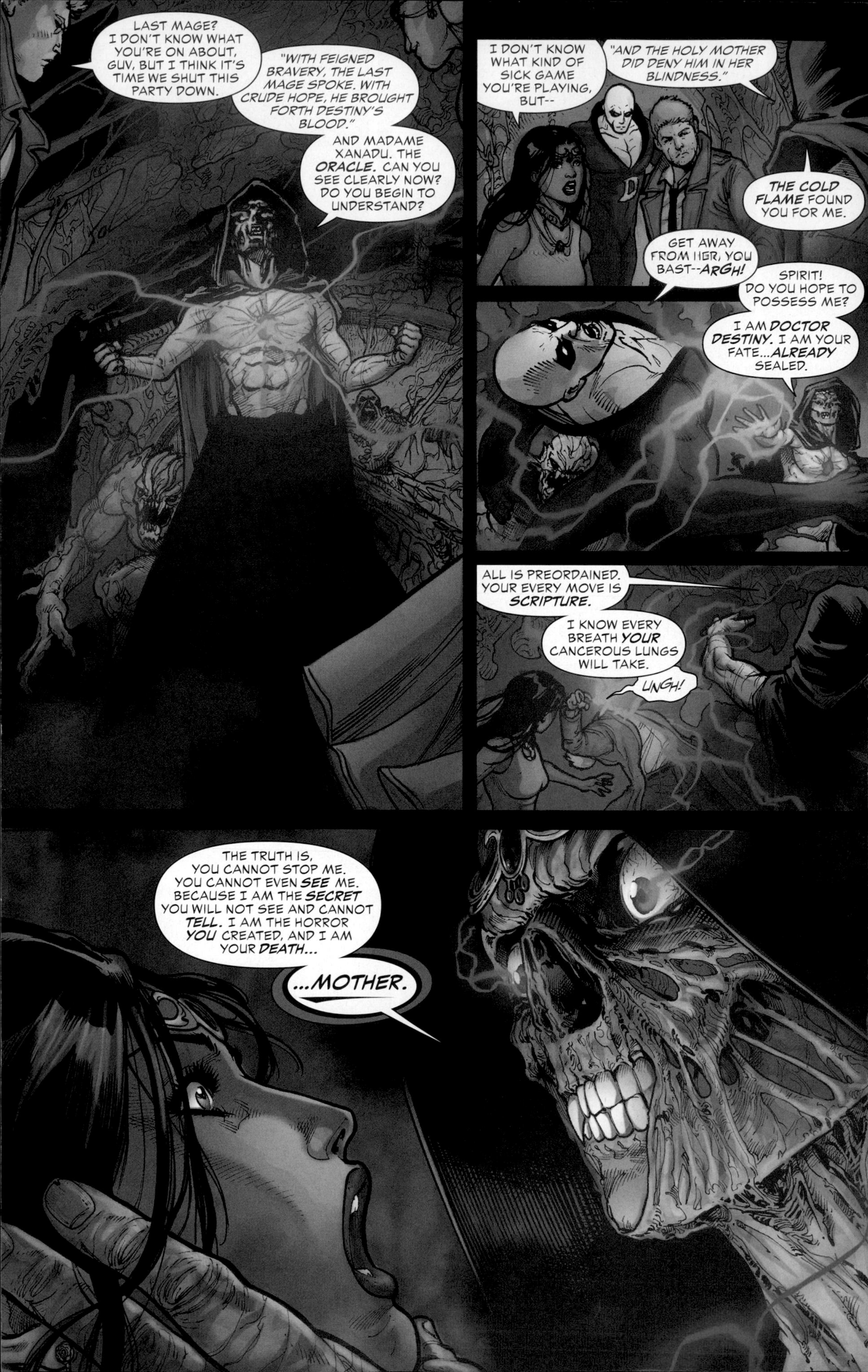
LAST MAGE? I DON'T KNOW WHAT YOU'RE ON ABOUT, GUV, BUT I THINK IT'S TIME WE SHUT THIS PARTY DOWN.
"WITH FEIGNED BRAVERY, THE LAST MAGE SPOKE. WITH CRUDE HOPE, HE BROUGHT FORTH DESTINY'S BLOOD."
AND MADAME XANADU. THE ORACLE. CAN YOU SEE CLEARLY NOW? DO YOU BEGIN TO UNDERSTAND?
I DON'T KNOW WHAT KIND OF SICK GAME YOU'RE PLAYING, BUT--
"AND THE HOLY MOTHER DID DENY HIM IN HER BLINDNESS."
THE COLD FLAME FOUND YOU FOR ME.
GET AWAY FROM HER, YOU BAST--ARGH!
SPIRIT! DO YOU HOPE TO POSSESS ME?
I AM DOCTOR DESTINY. I AM YOUR FATE...ALREADY SEALED.
ALL IS PREORDAINED. YOUR EVERY MOVE IS SCRIPTURE.
I KNOW EVERY BREATH YOUR CANCEROUS LUNGS WILL TAKE.
UNGH!
THE TRUTH IS, YOU CANNOT STOP ME. YOU CANNOT EVEN SEE ME. BECAUSE I AM THE SECRET YOU WILL NOT SEE AND CANNOT TELL. I AM THE HORROR YOU CREATED, AND I AM YOUR DEATH...
...MOTHER.

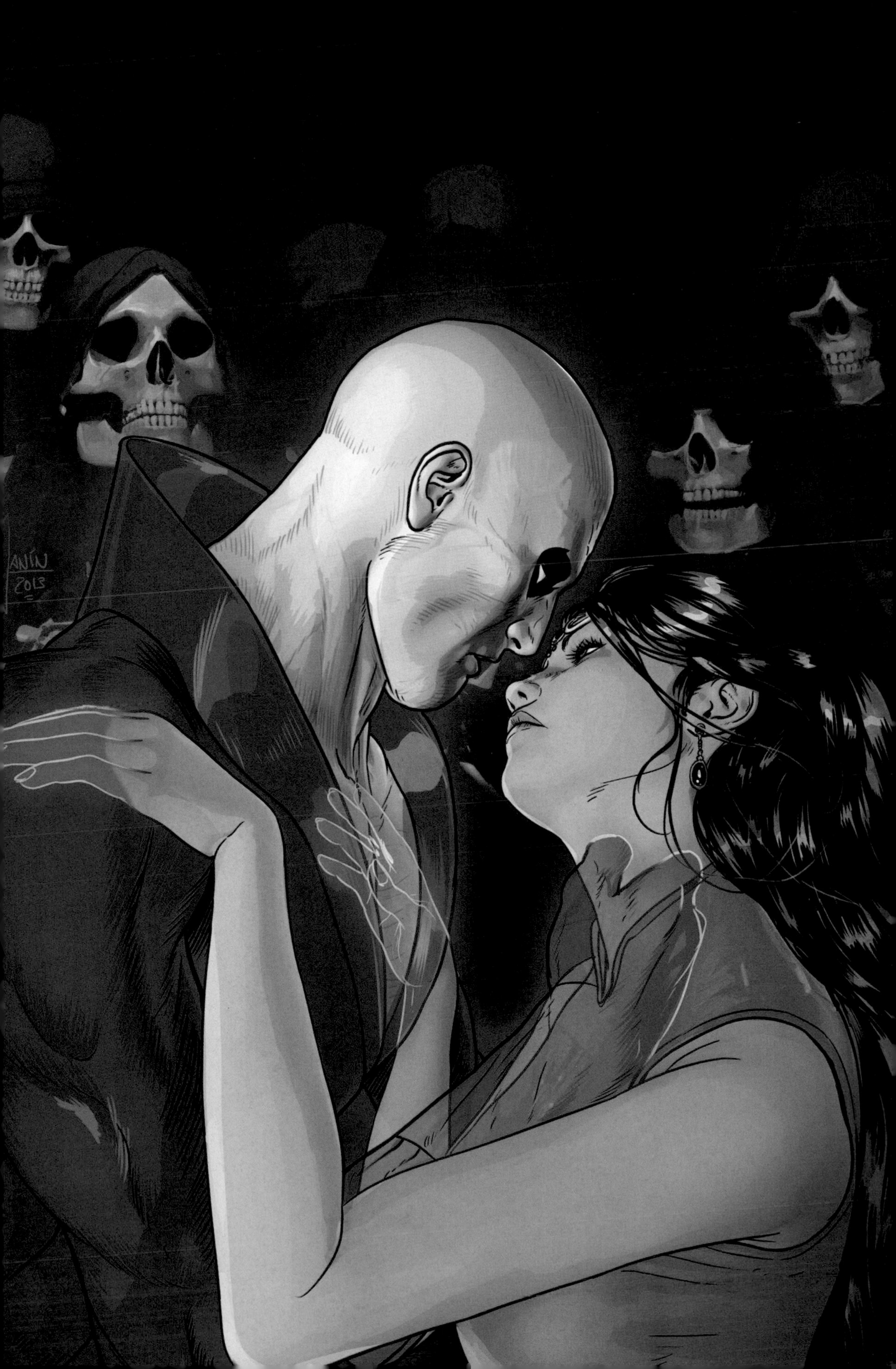
ANÍN
2013

HORROR CITY part three
DIE DIE DIE, MY DARLING

RAY FAWKES
JEFF LEMIRE
writers

MIKEL JANIN
artist

VICENTE CIFUENTES
finishes (pages 11-20)

MIKEL JANIN
cover artist

SWAMP THING created by LEN WEIN & BERNIE WRIGHTSON

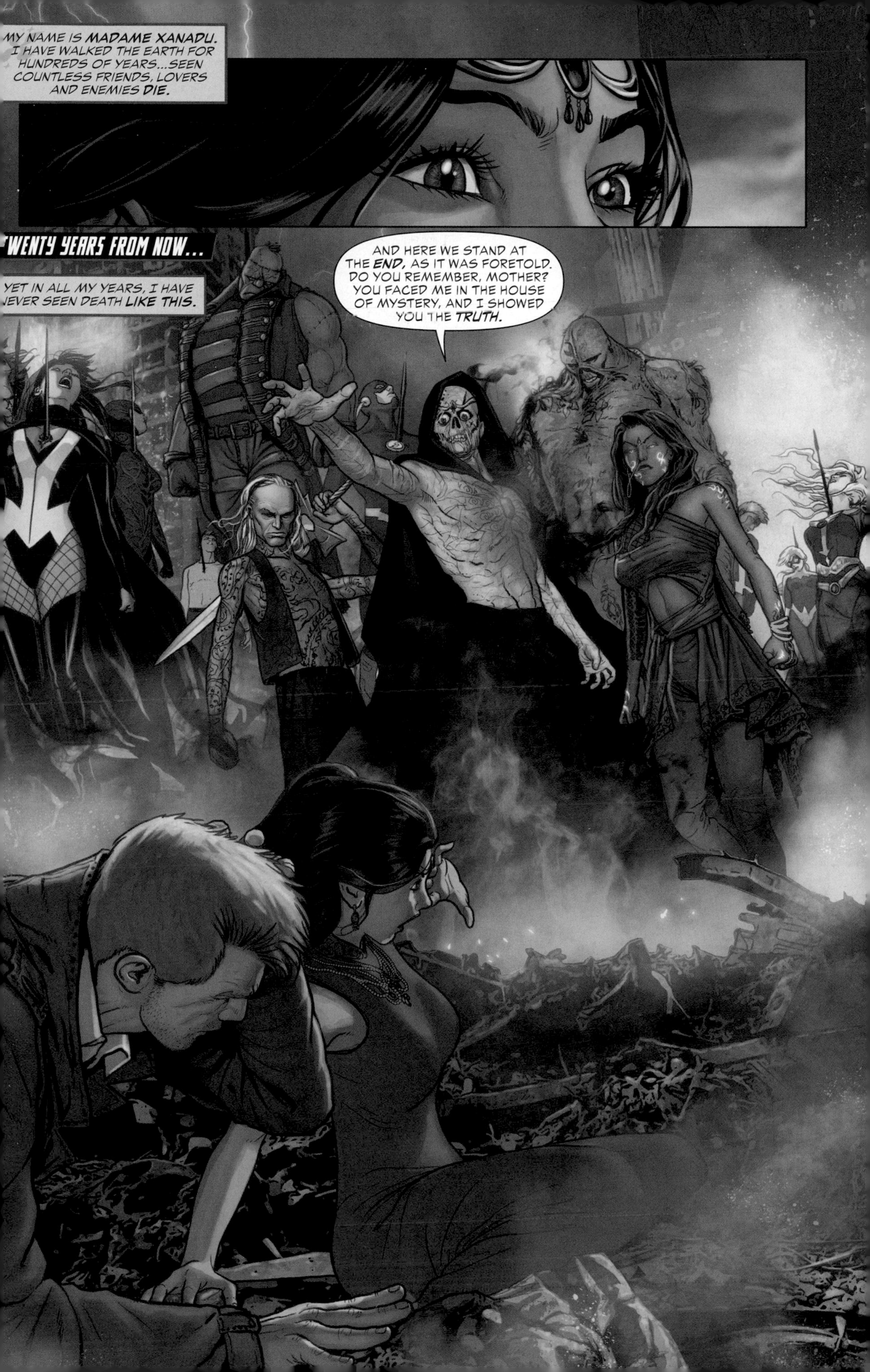
MY NAME IS MADAME XANADU. I HAVE WALKED THE EARTH FOR HUNDREDS OF YEARS...SEEN COUNTLESS FRIENDS, LOVERS AND ENEMIES DIE.
WENTY YEARS FROM NOW...
YET IN ALL MY YEARS, I HAVE NEVER SEEN DEATH LIKE THIS.
AND HERE WE STAND AT THE END, AS IT WAS FORETOLD. DO YOU REMEMBER, MOTHER? YOU FACED ME IN THE HOUSE OF MYSTERY, AND I SHOWED YOU THE TRUTH.

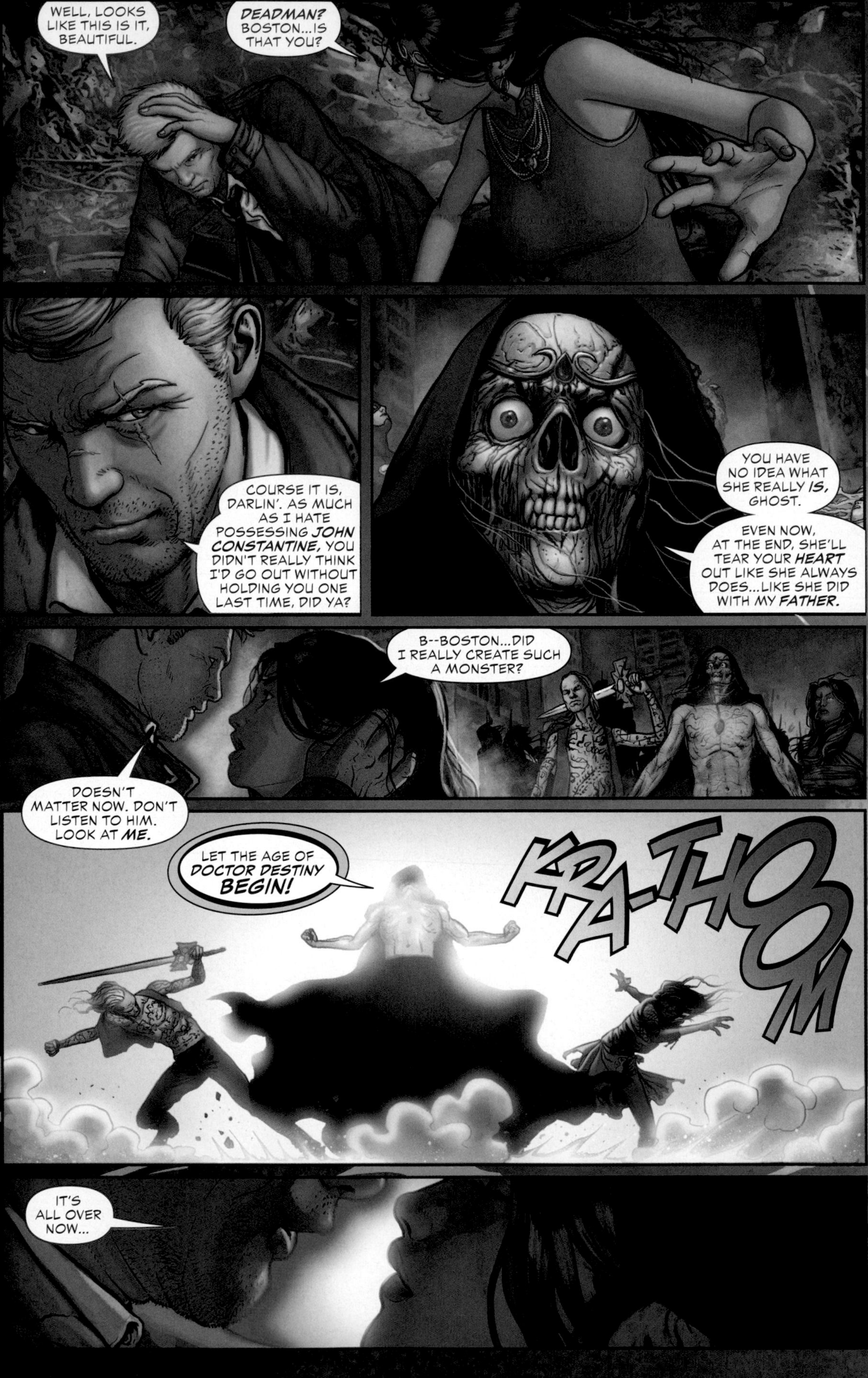

WELL, LOOKS LIKE THIS IS IT, BEAUTIFUL.
DEADMAN? BOSTON...IS THAT YOU?
COURSE IT IS, DARLIN'. AS MUCH AS I HATE POSSESSING JOHN CONSTANTINE, YOU DIDN'T REALLY THINK I'D GO OUT WITHOUT HOLDING YOU ONE LAST TIME, DID YA?
YOU HAVE NO IDEA WHAT SHE REALLY IS, GHOST.
EVEN NOW, AT THE END, SHE'LL TEAR YOUR HEART OUT LIKE SHE ALWAYS DOES...LIKE SHE DID WITH MY FATHER.
B--BOSTON...DID I REALLY CREATE SUCH A MONSTER?
DOESN'T MATTER NOW. DON'T LISTEN TO HIM. LOOK AT ME.
LET THE AGE OF DOCTOR DESTINY BEGIN!
KRA-THOOM
IT'S ALL OVER NOW...

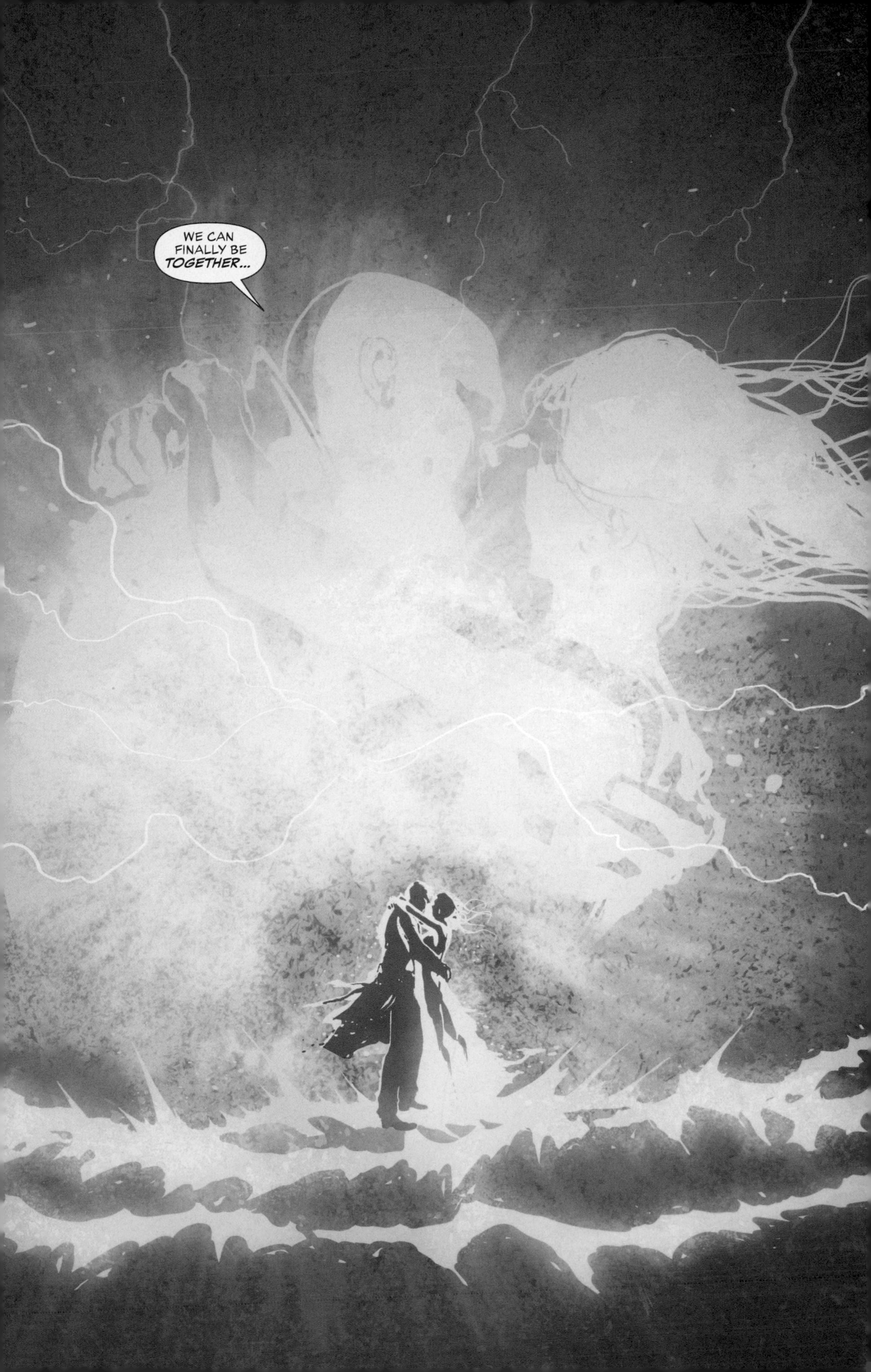
WE CAN FINALLY BE TOGETHER...

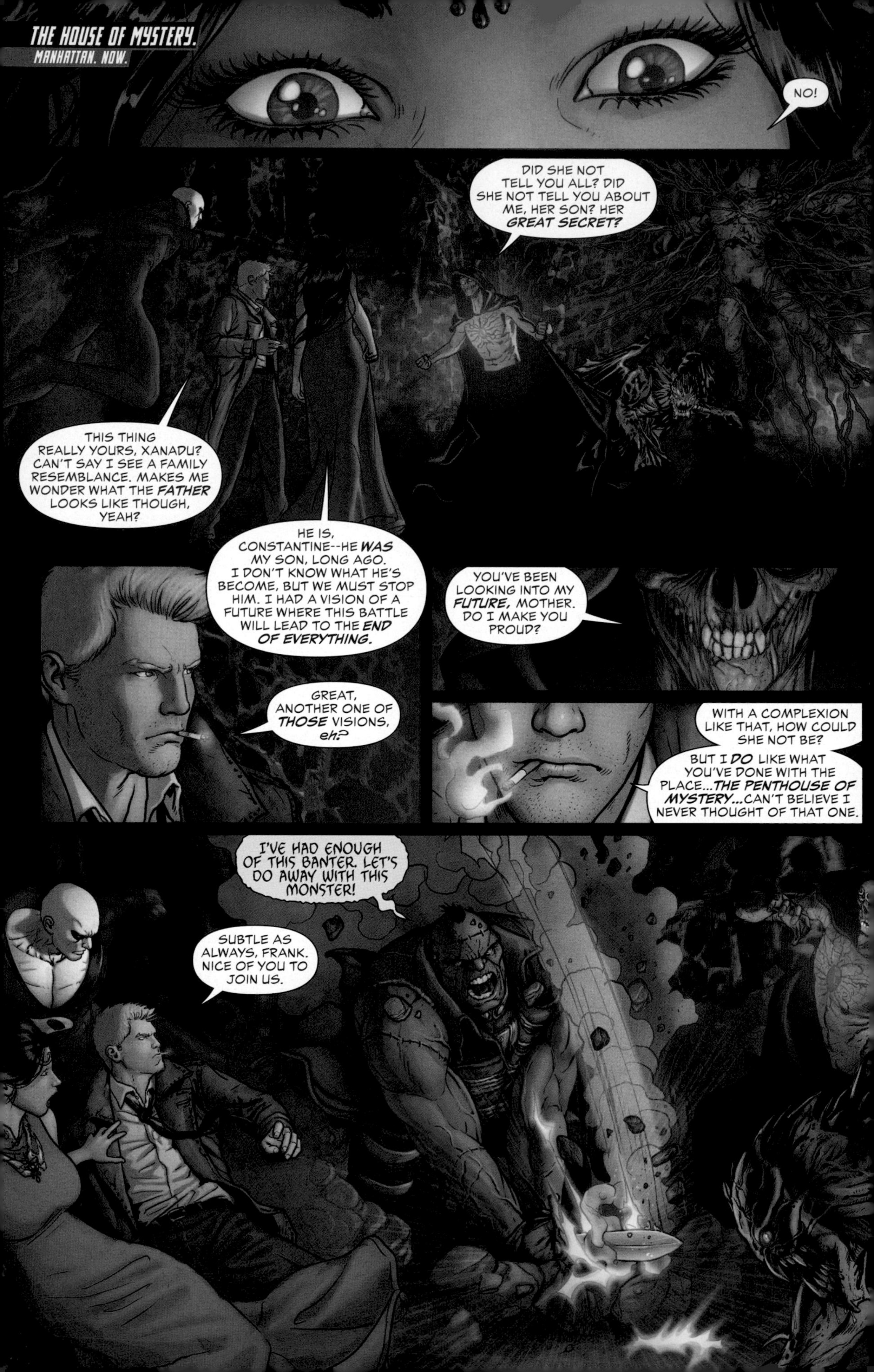
THE HOUSE OF MYSTERY.
MANHATTAN. NOW.
NO!
DID SHE NOT TELL YOU ALL? DID SHE NOT TELL YOU ABOUT ME, HER SON? HER GREAT SECRET?
THIS THING REALLY YOURS, XANADU? CAN'T SAY I SEE A FAMILY RESEMBLANCE. MAKES ME WONDER WHAT THE FATHER LOOKS LIKE THOUGH, YEAH?
HE IS, CONSTANTINE--HE WAS MY SON, LONG AGO. I DON'T KNOW WHAT HE'S BECOME, BUT WE MUST STOP HIM. I HAD A VISION OF A FUTURE WHERE THIS BATTLE WILL LEAD TO THE END OF EVERYTHING.
GREAT, ANOTHER ONE OF THOSE VISIONS, eh?
YOU'VE BEEN LOOKING INTO MY FUTURE, MOTHER. DO I MAKE YOU PROUD?
WITH A COMPLEXION LIKE THAT, HOW COULD SHE NOT BE?
BUT I DO LIKE WHAT YOU'VE DONE WITH THE PLACE...THE PENTHOUSE OF MYSTERY...CAN'T BELIEVE I NEVER THOUGHT OF THAT ONE.
I'VE HAD ENOUGH OF THIS BANTER. LET'S DO AWAY WITH THIS MONSTER!
SUBTLE AS ALWAYS, FRANK. NICE OF YOU TO JOIN US.

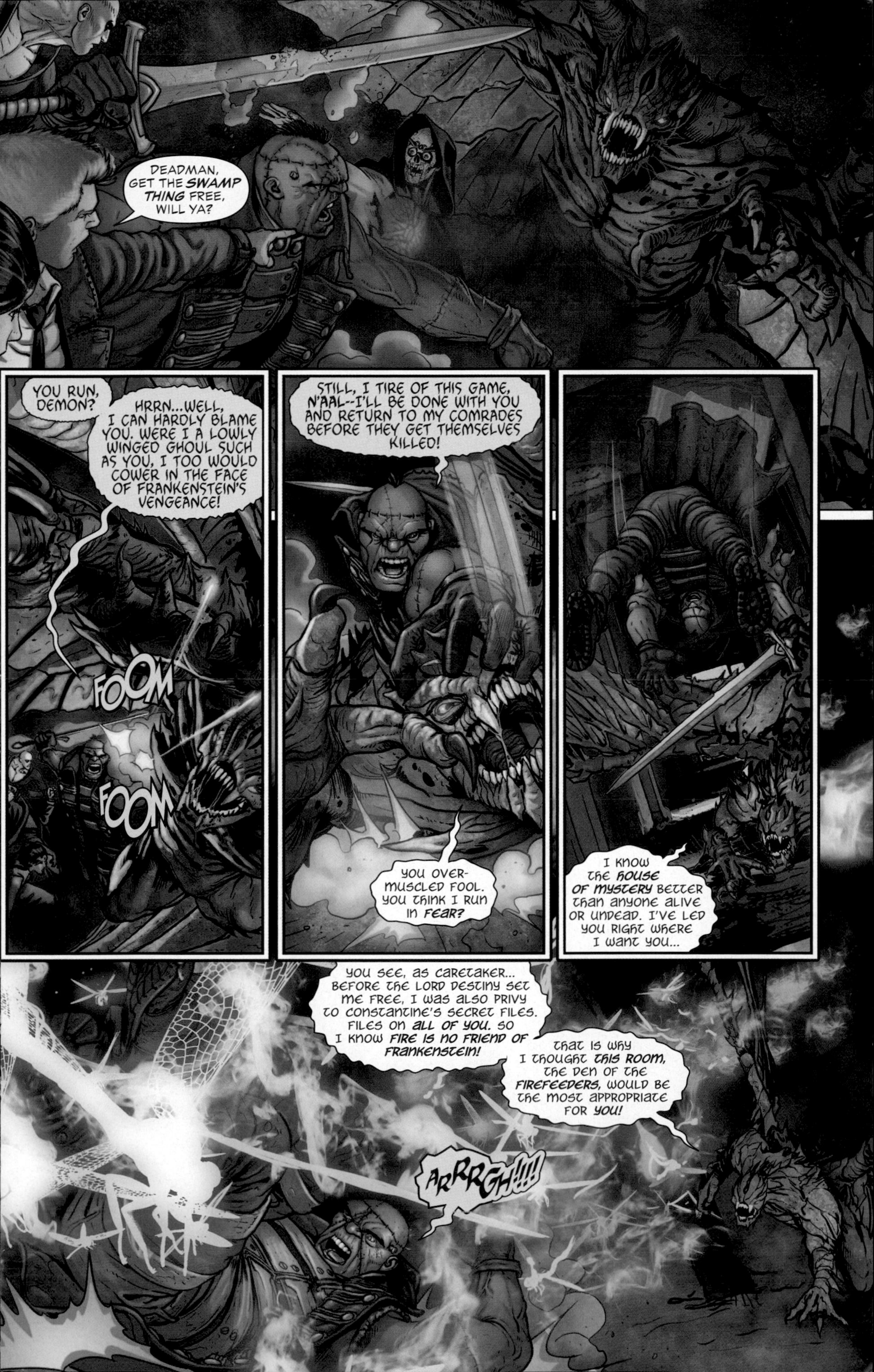
DEADMAN, GET THE SWAMP THING FREE, WILL YA?
YOU RUN, DEMON?
HRRN...WELL, I CAN HARDLY BLAME YOU. WERE I A LOWLY WINGED GHOUL SUCH AS YOU, I TOO WOULD COWER IN THE FACE OF FRANKENSTEIN'S VENGEANCE!
FOOM
FOOM
STILL, I TIRE OF THIS GAME, N'AAL--I'LL BE DONE WITH YOU AND RETURN TO MY COMRADES BEFORE THEY GET THEMSELVES KILLED!
YOU OVER-MUSCLED FOOL. YOU THINK I RUN IN FEAR?
I KNOW THE HOUSE OF MYSTERY BETTER THAN ANYONE ALIVE OR UNDEAD. I'VE LED YOU RIGHT WHERE I WANT YOU...
YOU SEE, AS CARETAKER... BEFORE THE LORD DESTINY SET ME FREE, I WAS ALSO PRIVY TO CONSTANTINE'S SECRET FILES. FILES ON ALL OF YOU. SO I KNOW FIRE IS NO FRIEND OF FRANKENSTEIN!
THAT IS WHY I THOUGHT THIS ROOM, THE DEN OF THE FIREFEEDERS, WOULD BE THE MOST APPROPRIATE FOR YOU!
ARRRGH!!!!

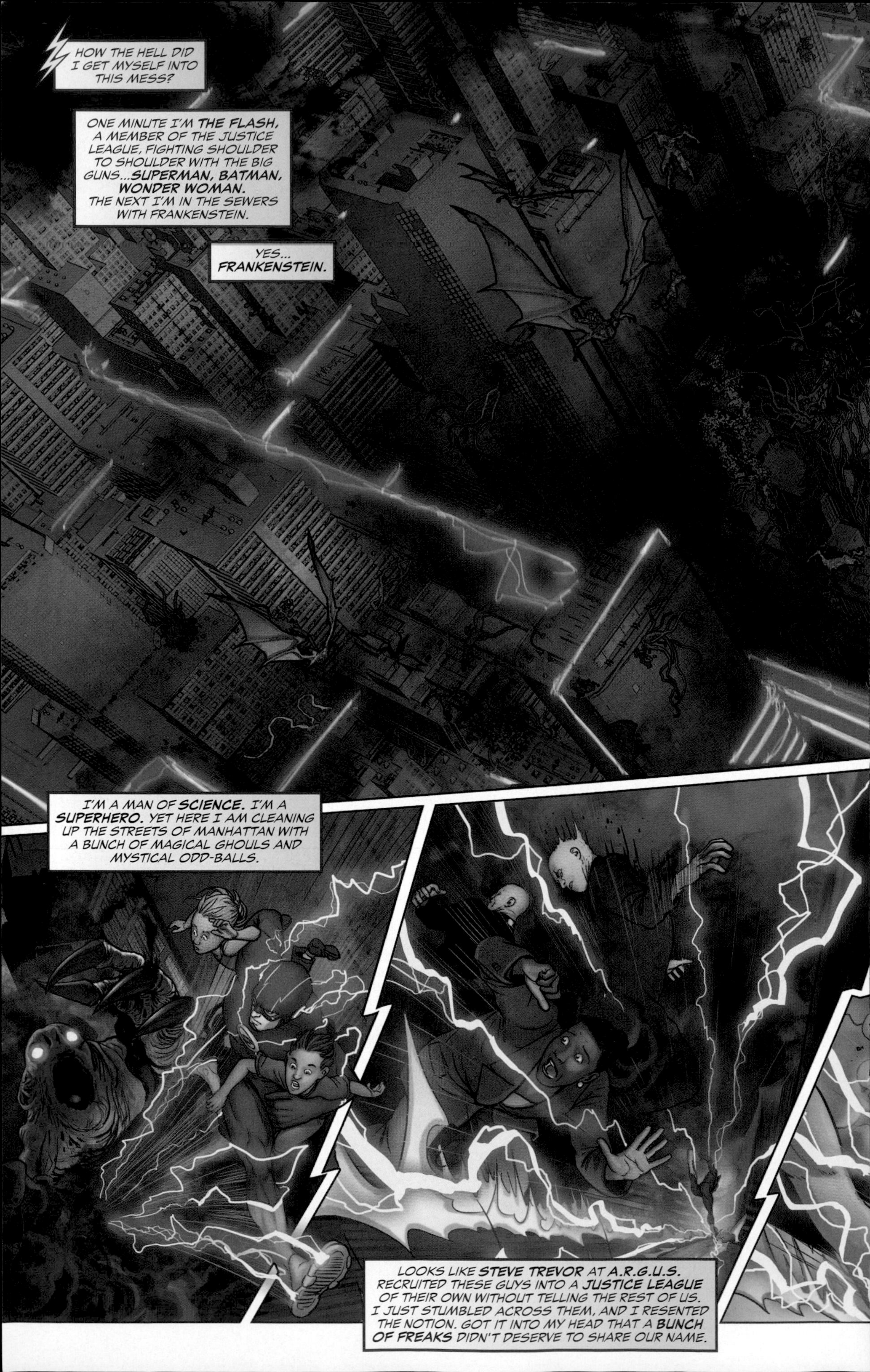
HOW THE HELL DID I GET MYSELF INTO THIS MESS?
ONE MINUTE I'M THE FLASH, A MEMBER OF THE JUSTICE LEAGUE, FIGHTING SHOULDER TO SHOULDER WITH THE BIG GUNS...SUPERMAN, BATMAN, WONDER WOMAN. THE NEXT I'M IN THE SEWERS WITH FRANKENSTEIN.
YES... FRANKENSTEIN.
I'M A MAN OF SCIENCE. I'M A SUPERHERO. YET HERE I AM CLEANING UP THE STREETS OF MANHATTAN WITH A BUNCH OF MAGICAL GHOULS AND MYSTICAL ODD-BALLS.
LOOKS LIKE STEVE TREVOR AT A.R.G.U.S. RECRUITED THESE GUYS INTO A JUSTICE LEAGUE OF THEIR OWN WITHOUT TELLING THE REST OF US. I JUST STUMBLED ACROSS THEM, AND I RESENTED THE NOTION. GOT IT INTO MY HEAD THAT A BUNCH OF FREAKS DIDN'T DESERVE TO SHARE OUR NAME.

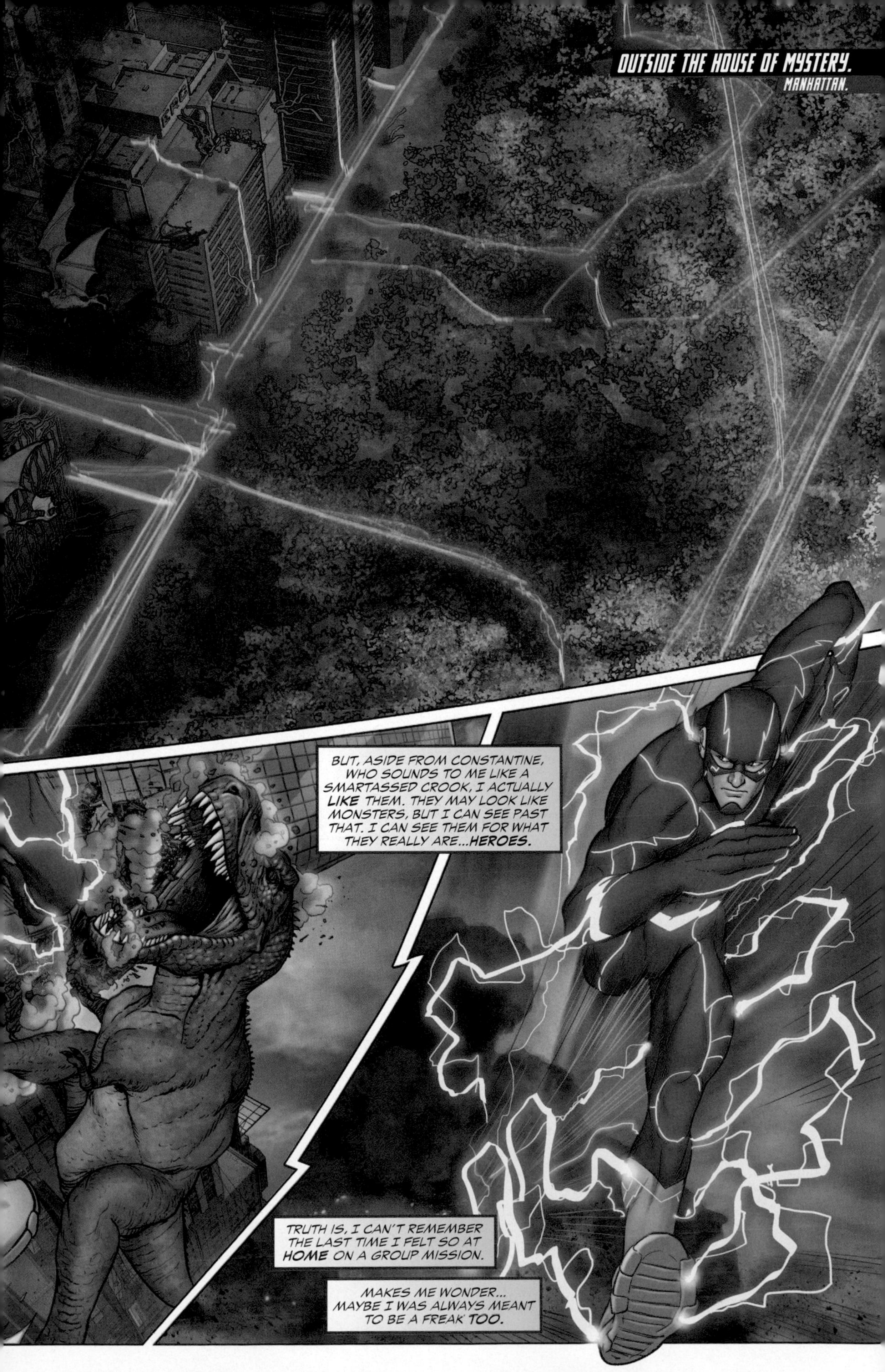
OUTSIDE THE HOUSE OF MYSTERY.
MANHATTAN.
BUT, ASIDE FROM CONSTANTINE, WHO SOUNDS TO ME LIKE A SMARTASSED CROOK, I ACTUALLY LIKE THEM. THEY MAY LOOK LIKE MONSTERS, BUT I CAN SEE PAST THAT. I CAN SEE THEM FOR WHAT THEY REALLY ARE...HEROES.
TRUTH IS, I CAN'T REMEMBER THE LAST TIME I FELT SO AT HOME ON A GROUP MISSION.
MAKES ME WONDER... MAYBE I WAS ALWAYS MEANT TO BE A FREAK TOO.

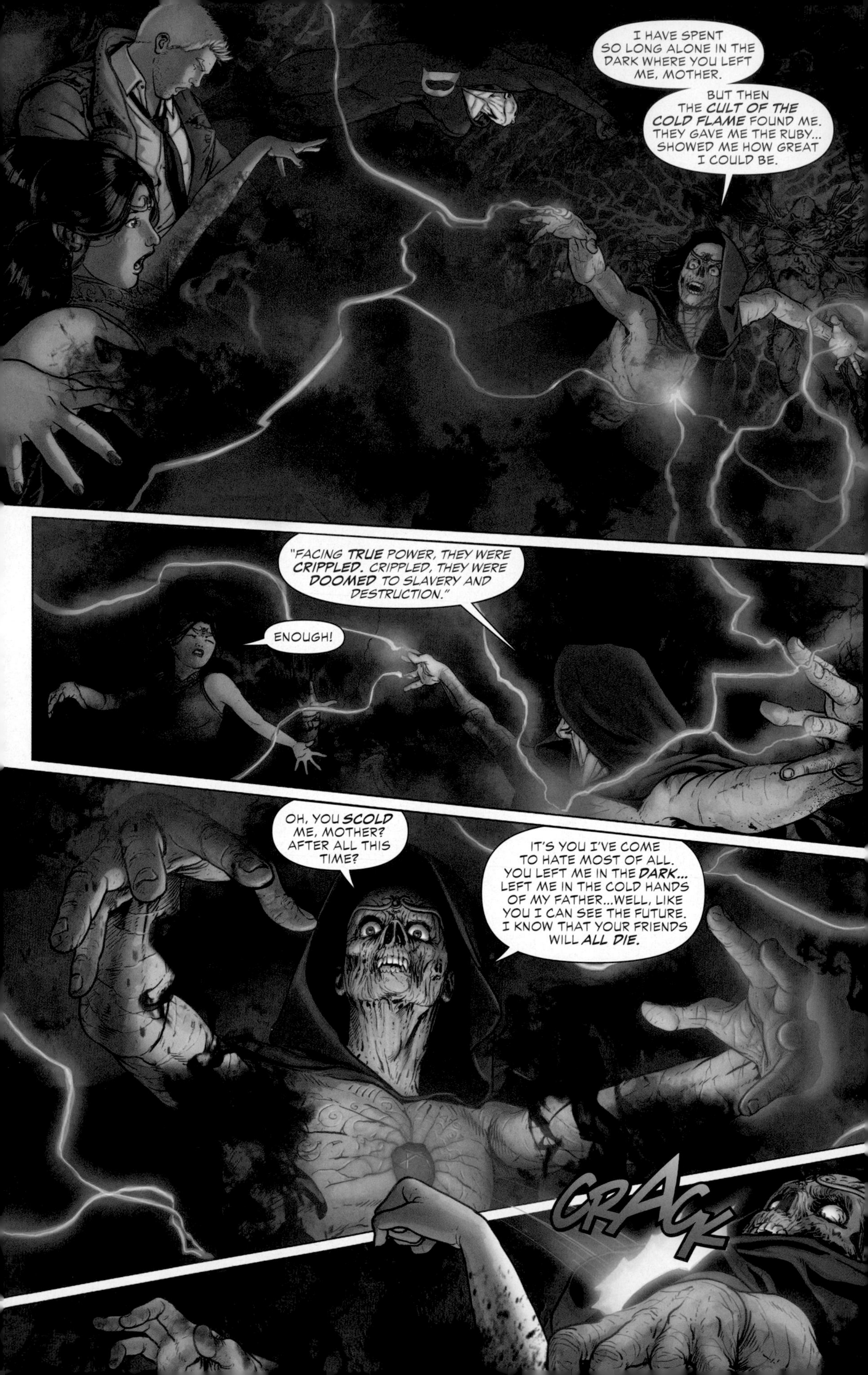
I HAVE SPENT SO LONG ALONE IN THE DARK WHERE YOU LEFT ME, MOTHER.
BUT THEN THE CULT OF THE COLD FLAME FOUND ME. THEY GAVE ME THE RUBY... SHOWED ME HOW GREAT I COULD BE.
"FACING TRUE POWER, THEY WERE CRIPPLED. CRIPPLED, THEY WERE DOOMED TO SLAVERY AND DESTRUCTION."
ENOUGH!
OH, YOU SCOLD ME, MOTHER? AFTER ALL THIS TIME?
IT'S YOU I'VE COME TO HATE MOST OF ALL. YOU LEFT ME IN THE DARK... LEFT ME IN THE COLD HANDS OF MY FATHER...WELL, LIKE YOU I CAN SEE THE FUTURE. I KNOW THAT YOUR FRIENDS WILL ALL DIE.
CRACK

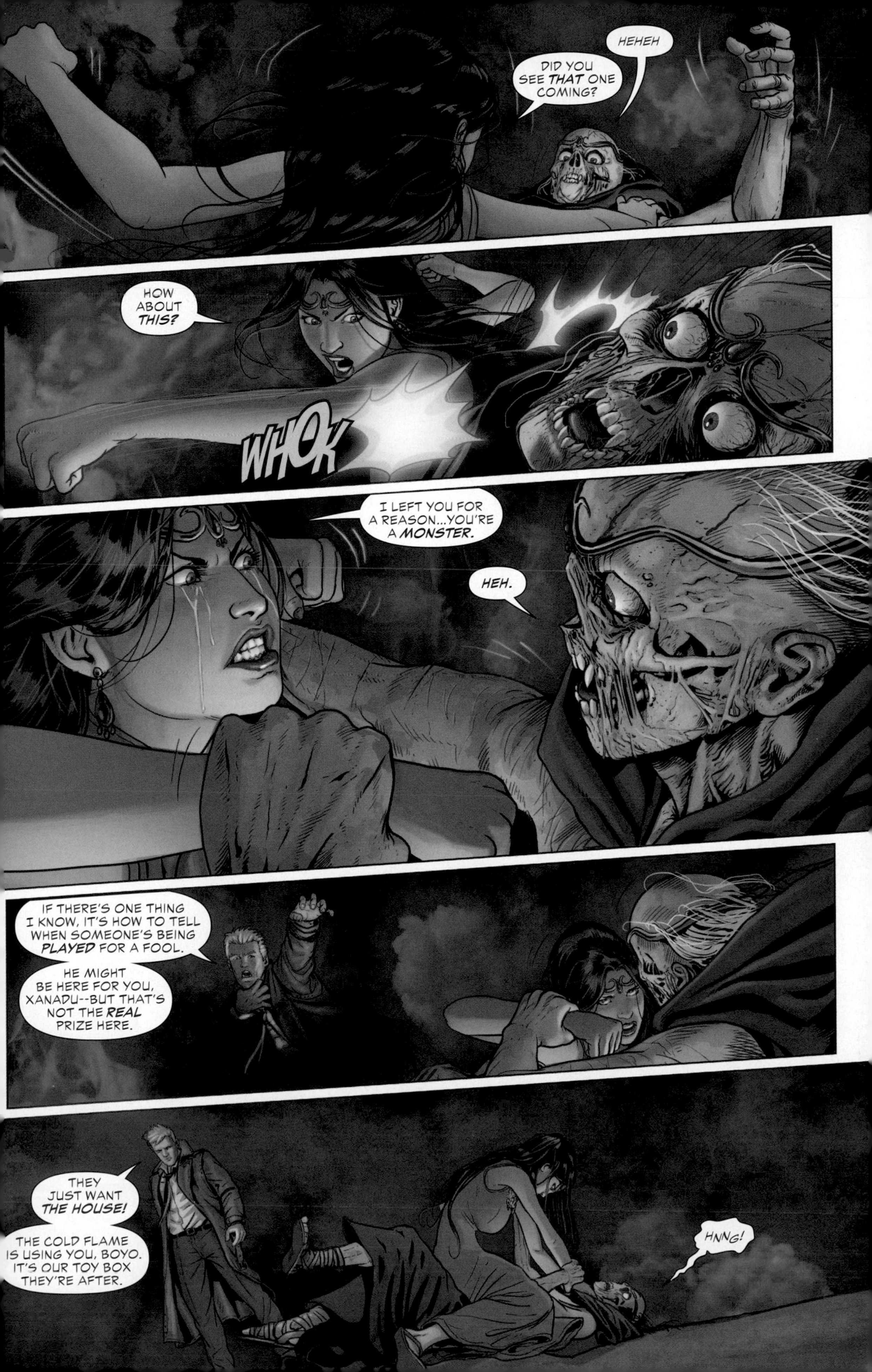
HEHEH
DID YOU SEE THAT ONE COMING?
HOW ABOUT THIS?
WHOK
I LEFT YOU FOR A REASON...YOU'RE A MONSTER.
HEH.
IF THERE'S ONE THING I KNOW, IT'S HOW TO TELL WHEN SOMEONE'S BEING PLAYED FOR A FOOL.
HE MIGHT BE HERE FOR YOU, XANADU--BUT THAT'S NOT THE REAL PRIZE HERE.
THEY JUST WANT THE HOUSE!
THE COLD FLAME IS USING YOU, BOYO. IT'S OUR TOY BOX THEY'RE AFTER.
HNNG!

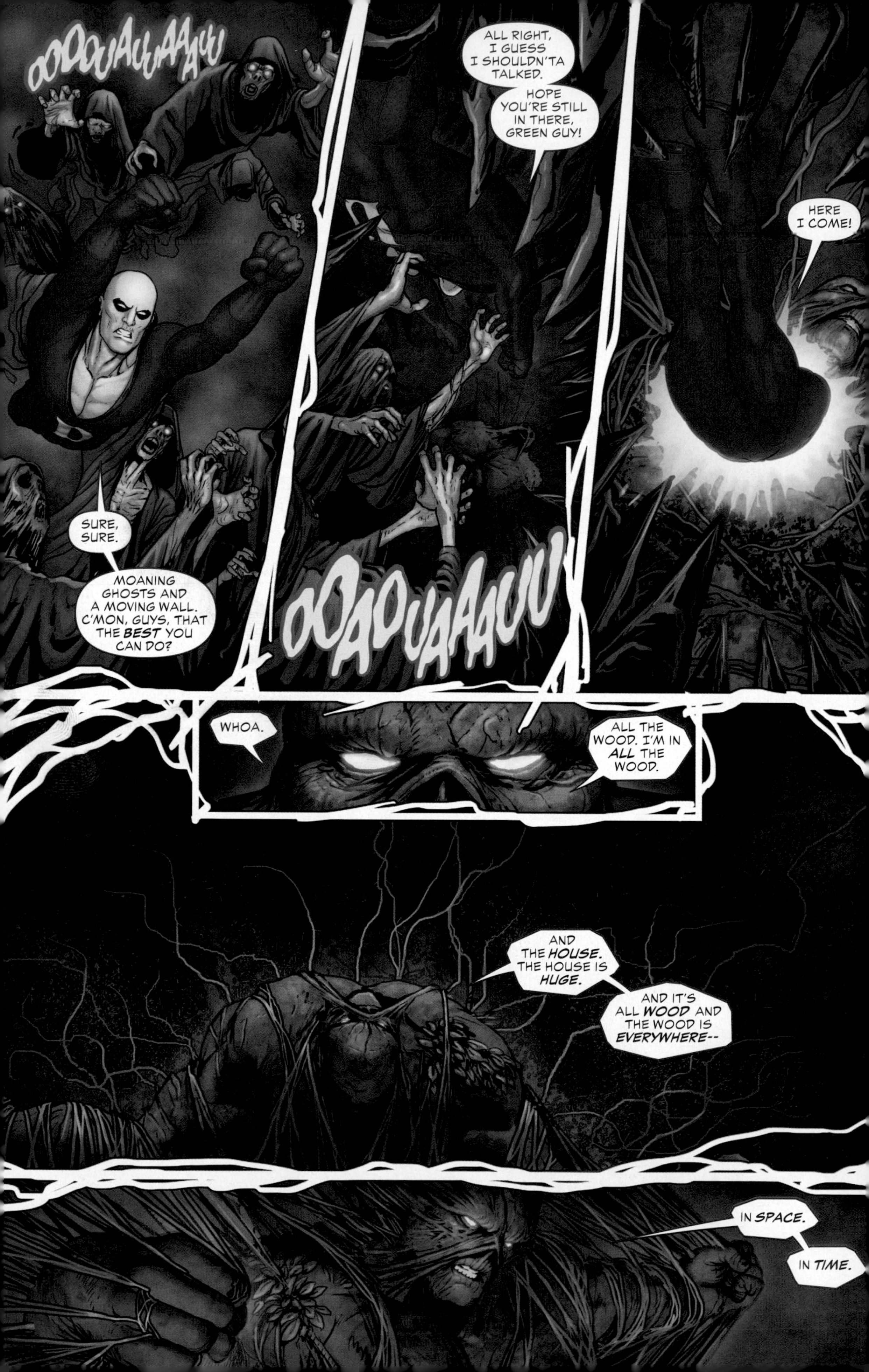
OOOOUAUUAAAUU
SURE, SURE.
MOANING GHOSTS AND A MOVING WALL. C'MON, GUYS, THAT THE *BEST* YOU CAN DO?
ALL RIGHT, I GUESS I SHOULDN'TA TALKED.
HOPE YOU'RE STILL IN THERE, GREEN GUY!
OOAOUAAAUU
HERE I COME!
WHOA.
ALL THE WOOD. I'M IN *ALL* THE WOOD.
AND THE *HOUSE*. THE HOUSE IS *HUGE*.
AND IT'S ALL *WOOD* AND THE WOOD IS *EVERYWHERE*--
IN *SPACE*.
IN *TIME*.

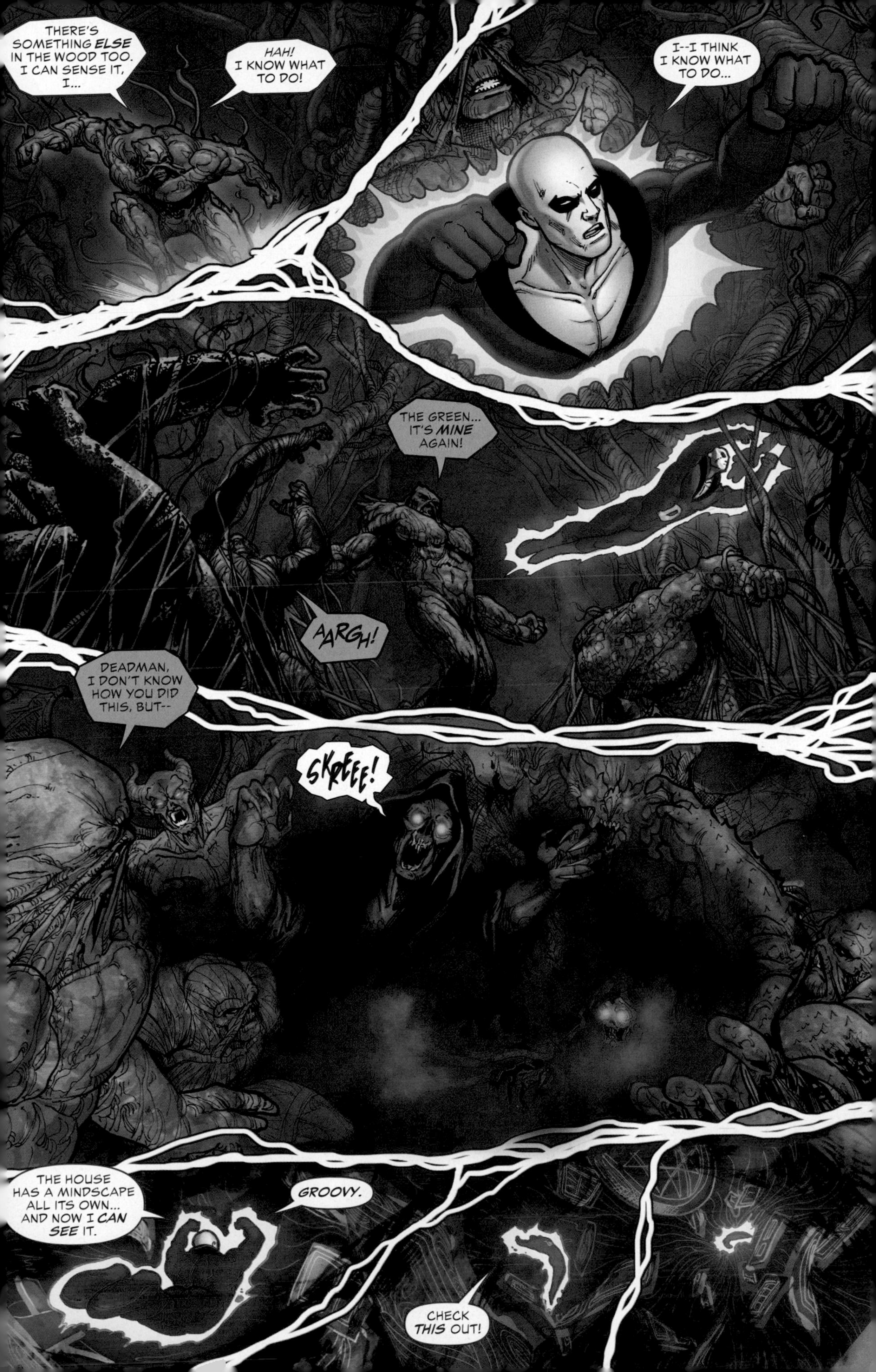
THERE'S SOMETHING ELSE IN THE WOOD TOO. I CAN SENSE IT, I...
HAH! I KNOW WHAT TO DO!
I--I THINK I KNOW WHAT TO DO...
THE GREEN... IT'S MINE AGAIN!
AARGH!
DEADMAN, I DON'T KNOW HOW YOU DID THIS, BUT--
SKREEE!
THE HOUSE HAS A MINDSCAPE ALL ITS OWN... AND NOW I CAN SEE IT.
GROOVY.
CHECK THIS OUT!

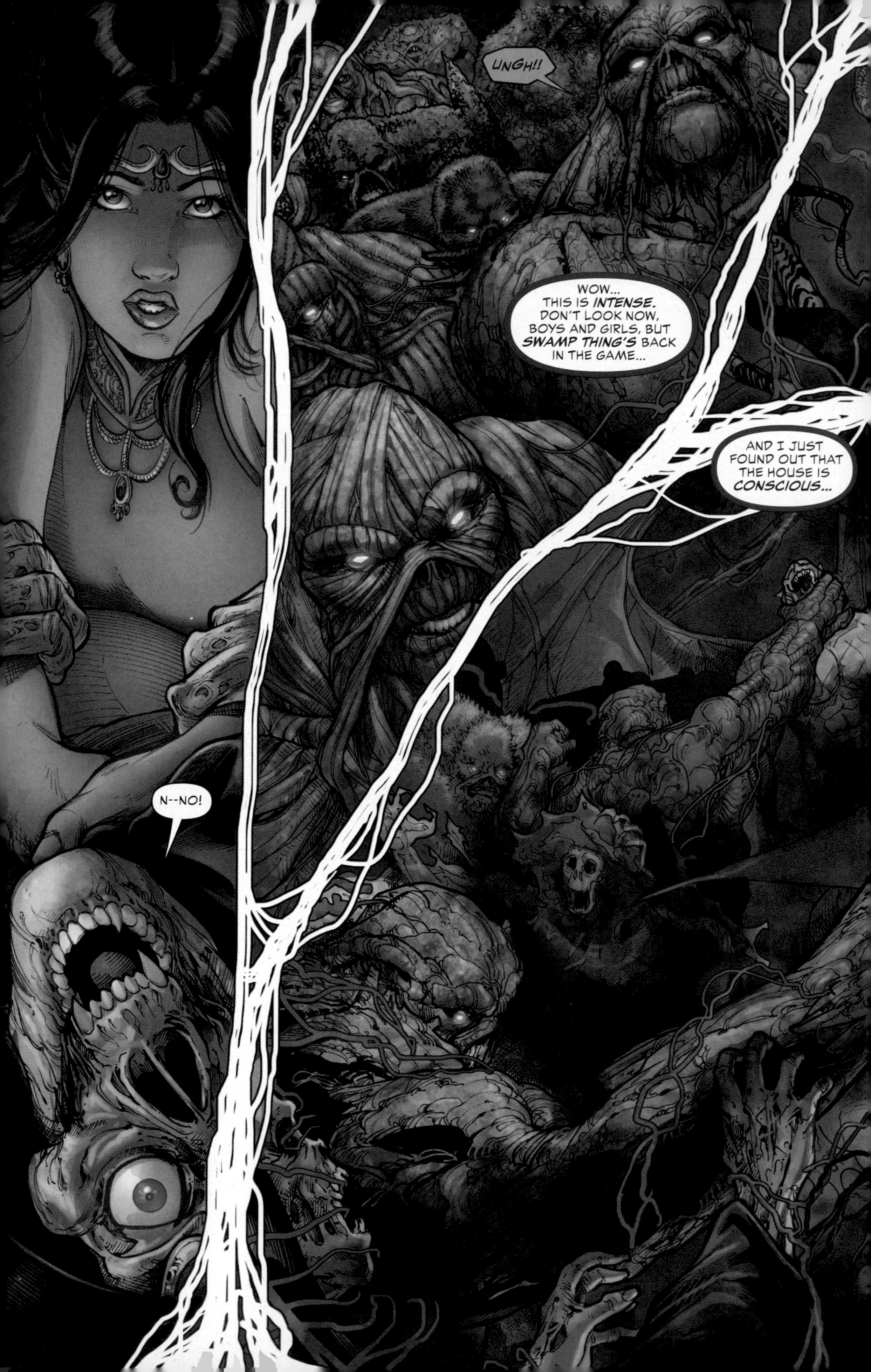
UNGH!!
WOW... THIS IS *INTENSE.* DON'T LOOK NOW, BOYS AND GIRLS, BUT ***SWAMP THING'S*** BACK IN THE GAME...
AND I JUST FOUND OUT THAT THE HOUSE IS ***CONSCIOUS...***
N--NO!

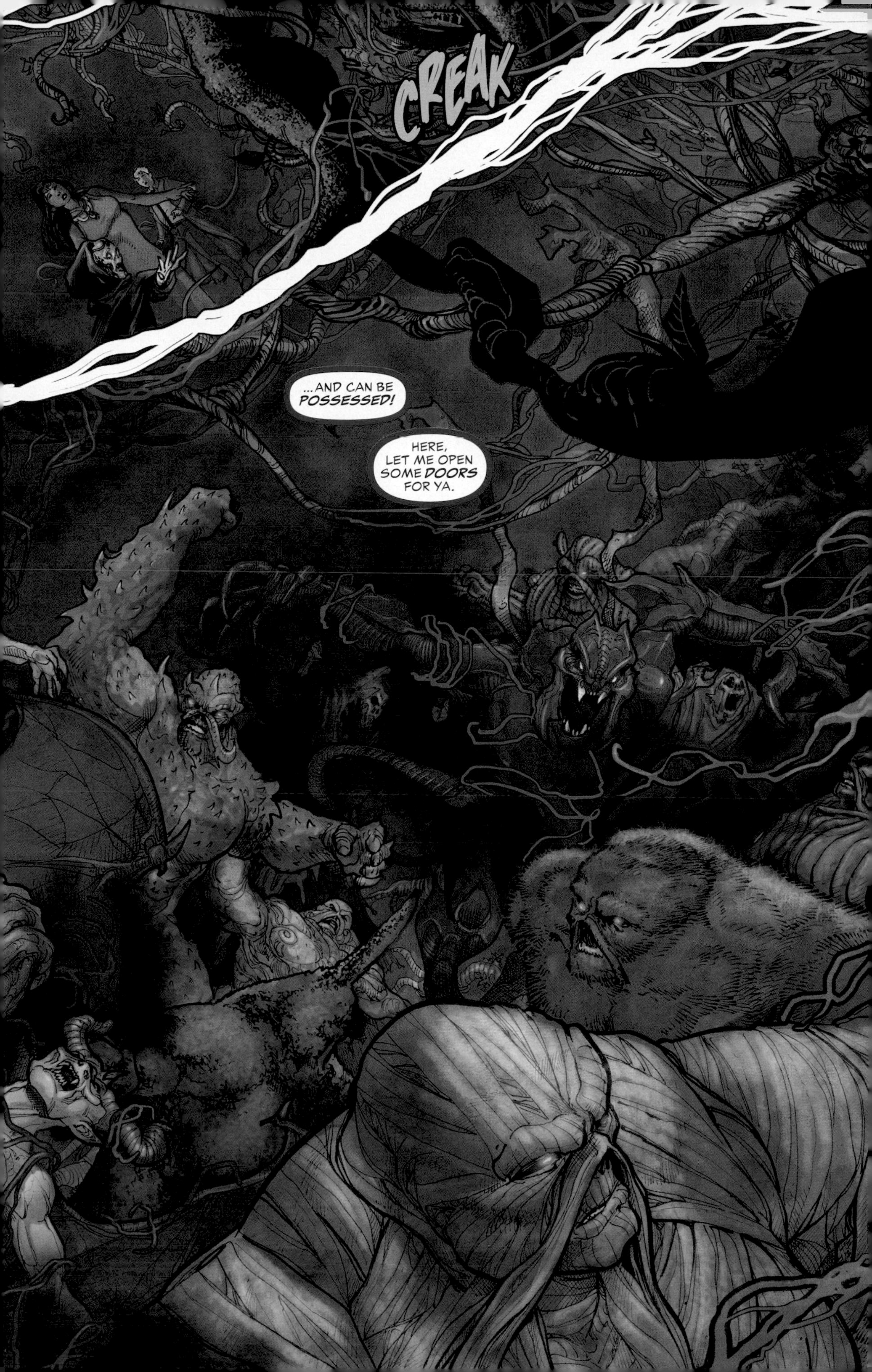
CREAK
...AND CAN BE POSSESSED!
HERE, LET ME OPEN SOME DOORS FOR YA.

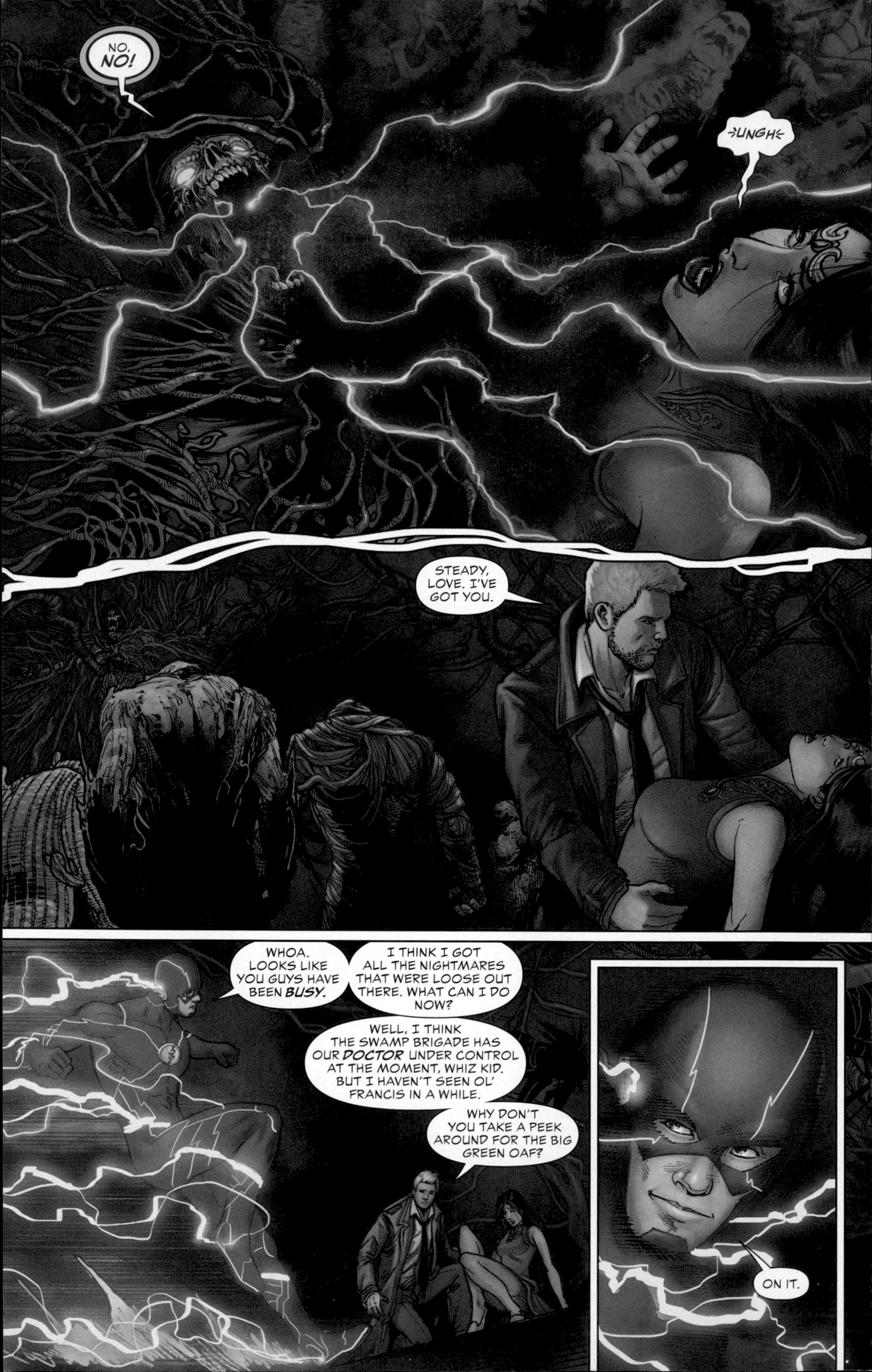

NO, NO!
UNGH
STEADY, LOVE. I'VE GOT YOU.
WHOA. LOOKS LIKE YOU GUYS HAVE BEEN BUSY.
I THINK I GOT ALL THE NIGHTMARES THAT WERE LOOSE OUT THERE. WHAT CAN I DO NOW?
WELL, I THINK THE SWAMP BRIGADE HAS OUR DOCTOR UNDER CONTROL AT THE MOMENT, WHIZ KID. BUT I HAVEN'T SEEN OL' FRANCIS IN A WHILE.
WHY DON'T YOU TAKE A PEEK AROUND FOR THE BIG GREEN OAF?
ON IT.

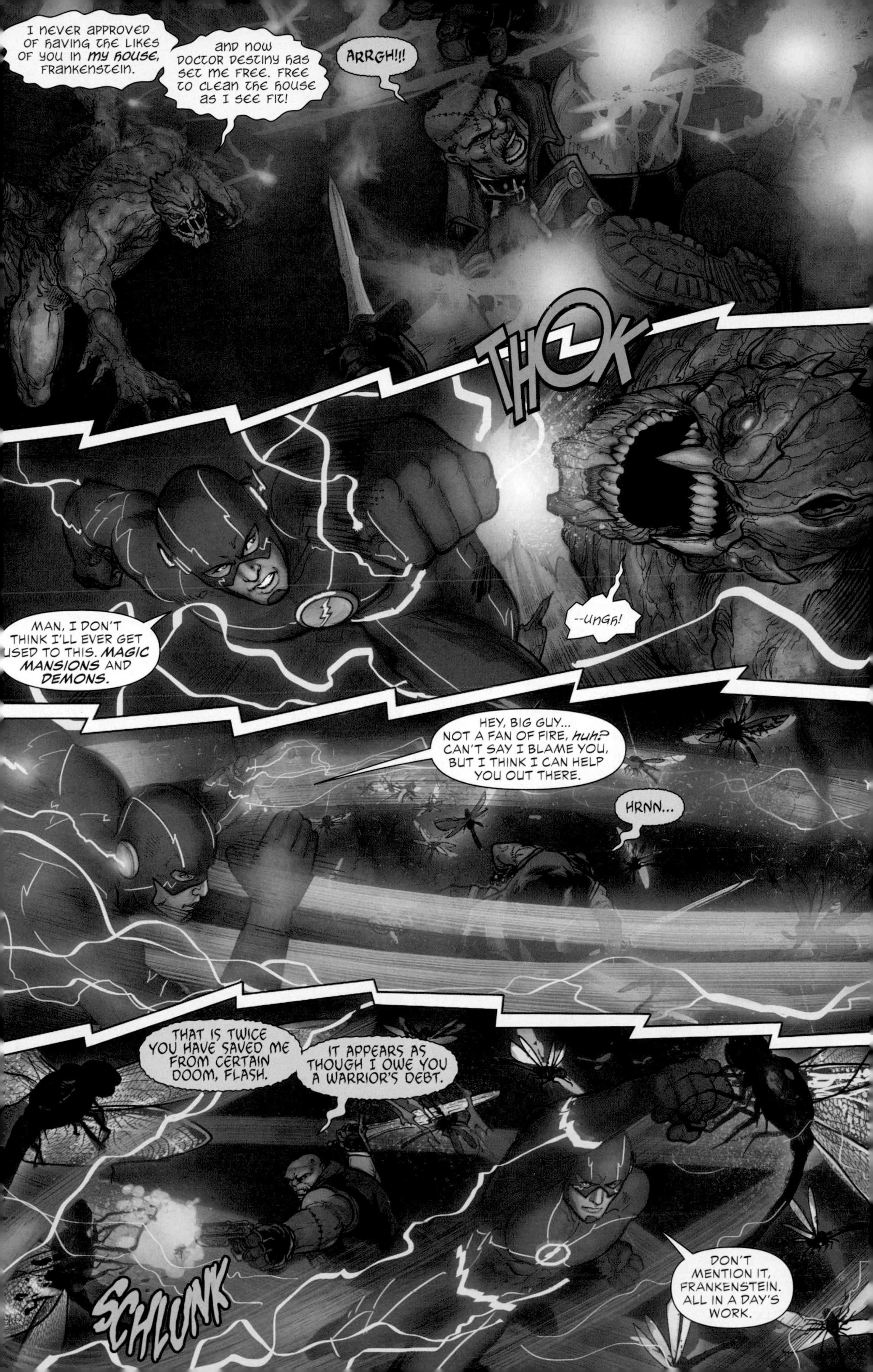

I never approved of having the likes of you in *my house*, Frankenstein.
and now Doctor Destiny has set me free. Free to clean the house as I see fit!
ARRGH!!!
THOK
MAN, I DON'T THINK I'LL EVER GET USED TO THIS. *MAGIC MANSIONS* AND *DEMONS*.
--UNGH!
HEY, BIG GUY... NOT A FAN OF FIRE, *huh?* CAN'T SAY I BLAME YOU, BUT I THINK I CAN HELP YOU OUT THERE.
HRNN...
THAT IS TWICE YOU HAVE SAVED ME FROM CERTAIN DOOM, FLASH.
IT APPEARS AS THOUGH I OWE YOU A WARRIOR'S DEBT.
SCHLUNK
DON'T MENTION IT, FRANKENSTEIN. ALL IN A DAY'S WORK.

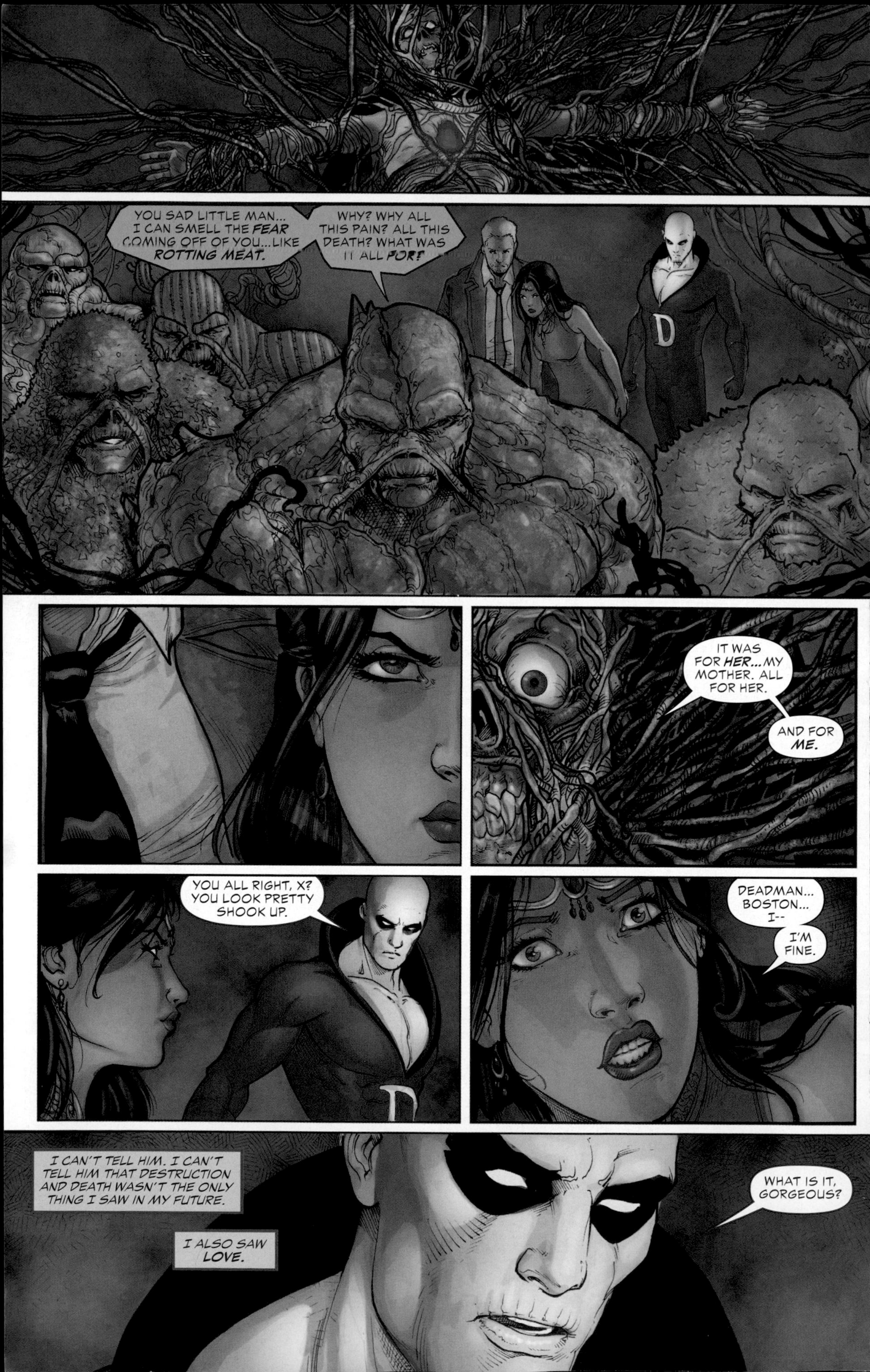
YOU SAD LITTLE MAN... I CAN SMELL THE FEAR COMING OFF OF YOU...LIKE ROTTING MEAT.
WHY? WHY ALL THIS PAIN? ALL THIS DEATH? WHAT WAS IT ALL FOR?
IT WAS FOR HER...MY MOTHER. ALL FOR HER.
AND FOR ME.
YOU ALL RIGHT, X? YOU LOOK PRETTY SHOOK UP.
DEADMAN... BOSTON... I--
I'M FINE.
I CAN'T TELL HIM. I CAN'T TELL HIM THAT DESTRUCTION AND DEATH WASN'T THE ONLY THING I SAW IN MY FUTURE.
I ALSO SAW LOVE.
WHAT IS IT, GORGEOUS?

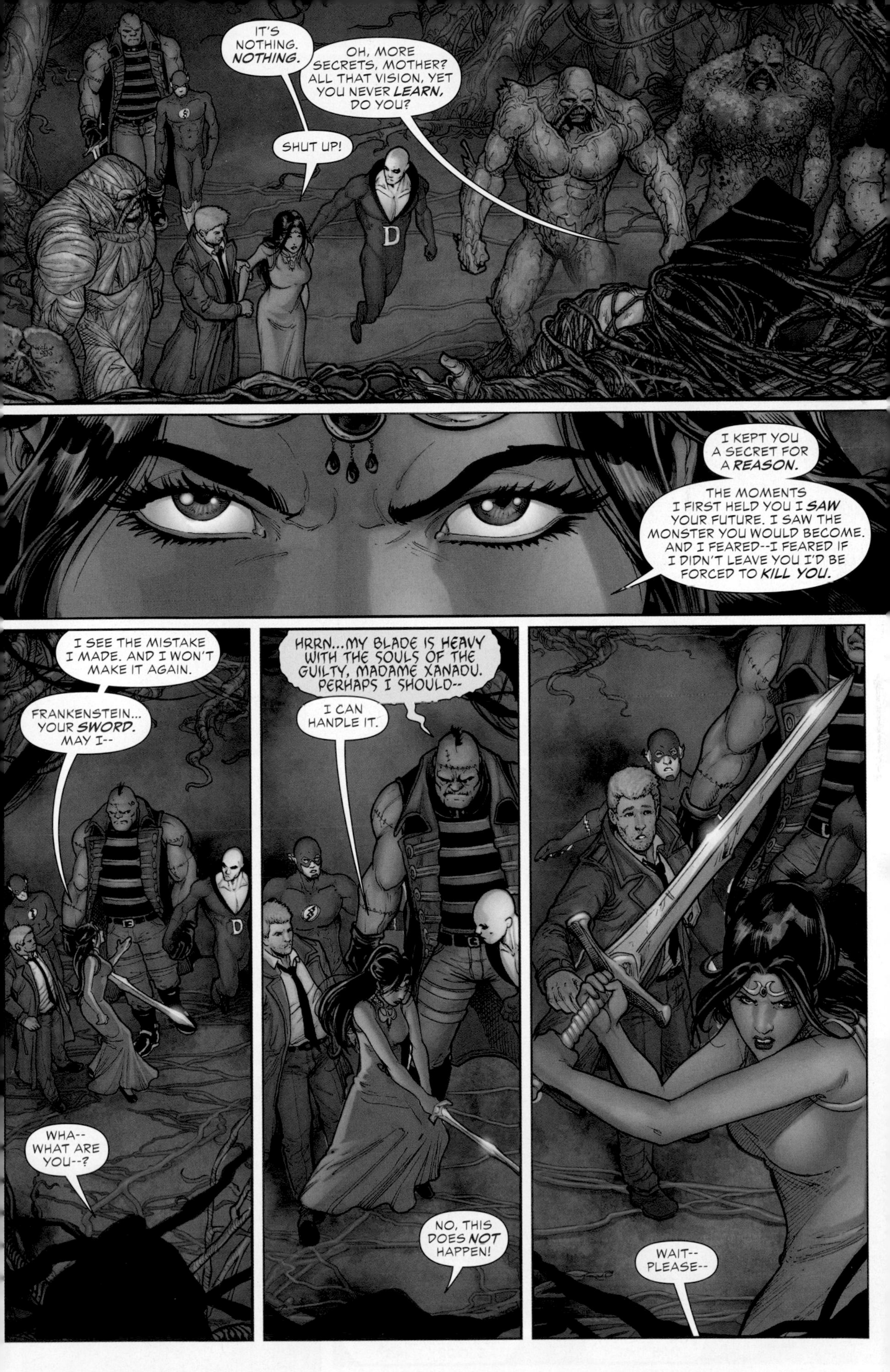

IT'S NOTHING. NOTHING.
OH, MORE SECRETS, MOTHER? ALL THAT VISION, YET YOU NEVER LEARN, DO YOU?
SHUT UP!
I KEPT YOU A SECRET FOR A REASON.
THE MOMENTS I FIRST HELD YOU I SAW YOUR FUTURE. I SAW THE MONSTER YOU WOULD BECOME. AND I FEARED--I FEARED IF I DIDN'T LEAVE YOU I'D BE FORCED TO KILL YOU.
I SEE THE MISTAKE I MADE. AND I WON'T MAKE IT AGAIN.
FRANKENSTEIN... YOUR SWORD. MAY I--
WHA-- WHAT ARE YOU--?
HRRN...MY BLADE IS HEAVY WITH THE SOULS OF THE GUILTY, MADAME XANADU. PERHAPS I SHOULD--
I CAN HANDLE IT.
NO, THIS DOES NOT HAPPEN!
WAIT-- PLEASE--

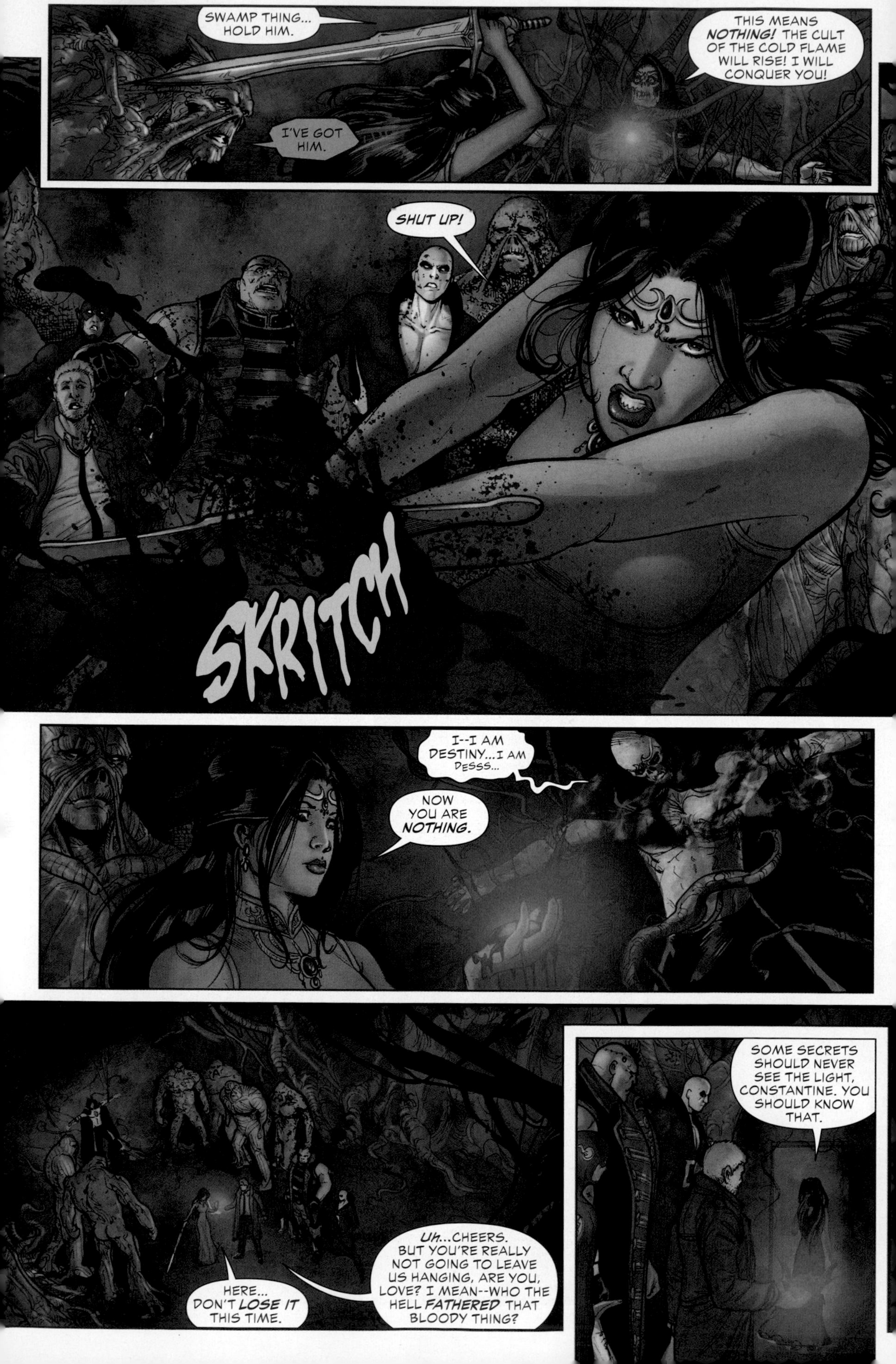

SWAMP THING... HOLD HIM.
THIS MEANS NOTHING! THE CULT OF THE COLD FLAME WILL RISE! I WILL CONQUER YOU!
I'VE GOT HIM.
SHUT UP!
SKRITCH
I--I AM DESTINY...I AM DESSS...
NOW YOU ARE NOTHING.
HERE... DON'T LOSE IT THIS TIME.
Uh...CHEERS. BUT YOU'RE REALLY NOT GOING TO LEAVE US HANGING, ARE YOU, LOVE? I MEAN--WHO THE HELL FATHERED THAT BLOODY THING?
SOME SECRETS SHOULD NEVER SEE THE LIGHT, CONSTANTINE. YOU SHOULD KNOW THAT.

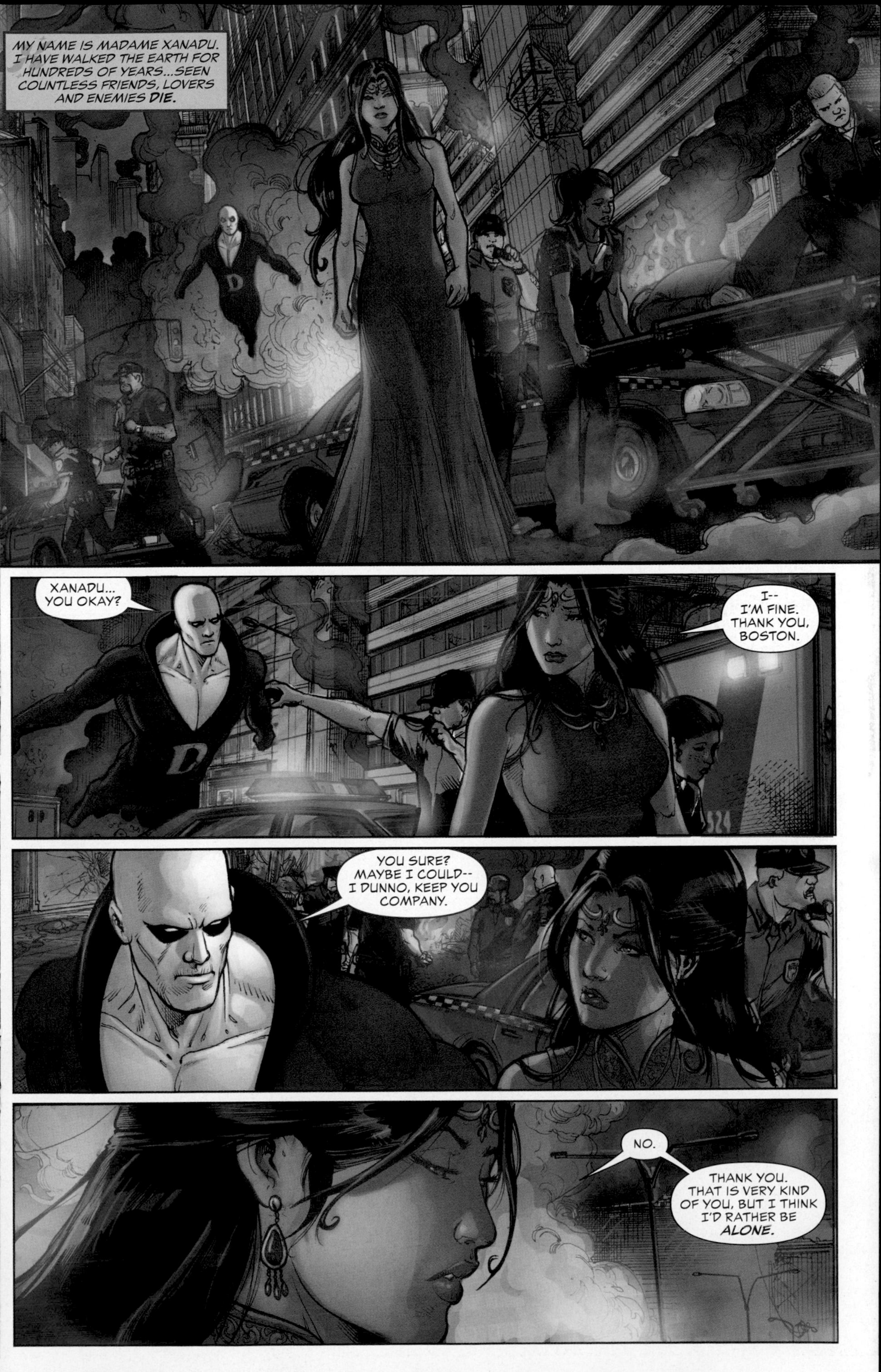
MY NAME IS MADAME XANADU. I HAVE WALKED THE EARTH FOR HUNDREDS OF YEARS...SEEN COUNTLESS FRIENDS, LOVERS AND ENEMIES ***DIE.***
XANADU... YOU OKAY?
I-- I'M FINE. THANK YOU, BOSTON.
YOU SURE? MAYBE I COULD-- I DUNNO, KEEP YOU COMPANY.
NO.
THANK YOU. THAT IS VERY KIND OF YOU, BUT I THINK I'D RATHER BE ***ALONE.***

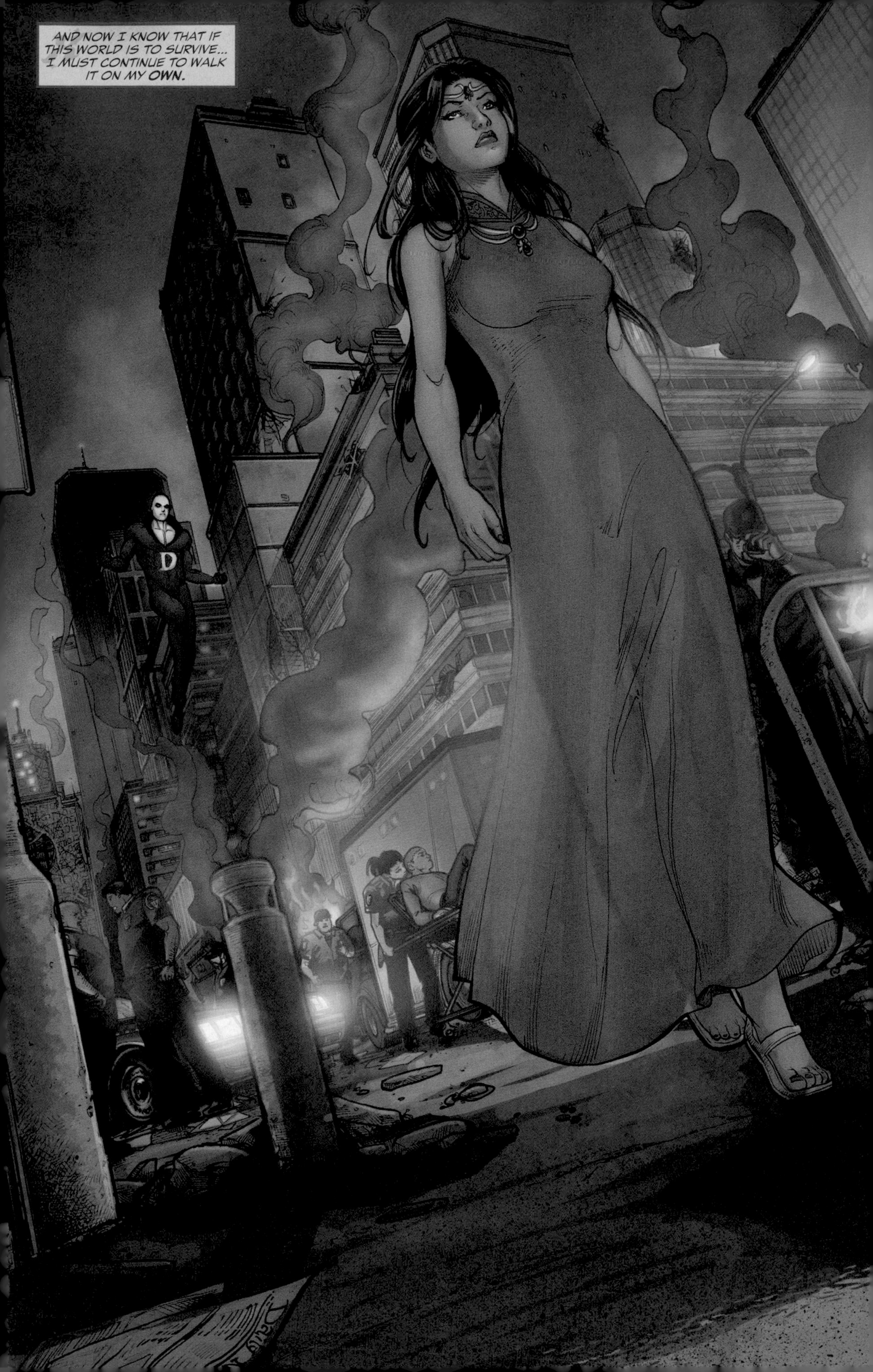
AND NOW I KNOW THAT IF THIS WORLD IS TO SURVIVE... I MUST CONTINUE TO WALK IT ON MY OWN.

JUSTICE LEAGUE DARK #14 cover sketch by Ryan Sook

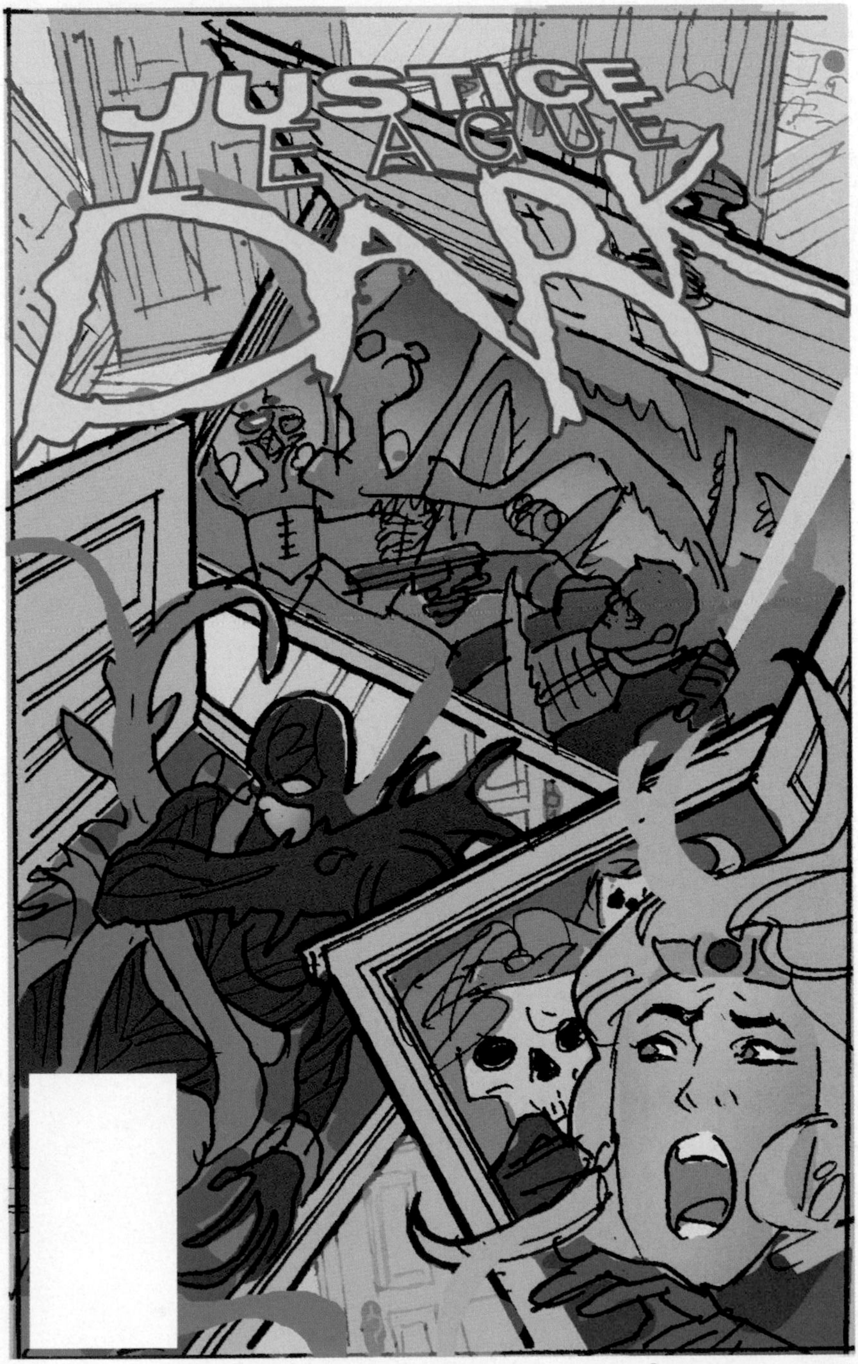
JUSTICE
LEAGUE
DARK

JUSTICE LEAGUE DARK #15 thumbnail cover sketches by Trevor McCarthy

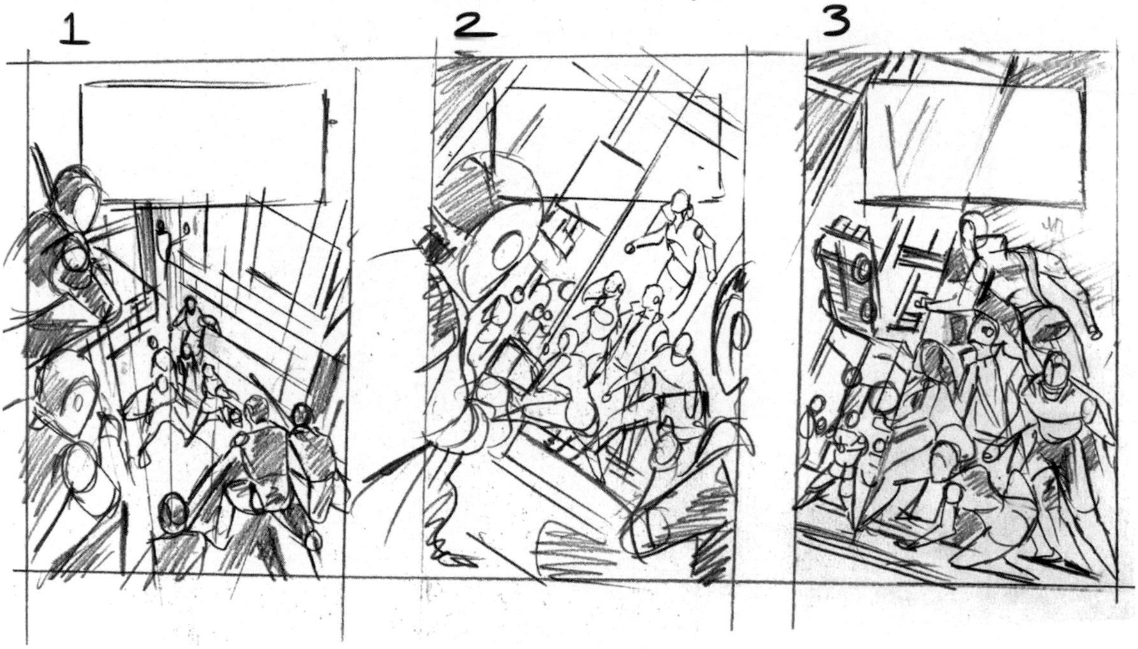
1
2
3

JUSTICE LEAGUE DARK #16 cover sketches by Mikel Janin

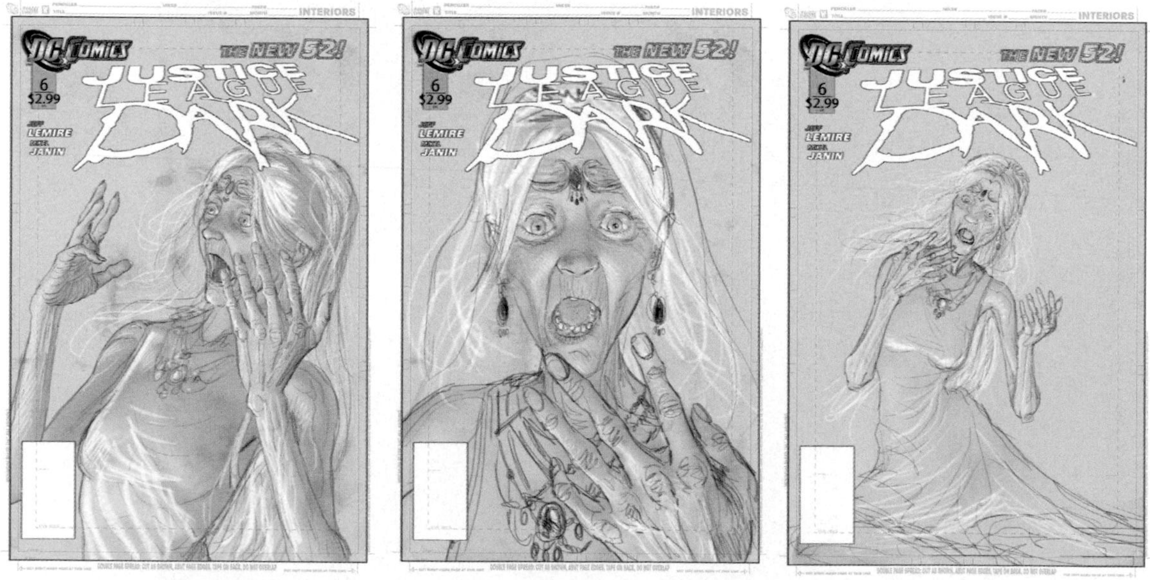
DC COMICS
THE NEW 52!
JUSTICE LEAGUE DARK
6
$2.99
JEFF LEMIRE
MIKEL JANIN
INTERIORS

JUSTICE LEAGUE DARK #17 cover sketches by Mikel Janin

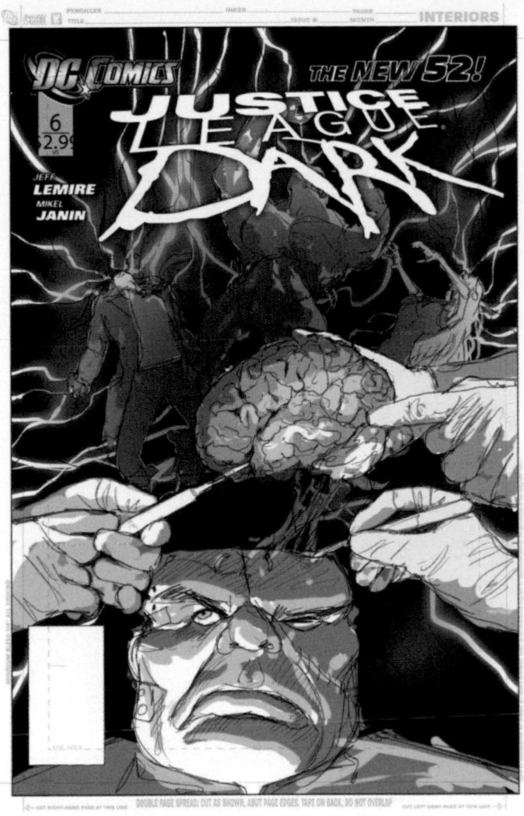
INTERIORS
DC COMICS
THE NEW 52!
JUSTICE LEAGUE DARK
6
$2.99
JEFF LEMIRE
MIKEL JANIN
DOUBLE PAGE SPREAD: CUT AS SHOWN, ABUT PAGE EDGES, TAPE ON BACK, DO NOT OVERLAP

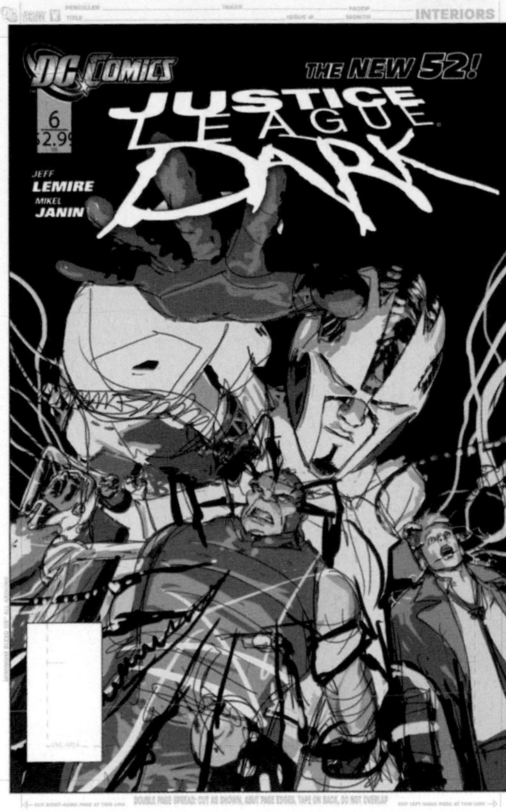
INTERIORS
DC COMICS
THE NEW 52!
JUSTICE LEAGUE DARK
6
$2.99
JEFF LEMIRE
MIKEL JANIN
DOUBLE PAGE SPREAD: CUT AS SHOWN, ABUT PAGE EDGES, TAPE ON BACK, DO NOT OVERLAP

JUSTICE LEAGUE DARK #18 cover sketches by Mikel Janin

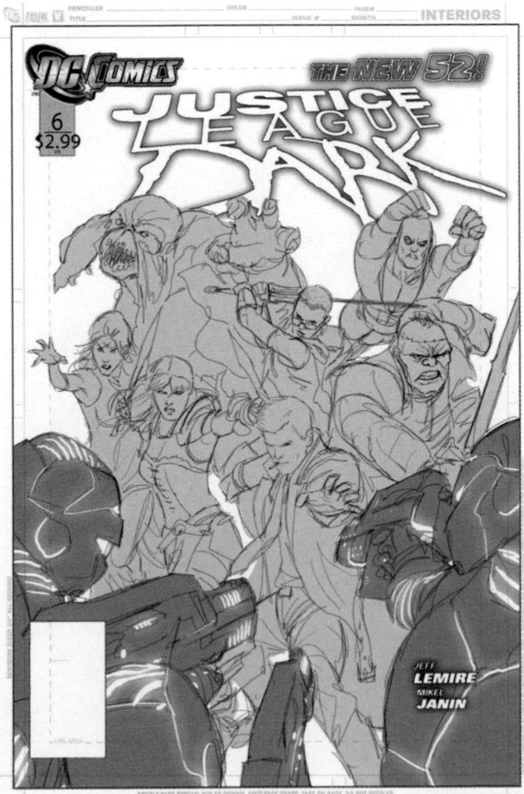
INTERIORS
DC COMICS
THE NEW 52!
JUSTICE LEAGUE DARK
6
$2.99
JEFF LEMIRE
MIKEL JANIN
DOUBLE PAGE SPREAD: CUT AS SHOWN, ABUT PAGE EDGES, TAPE ON BACK, DO NOT OVERLAP

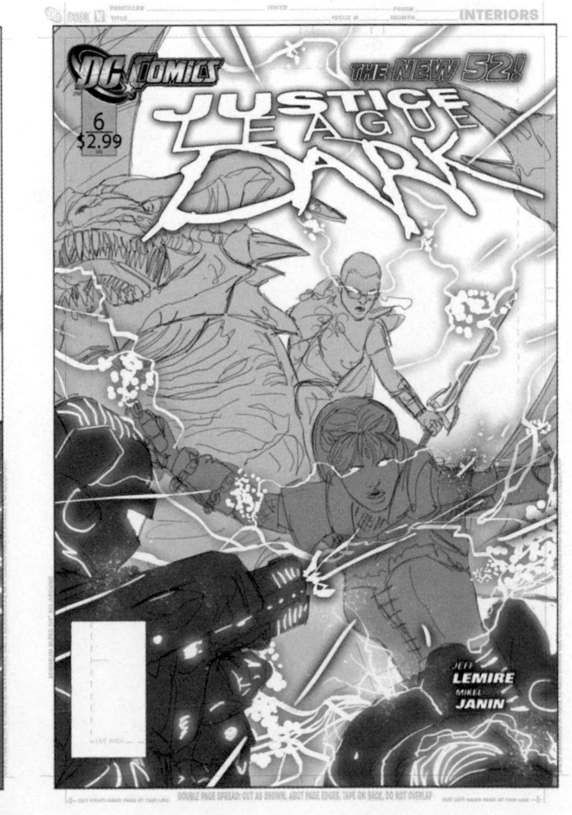
INTERIORS
DC COMICS
THE NEW 52!
JUSTICE LEAGUE DARK
6
$2.99
JEFF LEMIRE
MIKEL JANIN
DOUBLE PAGE SPREAD: CUT AS SHOWN, ABUT PAGE EDGES, TAPE ON BACK, DO NOT OVERLAP

JUSTICE LEAGUE DARK #19 rough cover sketch by Jeff Lemire

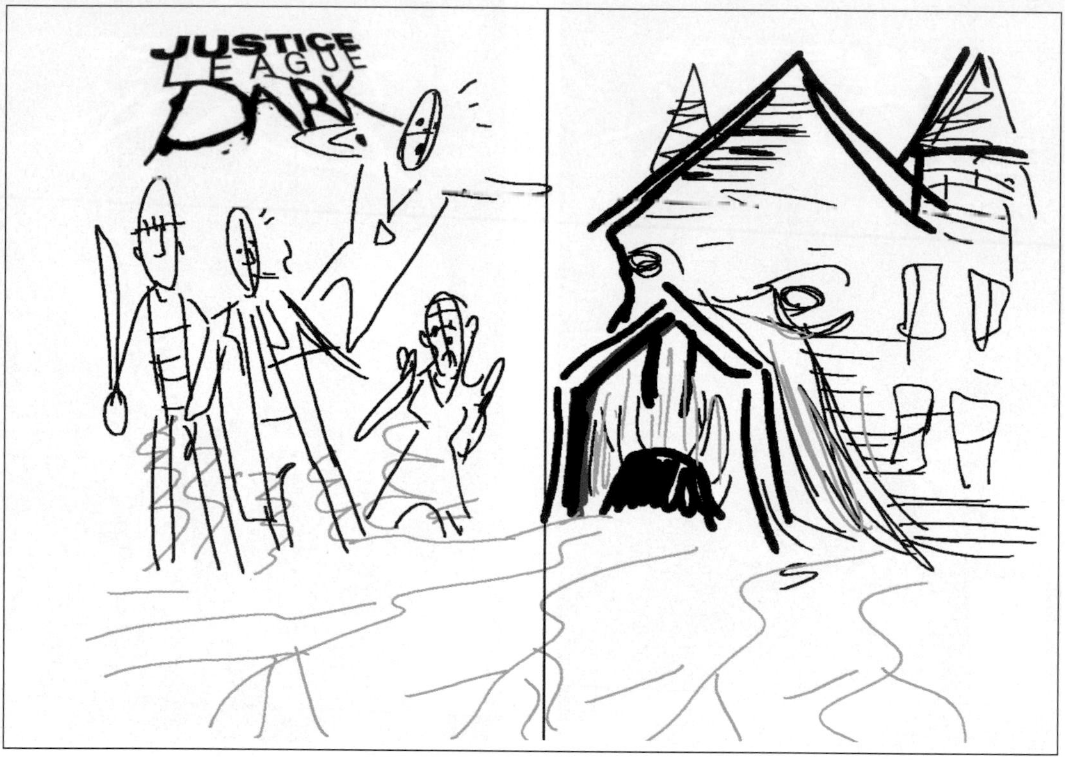
JUSTICE
LEAGUE
DARK

JUSTICE LEAGUE DARK #19 detailed cover sketch by Mikel Janin

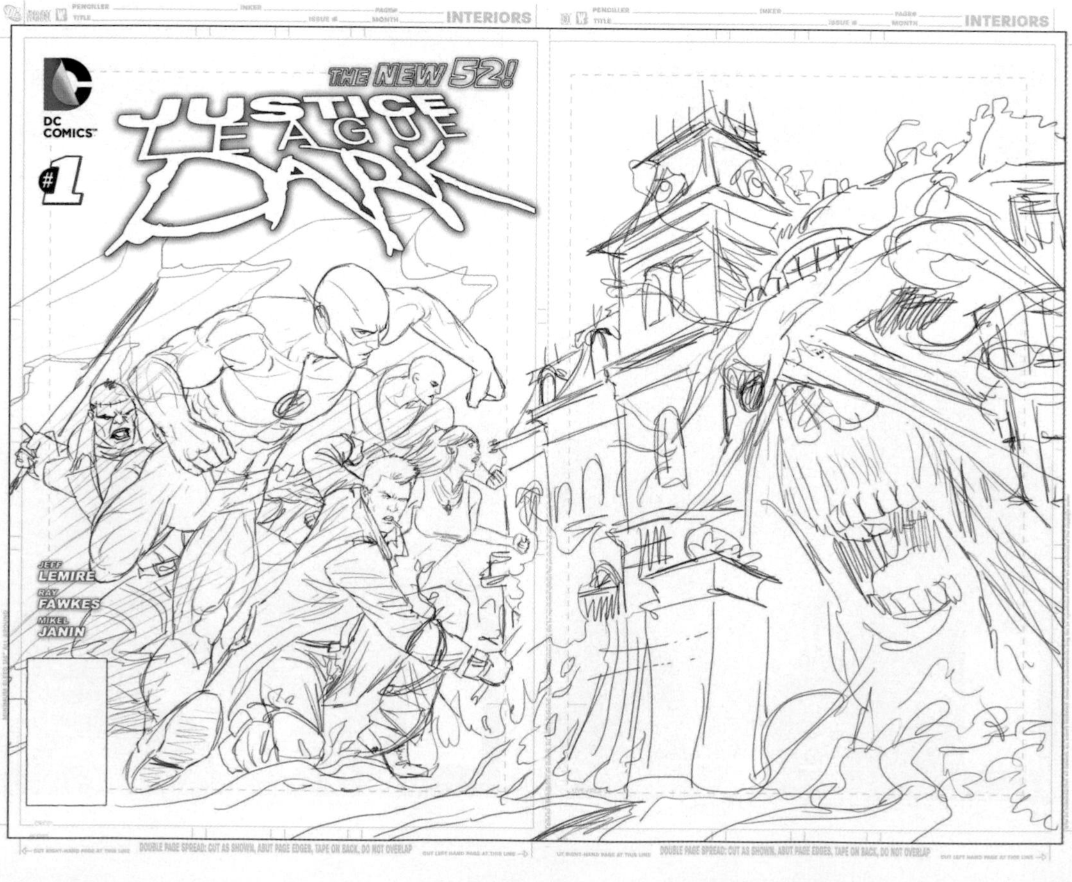
INTERIORS
INTERIORS
DC COMICS
THE NEW 52!
JUSTICE
LEAGUE
DARK
#1
JEFF LEMIRE
RAY FAWKES
MIKEL JANIN

JUSTICE LEAGUE DARK #20 cover sketches by Mikel Janin

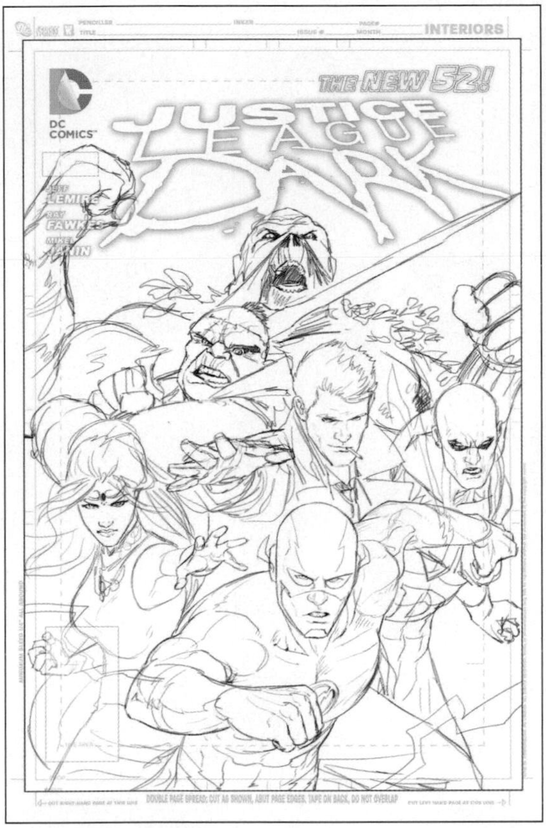
INTERIORS
THE NEW 52!
DC COMICS
JUSTICE LEAGUE DARK
JEFF LEMIRE
RAY FAWKES
MIKEL JANIN
DOUBLE PAGE SPREAD: CUT AS SHOWN, ABUT PAGE EDGES, TAPE ON BACK, DO NOT OVERLAP

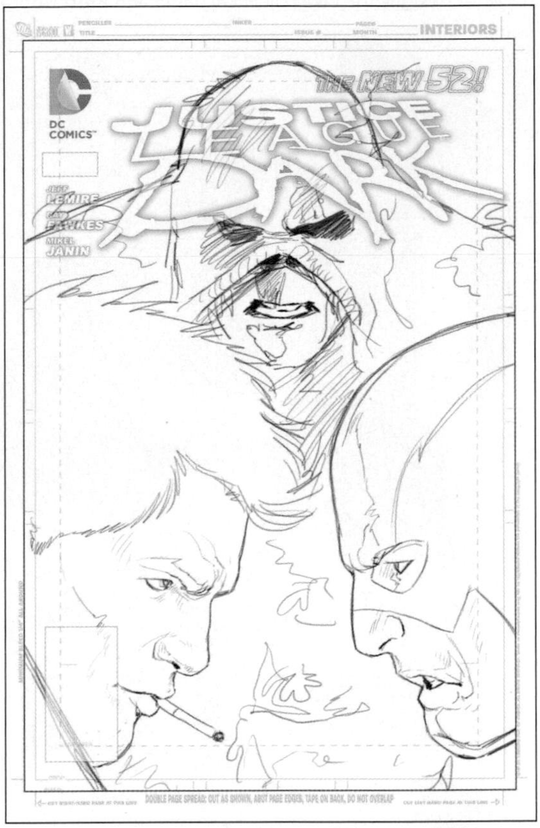
INTERIORS
THE NEW 52!
DC COMICS
JUSTICE LEAGUE DARK
JEFF LEMIRE
RAY FAWKES
MIKEL JANIN
DOUBLE PAGE SPREAD: CUT AS SHOWN, ABUT PAGE EDGES, TAPE ON BACK, DO NOT OVERLAP

JUSTICE LEAGUE DARK #21 cover sketches by Mikel Janin

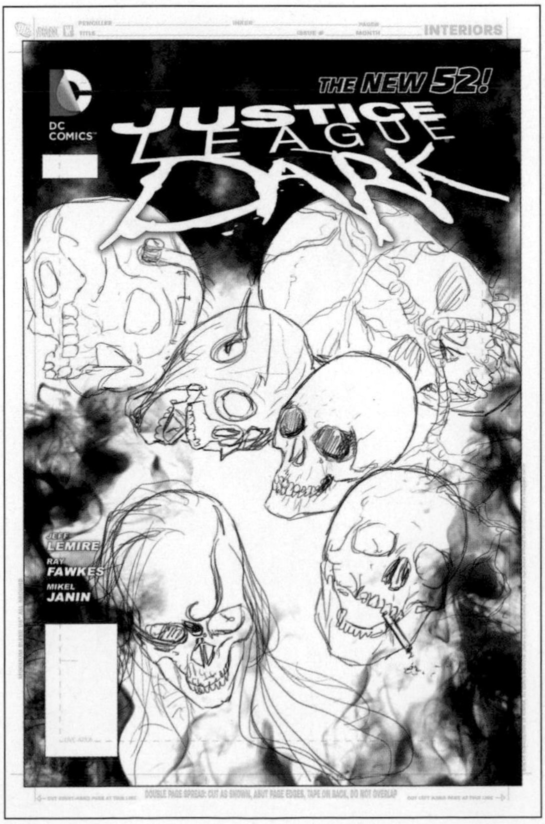
INTERIORS
THE NEW 52!
DC COMICS
JUSTICE LEAGUE DARK
JEFF LEMIRE
RAY FAWKES
MIKEL JANIN
DOUBLE PAGE SPREAD: CUT AS SHOWN, ABUT PAGE EDGES, TAPE ON BACK, DO NOT OVERLAP

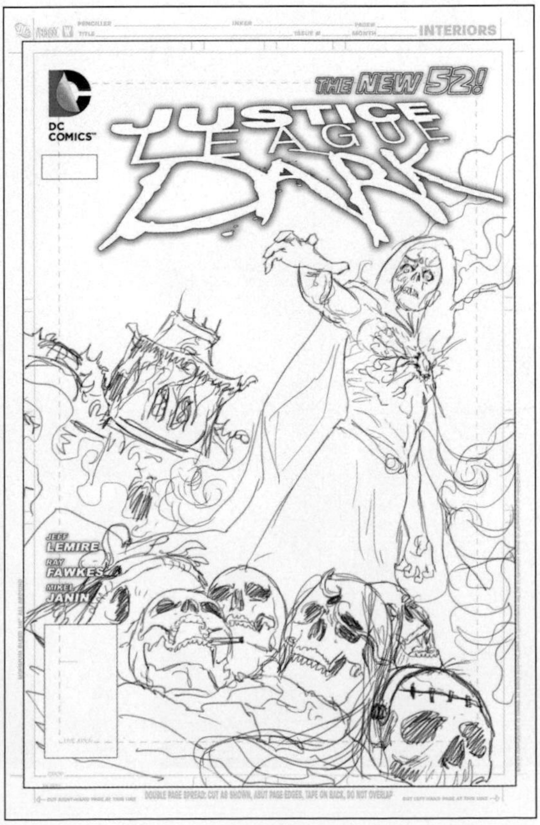
INTERIORS
THE NEW 52!
DC COMICS
JUSTICE LEAGUE DARK
JEFF LEMIRE
RAY FAWKES
MIKEL JANIN
DOUBLE PAGE SPREAD: CUT AS SHOWN, ABUT PAGE EDGES, TAPE ON BACK, DO NOT OVERLAP

Character designs for Vikar by Mikel Janin and Brett Booth (bottom right)

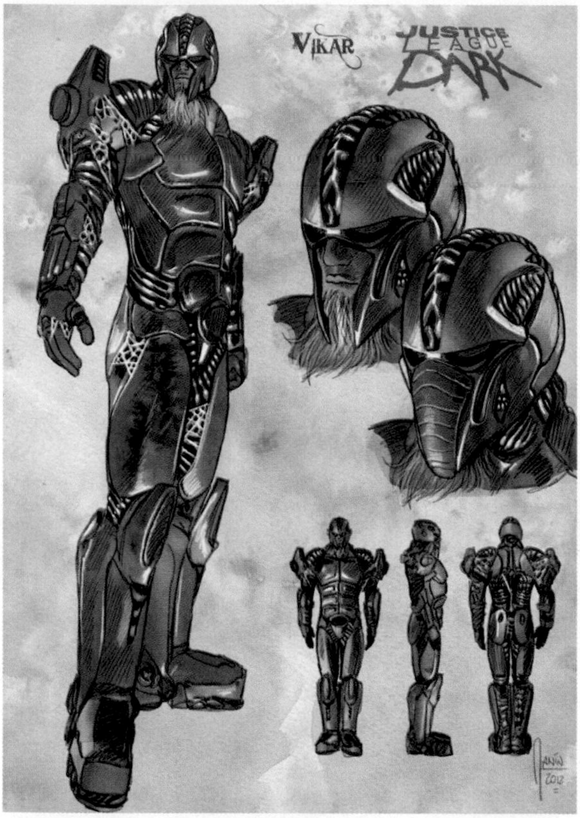
VIKAR
JUSTICE LEAGUE DARK

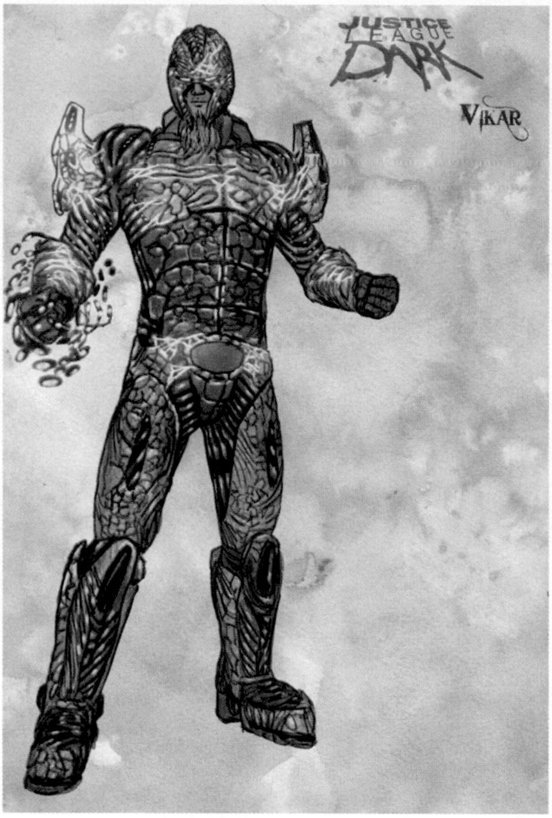
JUSTICE LEAGUE DARK
VIKAR

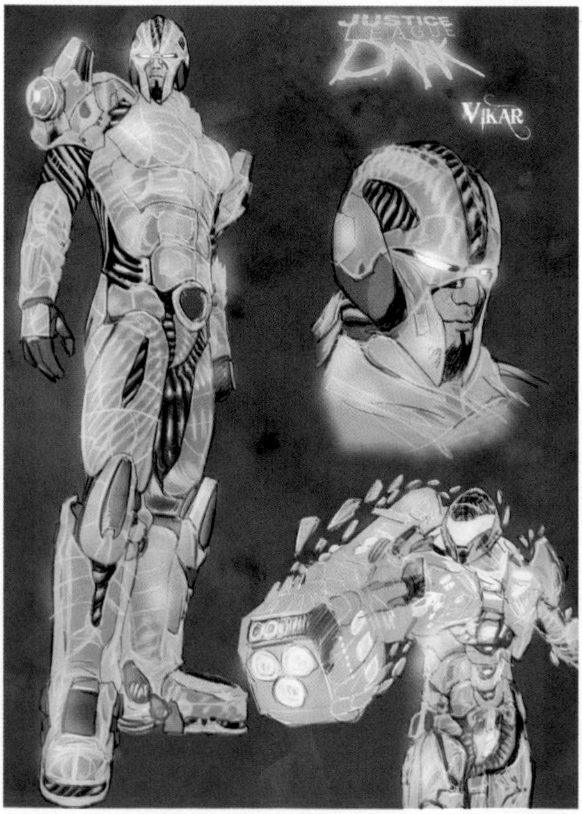
JUSTICE LEAGUE DARK
VIKAR

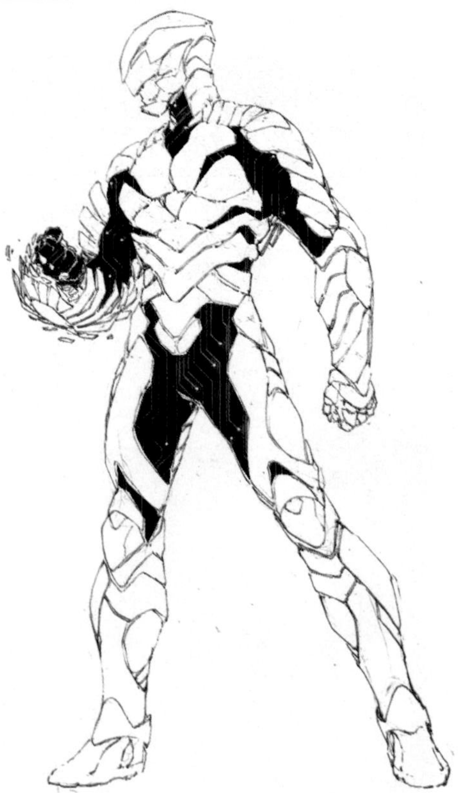

Character studies for Timothy Hunter by Mikel Janin

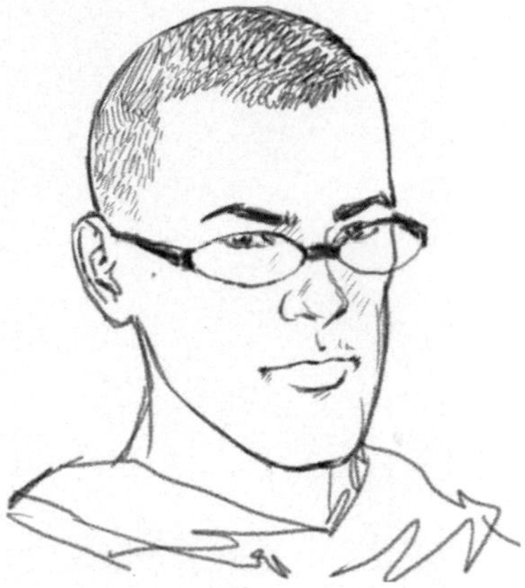

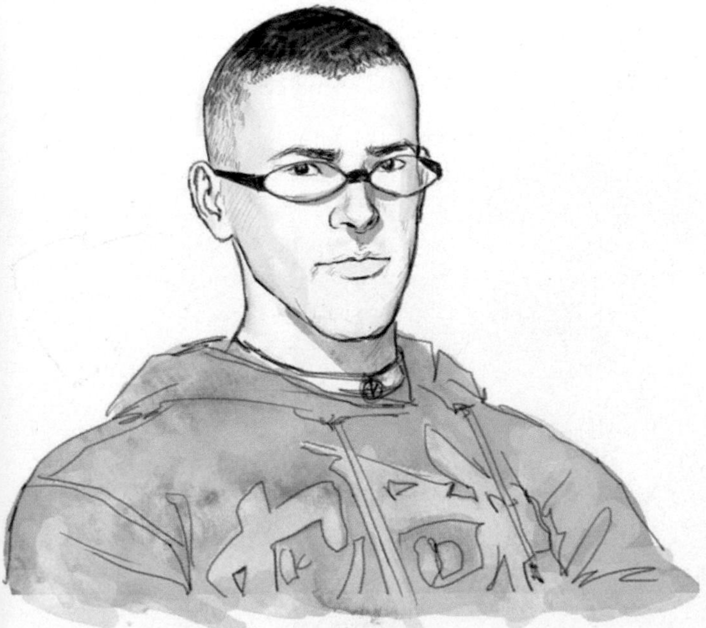

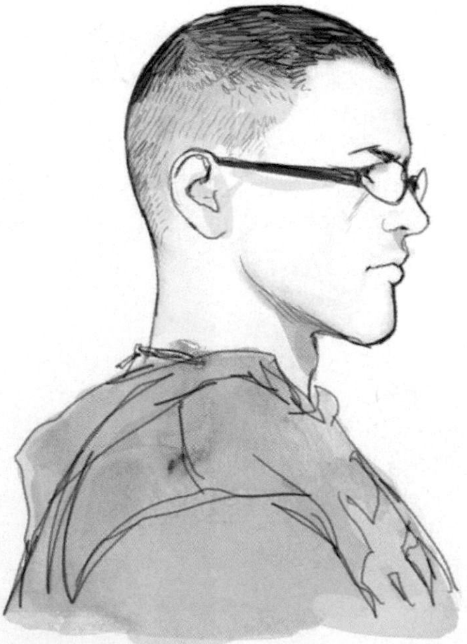

On Season Four of Syfy's special-effects make-up competition show *Face Off*, contestants were asked to design a character for a DC comic book. Below are the winning designs for Infernal Core by season winner Anthony Kosar, alongside the character's comics debut by artist Mikel Janin in JUSTICE LEAGUE DARK #16. Photos by Brett-Patrick Jenkins.

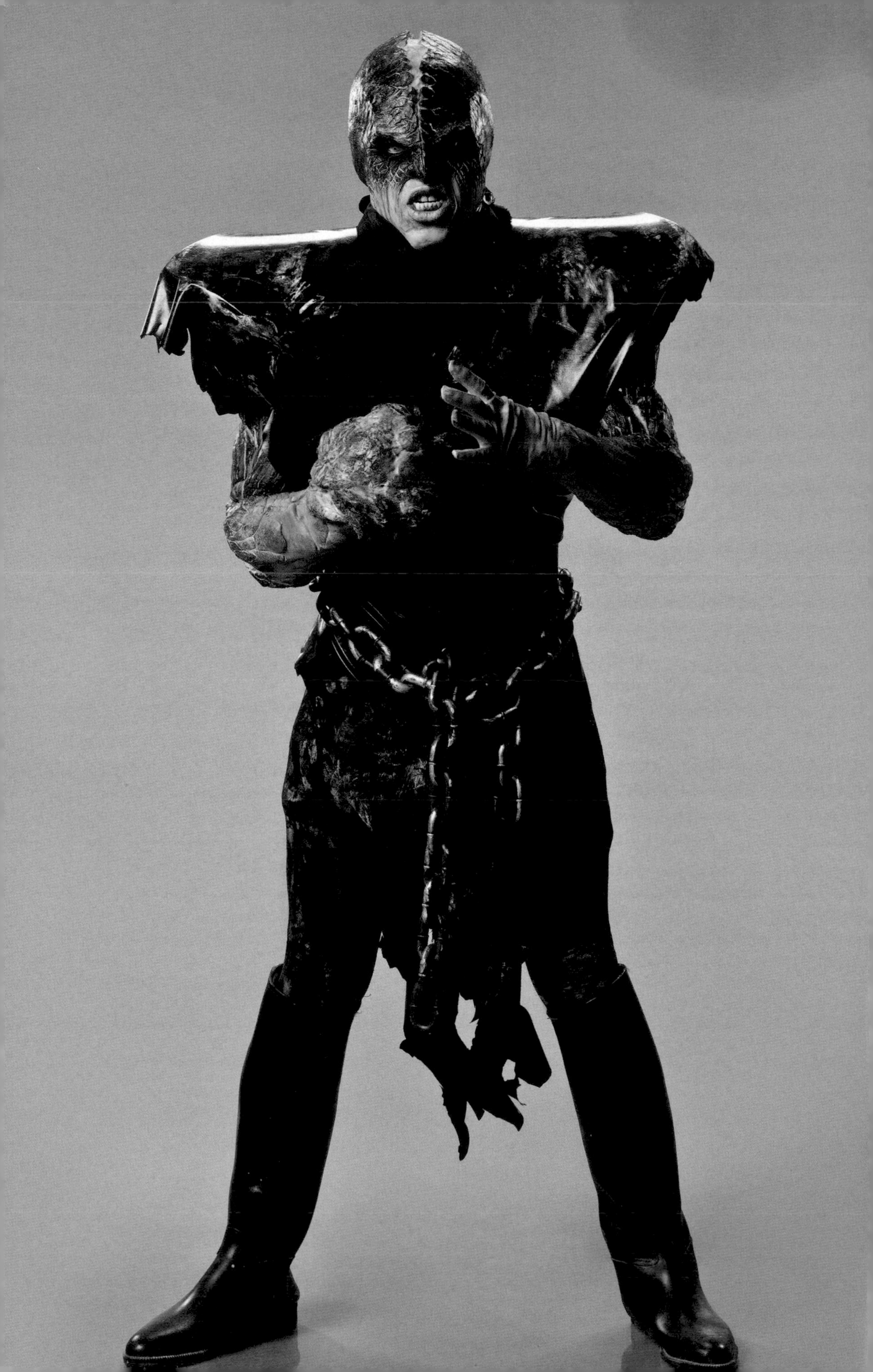

JUSTICE LEAGUE DARK #19 Full cover by MIKEL JANIN

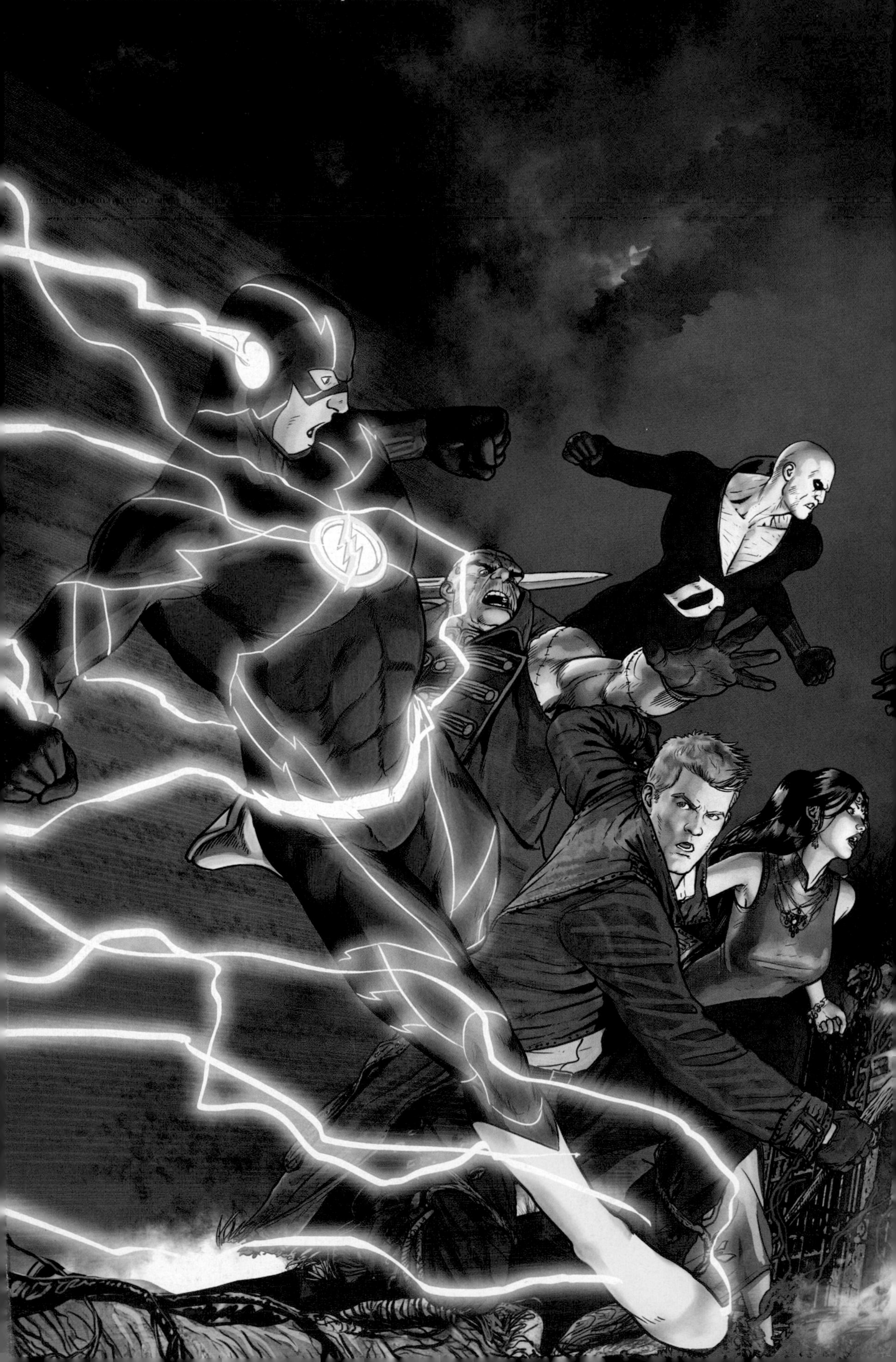

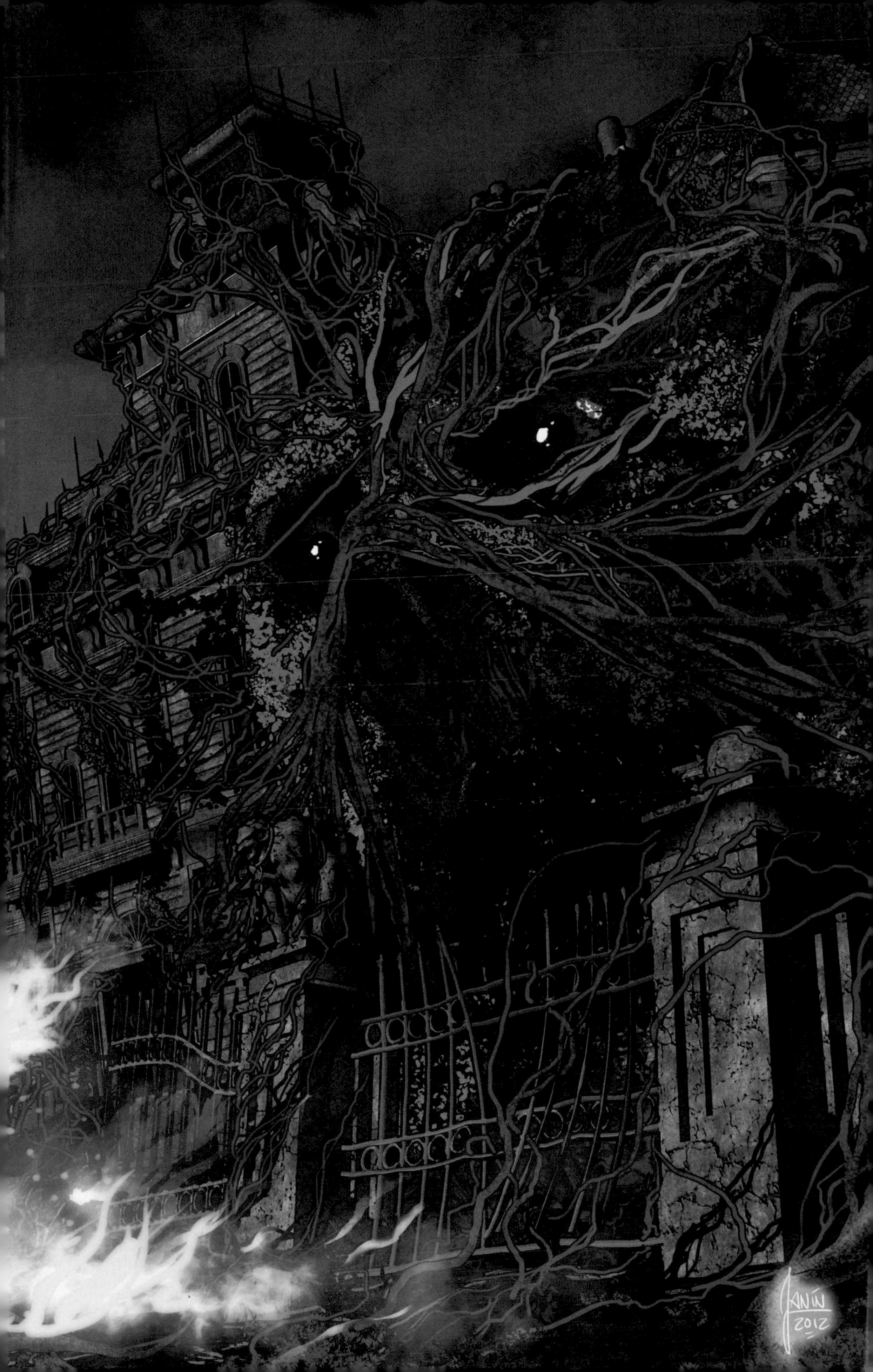
JANÍN
2012